D0850797

Medieval Dublin: the making of a metropolis

Howard Clarke, Editor

MEDIEVAL DUBLIN

THE MAKING
OF A METROPOLIS

IRISH ACADEMIC PRESS

The typesetting of this book was
produced by Gilbert Gough Typesetting for
Irish Academic Press, Kill Lane, Blackrock, Co. Dublin.

BRITISH LIBRARY CATALOGUING IN PUBLICATION DATA
Medieval Dublin: the making of a metropolis
1. Dublin. History
I. Clarke, H.B. (Howard Brian), *1940-*
941.8'35

ISBN 0-7165-2459-7

The companion volume to this book
is *Medieval Dublin: the living city*

ISBN 0-7165-2460-0

Printed in Ireland by
Betaprint Ltd

Contents

ESSAYS IN THE COMPANION VOLUME

List of illustrations

FIGURES IN THE COMPANION VOLUME

Acknowledgements

The essence of this book lies in the reprinted word. The editor and publishers here express their indebtedness to the officers and councils of the following learned bodies for permission to reprint material from their serial publications: the Amt für Vor- und Frühgeschichte at Lübeck (chap. 1), the Old Dublin Society (chaps. 4 and 6), the Royal Irish Academy (chap. 7), the Royal Society of Antiquaries of Ireland (chaps. 2, 5, 9, 11, 13 and 14), and the Society of Antiquaries of London (chap. 12). For clearance to reprint chap. 8 they are equally indebted to the Royal Irish Academy, as to the O'Brien Press Ltd. for chap. 10.

For permission to reproduce the following illustrations the editor and publishers are grateful to: Dublin City Archives for Fig. 15; Professor Herbert Jankuhn for Fig. 1; the National Library of Ireland for Figs. 5, 14, 31, 32, 55, 58 and 60; the National Maritime Museum at Greenwich for Fig. 16; the National Museum of Ireland for Figs. 8, 9, 10, 17, 18, 19, 20, 21, 22, 23, 24 and 25; and Mr. Leo Swan for Fig. 3. Ms. Mairead Dunlevy has kindly assented to the reproduction of Fig. 21, and Professor J.A. Watt and Gill & Macmillan Ltd. to that of Fig. 34 from *The Church in Medieval Ireland* (1972). The courtesy of the Right Honourable the Earl of Dartmouth is acknowledged for permission to print a copy of a map of Dublin Castle in his collections deposited in the Staffordshire Record Office (Fig. 33).

The editor wishes to thank Ms. Carine O'Grady for undertaking the arduous task of retyping some of the chapters and the staff of the Audio-visual Unit at University College, Dublin, for technical advice and for supplying photographic prints. Research on the notes, bibliographies and illustrations was conducted in the libraries of the Royal Irish Academy, Trinity College, Dublin, and University College, Dublin, as well as in the National Library of Ireland. For the unfailing helpfulness of their staffs the editor here expresses his appreciation. Others who have assisted in various ways are: Debbie Caulfield, Mary Clark, Senan Crowe, O.P., Siobhán de hÓir, Patrick Healy, Paula Howard, Joan Jennings, Patrick Johnston, Rhoda Kavanagh, F.X. Martin, O.S.A., Christine Meek, Uaininn O'Meadhra, Breandán Ó Ríordáin, Bride Rosney and Anngret Simms.

The Friends of Medieval Dublin are grateful to the Irish Academic Press for taking a lost sheep into its fold, there to be shepherded by Michael Adams, Martin Healy and Gerard O'Connor. Their professionalism and cheerful equanimity deserve far more praise than can be expressed here. Finally the editor and publishers wish to place on record the fact that the Associates of The Friends of Medieval Dublin – a group that provided invaluable financial and moral support at the time of the Wood Quay campaign – decided to assign the bulk of the residue of their funds towards the cost of producing this book. May they come to believe that the fruits of their expectations match their own generosity of spirit!

Abbreviations and conventions

16

Bk. Lec.	Mulchrone, K., (ed.), *The Book of Lecan: Leabhar Mór Mhic Fhir Bhisigh Leacain* (1937).
Bk. Leinster	Best, R.I., Bergin, O., O'Brien, M.A. and O'Sullivan, A., (eds.), *The Book of Leinster, formerly Lebar na Núachongbála*, 6 vols. (1954-83).
B.L.	British Library.
B.L., Add. MSS.	———, Additional MSS.
Cal. Chart. Rolls, 1226-57 [etc.]	*Calendar of the Charter Rolls, 1226-57* [etc.], 6 vols. (1903-27).
Cal. Christ Church deeds	'Calendar to Christ Church deeds', in *P.R.I. Rep. D.K. 20*, pp. 36-122; *P.R.I. Rep. D.K. 23*, pp. 75-152; *P.R.I. Rep. D.K. 24*, pp. 100-94. Index in *P.R.I. Rep. D.K. 27*, pp. 3-101.
Cal. Close Rolls, 1272-9 [etc.]	*Calendar of the Close Rolls, 1272-9* [etc.] (1900-).
Cal. Doc. Ire., 1171-1251 [etc.]	Sweetman, H.S., (ed.), *Calendar of Documents relating to Ireland, 1171-1251* [etc.], 5 vols. (1875-86).
Cal. Justic. Rolls Ire., 1295-1303 [etc.]	Mills, J., (ed.), *Calendar of the Justiciary Rolls, or Proceedings in the Court of the Justiciar of Ireland . . . 1295-1303* [etc.], 2 vols. (1905-14).
Cal. Papal Letters, 1198-1304 [etc.]	*Calendar of Entries in the Papal Registers relating to Great Britain and Ireland: Papal Letters, 1198-1304* [etc.] (1893-).
Cal. Pat. Rolls, 1232-47 [etc.]	*Calendar of the Patent Rolls, 1232-47* [etc.] (1906-).
Cal. Pat. Rolls Ire., Hen. VIII - Eliz.	Morrin, J., (ed.), *Calendar of the Patent and Close Rolls of Chancery in Ireland, Henry VIII to 18th Elizabeth* (1861).
Cal. Pat. Rolls Ire., Eliz.	Morrin, J., (ed.), *Calendar of the Patent and Close Rolls of Chancery in Ireland, 18th to 45th Elizabeth* (1862).
Cal. Pat. Rolls Ire., Jas I	*Irish Patent Rolls of James I: Facsimile of the Irish Record Commissioners' Calendar prepared prior to 1830* (1966).
Cal. Rot. Pat. et Claus. Hib.	Tresham, E., (ed.), *Rotulorum Patentium et Clausorum Cancellariae Hiberniae Calendarium, Hen. II - Hen. VII* (1828).
Cal. S.P. Ire., 1509-73 [etc.]	*Calendar of the State Papers relating to Ireland, 1509-1573* [etc.], 24 vols. (1860-1911).
C.G.G.	Todd, J.H., (ed.), *Cogadh Gaedhel re Gallaibh: the War of the Gaedhil with the Gaill, or the*

	Invasions of Ireland by the Danes and Other Norsemen: the Original Irish Text (1867).
Chartul. St. Mary's, Dublin	Gilbert, J.T., (ed.), *Chartularies of St. Mary's Abbey, Dublin . . . and Annals of Ireland. 1162-1370,* 2 vols. (1884-6).
Chron. Scot.	Hennessy, W.M., (ed.), *Chronicon Scotorum: a Chronicle of Irish Affairs from the Earliest Times to A.D. 1135, with a Supplement containing the Events from 1141 to 1150* (1866).
Civil Survey	Simington, R.C., (ed.), *The Civil Survey, A.D. 1654-56,* 10 vols. (1931-61).
Commons' Jn. Ire.	*Journals of the House of Commons of the Kingdom of Ireland . . .,* 28 vols. (1753-91).
Comparative Urban Origins	Clarke, H.B. and Simms, A., (eds.), *The Comparative History of Urban Origins in Non-Roman Europe: Ireland, Wales, Denmark, Germany, Poland and Russia from the Ninth to the 13th Century* (1985).
Cork Hist. Soc. Jn.	*Journal of the Cork Historical and Archaeological Society* (1892-).
Crosthwaite, *Obits*	Crosthwaite, J.C., (ed.), *The Book of Obits and Martyrology of the Cathedral Church of the Holy Trinity, commonly called Christ Church, Dublin* (1844).
D.N.B.	Stephen, L. and Lee, S., (eds.), *Dictionary of National Biography,* 66 vols. (1885-1901), reprinted with corrections, 22 vols. (1908-9).
D.H.R.	*Dublin Historical Record* (1938-).
E.H.R.	*English Historical Review* (1886-).
Extents Ir. Mon. Possessions	White, N.B., (ed.), *Extents of Irish Monastic Possessions, 1540-1541, from Manuscripts in the Public Record Office, London* (1943).
Féil-sgríbhinn Eóin Mhic Néill	Ryan, J., (ed.), *Féil-sgríbhinn Eóin Mhic Néill: Essays and Studies presented to Professor Eóin MacNeill on the Occasion of his Seventieth Birthday* (1940).
Frag. Ann.	Radner, J.N., (ed.), *Fragmentary Annals of Ireland* (1978).
Giraldus, *Expugnatio*	Scott, A.B. and Martin, F.X., (eds.), Giraldus Cambrensis, *Expugnatio Hibernica: the Conquest of Ireland* (1978).
Gwynn & Hadcock, *Med. Relig. Houses*	Gwynn, A. and Hadcock, R.N., *Medieval Religious Houses: Ireland* (1970).

Hist. & Mun. Doc. Ire.	Gilbert, J.T., (ed.), *Historic and Municipal Documents of Ireland, 1172-1320* (1870).
H.M.C. Rep. 9 [etc.]	*Historical Manuscripts Commission, Ninth* [etc.] *Report*, appendix, part 1 [etc.] (1884-).
I.E.R.	*Irish Ecclesiastical Record*, 5th series, 109 vols. (1913-68).
I.H.S.	Irish Historical Studies (1938-).
Kildare Arch. Soc. Jn.	*Journal of the County Kildare Archaeological Society* (1891-).
Marlborough, *Chronicle*	Henry of Marlborough (Marleburrough), 'Chronicle of Ireland', in Ware, J., (ed.), *Historie of Ireland*, vol. 3 (1633), pp. 207-23; reprinted in Ware, J., (ed.), *Ancient Irish Histories*, vol. 2 (1809), pp. 1-32.
Med. Studies presented to A. Gwynn	Watt, J.A., Morrall, J.B. and Martin, F.X., (eds.), *Medieval Studies presented to Aubrey Gwynn, S.J.* (1961).
Nat. Mus. Ire.	National Museum of Ireland.
N.H.I.	*A New History of Ireland* (1976-).
N.L.I.	National Library of Ireland.
Ormond Deeds, 1172-1350 [etc.]	Curtis, E., (ed.), *Calendar of Ormond Deeds, 1172-1350* [etc.], 6 vols. (1932-43).
Pipe Roll 5 Hen. II [etc.]	Pipe Roll Society, *The Great Roll of the Pipe for the Fifth Year of the Reign of King Henry the Second, A.D. 1158-1159* [etc.] (1884-).
P.R.I. Rep. D.K. 1 [etc.]	*First* [etc.] *Report of the Deputy Keeper of the Public Records in Ireland* (1869-).
P.R.O.	Public Record Office of England.
Proc. King's Council, Ire., 1392-3	Graves, J., (ed.), *A Roll of the Proceedings of the King's Council in Ireland for a Portion of the 16th Year of the Reign of Richard II, 1392-93* (1877).
P.R.O.I.	Public Record Office of Ireland.
Reg. All Saints, Dublin	Butler, R., (ed.), *Registrum Prioratus Omnium Sanctorum juxta Dublin* (1845).
Reg. Kilmainham	McNeill, C., (ed.), *Registrum de Kilmainham: Register of Chapter Acts of the Hospital of Saint John of Jerusalem in Ireland, 1326-1339* . . . (1932).
Reg. St. John, Dublin	Brooks, E. St. J., (ed.), *Register of the Hospital of S. John the Baptist without the Newgate, Dublin* (1936).
Reg. St. Thomas, Dublin	Gilbert, J.T., (ed.), *Register of the Abbey of St. Thomas, Dublin* (1889).

R. Hist. Soc. Trans.	*Transactions of the Royal Historical Society* (1872-).
R.I.A.	Royal Irish Academy.
R.I.A. Proc.	Proceedings of the Royal Irish Academy (1836-).
Rot. Parl.	*Rotuli Parliamentorum* [1278-1503], 7 vols. (1783-1832).
R.S.A.I. Jn.	*Journal of the Royal Society of Antiquaries of Ireland* (1849-).
s.a.	*sub anno, sub annis* (under the year/years).
Sheehy, *Pontificia Hib.*	Sheehy, M.P., (ed.), *Pontificia Hibernica: Medieval Papal Chancery Documents concerning Ireland, 640-1261,* 2 vols. (1962-5).
S.P. Hen. VIII	*State Papers . . . King Henry the Eighth,* 11 vols. (1830-52).
Stat. Ire., John - Hen. V	Berry, H.F., (ed.), *Statutes and Ordinances, and Acts of the Parliament of Ireland, King John to Henry V* (1907).
Stat. Ire., Hen. VI	Berry, H.F., (ed.), *Statute Rolls of the Parliament of Ireland, Reign of King Henry VI* (1910).
Stat. Ire., 12-22 Edw. IV	Morrissey, J.F., (ed.), *Statute Rolls of the Parliament of Ireland, 12th and 13th to the 21st and 22nd Years of the Reign of King Edward IV* (1939).
s.v.	*sub verbo, sub verbis* (under the word/words).
T.C.D.	Trinity College, Dublin.
Theiner, *Vetera Mon.*	Theiner, A., *Vetera Monumenta Hibernorum et Scotorum Historiam Illustrantia . . .* (1864, reprinted 1969).
U.J.A.	*Ulster Journal of Archaeology* (1853-).
V.C.H.	The Victoria History of the Counties of England (1900-).
Wood, *Athenae Oxon.*	Wood, A., *Athenae Oxonienses: an Exact History of All the Writers and Bishops who have had their Education in the University of Oxford,* 2 vols. (1691-2), ed. P. Bliss, 4 vols. (1813-20).

Introduction

H . B . C L A R K E

> We are standing in the historic council chamber of saint Mary's abbey
> where silken Thomas proclaimed himself a rebel in 1534. This is the
> most historic spot in all Dublin. . . . In the still faint light he moved
> about, tapping with his lath the piled seedbags and points of vantage on
> the floor. . . . With J.J. O'Molloy he came forth slowly into Mary's
> abbey where draymen were loading floats with sacks of carob and
> palmnut meal. . . .[1]

In 1904, the year in which *Ulysses* is set, nos. 2-5 Mary's Abbey were the
offices of Alexander & Co., seed merchants. Their warehouse at the rear
contained not only seedbags, but also a remarkable medieval relic — the
chapter-house of a Cistercian abbey that had been dissolved long before
during the reign of King Henry VIII. The dissolution of the religious houses
and hospitals represented the decisive beginning of the ruination of medieval
Dublin, a process that has continued relentlessly and almost unhindered
down to the present day. What has survived has done so mainly by chance,
as the archaeological excavations that have been conducted over the past
quarter of a century have revealed so dramatically. James Joyce's gesture to
the medieval past of the city immortalized in his masterpiece is a literary
allusion, not an historical evaluation. Indeed one might dissent from the view
that this chapter-house 'is the most historic spot in all Dublin', but Joyce,
like most Dubliners of his time, was not in a position to be well informed
about the history of the medieval city. The first aim of this collection of
essays, therefore, is to provide Dubliners, present and future, with a means
to remedy that situation, in order that the historical dimension of a much
earlier Dublin might attain an equally enduring, if not an equally renowned,
immortality.

In recent years the controversy surrounding the archaeological excavation
and historical conservation of Dublin has drawn attention to the need to
promote research on the city's medieval past. Hitherto most of the best
writing on the history of medieval Dublin has lain inside the covers of learned
periodicals and is unknown to all but a few scholars, both amateur and
professional. In this collection 28 essays have been selected, edited and

reprinted, with minor corrections and some new illustrations. The selection
is catholic in the sense that these essays are representative of a broad spectrum
of substance and opinion; they illustrate the extraordinary versatility of one
European city in the Middle Ages, as well as a range of expertise that no
single individual can now hope to command. The essays are grouped as
chapters of this book under four headings: historical and topographical
development; buildings and monuments; religious life and institutions; and
secular life and institutions. To make it possible for the reader to use the book
analytically, a comprehensive index of personal names and place-names has
been provided. The collection is intended both as a tribute to some of this
country's most distinguished medieval scholars and as a further contribution
by The Friends of Medieval Dublin to their declared policy of diffusing
knowledge of the early history of the capital of the Republic of Ireland.

From kingdom to capital

Medieval Dublin shares with York in England an historical development
from Scandinavian kingdom to regional capital. The Scandinavian ruling
dynasties of Dublin and of York were closely interrelated, but the kingdom
of Dublin was established earlier than, and far outlived, its rival.[2] Well before
the combined Anglo-Norman and Irish capture of Dublin in 1170, its Viking
and Hiberno-Norse inhabitants had been playing an important, though inter-
mittent, role in the affairs of the neighbouring island of Britain. Having been
incorporated into the empire of King Henry II and his sons, Dublin was to
acquire the chartered status of a typical English borough of the larger sort.
No longer a semi-independent kingdom, it now functioned as the principal
administrative centre of the feudally dependent lordship of Ireland. The
townspeople's fortunes thereafter rose and fell with those of the English
colony. As is widely known, the territory effectively controlled by the Dublin
administration had shrunk by the end of the Middle Ages to the area first
designated in 1446 as the Pale. Dublin had become the capital of a border
region that was notably smaller than the north of England. Both regions were
under external threat and both were to witness the construction of a considerable number of fortified dwellings that are generally called tower-
houses in Ireland and pele-towers in England.[3] Medieval Dublin was not a
capital city in the modern sense of a permanent concentration of all or most
of the institutions of a national government. The king's representative in
Ireland, like the king himself in England, was essentially peripatetic.[4]
Nevertheless the exchequer was located for most of the colonial period at
Dublin,[5] the castle was the biggest royal stronghold in the country, and over
half of the Irish parliaments between 1264 and 1494[6] met at Dublin. Like
York in the north of England, Dublin had no peer in the Pale of Ireland.[7]

The emergence of the concept of the Irish Pale, which coincided with the final stages of the Hundred Years War, was soon followed by the appointment of Richard, duke of York, as the king's lieutenant on 9 December 1447. Dynastic accident and dynastic rivalry meant that the fortunes of Dublin and of York were once again intertwined. Thus, for example, the duke of York left Dublin in the summer of 1460 to march on London and claim the English crown as his by right of inheritance, only to be defeated at the battle of Wakefield on 30 December and to have his head impaled on the city wall at York, crowned with a paper cap. The period of Yorkist rule in England from 1461 to 1485 was marked by an intensification of defensive measures at Dublin. When Edward IV assumed the English crown on 4 March 1461 and when Earl Thomas FitzGerald was sworn in as justiciar on 1 May in the same year, the Yorkist cause had triumphed both in England and in Ireland. At the other end of this period, on 14 June 1485, King Richard III made over the annual sum of £49 6s. 8d. out of Dublin's city rent (or farm of the borough) for a period of 60 years, to be expended on military works and on paving.[8] Only weeks before the battle of Bosworth, the house of York was taking a very long-term view of Dublin's affairs. On 20 April 1486 the new king, Henry Tudor, confirmed at Westminster all of Dublin's royal grants, from John's in 1200 to Richard's in the previous year.[9] Less than a year later a pretender to the English throne, Lambert Simnel, was lodging in the Dublin house of the earl of Kildare. On 24 May 1487 the boy was crowned by Archbishop Walter FitzSimons in Christ Church Cathedral as King Edward VI of England.[10] In the circumstances it was politic to forgive the Dubliners for this momentary lapse from grace. On 25 May 1488, virtually a year to the day since the pretender's coronation, Henry VII pardoned the 'citizens, men, inhabitants, and entire commonalty of Dublin, for all past offences, forfeitures, outlawries, etc.'.[11] Dublin and its hinterland would survive to form the chief base for post-medieval attempts by English administrations to grapple with the Irish question.

Historiographical perspective

The oldest contribution to this collection of essays (chap. 9) dates back a century to 1890; the most recent (chap. 3) has been rewritten for this book.[12] Thus our selection spans roughly one hundred years of an evolving historiographical tradition in Ireland. Such a relatively large sample can be divided chronologically into three groups, each representing a major stage in this evolutionary process. Both the historical content of the contributions and the historiographical context of the contributors reflect in subtle ways the origins, birth and development of one of Europe's newer nation States. A complete analysis would occupy an inordinate amount of space, but the following contextual framework will, it is hoped, offer some guidance to the user of this collection and give some indication of the value of a dispassionate historiographical perspective.

1. *Unionist and Protestant ascendancy versus nationalist and Catholic monolith to 1921*   The 19th century was a great age of scientific curiosity and discovery in many different fields of human endeavour, not least the investigation of the prehistoric and historic past. More people with education and 'leisure' were able both to edit texts and to make use of printed editions as they became available.[13] This, of course, is true of most European countries, but in Ireland there was a particular cultural gloss that was due to the preponderance of Anglo-Irish antiquarians and historians.[14] The first Dublin-related texts to be edited were the Book of Obits and Martyrology of Christ Church Cathedral and the register of All Saints' Priory, published respectively in 1844 and 1845, on the eve of the great famine.[15] Thereafter the pre-1921 period was dominated by two outstanding editors of medieval records. The first and better known was Sir John Gilbert, who even as a young man wrote a three-volume 'history' of Dublin.[16] Eleven years later his *Historic and Municipal Documents of Ireland*, based essentially on the archives of Dublin, was published in the Rolls Series.[17] During the 1880s Gilbert edited for the same series the cartularies and register respectively of the two wealthiest monasteries in the medieval city, St. Mary's Abbey and St. Thomas's Abbey.[18] Beginning in 1889 he published the initial volumes in what would become the indispensable collection of material on the history of Dublin, the *Calendar of Ancient Records*, which was eventually completed in 1944 under the editorship of Lady Gilbert.[19] In the year before his death in 1898 Gilbert issued an edition of the oldest register of the archbishops of Dublin.[20] By any standards and notwithstanding any criticisms that may be made of his work, his was an extraordinarily productive career.

The second editor of note was H.F. Berry, who in 1918 took the name of Twiss and whose non-editorial writings are here represented by chap. 24. An archivist by profession, Berry edited and translated an important register of wills and inventories in 1898.[21] Otherwise, apart from much other pioneering work, he concentrated on calendaring the records of one Dublin guild and three Dublin parishes, most of which are late medieval in date.[22] At the same time J.L. Robinson was calendaring the records of St. John's parish.[23] The other major text to find an editor and translator during the period of the Anglo-Irish ascendancy was an account roll of Holy Trinity Priory — the house of Augustinian canons regular attached to Christ Church Cathedral.[24] Between 1888 and 1895 an invaluable collection of deeds belonging to the same cathedral was calendared and indexed.[25] Although a summary in English is not an adequate substitute for an accurate and full Latin transcript, this enlightened procedure would avert the absolute tragedy of total loss in 1922 when these deeds, along with so many other irreplaceable medieval records, were destroyed in the violence that accompanied one stage in the birth of independent Ireland. Two Christ Church books were also calendared in this period,[26] with the result that the amount of accessible material relating to the older of Dublin's two medieval cathedrals is as considerable as its value remains unrealized to this day.

While Gilbert was writing his *History*, Dublin, though by then a 'deposed capital',[27] was acquiring many of the trappings of a Victorian city. Building operations and the digging of trenches for underground services in the late 1850s presented an opportunity to T.M. Ray to collect medieval artefacts and to record archaeological observations.[28] More dramatic was the accidental discovery between 1845 and 1866 in the course of railway and other construction of an extensive pagan Viking cemetery at Islandbridge-Kilmainham. Unfortunately no scientific excavation was conducted and only a proportion of the grave-goods has been preserved and published.[29] Another burial-place of the Viking Age was discovered under a mound at Donnybrook in 1879. Here were found the remains of between 600 and 700 people of both sexes and all ages, many showing signs of violent death, accompanied by the skeleton of one Scandinavian warrior at whose feet were the bones of two ritually murdered females.[30] Three years later the first known attempt to compile a map of medieval Dublin appeared in print under a title that reflects the technical constraints and romantic spirit of much Victorian historical cartography.[31] This map seems to have languished in relative obscurity, but its intellectual successor, produced by L.R. Strangways, was to reach a wider public and to enjoy a comparatively long life.[32] A further notable landmark of this period was C.T. McCready's compendium on Dublin's street names.[33]

These pioneering works in the fields of archaeology, cartography, historiography and the editing of medieval texts formed part of the intellectual background of the authors of the five oldest contributions to the present volumes (chaps. 9, 13, 14, 16, 24). So, too, did the restoration of the two cathedrals, a process that lies behind Thomas Drew's investigation of the precinct of Christ Church (chap. 9).[34] In his company, at this historic spot in the heart of medieval Dublin, we breathe the antiquarian air of a bygone age. There is a poignant contrast between the leisurely discursiveness of the text and 'the hungry army of unemployed' who, early in 1886, were engaged to excavate the site; between enlightened philanthropy and desperate poverty.[35] There were even those who made fun of their efforts, but crass ignorance of this kind is with us still a century later. In 1892 A.L. Elliott presented St. Thomas's Abbey as 'an ecclesiastical fort of English power . . . governed on a thoroughly Erastian principle' (chap. 16).[36] We hear about the 1392 conspiracy in which one of the canons bribed the mayor and a merchant to aid him in an attempt on the abbot's life. The fate of this powerful and wealthy community was ultimately determined by Henry VIII, 'one of whom no Catholic, Protestant or Roman, has reason to be proud'. The essay brings the story down to the court-house in Thomas Court — 'a meagre monument of monasterial might'.

In 1229 the citizens of Dublin made a decisive advance towards self-government when King Henry III granted them permission to elect a mayor. As the 'major' (Latin *maior*) administrator in the city he was to hold office for a year, but could be re-elected. Dublin's first mayor was Richard Muton and thereafter in the Middle Ages the municipality was headed by a mayor and two provosts, the latter being called 'bailiffs' as from 1292. By printing a list of these officers down to the time of the earliest surviving assembly roll (1447), Berry performed a considerable service for those who might follow in his steps (chap. 24).[37] As he recognized, undated documents witnessed by this triumvirate can be assigned with a fair degree of accuracy to a two-year period, since the annual term of office generally ran from Michaelmas to Michaelmas (29 September). The list is no doubt still capable of refinement and it is to be hoped that the resurrection of this pioneering exercise will act both as a guide and as a stimulant to further research. If the mayor was the human figurehead of the medieval city, its physical focal point was the High Cross situated at the ridge-top road junction south-west of Christ Church Cathedral. Shown in miniature on Speed's map of Dublin engraved in 1610, the only detailed drawing of this former monument was made in 1794 and published by H.S. Crawford in 1911 (chap. 14).[38] The final pre-independence contribution to the present collection dates from 1917 and comes from the busy pen of H.J. Lawlor, then Professor of Ecclesiastical History at Trinity College and subsequently dean of St. Patrick's Cathedral (chap. 13).[39] One of the last pre-Reformation archbishops of Dublin, William Rokeby (1512-21), was a Yorkshire man and towards the end of this fine piece of detective work yet another link was established between the Pale of Ireland and the north of England.

2. Independence and nationalism, 1921-72   On 6 December 1921, with the signing in London of the Anglo-Irish treaty, the modern Irish State was effectively (though not technically) born;[40] at midnight on 31 December 1972 the Republic of Ireland, along with Denmark and the United Kingdom, adhered to the European Economic Community (now the European Community). Independence began inauspiciously amid bitterness and re-crimination, and was to be accompanied by partition and civil war. During the course of that war much of the country's (colonial) recorded past was obliterated in the explosions and fire at the Four Courts, which then housed the Public Record Office. Original documents that had not been calendared, printed or transcribed were lost irretrievably in an act of gross barbarism. Against this sombre background, fewer Dublin-related texts remained to be published in full than would otherwise have been the case.[41] First among the major collections of documents came the register of the priory of St. John of Jerusalem at Kilmainham (1932), followed by that of St. John the Baptist's Hospital outside Newgate (1936).[42] Both of these manuscripts are preserved in the Bodleian Library at Oxford. Next came the cartulary of St. Patrick's Cathedral known as the *Dignitas Decani* (1957), which had already been calendared back in the period of the Anglo-Irish ascendancy.[43] A more comprehensive calendar of the register of Archbishop John Alen (1529-34) — the *Liber Niger Alani* — was published by Charles McNeill in 1950.[44] In the immediate post-Emergency years English versions of an invaluable and still unexplored series of deeds preserved in the library of Trinity College were produced by stages.[45] The 1960s saw more work being done on charters relating to the archdiocese — those of the Lord John and those in the *Registrum Novum* of Christ Church Cathedral.[46] At the same time the essential elements of Dublin's royal charter sequence were being printed in accordance with modern editorial standards, along with the Dublin and Waterford Laws and Usages as parallel texts.[47] Finally remnants and traces of one set of rolls destroyed in 1922 and reflecting the activities of the medieval exchequer were expertly surveyed in 1966.[48]

In independent Ireland academic life began to feel the impact of the National University, which had been established under an act of parliament and incorporated by a charter in 1908, as well as that of a number of new institutions of higher learning, such as the Irish Manuscripts Commission (1928) and the Dublin Institute for Advanced Studies (1940). In 1931 another distinguished body, the Royal Archaeological Institute of Great Britain and Ireland, held its summer meeting in Dublin. One result of this was a general map of the medieval town, by H.G. Leask, which sadly was to remain all but unknown for several decades.[49] The historiography of Dublin achieved its own independence with the foundation in 1934 of the Old Dublin Society, whose proceedings have been recorded since 1938 in the pages of the *Dublin Historical Record*. It is therefore fitting that a number of the contributions to the present collection dating from this period should come from this source (chaps. 4, 6, 18, 20, 21, 23, 28), as well as from the *Journal of the Royal Society of Antiquaries of Ireland*, which has a long and honourable tradition of publishing important work on the history of Dublin (chaps. 5, 17, 19, 22, 25-7). That the latter continued this tradition, and that it did so under such a non-republican title, testify to the salient point that 'in many respects, indeed, continuity rather than change characterized independent Ireland'.[50] But by the end of this period change was in the air, even if only symbolically, as when in 1972 Archbishop Dermot Ryan became the first Roman Catholic prelate to attend a service in Christ Church Cathedral since the Reformation, or when in 1973 Ireland opened up diplomatic relations with the U.S.S.R.[51]

The selection for the period 1921-72 starts with a workmanlike description of the city seals, with due prominence being given to the common seal of the 13th century (chap. 25).[52] Such a subject had a certain topicality at a time when the authority of the new State itself was being questioned and had just been put to a severe test. Equally workmanlike is McNeill's account of the hospital of St. John the Baptist, which was based on the then still unedited register (chap. 17).[53] Next we move to 1938, when the very first article to be published in the *Dublin Historical Record* was contributed by R. Dudley Edwards (chap. 23).[54] Again self-government was a topical theme, despite its municipal context and the readily acknowledged debt to a recent English publication.[55] This essay is remarkably prescient in its appreciation of the value of comparative history and may be said to represent a forerunner of the writings of other scholars in the 1970s and 1980s. The last inter-war item is from the same source and deals with a phenomenon that permeates much of Dublin's long history down to the present day — poverty (chap. 28).[56] From this piece one senses how slowly and imperceptibly daily life for the masses ceased to be medieval and became 'modern'. We hear of the wiley Barnaby Rathe who in the reign of Queen Elizabeth I preferred a life of relative ease in the house of St. John to the impossible and unrewarding task of killing pigs as pests and ridding the city of its equally pestilential beggars. As late as 1659 idle boys and women were being imprisoned in a large cage in Cornmarket prior to examination and punishment by the justices.

During the Emergency in the Republic, life continued to be lived and history continued to be written. The first item in this sub-group relates to a subject on which a great deal of light has since been cast by archaeological excavation — Norse Dublin (chap. 4).[57] Again the possibility of a comparative dimension is introduced and a row of 'garths' or tenements of the kind adverted to by the author has indeed been uncovered along the western side of Fishamble Street. These particular tenements could be traced back to the early tenth century — to the 'time that Dublin became a real town instead of a mere fortress', according to both Edmund Curtis and more recent scholars. Next in chronological order comes an essay on the Bachall Ísu, the celebrated staff associated with St. Patrick (chap. 21). Protected and venerated by the Anglo-Normans and their Anglo-Irish successors throughout the Middle Ages, 'it remained for an Englishman to destroy the greatest treasure Ireland possessed [which] was the most unpardonable piece of vandalism perpetrated by the so-called Reformation Church in Dublin'.[58] A third wartime publication is interesting partly for its information about prices in the mid-14th century (chap. 20).[59] In those days, on the eve of the Black Death, 'money wages were very low; bailiffs got 6*s*. 8*d*. a year, ploughmen

5*s*., and drivers of plough-teams 4*s*.'. A woman who was hired to bind sheaves of corn in the stackyard was paid 6*d*. plus her board for 12 days' work. Two men received 4*d*. for spending two nights on hilltops near *Clonkeen* (Deans Grange) on the lookout for hostile Irishmen. Such details serve to remind us of the vast gulf between medieval and contemporary monetary values.

One salutary medieval custom is mentioned in the first post-war contribution to our selection (chap. 18)[60] — the practice whereby 'the newly-elected mayor each year proceeded in state with his officers to St. Saviour's to listen to a sermon from the prior on civic duty and the rights of magistrates'. The liturgy of Dublin's Dominican friars came to include 'a special prayer for the health and happiness of the mayor, his officials and the citizens in general'. Next in order of publication we have a view of pre-Norman Dublin as it appeared 40 years ago (chap. 5).[61] Archaeology is given its rightful place, despite the fact that virtually no *scientific* excavation had yet been undertaken. The dark subsoil formed by many centuries of accumulated occupation debris is misinterpreted as an ancient bog, as it had been in the 19th century. The crucial importance of the immemorial ford and of the derivative place-name Áth Cliath is recognized, but the origins of the name Dubhlinn are left in the realm of legend. Just as the River Liffey was a vital seaway in the Middle Ages, so also was it a valuable fishery, especially for salmon. The latter attribute is reflected in the origin of the place-name Leixlip, which is probably the Norse *laxhløypa*, 'salmon's leaping-place'.[62] The river's fisheries form the subject of one of the essays illustrating secular life and institutions (chap. 27).[63] It will come as no surprise to present-day fishing enthusiasts that these waters were a constant source of friction as well as fish, though in deference to our medieval predecessors it should be noted that not to eat meat on Fridays and during Lent was a standard obligation. Punishments for those who infringed fishing rights and entitlements could be picturesque if undignified: in 1425 John Dyrre, a northsider, was sentenced sixfold for withholding his tithes to 'be beaten round St. Michan's Church, naked save for a loin-cloth, by the curate'. In the aftermath of the Mother and Child Scheme débâcle could there have been, even then, people who thought that this was an appropriate procedure?[64]

Most of the tithes of the Liffey fisheries belonged to the prior and convent of Holy Trinity, the monastery attached to Christ Church Cathedral as from *c*. 1163. This takes us back to the beginnings of a pivotal and venerable institution, as they are described by one of Ireland's most accomplished medieval scholars, Aubrey Gwynn (chap. 15).[65] Among the commonest misconceptions about the history of Dublin is that the older of the two cathedrals was founded in 1038, a date whose unlikelihood was demonstrated lucidly and conclusively by Gwynn as long ago as 1941.[66] His argument is

rehearsed more briefly here, as is some of the evidence for the development
of a close ecclesiastical association between the early diocese of Dublin and
major English churches such as those at Canterbury and Worcester. Seen in
this light, the coming of the Anglo-Normans to Ireland in the late 1160s 'was
in the logic of events, as foreshadowed by the career of William the
Conqueror',[67] rather than a bolt from the blue. Thus Dublin's second bishop,
Patrick, who was trained as a Benedictine monk at Worcester, may have been
a prime mover in the plan for a native Irish hierarchy, which came to fruition
in the first instance at the synod of Ráith Bressail in 1111.

Tension between ecclesiastical and secular authority surfaces in the context of the water supply to medieval Dublin in an article published post-
humously in 1958 (chap. 6). To modern eyes it may seem extraordinary that
the main supply to the entire city was to some degree dependent on the
goodwill of the inmates of St. Thomas's Abbey and that the precious water
was shared in the proportion 2:1 in favour of the canons. The background to
this state of affairs and the ingenious nature of the extensive engineering
works south-west of the city are explained by Valentine Jackson, who was
himself a water engineer.[68] In the Middle Ages there was tension, too, within
the Church: for example, between the chapters of Christ Church and St.
Patrick's. In Latin Christendom the city (as distinct from the diocese) was,
apparently, unique in its possession to *two* cathedrals, which were both
literally and figuratively within shouting distance of one another (chap. 19).[69]
Though capable of vehement expression of nationalist sentiments, Michael
(formerly R.H.M.) Dolley's numismatic expertise took him to the museums
and private collections of many other nations. It is fitting that his work should
be represented here and the chosen specimen, dating from 1963, focuses on
18 coins minted in Dublin yet preserved in the Hermitage Museum at
Leningrad (chap. 22).[70] During the winter of 1961-2 the Office of Public
Works investigated some of the ground lying beneath the new east range of
the castle, thereby inaugurating the great series of archaeological excavations
that has yielded, among so much else, a significant number of medieval coins.
The Hiberno-Norse currency minted at Dublin from 997 onwards demonstrates the important fact that the townspeople were in close contact with the
English economically and politically even earlier than they were eccle-
siastically. In the Middle Ages, as today, Mammon sometimes preceded God.
The latest item from the period 1921-72 shows the extent of the modelling
of governmental institutions in colonial Ireland on those of the mother-
country (chap. 26).[71] The chief governor or his deputy took the place of the
king — 'at one and the same time the military chief of the colony, the head
of its civil administration, and its supreme judge, subject always, of course,
to the overriding power of the king, whose deputy he was'. In the colony's
heyday there was ample scope for the justiciar to itinerate, but by the closing

decades of the 15th century the king's lieutenant or deputy to the lieutenant (as he was now usually known) was increasingly confined to Dublin and to its hinterland, the Pale. Some of these royal representatives were prelates from the same area — archbishops of Dublin, bishops of Meath, priors of Kilmainham.[72]

3. Interdependence and internationalism from 1973   Ireland's adherence to the European (Economic) Community from 1973 marked a decisive stage in a growing sense of interdependence and internationalism not only technically but also psychologically, despite the fact that her ex-colonial mother-country joined this supranational body at precisely the same time. Dublin, the national capital of the Republic, has become progressively internationalized, to the extent that the castle, which was for so long the headquarters of British administrations in Ireland, has been adapted to function as an international conference centre, especially on those occasions when the chairmanship of the Council of Ministers falls to this country. Even in the relatively arcane world of medieval studies, Dublin has been the venue for a whole series of international conferences, including the Seventh Viking Congress in August 1973;[73] colloquies on Visigothic Spain in May 1975, on Columbanus and Merovingian monasticism in May 1977, and on urban origins and colonization in non-Roman Europe in May 1978;[74] colloquies on Ireland and Europe in the early Middle Ages in May 1981 and in August 1984;[75] and a conference on domestic architecture in medieval Europe in September 1988. A parallel development has been greater emphasis on interdisciplinary approaches, particularly in the range of disciplines represented by archaeology, history and historical geography. This academic combination has formed the intellectual and methodological core of the Dublin Historic Settlement Group, which has been meeting regularly at University College, Dublin, since 1975.

To-date since 1973 only one small original document pertaining to medieval Dublin has been published.[76] On the other hand there has been a good deal of progress on the cartographical front. In 1978 the first large-scale, scientific map of the medieval city was published by the Ordnance Survey, while five years later a definitive study was produced of the oldest extant map of Dublin.[77] Most dramatic of all, however, have been the results of the various archaeological campaigns since 1961-2 by the National Museum of Ireland, the Office of Public Works, and the Dublin Archaeological Research Team.[78] The analysis of this abundant and exceptionally well-preserved material requires the skill of many different specialists, both inside and outside the normal scope of archaeology. This scholarly interdependence is reflected in the authorship and subject matter of the three fascicles that have so far been issued under the auspices of the Royal Irish Academy.[79] Almost inevitably, given the inadequacy of the legislation governing archaeological sites and national monuments in Ireland, conflicts of interest arose, most notably between Dublin Corporation and The Friends of Medieval Dublin over the Wood Quay site.[80] This controversy, together with the spectacular quality of what was recovered by means of controlled archaeological techniques,[81] had the effect of internationalizing medieval Dublin as never before.

Eight items have been selected to represent this period of increasing intellectual diversification and sophistication (chaps. 1-3, 7, 8, 10-12), beginning with a landmark in our understanding of the walls, wall towers and gateways of the medieval city (chap. 10).[82] Next in order of publication is a detailed study of post-medieval reclamation of land just outside the city wall (chap. 7).[83] This study is important methodologically for its use, in addition to early maps, of leases dating from the late 16th century onwards in order to throw light on the medieval past. The techniques here demonstrated have much to recommend them and more work of this kind remains to be done.[84] This particular piece of reclamation is historically significant in that 'the building of the first custom-house was the first stage of the eastward movement of port facilities and trade, a trend that has continued in Dublin to the present. . . . Centralization of trade at the first custom-house and wharf made the area a major focal point in the city, a role which was emphasized by the building of a replacement for Essex Bridge and the improvement of the north-south axis in the 18th century'.[85] Another effective demonstration of the relevance of materials dating from post-medieval times is J.B. Maguire's essay on 17th-century plans of Dublin Castle (chap. 11).[86] One of these plans was discovered relatively recently in an English county record office.

By the mid-1970s two directors of excavations from the National Museum of Ireland were in action — Breandán Ó Ríordáin and P.F. Wallace — and the first short-term reports were being published. The example chosen here was a paper delivered to the Viking Congress held in Dublin in 1973 (chap. 8).[87] The emphasis lies mainly on the evidence of craftworking recovered from the Christchurch Place excavation. Next in sequence came an interpretation of the topographical development of early Dublin (chap. 2).[88] Both the comparative dimension and interdisciplinary approaches were highlighted; contours appeared on an historical reconstruction map of medieval Dublin for the first time; the full significance of the double place-name Baile Átha Cliath and Dublin was explained; and a remarkable relict feature still preserved in the modern street pattern was identified on the basis of the pioneering work of Leo Swan.[89] The internationalization of Irish historiography is exemplified in a quite different idiom by chap. 12, which deals with the sculpture of Christ Church Cathedral.[90] The styles and themes of this sculpture 'provide a very precise illustration of the way English ideas infiltrated into Ireland after the Anglo-Norman invasion'. The present collection opens with an article that was published initially in German in a periodical based at Lübeck in the Federal Republic of Germany (chap. 1).[91] A direct comparison is made between medieval Dublin and medieval Lübeck. Finally, and most appropriately, we return to archaeology with Wallace's review of the origins of Dublin in a north-western European context (chap. 3). As an archaeologist of international repute and as the newly-appointed Director of the National Museum of Ireland, his contribution represents an intellectual synthesis that this book is intended both to commend and to commemorate.

Editorial principles

In general the authors have been allowed to speak for themselves. The actual texts contain few editorial intrusions (in square brackets)[92] other than standardizations of names, minor corrections and stylistic emendations. Dates have been revised silently in accordance with *A New History of Ireland*, vols. 8 and 9, which have also acted as models for the spelling of proper names. Each set of references or bibliography is preceded by editorial notes. These state the precise source, any major changes or omissions, and provide a bibliographical update. Some of the contributions have been supplied by the editor with headings to indicate the chief subdivisions of the text. Recent reprints of ancient and not so ancient works have been noted. Where modern editions of primary sources that postdate a contribution exist, the appropriate reference has been given. The list of abbreviations and conventions is based on that in vol. 2 of *A New History of Ireland*.

Whereas the texts have, for the most part, been reprinted in full and the notes and bibliographical references have sometimes been expanded, the illustrations have had to be severely rationalized for technical reasons. Some of the originals are substandard; others are unsuited to the present format. The main principles that underlie the choice of illustrations for this book are clarity of reproduction and necessity for a proper understanding of the text. In conformity with these principles, a small number of new illustrations have been provided. The index is confined to personal names and place-names; the inclusion of thematic entries would have resulted in an intractable Slough of Despond. There is no entry for Dublin itself, apart from the place-name forms Áth Cliath and Dubhlinn. These take us back to the beginnings of the recorded history of this justly famous and fascinating city, whose very street names were of greater interest to James Joyce than 'the riddle of the universe'.[93]

PART I

Historical and topographical development

Medieval Dublin in a European context: from proto-town to chartered town

ANNGRET SIMMS

In a European context the early growth phases of Irish towns are of importance in three different respects: first, for the study of early forms of urban development outside the romanized zone; secondly, for the question of the development of towns in areas where contacts and conflicts between different ethnic groups took place; thirdly, for comparison with other 'maritime city States' (*Fährmännerstadtstaaten*) that existed in northern Europe in the early Middle Ages. The first, and as far as I know the only, attempt to illustrate the close connexion between the development of trade, towns and territorial States in northern Europe in the Middle Ages, and which included the Irish coastal towns, was made by W. Vogel in 1931.[1] Later contributions, such as the pioneering works of H. Jankuhn,[2] are limited to early medieval overseas trading settlements in the Baltic and North Sea regions. In the volumes of collected essays published mainly in German under the title *Vor- und Frühformen der europäischen Stadt im Mittelalter*[3] are to be found contributions on the early forms of Scandinavian and Slavic towns. In the English collection of essays, *European Towns: their Archaeology and Early History*, the late T.G. Delaney provided a preliminary survey of city centre excavations in Ireland and alluded to the problem of the early growth phases of the Irish town.[4]

This contribution has two aims. The first is to establish that proto-urban forms developed not only in central and northern Europe, that is, in the Slavic and Germanic areas of settlement, but also in the north-western border region of Europe, as in Ireland in the ninth and tenth centuries. In coastal areas these were the Viking overseas trading settlements (Fig. 1). In contrast to the early overseas trading settlements of the Vikings in Scandinavia, Århus excepted, their Irish counterparts have developed between the Viking Age and the present day into the more important towns and cities of the country. The second aim is to make possible a comparison between the historical topography of early medieval Dublin and that of overseas trading settlements on the Continent. A good example would be Lübeck, whose growth into a town also took place in the context of tensions between two different ethnic groups.

A new appraisal of the early history of Irish towns

The significance of early medieval Dublin was already known to historians of the last century from literary sources,[5] but clear evidence for the Viking settlement at Dublin came only with the city centre excavations of the last 20 years. The first excavation was carried out in 1961-2 at the castle, under the auspices of the Office of Public Works (the State agency for the protection of national monuments). The results, unfortunately, were never published. Further excavations on several productive sites were undertaken by the National Museum of Ireland, under the direction of the archaeologists B. Ó Ríordáin and P.F. Wallace for which preliminary reports have been published.[6]

The historical importance of the Dublin city centre excavations became widely known through the activities of an interdisciplinary research group, The Friends of Medieval Dublin, founded in 1976. Towards the end of 1977

1 Map of trade routes in central and northern Europe during the Viking period
(after H. Jankuhn).

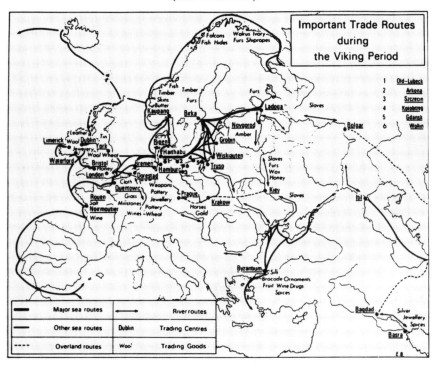

the group faced a crisis when Dublin Corporation attempted to flatten the by no means completed excavations of the Viking settlement between Christ Church Cathedral and Wood Quay, in order to build four skyscrapers to serve as Dublin's new civic offices. Public pressure ensured that the excavations were resumed for a brief period. In 1978 F.X. Martin, Professor of Medieval History at University College, Dublin, and chairman of The Friends, went to court and managed to have the excavation site north of Christ Church Cathedral up to the medieval town wall declared a national monument. In spite of this the Corporation sought, with the aid of formal legal provisions, to break off the excavations prematurely. There was a protest demonstration, in which about 17,000 people took part for the preservation of their Viking town. In May 1979 the Council of Europe passed a resolution calling on the Irish government to preserve the Viking settlement at Wood Quay as a European monument. The Irish government did not react, but rather conceded a stay of execution by which the excavations could continue until the end of March 1980. This was extended to the end of September owing to strong political pressure from the city council. At present (1980) a debate is being prepared in the European Parliament about the premature ending of the Dublin excavations and the government's failure to preserve the structural finds *in situ* as a European cultural monument.[7] The finds from Dublin formed an important part of the great Viking exhibition that was held in the British Museum in 1980.

The enthusiasm of the Irish for the beginnings of their urban life is a new phenomenon. Until recently the official wisdom was that Irish towns were solely the result of the various phases of colonization, all of which had come into conflict with the native Celtic population. From the ninth to the 12th century the colonizers were the Scandinavians, from the late 12th century onwards the Anglo-Normans, and in the 17th century the English. A quotation from F.H.A. Aalen's book illustrates the old standpoint: 'Before urban life could take root on Irish soil a radically new cultural and economic milieu was needed and this could only come from outside'.[8] This statement echoes the opinion of the Celtic scholar D.A. Binchy, who claimed that urban civilization had more or less to be foisted upon the Irish by conquerors from outside.[9] Recently the exponents of this hypothesis have been subjected to severe criticism. They have been accused of suffering from an 'invasion neurosis'.[10] We now know from studying the sources that at the time of the arrival of the Vikings in Ireland settlements already existed that, judging by their form and function, were of the nature of proto-towns.[11] These were the big monastic settlements. Much research remains to be done on the functional relationship between these big monastic settlements and the Scandinavian overseas trading settlements of the 11th and 12th centuries.

This new approach has been demonstrated on a map entitled 'Origins of

Principal Towns' and published in the *Atlas of Ireland*, which I compiled in co-operation with the historian K. Simms.[12] This map is based on two variables: first, the definition of what constitutes a town; secondly, the determination of the important growth phases for the development of towns in Ireland. To borrow from Jankuhn's terminology, we must differentiate between 'towns of the old kind' (*Städte alter Art*) and 'chartered towns of the new kind' (*Rechtsstädte neuer Art*).[13] With regard to proto-towns we distinguished between early Irish monastic settlements, Viking trading settlements, and later Irish market settlements. Dublin's medieval growth phases belong to three categories: as a Viking overseas trading settlement it belongs to the proto-town category; from the first half of the tenth century to the second half of the 12th century it functioned as a town without a charter; and under Anglo-Norman influence it became a town with a charter. Just what role was played by Early Christian, Gaelic Dublin, whose monastic settlement was subsumed into Scandinavian Dublin, is still being researched.[14] One process was especially important for the later development of Ireland: owing to the foundation of Viking overseas trading settlements along the coast and their successful further development, the centre of gravity of settlement in Ireland shifted towards the east coast.

Certainly the deep-rooted belief in Ireland, which has only recently weakened, that towns were really something un-Irish, has contributed in the past to a neglect of the historic townscape. Emotionally people simply associated towns with colonial rule. The first group of colonizers, namely the Vikings, has got a particularly bad press. They came to Ireland in the ninth century as pirates from the Norwegian fjords and settled on the big river estuaries. Using fortified military camps as their bases they sallied forth to plunder Irish monasteries and to capture Irish slaves. Consequently they were presented only as a great threat in the contemporary Irish annals. In the prayer of an Irish monk of the ninth century the following lines are to be found, illustrating the fear of Viking raids:

> The wind is rough tonight / tossing the white-combed ocean;
> I need not dread fierce Vikings / crossing the Irish Sea.[15]

But by the early tenth century the Viking pirates had evolved into merchants and craftsmen, farmers and fishermen. In co-operation with the native population they made a considerable contribution to the economic and cultural development of Ireland. Nationalist historiography in Ireland, however, has limited itself to a description of the youthful sins of the Vikings and has ignored the more mature achievement, the cultural contribution. But in recent times this has changed — so much so, indeed, that we may even speak of a new historical consciousness.

Through their long colonial history the Irish suffered from a lack of self-confidence. Thus it is important to draw attention to the fact that in the tenth and 11th centuries Dublin was one of the most outstanding trading settlements of its day. It is more important still to realize that urban life at that time was not an innovation that the Vikings brought with them ready-made from Scandinavia. Rather the Viking towns are the product of the Viking Age and are not conceivable without interaction with the respective native population, be it the Irish on the western edge or the Russians on the eastern edge of Europe. This marked fusion of native Irish and Viking elements in 11th- and 12th-century Dublin is defined by historians by the term 'Hiberno-Norse'.

Proto-town origins and early growth

The classic works of synthesis on medieval Dublin were written in the 19th century by an archivist and a merchant, and have recently been reprinted.[16] These works do not include any maps of medieval Dublin. In 1931 the architectural historian H.G. Leask made the first exact attempt to show medieval remains in the modern city on a map, which was tucked away in an excursion report.[17] A pioneer with an individual stamp was the medical doctor and amateur historian G.A. Little, who in a book about early medieval Dublin speculated on the existence of a big, pre-Viking, Gaelic settlement.[18] His conclusions, however, far exceeded what could be proved from the source material. J. Ryan, on the other hand, wrote a painstakingly researched article on the political history of Gaelic and Viking Dublin, but failed to deal with topographical questions.[19] More recently we are indebted to the archaeologists Ó Ríordáin and Wallace, and to the surveyor P. Healy, for references to the topography of medieval Dublin. The latter illustrated the course of the medieval town wall cartographically, while the historical geographer N.T. Burke reconstructed the course of the north-eastern town wall with the help of title-deeds and leases.[20] A comparative analysis of the Viking kingdoms of York and Dublin was produced by the historian A.P. Smyth in 1975-9.[21] The recent publication, written by geographers and called *The Development of the Irish Town*, contains no case-studies.[22]

In order to create a basis for a more precise knowledge of medieval Dublin, The Friends have brought out two large-scale maps, which were printed by the Ordnance Survey.[23] The cartographical supplement to *A New History of Ireland* contains two small-scale maps showing the growth of medieval Dublin.[24] The historian H.B. Clarke has attempted to reconstruct the settlement of pre-Viking Dublin, whilst I have tried to delineate medieval Dublin with the help of a town-plan analysis of the first accurate contemporary plan of Dublin drawn up by John Rocque and published in 1756.[25] In both cases documentary and archaeological sources were taken into account. The following presentation is based largely on the results of this work.

The ground level in present-day Dublin is higher than in the early medieval period, because over the centuries rubbish and waste have accumulated. North of Christ Church Cathedral archaeologists have worked at a section about 9 m. high, which was created by mechanical excavation. This section was made up exclusively of the remains of earlier layers of settlement. The remains of Viking houses from the tenth and 11th centuries were found and over them lay those of Anglo-Norman houses from the 13th century. In the riverside area by the Liffey the original configuration of the ground has also been altered considerably through infilling. Nevertheless the contour lines provide some valuable hints about locational factors for the first settlement. A long, narrow hill or ridge is apparent, roughly 16 m. high, which runs parallel to the south bank of the Liffey as far as its confluence with the Poddle. This corresponds fairly closely to the height of the hill on which Lübeck stands.

The hill at Dublin is made up of boulder clay and the streets that now radiate from the hill in a northerly, southerly and easterly direction exhibit a marked fall in gradient. Strategically speaking, the choice of a spur for a hill-top town was ideal. No wonder the Vikings chose this site on which to build their military camp. In addition the spur lay at the point of entry of a tributary into the Liffey. Such a riverside location, where a smaller stream flows into a larger one, fulfilled all of the conditions for the smooth operation of loading techniques for early medieval ships. As D. Ellmers has pointed out, 'the banks of the side-stream provided the necessary firm ground for the ships to be beached, while the estuary afforded protection against the current and waves emanating from the mainstream'.[26]

Quite apart from the favourable strategic location, the chosen site also had the advantage that it was an important road junction. Just before the mouth of the Liffey there was a river-crossing that was central to the road network of the pre-Viking period. It was a ford, by which the long-distance road from Tara, the seat of the Irish high-kings, ran on its way to the kingdom of Leinster, which lay south of the Liffey.[27] Here, too, parallels may be drawn with Lübeck, whose location was influenced to a significant degree by the course of a long-distance trade route of the Slavic period.

In the early Middle Ages the Liffey estuary was much wider than it is today. The geological map shows the line between alluvium and boulder clay, which has been reproduced on Fig. 4.[28] It is uncertain at which point in time this line actually represented the river-bank. Excavations have shown that in the Hiberno-Norse period (the 11th and 12th centuries), when the town wall was built of stone, the water of the Liffey came very close to this wall (Fig. 3, no. 7). It is worth mentioning that north of the Liffey both churches of the pre-Norman period, St. Michan's and St. Mary's Abbey, are located just off the alluvium on boulder clay. The priory of All Saints, whose foundation predates the Anglo-Norman invasion, makes this reconstruction of the river-bank appear questionable. After the dissolution of the monasteries in the 16th century, it became the site of Trinity College, Dublin. Here, at least, the mid-12th-century coastline must have run north of the line separating the alluvium from boulder clay. A permanent bridge over the Liffey must have already existed by 1014, because at that juncture the *pons Ostmannorum* (as it was later known) is mentioned in connexion with the battle at Clontarf, which lies about 2 km. north-east of Dublin. The 'thing', a public assembly of free men, was an important institution at major Viking settlements and at Dublin the Thingmount was demolished only in the late 17th century. The district between the eastern course of the town wall and the Thingmount was built on after drainage work earlier in the same century.[29]

The River Poddle in the early Middle Ages meandered between widely spaced contours and split up into a mainstream and a side-stream. The island thus created was to be the site of St. Patrick's Cathedral (Fig. 4). The confluence of the Poddle with the Coombe stream was probably the lowest point at which the Poddle was fordable. In addition it was an important intersection for long-distance routes. Long-distance routes were called in Irish *slighte*, a derivation from the Old Irish verb *sligid*, which means 'to fell'.[30] The Slige Dála, which came from Cork, and the Slige Chualann, which came from Waterford, joined one another near the crossing-point of the Poddle and led northwards across the Liffey in the direction of Tara (Fig. 4).

Between the Poddle and the Steine, i.e. east of the major road intersection, there were a number of church sites and holy wells, which seem to have been Gaelic foundations from pre-Viking times. These are St. Patrick's (now a Protestant cathedral), St. Brigit's and St. Michael le Pole's (both pulled down in the 18th century), St. Kevin's (now a ruin) and St. Peter's (now vanished) (Fig. 4). St. Peter's stood in a curve in the street that is reminiscent of early Irish monastic enclosures in other locations. These enclosures have frequently been delineated with the help of aerial photography.[31] Clarke has discussed the documentary sources that suggest that an Early Christian monastic settlement was to be found here.[32] The eastern part of this former enclosure was drastically altered in the 17th century, when a new town quarter was laid out.[33]

South of the spur, beyond the Poddle, we find a hollow that is denoted by the 35 ft. contour line. The same contour represents the course of the old river-bank along the town wall at Wood Quay. In early medieval times this hollow is likely to have been flooded at high tide. It has been suggested that this was the 'black pool' (*linn dubh*) from which the Irish place-name Dubhlinn originated. This place-name was evidently adopted by the Vikings for their first settlement from the existing Gaelic population. F. Henry and more recently Clarke have suggested that the name Dubhlinn referred to the Early Christian monastic settlement south of the black pool.[34] Ample proof of this can be found in the Early Christian literature: for example, the Martyrology of Donegal records the death of bishops of Dubhlinn from the seventh century. Clarke believes that this interpretation of the word Dubhlinn would explain why *two* Irish place-names for Dublin were used in the annals: Dubhlinn, the monastic settlement at the black pool, and Áth Cliath, the settlement at the ford (Fig. 4).[35] He cites a passage from the medieval biography of St. Mo Laga, where it says: ' . . . et ad ciuitatem maritimam, quae Dun Dubhlinne seu Ath Cliath appellatur'.[36] Down to the present day the official Irish version of 'Dublin' is Baile Átha Cliath. According to Clarke the oldest contemporary references to Áth Cliath appear in a sixth-century Irish praise poem and in Adomnán's seventh-century biography of St. Columba.[37] The same author postulates that, in addition to the Irish monastic settlement and the settlement on the ridge associated with the ford, there may have been a pre-Viking ring-fort.[38] To-date, however, no archaeological evidence has been found that might confirm the existence of such a ring-work.

According to the Annals of Ulster the first Vikings at Dublin landed with their ships, apparently 60 of them, at the mouth of the Liffey in the year 837.[39] A few years later they built themselves a fortified landing-place, which is known in Irish as a *longphort*. It has already been pointed out with the aid of the contour map that the ridge south of the Liffey was ideally suited, for strategic reasons, as a location for the first Viking settlement. This settlement had the function of a military camp, or pirates' nest, to be more precise. Excavations have confirmed that this was the site of the tenth-century Viking settlement, but the question remains open whether that settlement had expanded from the ridge towards the river or the other way round. With a harbour settlement one is inclined to believe that the latter may be the case. It is equally unclear whether a fortification existed in the Viking period on the site of the present castle, or whether that possibility should be discounted.

In the year 902 the Irish managed to eject the Vikings from Dublin and to burn down their settlement. This was the result of a complicated political scenario, which already included the alliance of Vikings and Irish *against* other Vikings and Irish.[40] Fifteen years later the Vikings returned with reinforcements. This time they laid out settlements at Dublin, Wexford, Waterford, Limerick and presumably Cork as well. Evidently these settlements began to fulfil trading functions within a short time and they became important centres of craft production, as the Dublin excavations have made clear. The excavations have also shown that this later Viking settlement nucleus beside the Liffey was protected by two parallel earthen banks (Fig.

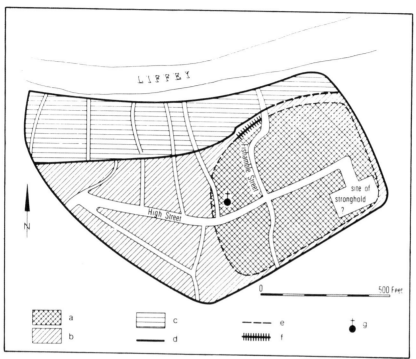

2 Map of the growth stages of the walled town. This is a conjectural reconstruction based on town-plan analysis and on archaeological discoveries.

KEY: a. Viking encampment; b. extension of the Viking settlement into a trading station, with a town wall of *c.* 1100; c. Anglo-Norman reclaimed area in the Liffey estuary, with extensions to the town wall of *c.* 1300; d. town wall; e. probable course of the earthen defences; f. point at which three parallel earthen banks were uncovered archaeologically; g. Christ Church Cathedral, first built as a wooden church *c.* 1030 and rebuilt in stone in the early Anglo-Norman period.

3, no. 6). The first of these earthen banks, according to Wallace, is dated *c.* 950 and the second *c.* 1000, the latter having several structural phases.[41] These wooden and earthen constructions represent Dublin's first fortifications. Thus Dublin may be classed among the better known early medieval trading settlements, protected by earthen banks. Two further examples would be Haithabu in Germany and Birka in Sweden.

From the point of view of a settlement historian it is of great importance to determine when the transformation of Dublin from a 'pirates' nest' into a trading settlement took place. Apparently this happened around 950, according to the evidence of the archaeological finds. From the end of the tenth century the Dubliners were minting their own coins. In the course of the Dublin excavations a silver coin dating from 997 and a gold coin dating from 995 were found. The Annals of the Four Masters report that in 989, when Dublin was temporarily under Irish overlordship, the high-king Máel Sechnaill levied a tax of one ounce of gold on each house plot in the town. This fact leads one to conclude that by then individual property units had emerged inside the settlement.

Dublin developed into one of the most important Viking trading settlements of its time. But it should be remembered that Dublin's primary function was not that of a market serving a large hinterland; rather it was an emporium, that is a point of interchange with a key position in a system of commercial exchange between northern Europe and the Mediterranean region. Dublin was particularly involved in the trade in slaves and in silver.[42]

The expansion of the settlement westwards along High Street took place in the period of Dublin's development into a trading centre, in the second half of the tenth century (Fig. 2). The excavations at High Street and Christchurch Place have revealed, 2.50 m. beneath the present-day road surface, material remains of the tenth- and 11th-century Viking settlement. This material finds its parallels in the results of excavations at other settlements of the Viking Age, such as Birka, Haithabu and Duurstede.[43] The excavations at Fishamble Street provided clear evidence of trade with France that predates the Anglo-Norman invasion: grey pottery of French origin such as glazed sherds from Andenne and red-painted pottery from Normandy.[44] In addition Wallace has excavated wooden houses from the tenth and 11th centuries at Fishamble Street (Fig. 3, no. 10). They are almost rectangular, about 6 m. by 4 m., and consist of wood, mainly post-and-wattle work. The street fronts of these houses correspond to the course of present-day Fishamble Street! Máel Sechnaill's tax of the year 989 must refer to these house sites. They stood on long, narrow plots, at the end of which there were indications of outhouses. Whether these houses were those of traders with an adjacent landing-place for ships, as excavations have shown for Hamburg and Kaupang, is not yet clear. It is still an open question at which stage the harbour was shifted from the confluence of the Poddle and the Liffey. Nor do we know whether the Vikings had already built jetties at Dublin, or whether they simply dragged their ships up the earthen banks that had been built for the purpose of protection.

The excavations along High Street have shown that the growth of the settlement was due primarily to the productive capacity of the craftsmen. Artisans' quarters have been revealed that produced, amongst other things, combs (in High Street alone 600 were found), footware and metal-work in the form of brooches. Their ornamentation corresponds to the Hiberno-Norse form of the Ringerike style.[45] The influence of Scandinavian art on that of the native Irish is a wide field of investigation.[46]

At the time when Dublin was developing into a trading centre, a marked

3 The Wood Quay archaeological site, 1977.
KEY: 1. Christ Church Cathedral; 2. High Street; 3. Fishamble Street; 4. Winetavern Street; 5. Wood Quay; 6. earthen banks; 7. town wall of *c.* 1100 and later; 8. part of the area reclaimed from the river in the 13th century; 9. site of the quay wall of *c.* 1300; 10. site of the row of Viking and Hiberno-Norse house plots.

integration between the Scandinavian and the Irish inhabitants occurred. An immediate consequence of this was that King Sitric Silkbeard introduced Christianity in the early 11th century. The first Scandinavian church, a wooden structure, was erected on the site of Christ Church Cathedral (Fig. 3, no. 1). Judging from their names, the first five bishops of Dublin were Irishmen. But they did not adopt the Irish system, in which abbots exercised the functions of bishops; rather they had their bishops consecrated at Canterbury and opted for the Roman diocesan system.[47] It has been claimed that it was through this connexion of the Irish Scandinavians with Canterbury that 'greedy Norman archbishops' first became aware of Ireland and that the idea of an invasion, which came to pass in 1169, was born.[48]

Around the turn of the 11th and 12th centuries the earthen banks, which enclosed the considerably enlarged area of settlement along High Street (according to observations made beneath the road surface at the western gate), were replaced by a wall consisting of limestone blocks (Figs. 2; 3, no. 7). The town wall of Hiberno-Norse Dublin enclosed an area of about 12 hectares. By continental standards this was not much: contemporary Duurstede in Holland covered about 100 hectares. At Cologne the merchants' settlement on the Rhine, which was surrounded by a wall in the tenth century, covered 25 hectares, but by the 12th century this had increased to a total walled area of 200 hectares. More appropriate would be a comparison with contemporary Scandinavian trading settlements: the defensive works enclosed 11.7 hectares at Birka and 24.3 hectares inside the rampart at Haithabu.[49] On the other hand the Slavic *suburbia* had even smaller enclosed settlement areas: for example, Gdansk and Opole in Poland had between 1 and 2 hectares while Poznan had 5-7 hectares.[50] These town walls at Dublin were far from being directed exclusively against Gaelic enemies, for contrary to all expectations the Viking towns exhibited little solidarity with one another. Quite the reverse! In 1087 the men of Dublin razed Waterford to the ground; in 1088 the men of Dublin, Wexford and Waterford were driven off by the Irish sept Uí Echach Muman as they were about to attack Cork.[51] Vikings and Irish allied against Vikings and Irish if political capital and booty could be seen in it.[52] Despite the political turbulence, however, trade and handicrafts at Dublin could develop to such a degree that preconditions for the growth of early urban modes and functions were created.

Anglo-Norman Dublin: a chartered town

After the capture of Dublin by the Anglo-Normans (21 September 1170), King Henry II of England issued a charter in 1171-2 by which Dublin was handed over to the men of Bristol for development. Thus this settlement, which was already exercising urban functions, acquired a legal identity for the first time, if only in the sense that foreign burgesses living there enjoyed the liberties of a foreign town. From now on Dublin belonged to the chartered towns, that is 'towns of the new kind'.

The town itself acquired a municipal identity by a charter of 1192, which contains several useful topographical allusions. There is a reference to houses outside the Hiberno-Norse walls: by common consent the inhabitants were to lay out new messuages, some of which were 'on sands and mudbanks' (*in sabulis et glisseriis*).[53] By this is probably meant the land between the old town wall and the river, which was reclaimed in order to cater for the deeper draught of the bigger Anglo-Norman ships. With the help of wooden quay-sides, which Wallace has excavated and dated to between 1180 and 1300, this process of reclamation could be reconstructed accurately (Fig. 3, nos. 8, 9). In the early 14th century the town wall was extended down to the river and as a result the area enclosed by the walls increased to 18 hectares (Fig. 2). The Anglo-Normans improved, or perhaps even replaced, the existing town walls. Henry III provided money to this end in 1221: '. . . in aid of enclosing that city, and for the security and protection of it as well as the adjacent parts'.[54] The numerous town gates originated in all probability in the Anglo-Norman period (Fig. 28).

The size of the original burgage plots may be gleaned from contemporary documents. In the register of Archbishop Alen of Dublin there is an entry for the period between 1228 and 1255: 'land with buildings in New Street which was formerly Bartholomew the baker's, lying between the lands of Arnulph Marescall and William Wulf, and containing in front 30 ft.'.[55] In the same register an entry for the year 1336 runs: '. . . in St. Patrick's Street . . . containing in front 54 ft., in rear 66 ft., and extending in length . . . five score and 19 ft.'.[56]

The 13th century was for Dublin a period of economic prosperity and so a large number of public buildings, which are shown on Clarke's map,[57] came to be built. The most significant was Dublin Castle (Fig. 28, nos. 1-7), which remained the centre of English power in Ireland until the coming of independence in 1921. Artisanal quarters from the Scandinavian period continued to prosper and new ones were added (e.g., in Castle Street, known as Lormeria, horse spurs and other small iron objects were being produced). Street markets developed, of which the most important was the corn market next to the western gate, inside the town walls. A good indication of the sharp rise in population in this period is the large number of newly founded churches and religious houses. The spatial growth led to a fusion between the old Viking settlement nucleus on the ridge and the former Gaelic monastic settlement south of the ridge in the 13th century. Settlement along the main arterial roads to the north and west also grew denser. This expansion beyond the town walls can be seen clearly on the earliest surviving map of Dublin, by Speed, which dates from 1610. But here we must leave the high medieval period of growth. Its further topographical development may be gathered in broad outline from Clarke's map and from my town plan analysis based on medieval sources.[58]

In order to investigate the question of ethnic stratification, it should be borne in mind that the Anglo-Normans deported the remaining descendants of the former Viking inhabitants of Dublin to Oxmantown (derived from Ostmantown), which lay on the north bank of the Liffey. Exactly when this took place is not clear. Nor was the native Gaelic population allowed to become integrated with the new settlers, as had been possible in Hiberno-Norse Dublin: for example, the Anglo-Normans forbade the Irish to be members of guilds.[59] Thus, despite significant growth in the first century of Anglo-Norman domination, Dublin began to decline in international importance. This was so because from now on it was the administrative capital of a colony that had to serve English interests.

The three phases of growth inside the medieval town wall

In conclusion we may say that the walled part of the medieval town experienced three phases of growth, as shown on Fig. 2. The first was the Viking military camp of the ninth century, which after its destruction was rebuilt in the early tenth century as the core of the new and developing trading settlement. Secondly came the expansion of the Viking settlement nucleus along High Street in the tenth and 11th centuries, when Dublin became an international trading centre and was from time to time under Gaelic overlordship (the Hiberno-Norse period). Thirdly the Anglo-Normans enlarged the town by means of land reclamation on the south bank of the Liffey in the 13th century, in order to provide a deeper berthage for their ships.

The early walled town of the Hiberno-Norse period, which the Anglo-Normans took over and extended, was preceded not only by the Viking *longphort* but also by two Gaelic settlement nuclei in close proximity to one another. These were the ford settlement of Áth Cliath and the monastic settlement of Dubhlinn (Fig. 4). The fact that the churches of St. Brigit and St. Michael le Pole were pulled down only in the 18th century, and that other churches from the Gaelic monastic period still survive in some form, leads one to suppose that the Viking and the Gaelic settlements coexisted for a time. Especially for the first generation of Vikings, the inhabitants of the ford and monastic settlements must have been important for the rendering of services.

The early development stages of Dublin and Lübeck have a number of points in common. Both towns had a pre-urban core that was ethnically different in composition from the later chartered town. An obvious topographical similarity between the two towns lies in the choice of location on a ridge at the confluence of two rivers shortly before the outlet into the sea. Both towns grew up along a straight road on the crest of the ridge and almost entirely surrounded by water. In both towns the castle was built in a dominant position at one end of the ridge, with the cathedral towards the other end. Castle and cathedral were linked by a straight road. Had the original Viking settlement at Dublin not developed in the area of the present-day castle, but rather on the site of Christ Church Cathedral, the highest point inside the walled town, then the street pattern would probably have evolved in a concentric fashion around the church, which it clearly did not. Can one apply this argument to Lübeck and conclude that there the castle site is the older habitation area in comparison with the market-place? This has already been proved archaeologically. Whether the first settlement developed from the river-bank uphill, or from the top of the ridge downhill, or from a combination of the two locations, remains an open question for both towns.

To what extent did similarities in the historical topography of Dublin and Lübeck reflect typological homogeneity among early medieval overseas trading settlements? The answer would require a precise comparative analysis. This contribution attempts merely to narrow the information gap, which has existed for far too long, in relation to the initial phases of Irish towns. The imminent publication of the archaeological results from Dublin will in future play an important part in this debate.[60]

In marked contrast to Lübeck, with its great variety of medieval buildings still extant, Dublin's medieval past can be reconstructed only with the help of documents, old maps and archaeological finds. The only medieval monuments still standing are the cathedrals (both of which were extensively renovated in the 19th century), remnants of a few churches, sections of the town wall, and the largely preserved street pattern. The medieval part of Dublin suffers from 'planning blight' (*Planungswüste*) and much of it is in disrepair. The origins of this decline can be found in the 16th and 18th centuries. In the 16th century the dissolution of the monasteries led to the destruction of the old buildings; later, in the 18th century, the centre of the new 'Georgian town' was shifted to a north-south axis, east of the medieval core, and this area has remained the commercial hub of the city to the present day. Dublin's medieval origins were more or less forgotten, until the city centre excavations of the last 20 years raised the historical consciousness of her citizens about the early medieval history of Dublin.[61]

The topographical development of early medieval Dublin

H . B . C L A R K E

This contribution to an understanding of the circumstances in which Dublin developed in the early Middle Ages is based primarily on topographical analysis. The questions to be asked and, if possible, answered have to do with the location and interrelation of historical features and sites on the ground. For the historian there are two ways of exploring the topography of medieval Dublin. One is to examine modern large-scale maps for relict features still preserved in the pattern of buildings, property boundaries and streets. The other is to plot known medieval features and sites on maps in order to build up a sequential picture of Dublin's origins and early growth. Ideally we should be able to produce maps depicting the settlement plan at regular intervals, say of one or two centuries, but in this preliminary investigation maps representing Dublin in its Gaelic and Scandinavian stages will be used as illustrations. We are thus engaged on an exercise in the dimensions of space and time.

The evidence for early medieval Dublin has come, and will continue to come, from the ground and from documents. The elucidation of the problems posed by this evidence is the business of archaeologists, historians and historical geographers working together. Auxiliary disciplines and techniques have an important role as well: for example, the study of coins and of place-names and the photographing of sites from the air. The difficulties inherent in the co-ordination of these types of evidence are not to be under-estimated.[1] Many Dubliners are by now aware that excavations in the medieval core-area of the modern city have yielded a wealth of archaeological material in the form of buildings, pathways, carved antlers and bone, leather-work, woodwork and much more besides. When this material has been analysed and published in full, our knowledge of Norse, Hiberno-Norse and Anglo-Norman Dublin will increase dramatically. Two important qualifications are necessary here. First, the areas so far excavated represent only part of the Scandinavian settlement and only a small part of the Anglo-Norman town, much of which was situated outside the walls. Secondly, the dating range of the material recovered is generally late ninth century to early

14th century:[2] no evidence of pre-Norse habitation has yet come to light. The documentary investigation of early medieval Dublin has been equally limited. From the middle of the 19th century down to *c.* 1920 Scandinavian and Anglo-Norman Dublin excited a good deal of interest that resulted in the publication of basic information about the city's medieval past. Two of the most impressive and substantial works written in this period have recently been reprinted, for they have hardly been superseded.[3] To emphasize that more remains to be done brings no discredit upon these pioneers in the field of scholarship.

With one exception, mentioned below, all existing books dealing with the medieval period share a particularly serious deficiency: they lack maps that illustrate the town's topographical plan and development. This is true of Gilbert's *History of the City of Dublin*, despite the fact that the entire work, published in three volumes, was arranged topographically. The most informative small-scale general map of medieval Dublin lies hidden away in an account of the summer meeting of the Royal Archaeological Institute of Great Britain and Ireland at Dublin in July 1931.[4] Maps are not altogether lacking. Time and again the inset to John Speed's map of Leinster has been reproduced in later works.[5] As the earliest depiction of Ireland's leading town Speed's map is of inestimable value, but it cannot be expected to stand duty for purpose-designed maps of Dublin in the Middle Ages. Thus many basic features of the topographical development of medieval Dublin have still not been ascertained. The prevailing uncertainty applies equally to the solitary book on pre-Norse Dublin.[6] This challenging interpretation, infused with a spirited sense of nationalism that distorted the author's view of the period, remains an invaluable storehouse of references to the documentary sources. But in an attempt to plot all pre-Norse sites, they were superimposed in red on Pool and Cash's version of Speed's map, which is not an exact copy of the original.[7] The magnetic attraction of the map he prepared might have gratified Speed, yet there is no substitute for a blank sheet of paper when embarking upon a reconstruction of the origins and early growth of this or any other modern city.

Continental background

In common with the origins of most important European towns, those of Dublin are shrouded in obscurity. Our problem relates to the wider history of medieval towns. During this century there has been much debating among historians as to why towns grew in the early Middle Ages, that is to say, between A.D. 400 and 1000.[8] One safe conclusion is that a monocausal explanation can no longer be sustained. In fact various processes can be distinguished in the normally inadequate documentation. Examples of these are as follows: town growth on a former Roman site that had been made the seat of an archbishop or a bishop; town growth in association with a royal palace, to which an artisanal and/or merchant community was attached; town growth in association with a big monastery, again to which an artisanal and/or merchant community was attached; town growth in England and Germany on a site fortified in the first half of the tenth century. In each case a specialized group of non-producers formed eventually the nucleus of an urban settlement. In other words the episcopal household, royal household, monastic community or military garrison gave support to dependent crafts-men and/or traders, in so far as the former represented concentrations of influence, power and wealth. Scholars have come to adopt particular terms by which to refer to such combinations: pre-urban cores, pre-urban nuclei, proto-towns. Whilst all these terms lack elegance, they are expressive of settlements or settlement clusters that cannot strictly be described as towns, but which in the course of time were transformed into towns. The pre-urban core was a vital stage in the evolution of innumerable European towns.

That early Irish history needs a stronger comparative dimension is hard to deny. The study of comparative linguistics has admittedly drawn attention to a common Indo-European social order that is reflected in the languages of peripheral countries such as Ireland and India,[9] but for the purposes of comparative history the closest models are likely to be much nearer home. For suitable models the most promising region is central Europe between the Elbe and Vistula rivers, corresponding roughly to the modern States of East Germany and Poland. Down to the 12th century this was the territory of the western Slavs, infiltrated to some extent by Germans in the tenth century. Prior to the great age of high medieval colonization this region and Ireland reached a comparable stage in their economic, social and political devel-opment. Currently Polish scholars are emphasizing the indigenous evolution of urban centres in the early Middle Ages.[10] At least a dozen places have yielded concrete archaeological evidence, whilst others are mentioned in the scanty documentation.[11] Among the best examples are Gdansk and Opole, dating from the late tenth century onwards.[12] Many Polish town sites are low-lying and beside a lake or river or near the sea, reflecting the importance of fishing and of water transport. Some included a major stronghold built of earth and timber. At Liubice, the predecessor of the later Hansa city of Lübeck, a stronghold about 100 m. in diameter was the headquarters of the Obodrite princes and was associated with subsidiary settlements for crafts-men, farmers and merchants.[13]

Tenth-century German colonization east of the Elbe resulted in the estab-lishment of fortified settlements in hostile territory. One of these was Magdeburg, situated at a crossing-place for long-distance routes of the River Elbe. Here the complex historical sequence includes a Saxon lord's house, a

Carolingian stronghold and a tenth-century royal palace, all on the same site and, together with the adjacent monastery of St. Moritz, forming the pre-urban core of Magdeburg. In 968 a cathedral was constructed for the new archbishopric and by the year 1000 a regular market had been instituted. A number of villages were located not far from the evolving town, supplying its inhabitants with food and other necessities.[14] This example, as will be seen, has a fairly close parallel in Dublin. More generally, before the high medieval German expansion in central Europe there were already settlements that may be classified either as pre-urban cores or, from the tenth century onwards, as genuine towns equipped with market facilities and merchant communities.

Gaelic Dublin: Áth Cliath

We turn now to a case-study of Dublin. Towns have evolved for many historical reasons, but their precise location is always related to the peculiar properties of the natural landscape. Ideally we should be in a position to reconstruct the environment of Dublin before any settlement had taken place. In practice this is a difficult undertaking in the absence of appropriate

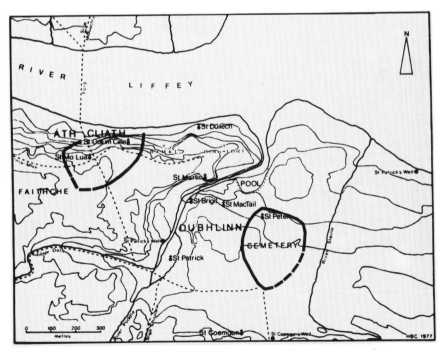

4 Map of Gaelic Dublin. The contours of the boulder clay area are shown at 5 ft. intervals, starting at 30 ft. O.D.

research, but in one important respect a tentative reconstruction is possible. Some indication of the previous alignment of the coastline and major rivers is provided by a modern drift map showing the boundary between boulder clay and alluvium.[15] The presence of deposits of alluvium suggests that, at some stage in the recent geological past, water covered parts of the modern city. The accuracy of this geological dividing line depends on the number of borings and recorded observations, and even as an indicator of drift deposits this boundary should be regarded as approximate. From an historical point of view no date can be attached to this earlier coastline, but the alluvial deposits may well correspond to the area occupied by the bay and by the rivers flowing into it until the extensive infilling of medieval and modern times. As a consequence of centuries of infilling the pattern of contours in the alluvial area is now exceedingly artificial. Nevertheless several interesting observations can be made about estuarine conditions near the site of Dublin (Fig. 4).

First, Dublin Bay opened out immediately east of the town: access to the sea was much more direct than nowadays. Very possibly the bay was fringed by slobland that was dry and firm for much of the time. Secondly, the River Liffey was broad, shallow and tidal. Rising as it does in the near-by mountains, the river until recently was subject to flash floods — sudden onrushes of water occasioned by heavy rain in the upper reaches. This characteristic of the Liffey may explain two historical phenomena. Whereas the name Liffey was applied originally to the plain west of Dublin,[16] the old name for the river was Ruirthech, meaning 'tempestuous'.[17] And in the year 770 a victorious army of the Ciannachta was drowned while crossing the river 'in the full of the sea',[18] which of course might equally refer to an oncoming tide. Thirdly, the River Poddle, a major influence on the topographical development of early Dublin, was probably subject to tidal movements as far as an island defined by the main channel and a minor channel branching off near the lowest convenient crossing-place. In the 18th century this crossing was called either Poddle or Cross Poddle,[19] the latter name appearing on the wall of a building in James Malton's aquatint of the west front of St. Patrick's Cathedral. The lower reaches of the Poddle were marshy and there are many allusions to flooding in the locality. As late as 1603 the river presented something of an obstacle to the mayor and his party when riding the franchises.[20] Fourthly, a pool scoured out by tidal movements almost certainly existed on the site of the later castle garden. This open area was not built upon presumably because the ground was too wet. Although not delineated on the drift map, the depression depicted as the pool on Figs. 4 and 7 shows up clearly on a large-scale contour map. This pool is recalled in the names of three structures in the Anglo-Norman town: the church of St. Michael le Pole, the Pole Gate and the Pole Mill. Even in the late 18th century the Poddle was still capable of inundating New Street and a tradition lingered that water was able to 'beat at full tide against the rising ground at Ship Street'.[21] The name Ship Street, incidentally, is a corruption of Sheep Street (Latin *vicus ovium*) and is therefore unconnected with the present argument. This 'black pool' (*linn dubh*), as is well known, gave rise to the English name of the medieval town and of the modern city. The allusion in an early poem to the 'mouth of the black pool' (*inbher Duibhlinne*) could represent the Poddle's outlet to the River Liffey and Dublin Bay.[22]

The proximity of the bay, the breadth of the Liffey, the obstacle presented by the Poddle and the haven afforded by the pool were crucial to the siting of Dublin. All are deserving of more detailed investigation. A partial investigation of another pertinent factor was conducted more than a generation ago in the context of the whole country, namely, long-distance routes in early medieval Ireland.[23] The composite map illustrating this analysis suggests that, despite Tara's position as the focal point of several roads, the focal point of the *slighte* or great routeways in early historical times was Dublin. Dublin was situated at the junction of the Slige Chualann from Leinster, the Slige Dála from Munster, the Slige Mór from Connacht and the Slige Midluachra from Ulster.[24] If this analysis is correct (the text, unfortunately, does not provide sufficient explanation for the map), nothing could demonstrate more forcefully the pivotal position in Ireland's economic and political structure of Dublin and its immediate neighbourhood. Certainly the geographical distribution of the major early churches seems to be related to the great routeways. There are several incidental references to the possible use by travellers of these roads: for example, the journey of Conall Corc from Munster to Dublin (Áth Cliath), where he saw ships about to sail, recorded in the Cycle of Crimthann of the eighth or ninth century.[25] The Slige Dála approached the Poddle crossing by following a small tributary flowing along The Coombe (meaning 'valley'). A zigzag in this stream is indicated by the pattern of contours and by the sequence Cork Street, Ardee Street and The Coombe. A complete list of similar references would help us to assess Dublin's importance in the early medieval period.

Now the north-south route comprising the Slige Midluachra and the Slige Chualann had to cross the Liffey *and* the Poddle. This necessity gave rise to a ford across the shallow Liffey, which according to the Triads was one of the three notable fords in Ireland.[26] The exact location is unknown, but it is likely to have been influenced by the position of the Poddle crossing. Immediately north of the Liffey the only streets that look ancient on the 1:2,500 Ordnance Survey map are Bow Street and Church Street, being irregular in their width and gently curving. Significantly enough these streets pass on either side of St. Michan's Church, which was the sole parochial church for Dublin's left-bank suburb in the Middle Ages. Bearing all these factors in mind the alignment represented by Bow Street, St. Augustine Street, Francis Street, Dean Street and New Street is the most probable course of the early medieval north-south route. This ford is commemorated in the modern Irish name for the city, Baile Átha Cliath, a place-name formation first documented in 1368.[27] Hitherto the Irish name was simply Áth Cliath. The word *cliath* refers presumably to rafts of hurdle-work staked to the river bed, weighted down by massive stones, and designed to provide a footway for people and domestic animals across the mud flats at low tide. To judge by the breadth of the alluvial deposits at this point, the distance was approximately 300 m. The technique of depositing rafts across unstable ground is prehistoric and, though traces of the Liffey ford have not yet been found, large hurdles of wattle-work were used as floors in the houses of Hiberno-Norse Dublin.[28] A programme of research excavation conducted in the right places would almost certainly uncover the substantial remains of the postulated rafts. This 'ford of hurdle-work' (*áth cliath*) was not a bridge, as some writers have imagined,[29] and should be distinguished sharply from any such structure. In crossing a ford one gets one's feet wet; in crossing a bridge one does not. Another ford is recorded in the late medieval period opposite Dame's Gate and leading to St. Mary's Abbey. In the year 1455-6 an order was issued that this ford be blocked by a wall to prevent 'enemies' from entering the town.[30] This is a striking reminder of how shallow the Liffey must still have been centuries after the construction of the first bridge.

The intersection of three long-distance routes on a prominent ridge overlooking an important ford is an obvious location for human settlement. The prose version of the *Dindshenchas* collection of traditions about Irish topography says that (the settlement) Áth Cliath was so named from its association with the ford and that hurdles were placed here in the reign of King Mes Gedra to enable the sheep of Athaine Ailgesech to cross over to Howth.[31] The earliest contemporary reference to Áth Cliath is to be found in a sixth-century praise poem,[32] followed by another in Adomnán's *Life of Colum Cille*, written probably between 688 and 692.[33] The historical and literary sources contain numerous allusions to this place, which must have been the primary settlement in the district. It is possible to speculate a little further by pointing to a network of roads, lanes and property boundaries in the Cornmarket area of the modern city, which may be a distant reflection of a proto-clachan or irregular settlement cluster defined by an earthen bank and fosse. Two churches that *may* date back to Early Christian times were situated within this area. One was dedicated to St. Colum Cille, who died in 597. This building is typical of Dublin's oldest churches in that, apart from the dedication to an Irish saint, little or nothing is known about it before 1170.[34] Uncertainty prevails even with regard to dedications, for those first documented in the Anglo-Norman period were not necessarily original. But to assume that at least one Christian church was built to serve the community at Áth Cliath after the conversion is not unreasonable. More mysterious, but no less suggestive, is a chapel dedicated to St. Mo Lua, unmentioned until the beginning of the 17th century when it lay in St. Catherine's parish.[35] By that time the building had little significance, but on a map of early medieval Dublin its position at the crossroads overlooking the ford conjures up a picture of a wayside chapel or shrine. Of the several St. Mo Luas in Irish hagiography, one is linked in tradition with St. Colum Cille and both these men with western Scotland. Early Christian Ireland may have had many such places of worship, just as travellers were accustomed to put up for the night in humble dwellings. In this regard we need only recall St. Patrick's Confession, in which the author refers to a cottage where he took lodging.[36]

One of the most puzzling aspects of the origins of Dublin is the question of lordship. In view of the multiple kingship characteristic of Ireland in the early Middle Ages, it is hard to believe that at least some petty king was not installed at the meeting point of the great routeways. Dublin lay in Leinster, whose provincial kingship was monopolized from 738 to 1042 by the Uí Dúnlainge of the Liffey plain, based on the great stronghold at Ailenn, near Kildare.[37] One of the population groups nearest to Dublin comprised two branches of the Cualann. Indeed the prose *Dindshenchas* refers specifically to Áth Cliath Chualann.[38] The ale of their territory, Cualu, was renowned for its quality[39] and the district may have been producing barley and other grains. One incident in the political history of the Cualann, the use at the battle of Selg in 709 of mercenary troops drawn probably from the Isle of Man,[40]may be a reflection of links between Dublin and that island. In later times the Uí Dúnchada, whose royal seat was at Liamain (Newcastle Lyons), extended their power towards Dublin.[41] But across the Liffey was another major political unit, Brega. North of the river dwelt the Gailenga who, together with the Ciannachta south of the Boyne, were regarded by the Uí Néill as being in the front line of attacks from Leinster.[42] Áth Cliath, then, was a border settlement that must have been of some political importance in the struggles between the kings of Cashel and the Uí Néill. There are signs that the Norse kingdom of Dublin was seen in this light. According to a late source, the Book of Rights, it was customary for a king of Cashel to give the king of Dublin 10 women, 10 horses and 10 ships in exchange for one month's sustenance and escort into Leinster. Such customary arrangements were not in the least outlandish in the context of an indigenous economy in which most exchanges were of favours, gifts and services. A poetic version alludes to entrenched Áth Cliath and to the prosperous ford.[43] Late sources advert also to a major stronghold at Dublin. The Book of Leinster (*c.* 1160) in a poem describes Dún Duibhlinne as one of the seven Wonders of Ireland.[44] The Life of St. Mo Laga equates Dún Duibhlinne with Áth Cliath.[45] But again these are probably references to the Scandinavian stronghold of the mid-ninth century or later. Before we reach a conclusion on this point, four other pieces of evidence need to be considered.

Two more reputedly early churches are associated with the area between the Liffey and the Poddle. One, dedicated to the popular cult figure St. Martin,[46] was replaced by St. Werburgh's after the Anglo-Norman settlement. The other, known only from the old name for the northern section of Fishamble Street, St. Tullock's Lane, may have been dedicated to St. Duilech, a recluse with more certain connexions with Balgriffin.[47] If such a church did exist it was probably refounded afresh and dedicated to St. Olaf in the 11th century, with the christianization of the Norse townsfolk. There is documentary proof that St. Olaf's (Olave's) Church was situated on the western side of Fishamble Street near the pronounced double bend in the road.[48] The third piece of fragmentary evidence relates to a curious feature of the Anglo-Norman town: the presence of three Ram Lanes leading off High Street.[49] Little suggested that these were a relic of the *rámat* before the stronghold, in its extended meaning of an open space in front of a king's residence.[50] To evaluate this kind of evidence is a hazardous task, but topographically the Ram Lanes were in an appropriate position. Fourthly a much larger expanse of ground is described in the sources as the 'green' (*faithche*) of Áth Cliath, that is to say, the local lord's territorial preserve or domain. Again, if a stronghold did stand at the eastern terminus of the great Slige Mór, a dependent relationship involving Áth Cliath is to be expected. In the terminology of Slavic historiography Áth Cliath may have been a service settlement attached to the prince's stronghold and supplying food and other necessities to his household. In the terminology of Irish historiography Áth Cliath may have been a proto-clachan co-existing with the near-by ring-fort and fulfilling precisely the same functions.[51]

Many previous writers have assumed that a pre-Scandinavian ring-fort occupied the site of the later castle. That they may have been correct in their assumption is supported by the example of several Ulster towns,[52] but the evidence is mainly circumstantial. In the case of Dublin topographical analysis favours this hypothesis: the defensive properties of a site surrounded on three sides by water; the postulated *rámat* on the western side; and the two churches, for many early churches were built under royal patronage near a king's fortress.[53] The safest conclusion is that, while documentary sources do not provide adequate proof, no possibilities should be ruled out before the completion of a concerted programme of research survey and excavation. Whatever the outcome of such a programme, the later stronghold was known in Irish not as Dún Átha Cliath but as Dún Duibhlinne. To appreciate the full significance of this we shall now cross over the River Poddle.

5 Anonymous drawing of the round tower of
the church of St. Michael le Pole, 1751.

Gaelic Dublin: Dubhlinn

On the right bank of the Poddle three or four churches with Irish dedications
were standing when the Anglo-Normans captured Dublin in 1170. One, St.
Patrick's, was destined to become a cathedral; the others were to become
parish churches. These were dedicated to St. Brigit, St. Cóemgen (Kevin)
and possibly St. Mac Táil, all persons associated with places in northern
Leinster (Kildare, Glendalough and Kilcullen respectively). In 12th-century
documents St. Patrick's is described as being 'on the island' (*in insula*), that
is to say, between the two branches of the River Poddle. The course of the
lesser, eastern channel is uncertain, but an 'ancient watercourse' beneath the
choir is marked on Thomas Drew's plan of St. Patrick's Cathedral.[54] This
church was near the Poddle crossing and could have been the focal point of
another proto-clachan settlement. Little and others believed that St. Michael
(le Pole) was an Anglo-Norman corruption of a dedication to St. Mac Táil,
who died in 664.[55] Nevertheless there is evidence to suggest that the cult of
St. Michael was developing in Ireland by the eighth century: for example,
the foundation legend of Tallaght.[56] The outstanding fact about this church
is that near by stood a round tower that was demolished as late as 1778-89
(Fig. 5).[57] Not far from St. Cóemgen's and St. Patrick's there may have been
holy wells with complementary dedications, whilst east of the little River
Steine St. Patrick's Well still survives. None of these wells, however, can be
proved to date from an early period.[58] The interrelation of all these churches
and holy wells has never been fully resolved. An answer will be apparent to
anyone who looks carefully at a detailed map of the modern city. The
alignment of Peter Row, Whitefriar Street, Upper and Lower Stephen Street,

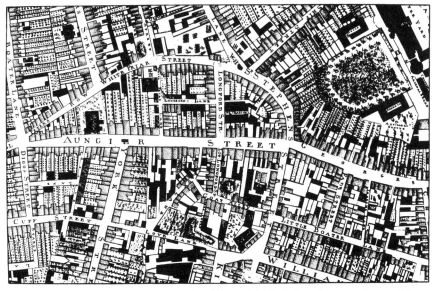

6 Extract from John Rocque's map of Dublin, 1756. North is at the top and part of the castle appears in the top left-hand corner.

Johnson Place and a former property boundary due east of Lower Mercer Street preserves the characteristic outline of an ecclesiastical enclosure (Fig. 6). The Whitefriar Street section has been broken in recent times by a building containing flats. The property boundary was noticeably out of alignment with the street block to which it belonged and continued the line from Johnson Place. The remainder of the outline has been destroyed, at least on the surface, by redevelopment of the York Street area. In shape this street outline is reminiscent of numerous enclosures as seen from the air and which are particularly common in midland and eastern Ireland.[59] This example has a north-south axis of approximately 335 m. and an east-west axis of 260 m., somewhat smaller than the dimensions of Duleek or Kells.[60] A few similar enclosures survive in the street patterns of Irish cities and towns; most are recognizable in the countryside in the form of curving walls, banks, ditches, hedges or crop-marks. To this astonishing historical feature of present-day central Dublin I have found only one reference in print — to 'a rathlike site surrounded by a ring of old streets which still retains its remarkable outline'.[61] This was not a rath, but no better demonstration could be made of the value of studying modern large-scale maps for relict features of the past.

None of the churches and wells just mentioned lay inside the enclosure, which may have served principally as a graveyard and sanctuary. This would explain its preservation throughout the medieval period, when the pattern of streets and lanes that eventually emerged went around rather than across the site. Three tombstones from a lost Celtic cemetery were built into the fabric of St. Patricks's Cathedral in the 13th century and another grave-slab was discovered at Lower Mount Street in 1916.[62] The best evidence that there is something significant about this street outline is that it corresponded to the medieval parish of St. Peter and that to this day the surviving portion represented by streets is part of the boundary of the modern parish. St. Peter's Church is undocumented before the 1170s, but seems to have been in existence when the Anglo-Normans arrived. In Anglo-Norman documents it is called St. Peter's on the Hill (*de la Hulle, de Monte*), that is to say, on rising ground overlooking the pool.[63] In fact the terrain continues to rise in a southerly direction towards modern St. Peter's, before falling again at Redmond's Hill. All this is to suggest that the postulated Christian cemetery may have contained a church dedicated to St. Peter, a popular early medieval cult figure throughout Europe. The apostle's traditional role as keeper of the keys would have made this a fitting dedication for a graveyard church, whilst a consciousness of the pope as St. Peter's successor was present in Ireland as in other parts of western Christendom.[64]

Even though dedications were unusual in the early stages of Irish monasticism,[65] all five churches on the right bank of the Poddle could have been founded by the year 700. This would help to explain another interesting historical feature, the rather dubious references to bishops of Dublin, the first of whom, Livinius, died in 633. Continental hagiography is in this respect unreliable,[66] but the existence of bishops is not inherently unlikely. The Martyrology of Donegal mentions another, Rumoldus, who is described as 'bishop of Dubhlinn, which is called Áth Cliath'.[67] More suggestive still are the references to an Abbot Beraid, who died in 650, and to an Abbot Siadal, who died in 790 and who is listed as a bishop in the martyrologies.[68] Now the early Irish Church was characterized by a gradual shift from episcopal to abbatial control, a process whose chronology varied from place to place. In general, however, the preponderance of abbots over bishops became decisive at some stage in the seventh century.[69] The evidence under review seems to point to the evolution of a monastic community on the right bank of the Poddle and south of the pool.[70] Indeed a striking concentration of monastic sites is to be found in and near the lower Liffey valley, namely Clondalkin, Finglas, Glasnevin, Kilmainham, Santry and Tallaght, with Swords and Lusk farther north.[71] Dublin should surely be numbered among them. And what stands out in the scanty documentation is the consistency with which Dubhlinn rather than Áth Cliath is cited as the seat of these shadowy ecclesiastical figures.

Consistent, too, is the question of approach roads to the enclosure. The Slige Dála continued eastwards from the Poddle crossing towards the south-western corner, the most probable location for the main entrance. In later times this stretch of road was called Great Boater/Butter Lane, from the Irish word *bóthar*, and is represented by present-day Upper Kevin Street and Bishop Street.[72] A Butter Cross also commemorated this earlier *bóthar*.[73] There is no indication as to the origin of this stone cross, but market crosses stood on or just outside the boundary of the ecclesiastical enclosures at Kells and possibly Armagh and Duleek.[74] Another road is likely to have approached the enclosure from the south, along the line of Camden Street, Wexford Street and Redmond's Hill. This route led to Enniskerry and Glendalough past the Scalp, which might account for the reputation in the Triads of the 'pass of Dublin' in the sense of a defile through mountains or a way cut through dense woodland.[75] It might also account for another puzzling documentary allusion, in a tract composed by Cuán ua Lothcháin, who died in 1024, entitled Restrictions and Prerogatives of the Kings of Éire. According to this text the Leinster kings were prohibited from passing with an army on a Monday along the 'road to Dublin'.[76] Does the tract imply, therefore, that the monastic community and/or its Scandinavian successors exercised prescriptive rights over this approach road? True or not, topographical analysis creates credible explanations for otherwise meaningless allusions.

Despite all the defects of the evidence this interpretation resolves the one uncompromising and undeniable fact about early medieval Dublin: the existence of two place-names associated with two distinct geographical features, a ford and a pool. Our conclusion must be that by the eighth century two settlement clusters had evolved on either side of the River Poddle. Áth Cliath was a farming and fishing community, possibly dependent upon a near-by stronghold and certainly controlling the ford and major routes. Dubhlinn was an ecclesiastical or quasi-ecclesiastical community ruled by bishops and/or abbots and may have acted as a magnet for craftsmen to settle in the immediate neighbourhood.[77] The presence of craftsmen, if proven, would be important, for they represent not only different productive processes but also a division of non-agricultural labour that must form the basis of any argument in favour of monastic 'towns'. All this serves to remind us of Armagh, with its 'thirds' where craftsmen, students and traders congregated.[78] The treatment in the sources of Áth Cliath and Dubhlinn was not necessarily consistent, for contemporary writers may have been unfamiliar with the local topography. Occasionally the two names were run together in the form Áth Cliath Duibhlinne, reminiscent of the way in which the name Budapest has evolved from separate settlements on opposite banks of the River Danube. The two settlement clusters at Dublin were to form the nucleus of the Anglo-Norman town. Curiously enough the enclosure was later occupied by a Carmelite priory and St. Stephen's Hospital, besides St. Peter's Church. In other words the cemetery and sanctuary continued in ecclesiastical use throughout the Middle Ages, just as there are examples even now of country roads skirting ancient field monuments.[79] And thanks to an excellent recent investigation we know a good deal about the circumstances in which this sacrosanct site was eventually and decisively secularized.[80] Between 1660 and 1685 Francis Aungier, the first earl of Longford, developed an extensive planned suburb on land he had purchased. This development marked the beginning of that eastward shift of central Dublin which was to lead ultimately to the decay and destruction of the medieval core.

Scandinavian Dublin

Now that so much archaeological evidence for Norse and Hiberno-Norse Dublin has been recovered, there is an understandable reluctance on the part of a non-archaeologist to interpret the extant documentary sources. The Scandinavian period will here be passed over in a more summary fashion before a general conclusion is reached. Over 40 years after the first raiders appeared off the Irish coast a party of Scandinavians established a base at Dublin. According to the *Cogadh Gaedhel re Gallaibh*, a late and not always reliable source,[81] a fleet of 65 ships landed *c.* 837 at the black pool of Áth Cliath.[82] These seafarers needed sheltered waters for their ships and a defensible site on land, requirements that were satisfied by the pool and Poddle estuary on the one hand and by the eastern end of the ridge on the other. In 841 a fortified ship harbour (Irish *longphort*) was constructed. In recent excavations at Fishamble Street a gently curving and timber-revetted earthen bank has been uncovered at the lowest stratified level. The exact nature of this feature has still to be determined, but an obvious possibility is that it represents part of an early, if not the earliest, Scandinavian enclosure. The word *longphort* is a compound based on two Latin loan-words[83] and the *longphort* at Linn Duachaill (Annagassan), Co. Louth, was similarly situated at the confluence of two rivers.[84] Hereafter there are many references to the Dublin Norsemen and their semi-legendary leader, Turgéis.[85] One of the most interesting is the statement that *c.* 845 'a great fleet came into the south of Áth Cliath.[86] This makes sense in the context of a river pool south of the ridge on which Áth Cliath stood. The location and shape of the earliest Scandinavian stronghold have not yet been established, though the curving bank and a zigzag in the north wall of the later Hiberno-Norse town hint at a squarish enclosure surrounded on three sides by water (Fig. 7). An alternative explanation for the zigzag is that the builders were seeking a firm foundation of rock for the stone defences: again only a full-scale archaeological investigation can provide accurate knowledge. The initial defences were constructed presumably of earth and timber, at least on the landward side.

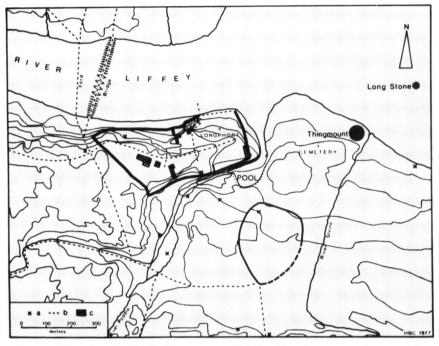

7 Map of Scandinavian Dublin. The contours of the boulder clay area are shown at 5 ft. intervals, starting at 30 ft. O.D. KEY: a. Gaelic site; b. earthen banks; c. excavated area with evidence of Hiberno-Norse habitation.

Whether the line along modern Essex Street was defended is unknown. Possibly an early quay associated with a slipway at the foot of Fishamble Street became a focal point of commercial activity. Undoubtedly the Dublin Norsemen had contacts with other parts of Ireland and north-western Europe, leading eventually to the transformation of the military base into a trading station comparable with Birka in Sweden and Haithabu in Schleswig-Holstein.

The 11th- or 12th-century Life of St. Cóemgen alludes to the 'town' (*civitas*) of Áth Cliath situated on an arm of the sea named in Irish Dubhlinn.[87] The allusion to a *civitas* poses a vital question: when did Dublin become a town? By the tenth century there are many signs of growth and prosperity. Early tenth-century Norse settlement in western Northumbria played a part in the commercial development of both Dublin and York.[88] Dublin's sister-town was probably wealthier and is currently producing similar archaeological material.[89] Before 1014 a permanent bridge may well have been built across the Liffey in conjunction with causeways from both banks of the river. The bridge is recorded indirectly in connexion with the later stages of the battle of Clontarf. One version says that 'the followers of Tadg ua Cellaig pursued them [the Dublin Norsemen] until they slew them at the head of the bridge of Áth Cliath, that is to say, the bridge of *Dub-Gaill*'.[90] In Latin sources the bridge is called *pons Ostmannorum*, with the implication that the 'men from the east' (the Scandinavians) were responsible for its construction. A location on or very near the site of the Anglo-Norman bridge can only be assumed, leading across to what became Oxmantown Street and later Church Street. The next reference to this bridge is again indirect and occurs in the Annals of the Four Masters under the year 1112.[91] With the settlement of the Norsemen the political geography of the area changed. Instead of being a border settlement Dublin became the focal point of a fairly wide territory on both banks of the Liffey, called Fingal, the land of the foreigners. Perhaps in association with the building of a bridge the original Scandinavian enclosure was apparently extended westwards towards Áth Cliath, so as to control the bridgefoot on the southern side as well as to contain an expanding population. At an unknown date the circuit was defended by a stone wall. Some works of fortification were undertaken after the capture of Dublin by Sitric Cáech in 917[92] and two years later Sitric's defenders annihilated the attacking army of King Niall Glúndub mac Áeda outside the town. In the autumn of 1013 the fortifications were capable of withstanding the siege of Brian Bóruma's formidable army.[93] The enlarged enclosure would have made Dublin about the same size as Birka (11.7 hectares) and about half that of Haithabu (24.3 hectares).[94]

Apart from major works of construction there are other signs of economic prosperity. In 989 Máel Sechnaill mac Domnaill, high-king of Ireland (980-1002 and 1014-22), captured Dublin after a 20-day siege and imposed a tax of one ounce of gold on each messuage (*garrdha*).[95] This may imply that uniform building plots characteristic of medieval towns had already been laid out, though recent excavations have not revealed much of the general street pattern of the Hiberno-Norse settlement. As from *c*. 997 a Dublin coinage of silver pennies appears, whereas hitherto English coins had been used.[96] The new coins were based on English models and were of high quality down to 1014.[97] This currency was not necessarily initiated for purely commercial purposes, for the pennies may have been struck in order to pay tribute to the Irish high-king. Some time in the Scandinavian period two imposing monuments that survived for many centuries were built: the Long Stone on slobland in the bay to commemorate the first landfall; and the Thingmount outside the town as a place for public assemblies and for judicial proceedings.[98]

All this in turn poses the problem of the fate of the Irish population and sites. Whereas at York the Danes allied with the local church almost immediately,[99] the Dublin Norse appear not to have adopted Christianity *en masse* before the beginning of the 11th century. What happened to the monastic community across the pool from the Scandinavian stronghold is completely obscure. Possibly the natives and foreigners co-existed for a time; certainly monastic life continued at Clondalkin and Tallaght.[100] The five churches on the right bank of the Poddle were still there in the 1170s, perhaps having been rebuilt in the 11th or 12th century. A century and three-quarters separates 837 from 1014 and many developments may have taken place of which we know little or nothing.

How often has it been asserted that the Scandinavians founded the major Irish towns! In the latest work on this subject we read that the Norse 'established and settled in a number of walled coastal towns, of which Dublin, Wexford, Waterford, Cork and Limerick were the most important'.[101] There is something essentially misleading about such statements, which in the case of Ireland may have given rise to a needless sense of inferiority. The ninth-century Scandinavians who founded a military base at Dublin were pirates and plunderers.[102] In those days towns were not usually founded as conscious creations by powerful lords, as they undoubtedly were founded in the 12th and 13th centuries. Rather they evolved from pre-urban cores. As it happened the freebooters were expelled from Dublin by the Irish for 15 years (902-17), whereupon a new generation of Scandinavians had to be recruited from Britain.[103] At a guess, therefore, the military base-cum-trading station evolved into a town during the tenth century.[104] Before then towns north of the Alps were rare.[105] If this is true of England and Germany, with their more developed agricultural economies, it is also likely to be true of Ireland. This is not to say, however, that agriculture was not practised in Ireland: the balance between field cultivation and livestock farming in medieval Europe was always relative. With regard to the concept of 'monastic cities', extreme caution should be exercised in thinking of such places as towns earlier than the tenth century. We should be well advised to recall the evolution of Magdeburg from a pre-urban core consisting of a royal palace and a monastery, north of which were established a cathedral complex and a market-place in the second half of that century and near which lay a number of villages. The elements that went to make up early medieval Dublin were not dissimilar. A pre-urban core is not the same thing as a town.

Against this background Gaelic *and* early Scandinavian Dublin constituted not so much a town as a complex pre-urban core or proto-town. Before we can be certain about this, much more research will have to be done. Every reader of this brief discussion will have observed that the evidence is fragmentary and obscure. What has been offered here is a series of hypotheses that future work may prove, or may disprove. Even if they are eventually dismissed, however, it is important for hypothetical reconstructions to be made from time to time. Whenever we excavate in the ground we need to be informed about the site, whilst always being prepared for the unexpected.

Despite the obvious defects of the evidence currently available for the topographical development of early medieval Dublin, a hypothetical reconstruction has been shown to be feasible. Indeed, with the injection of a topographical dimension, it is possible to make sense of virtually every documentary reference to Áth Cliath and to Dubhlinn. This reconstruction suggests in turn that Dublin in the early Middle Ages possessed what might be termed 'an Irish dimension' that has scarcely been appreciated by the majority of the inhabitants of this island. Among the honourable exceptions was the late George Little. But instead of the vast city he projected into the past, we have postulated the existence of two settlement clusters, each with an Irish name. The ancient ford lingered in the folk-memory of the indigenous population, hence the emergence of the place-name Baile Átha Cliath; to the seafaring foreigners of the ninth century the black pool was a vital asset, hence the adoption of Dubhlinn and its adaptation over the centuries to Dublin. What, we might well ask, is in a name?[106]

The origins of Dublin

P. F. WALLACE

There was a break in the continuity of the Viking settlement at Dublin between 902 and 917, during which many of the Scandinavians were forced into exile following their defeat by a successful alliance of Irish kings. As it is likely that a new type of settlement was undertaken on a new site on their return to Dublin, this break probably explains why we have found only the tenth-century town in our excavations and why no definite trace of the pre-902 settlement has been identified on any of the sites excavated to-date. Thus Dublin was founded twice over by the Scandinavians: first in 841 as a permanent trading-cum-piratical base or *longphort*, in which the Norse could remain over the winter months, and secondly c. 917 as a defended town or *dún* as it is later referred to by the Irish annalists. So far no definite archaeological evidence for either the location or the character of the ninth-century settlement has come to light. Only the later *dún* or tenth-century town is represented in the excavated evidence from the various sites on the slopes of the high natural crest above the south bank of the Liffey. Dublin was referred to as a *dún* at least as early as 937 — the year of the battle of *Brunanburh*.[1] A distinction between *dún* and *longphort* is made in connexion with Donnchad mac Briain's visit to Dublin in 1026, where the former term describes the town and the latter the Munster king's encampment outside the town.[2]

The ninth-century longphort

The *longphort* was almost certainly of more purely Scandinavian inspiration and character than was the later town of the tenth century. It may well have been an undefended *suburbium* with an attached fortified citadel on the lines of Birka or Haithabu. It seems probable that the extensive late ninth-century cemetery at Islandbridge-Kilmainham was the burial-ground for the inhabitants of the *longphort*. The spindle-whorls, iron tools, glass linen-smoother, weights and scales that were found in the cemetery, in addition to personal ornaments such as oval brooches and glass beads and weapons such as swords, spearheads and shield bosses, show that this was not just the cemetery of a military community but also that of a settled population involved in trade and commerce. It is possible that the enigmatic *longphort* was located near by, though the alternative possibilities that it was situated near the confluence of the Liffey and the Poddle in an unexcavated area of the old part of the city (Fig. 7), or that it has left little trace in the archaeological record, have also to be considered. The argument for an upstream location for the early settlement seems plausible, more especially since none of the levels uncovered in the National Museum's excavations can be said to date from before 900, though Wilson holds that 'there is no reason to suggest that the site of the town was shifted in the early tenth century'.[3] It is a dispute which can be settled only by future archaeological excavation in the right place. In the light of the experience of the early Scandinavian proto-urban settlements at Birka and Haithabu, where the cemetery is adjacent, and since a shift in location is consistent with the emergence of many European towns, it will not come as a surprise if the *longphort* turns up in the Islandbridge-Kilmainham area.

It is difficult to conceive of how the mid-ninth-century *longphort*, which Clarke pictures as 'not so much a town as a complex pre-urban core or proto-town',[4] could have had much of the character of the tenth-century town, with the streets, pathways, regulated property layout and enclosing defensive ramparts that we know from our Fishamble Street and other excavations. The mid-ninth-century Scandinavians who founded the *longphort* were pirates and plunderers,[5] who came from an area of Europe in which the idea of urbanization (though not necessarily of trade) was arguably not so advanced as in Ireland, where monastic and secular settlements had evolved outside the mainstream of northern and western European town development. Indeed, of the many different kinds of pre-urban social structure that may have contributed to the creation of the European medieval town around the beginning of the tenth century, such as the permanent and seasonal trading centres, fairs, markets and assembly sites, as well as the episcopal and monastic sites and fortified settlements of Slavic and Germanic types,[6] it must be admitted that early historic Ireland was itself in possession of almost all of them. Nevertheless the late involvement of Irish kings in trade and urban life and the slow evolution of centralized monarchy in Ireland, as well as the basically rural character of a society in which the main population centres had a primarily religious rather than a commercial *raison d'être*, meant that the medieval town did not evolve here but rather was introduced by the Vikings who first exploited Ireland's commercial potential on an organized scale. Even so the late emergence of towns in Norway, the non-appearance of towns in any of the areas settled by the western Vikings, and the settlement in farmsteads and shunning of towns in England by the Dublin Norsemen after their exile in 902 from Ireland[7] underline their non-urban instincts. The general Viking tendency to burn rather than to occupy towns in the North Sea area in the ninth century is hardly the mark of people who properly understood the full potential of such places.

It is necessary to see the foundation of Dublin in the light of contemporary historical developments and the acquisition of its urban character in the tenth century as the culmination of traditions (including non-Irish) that had been developing for about two centuries. The undoubtedly large part played by people of Scandinavian origin in the foundation of the tenth-century town of Dublin cannot be denied. Yet, as I hope to show presently, the concept of this town cannot have been derived from south-western Norway, whatever about elements of its character and the origins of the majority of its population. Before searching for the origins of the tenth-century town of Dublin, it is necessary also to see both the *longphort* and the town against the background of the Viking expansion westwards and to investigate why the Vikings came to Ireland and to the mouth of the Liffey in particular.

How can the *longphort*, the term by which the Irish sources describe the Viking settlement of 841, be defined? Recent writers have seen this settlement as 'a defended ship enclosure',[8] 'a shore fortress'[9] or 'a stronghold' or 'trading station'.[10] Lexicographers have defined *longphort* as 'a camp, encampment, temporary stronghold [or a] mansion, princely dwelling, stronghold, fortress'.[11] This does not advance our understanding of the shape, size and character of the *longphort*, much less its streets, buildings, stalls and defences. The answers to such surmises can come only from archaeological excavation and by reference to contemporary settlements in the archaeological record of other northern and western European countries.

The Dublin *longphort* was only one of a number of such settlements established by the Vikings in mid-ninth-century Ireland. There appear to have been others at Strangford Lough (Co. Down) and at Annagassan (Co. Louth). Their foundation can be seen as the culmination of a series of raids that became a serious and widespread menace in the 830s. The arrival of a fleet of 60 or 65 ships at the mouth of the Liffey was noted in 837.[12] The raids were intensified in the following decade.[13] It was a period of great turmoil over north-western Europe, where Vikings wrought havoc on the Frankish empire in the last uncertain decade of the reign of Louis the Pious.[14] This was about twenty years before the Great (Danish) Army ravaged eastern England.

One of the main reasons for the expansion of the Vikings in the ninth century was a need for new land due to a population explosion in the homelands, which itself had followed an expansion of tillage and farming in areas of woodland felled by more efficient iron axes. Other reasons include quarrels among Scandinavian kings and the ambitions of these and other leaders.[15] The wealth to be made in the flourishing eighth-century markets of the North Sea area and the degree of protection provided by Carolingian and Mercian kings to foreign merchants using them, as well as the increasing demands of western European aristocrats and churchmen for luxuries from the north, such as furs, ivory, amber, feathers, iron and animal skins, were factors which inspired the Scandinavians to become involved in trade and adventure.[16] Their evolution of swift, seaworthy, clinker-built ships enabled them to perform perilous journeys and to avoid lesser pirates, while their production and patronage of improved iron weapons made them invincible. The success of their initial raiding forays led inevitably to longer journeys, penetrating ever deeper inland, and eventually to their building of winter camps that may also have had a trading function. Dublin's *longphort* probably served as a *comptoir*, that is a safe refuge for ships, a storage place for provisions, and a collecting and dispatching depot for slaves. Smyth believes that the rapid rise of Dublin to the level of a famous trading emporium was due to the slave trade, which was to become 'a key factor in the economic life of Scandinavian Dublin' and the chief reason why Dublin was ruled by a dynasty of Scandinavian kings and not jarls, as might be expected for such a small territory. Smyth also believes that the Dublin leaders only 'creamed off' slaves from Ireland's monastic communities, but rarely destroyed these sources of so much of their income.[17] It was probably this slave trade that first established Dublin firmly on the trading network of western Europe and led to the initial inflow of silver into Ireland, where it was often ransomed by or traded with the native population, who produced silver jewellery especially in the first half of the tenth century. Apart from providing raiders with slaves and cattle, Ireland's monasteries were plundered for the portable valuables that were left in them for safe-keeping. These centres were 'the ancient equivalent of the bank strong-room'[18] and it is hardly surprising that countless intact, cut-up, and altered specimens of Irish ornamental metal-work found their way into Viking graves,[19] settlements,[20] and now feature in Scandinavian museums.[21] There is also historical evidence for an increase in the wealth of ninth-century Ireland,[22] which made it very attractive to the Vikings.

It is important to realize that first the *longphorts* such as those at Dublin and Annagassan and later, in the tenth century, the towns such as Dublin, Waterford and Limerick always remained the primary expressions of Scandinavian interest in early medieval Ireland. While each of these must inevitably have had a farming hinterland, from which foodstuffs, bedding, fodder, building and other raw materials were derived, the Vikings never undertook a concerted settlement plan in Ireland. This is obvious from their lack of impact on the landscape and from the comparative absence of place-names of Scandinavian derivation, except around the coasts,[23] and of Scandinavian loan-words to Irish, other than those relating to trade and markets.[24] It would appear that the Scandinavians settled and farmed extensively only in territories with few or no people, such as the Scottish Isles, the Faroes, Iceland and Greenland. They would not have contemplated anything like a conquest of Ireland. This is a concept of the high Middle Ages and finds its best expression in the Norman conquests of England and later of Ireland, and in the German expansion into the Slavic territories of east-central Europe. The multiplicity of Irish kings and their individual kingdoms would have made a military conquest of Ireland impossible in the Viking Age.[25] The Vikings' lack of a co-ordinated scheme of conquest is implicit in their own division and especially in the frequency of their alliances with Irish kings.[26] Their lack of Christianity until the late tenth century resulted in their 'bad press' at the hands of Irish scribes, while the deliberate post-1014 misinterpretation of the battle of Clontarf as a war between two nations — Viking and native Irish — has led to an over-estimation of their importance in Irish history.[27] For all their differences, it is also important to be mindful of the common non-romanized, Indo-European, rural culture that they shared with the Irish.[28]

It is not difficult to see why the mid-ninth-century Vikings chose the mouth of the Liffey as a base — a choice with which they persisted. It is excellently located on the west of the Irish Sea, which was soon to become a 'Viking lake' and to be traversed by both north-south routes from Scandinavia and Scotland to south-western Britain and beyond, and east-west routes from Dublin to the Isle of Man, Chester and York. Secondly it was at the mouth of a river that drained a rich hinterland and had a relatively safe tidal estuary. The slopes overlooking the south bank of the estuary both at Islandbridge-Kilmainham and at Fishamble Street led to summits that afforded commanding views of the river on the one hand, and of the flat hinterland to the south and west on the other. Both positions could easily be defended. Other factors, such as Dublin's location in a border area between two native kingdoms, may have been considered. Neutrality was a significant factor in the location of early 'ports of trade' in northern Europe[29] and in the location of monasteries in early historic Ireland.[30]

Before passing on to Dublin's place in the context of the urbanization of early medieval Europe, it has to be said that Clarke's view that the curving bank at Fishamble Street and the zigzag in the wall of the later Hiberno-Scandinavian town 'hint at a squarish enclosure surrounded on three sides by water', which he thought might be equated with the earliest Viking settlement,[31] has to be altered in the light of subsequent excavation that showed the bank to be tenth-century in date. It should be stated, however, that the recognition of the *longphort* levels may not be easy, since there is no guarantee that they are in the same splendid state of preservation as are the levels of the tenth-century town. The possibility that the ninth-century levels resemble those of any average 'dry' site has to be kept in mind.

There is little doubt that the settlement excavated on the south bank of the Liffey at the Fishamble Street, Christchurch Place, High Street and John's Lane sites is a tenth-century town, in the mainstream of the evolving town in contemporary northern and western Europe. Thanks to the uncovering of town remains in so many European countries, we need no longer rely on the existence of charters, constitutions and other urban institutions as the criteria by which we define 'towns'. The rigid definition of the historian of legal documents has been replaced by a composite definition, which accepts a settlement as a 'town' if it possessed a number of attributes from an historical, archaeological and locational standpoint.[32] This 'compound bundle of criteria' can be flexible and adjusted according to time and place.[33] External form and appearance, deliberate or gradual settlement, layout, and stratification of society, are among Haase's 'bundle of elements' which should be examined for town definition.[34] Settlements have been qualified as 'urban' by Reynolds if they afford a variety of non-agricultural occupations to a significant proportion of their inhabitants, serve as markets and administrative centres for the surrounding countryside, and are more or less distinguished 'from it both in their local government institutions and in the density of their population'.[35] Heighway's acceptance of a site as a town if it fulfilled more than one of 12 criteria seems to be much too open.[36] In reality a place should possess about three or four of these criteria to merit acceptance.[37] Five of Heighway's criteria (defences, street system, market, mint, plots and houses) rely on archaeological evidence and of these Dublin seems to have had all except a mint from the early tenth century. The mint was established in or about 997. History and historical geography will undoubtedly show that from an early date Dublin also fulfilled some of the other criteria. These include legal autonomy, a role as a central place, a relatively large and dense population, a diversified economic base, social differentiation, complex religious organization and a judicial centre. Archaeology can also be of help in the understanding of some of the latter, though those relating to legal status, religious organization and a judicial centre are obvious exceptions.

Doherty warns us against bringing to studies of the origins of the towns of early medieval Europe 'the preconceptions of the modern world' and follows an anthropological approach to the nature of the Irish monasteries, which he concedes 'were probably not urban in the sense normally understood in contemporary society' but, most importantly, he doubts if *any* town of the early medieval period was urban in the modern sense. He finds no difficulty in describing Ireland's major monasteries as towns in the tenth- to 12th-century period and believes that 'the monastic cities of Tibet or

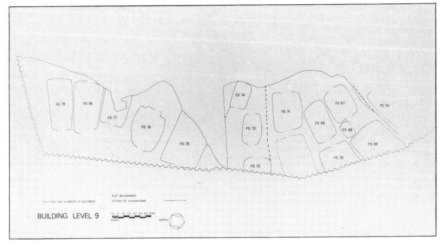

8 Plan of Fishamble Street, building level 9, showing the 11th-century plot layout.

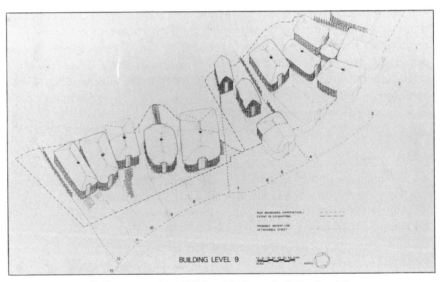

9 Reconstruction of Fishamble Street, building level 9.

Zanskar might bring us nearer to the atmosphere of town life in Ireland during this period'.[38] Such a model is also useful in conceptualizing what life was like in the congested bustle of tenth-century Dublin with its low-rise thatched buildings, though the contrast between Dublin, a trading settlement in the mainstream of the emerging European town, and the Irish monasteries in which the 'main function is religious' has to be remembered, regardless of inevitable coincidences of architecture (and possibly street plan), atmosphere and the overlap of certain functions and services in respect of their inhabitants and their hinterlands.

It appears from our excavations in Fishamble Street that tenth-century Dublin was established as a town with plots or properties (Fig. 8), a street layout, and an already evolved house form and construction pattern (Fig. 9) that would last at least until the Anglo-Norman invasion of almost two and a half centuries later. It was defended by an earthen rampart, if not from the beginning, from shortly after its establishment and, most significantly, it seems to have been set up *de novo* without reference to any previous form of settlement, at least on that site. No matter what physical and even planning details early tenth-century Dublin may have derived from the probably by now defunct *longphort* or from contemporary native monastic or secular settlements, the *concept* of a town was apparently introduced from outside Ireland. This concept seems to have evolved abroad and to have been introduced by what I would regard as saxonized Vikings on their return to Ireland after an enforced 15-year exile, which they spent mainly in the north of England. I believe that these are the important points in understanding the new settlement in early tenth-century Dublin, which for the Irish annalists was so different from the *longphort* that preceded it that they began to refer to it as a *dún* before the middle of the century.[39] It is necessary to look outside Ireland for the origins of this first Irish town and to conclude our quest by reviewing the evidence for the possible indigenous contributions to its evolution.

The origins of towns in Europe

While 'urban history does not begin with the Middle Ages',[40] it is doubtful whether the urban revolution of the fourth millennium B.C. in western Asia had a long-term impact on prehistoric Europe.[41] The process of urbanization that commenced in the islands of the eastern Mediterranean during the second millennium B.C. had a more direct impact on urban origins in barbarian Europe, not only because of the appearance of *oppida* which may 'represent the beginnings of an urban way of living in northern Europe',[42] but also because in the Roman world they led to the establishment of that lowest form of Roman urbanization, the *civitates*, some of which preserved a slender thread of urban continuity from the late antique to the early medieval periods in areas within the boundaries of the empire north of the Alps.

The continuity of a vigorous economy, international trade and urban life in the Eastern Empire between the fifth and ninth centuries[43] and the revival of east-west trade links in the seventh century[44] are paralleled by a changing situation in the North Sea-English Channel area, where

> a more modest kind of trade, ruder crafts, and more primitive towns also began to appear during the Barbarian Age along the other 'Mediter-

ranean' formed by the North Sea and the Baltic Sea: the Frisians, the
Anglo-Saxons, the Scandinavians, and the Rhinish [*sic*] Germans com-
peted for the opportunities arising along the frontier between half-
civilized barbarians and uncivilized ones, often alternating trade with
agriculture, piracy, and war.[45]

New commercial centres sprang up from the Somme to the Baltic and are
variously described in the sources as a *portus*, *vicus* or *wic*. Many of these
pre-urban trading emporia were the dwelling places of farmers who supplemented their incomes by seasonal indulgence in manufacturing crafts, trade
and piracy. *Wics* such as Quentovic, Duurstede and Haithabu were busy
centres of long-distance trade where 'merchant-peasants' sold their goods.
Earlier trading posts or 'incipient towns' such as Helgö and Paviken had a
more obvious agricultural base. Helgö, a fifth- to sixth-century Swedish
trading centre, was really a collection of farms and workshops and its
inhabitants engaged in only a minimal amount of long-distance trade, as may
be evidenced by the Irish crozier-head and Indian Bhudda that were unearthed there. Nevertheless it has been suggested that 'the beginning of the
process of urbanization in the Scandinavian region must be pushed back a
couple of hundred years earlier than hitherto thought[46] and it does appear that
sites like Helgö, Paviken and Löddeköpinge show that crafts were slowly
detaching themselves from an overwhelmingly agricultural community. In
Germany town life declined steadily throughout the Merovingian and
Carolingian periods, except that episcopal seats were established in some of
the old fortified Roman *civitates*. Carolingian kings had no fixed urban
abode, in contrast to the bishops, a situation that is paralleled in early
medieval Ireland, where monasteries overshadowed secular settlements.

Apart from the Church's re-use of the old *civitates* and *castra*, Germany
also experienced the gradual separation of artists and craftsmen from the
peasant population between the third and fifth centuries. Trading posts
populated by merchants and craftsmen emerged from the seventh century
onwards and preceded towns proper. Jankuhn sees three elements in these
trading posts that were to remain intrinsic characteristics of the fully developed medieval town: they were not directly dependent on agriculture, they
produced beyond their own needs, and they benefited from long-distance
trade.[47] Although they had little enduring impact on the shape, size and layout
of the northern European town as it subsequently developed, Jankuhn
believes that the legacy of the townsman as a freeman derives from the
undefended merchant settlements or depots for long-distance trade known
as emporia, which emerged on northern European coasts in the Vendel
period.[48] Many of these had to be abandoned by the mid-ninth century
because of their vulnerability to Viking and other attacks. Another and

apparently separate proto-urban settlement was the *portus*, which comprised a craftsmen's and traders' quarter (*suburbium*) nestling for protection outside the walls of a fortified baronial castle (*burgus*), especially in Flanders. Herteig saw this as 'the real beginning of an interesting development which culminated in the medieval town'.[49] The west Slavic region witnessed the emergence of similar merchants' and craftsmen's *suburbia* near the lord's castle,[50] though differences in settlement layout and social regulation, and subsequently in the process of citizen emancipation and the integration of the *suburbium* with the castle, mark these apart from the northern and western European town. This is not to deny the possibility that the semicircular ramparts that were later erected around settlements such as Århus and Haithabu were inspired by Slavic fortifications.[51]

The true town emerged when the suburban trading post or *suburbium* was unified with the fortified *burgus* within an earthen embankment in the tenth century. The fusing of the 'dual organism' of castle (or monastery) and merchants' settlement into a unit within a common defensive enclosure is well evidenced at Haithabu and Birka. Like Århus, Ribe, Odense, Lund and Sigtuna these were originally without defensive walls. The *portus* was an exchange point for goods that were brought from the east to what Reynolds terms 'a commercially supine Europe' by Venetians and Scandinavians.[52] The inhabitants of the *portus* were under the protection of a bishop or lord, from whom they later had to win their freedom. The characteristic walled appearance of the medieval town owes its origin to the earth-banked *portus* of northern Europe.

The idea of defending towns by the erection of earthen embankments was widespread in different parts of Europe in the late ninth and early tenth centuries. It was against a general background of Viking attack and threatened invasions that Alfred the Great and Edward the Elder in England and especially Æthelflæd and Æthelred in north-western England, as well as Charles the Bald in France, started to fortify towns in order to form systems of defence against the Viking menace. At a slightly later date Henry the Fowler defended German settlements against the Hungarians, just as Alfonso II had fortified Ovideo against Viking attacks on ninth-century Spain.[53] In keeping with the general necessity to protect wealthy settlements, the Scandinavians themselves began to defend their own *wics*. Semicircular earthen banks were built around Haithabu and Birka in the early tenth century and the new town of Århus was similarly provided for. The defence of York and Dublin, the main urban settlements of the Scandinavians in the west, within earthen banks can be seen as part of the general desire to protect urban property, a reflection of the regard placed on towns by kings that is itself proof of their realization of the potential wealth, military support, fleets, mercenaries, foreign luxuries and craft products that such places offered. The possible defence of Limerick and Waterford at the same time may be seen as a local echo of the same international trend.

It is interesting that while the idea of defending towns in this way was probably brought to Ireland by the Vikings from experiences in the homelands and especially in England, they did not *originate* the idea. Ironically the concept of defending urban settlements within ramparts seems to have originated among peoples who had to defend themselves from the Vikings. Nevertheless the defensive embankment erected in tenth-century Dublin was very different in form and scale from those which protected Scandinavian towns and it may reflect the interpretation by the Dublin Vikings of an international defensive requirement either to a native form and scale, possibly based on contemporary Irish royal raths, or to the scale of the urban defensive system first experienced in England. Some of the embankments (especially those built in England) completely encircled the settlements that they defended, while others (especially those in Scandinavia) defended their settlements on the landward side only by forming embanked crescents with no embankment on the side along the water, which was sometimes defended by stakes and piles or sunken ships in the water. This is the essential background against which the fortification of early tenth-century Dublin must be viewed. That the town was embanked along the waterfront, and at a date roughly similar to and *not later* than the towns of Scandinavia, suggests that the inspiration can hardly have been derived from that quarter. The resemblance of the Dublin embankments to those erected shortly before by the Anglo-Saxons to protect Mercian *burhs*, as well as their similarity to the defences at Anglo-Scandinavian York, point to an origin and inspiration much closer to Ireland than Haithabu or Birka.

The refoundation of Dublin c. 917

The first Scandinavian settlement at Dublin, the *longphort*, was probably most closely paralleled by the earlier or unwalled stages at Birka, Haithabu and other sites. It can be seen in the tradition of the *portus* or *vicus* in the Scandinavian or German sense. The proximity of tenth-century Dublin's merchants and craftsmen to a defended stronghold, or their situation within the defences of such a fortress, has to be seen in contrast to undefended trading stations or emporia such as Kaupang in south-western Norway, in which the inhabitants would have had a much more identifiable agrarian contact. No less than elsewhere, the true town of Dublin probably emerged with the fusion of the *suburbium* and the fortress within the same defensive enclosure in the tenth century. Such a fusion may have been envisaged by the founders of tenth-century Dublin if they did move to a fresh site. It is difficult to avoid the conclusion that the settlement unearthed in our ex-

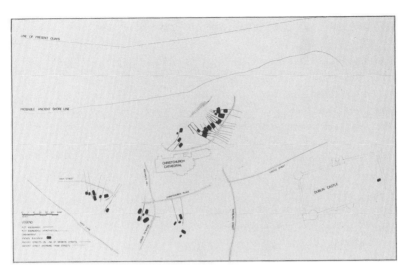

10 Plan of the layout of mid-11th-century Dublin as known from excavation.

cavations was a true town. It was laid out in plots that probably radiated around a street network (Fig. 10), it was defended by earthen embankments, and the term by which the Irish annalists described it changed from *longphort* to *dún* — all before the middle of the tenth century. The abundance of the historical and archaeological evidence for the commercial, administrative, political and ecclesiastical status of 11th-century Dublin leaves absolutely no doubt that we can speak of a true town from that time. Yet the apparent continuity of the lines of the property boundaries from the tenth-century levels to at least the end of the 11th century, the basic consistency of the principal house form over these two centuries, and the growing archaeological evidence for the wealth of Viking Dublin compels the acceptance of this settlement as a town from the beginning of its refoundation in or about 917. The apparent location of the new settlement on a fresh site and, to judge by contemporary evidence from other northern European (especially Viking) sites, its probably different layout from that of its ninth-century predecessor, the coincidence of significant political events in both England and Ireland, and the timing and place of the exile of Dublin's Vikings — all these factors suggest that this exile marked a real break, not only in settlement continuity but also in settlement form, and that the first real town of Dublin (and Ireland) can be dated from the refoundation of *c.* 917.

A combination of circumstances (from their point of view favourable in Ireland and, generally, unfavourable in England) seems to have prompted the Scandinavians to return to Ireland *c.* 914 and to Dublin *c.* 917. The defeat and death of Cormac mac Cuilennáin, king of Cashel and Ossory, as well as many Munster princes at the battle of Belach Mugna in 908 upset the balance of power in the south of Ireland, where there was to be no strong overlordship until the emergence of the Dál Cais later in the century.[54] It is hardly coincidental that all of the Scandinavian towns date from the early tenth century and that all are located in Munster and Leinster. The 'treaty' of Saint-Clair-sur-Epte in 911, by which Normandy was granted to Rollo and his Vikings, may have released many Scandinavians for fresh adventures. It is probably not coincidental that the 'large new fleet of Gentiles' that arrived at Waterford in 914 was the same as that which entered the Bristol Channel from Brittany earlier in the year.[55] Recent authorities agree that this was the year that the Scandinavian fleets returned to Ireland.[56] The outstanding leader, Ragnall, became involved in a war that devastated Munster in 914-15 and reached northern England in 914, causing Æthelflæd to build new fortresses at Eddisbury and Runcorn to check the threat to Mercia.

In 917 Sitric Cáech returned to Ireland to aid Ragnall[57] and to Dublin, which was probably re-established by him at this time. The death in 916 of the old high-king, Flann Sinna, who had resisted the Scandinavians at the end of the ninth century but whose long reign was eventually marred by the rebellion of his sons, also favoured the returned Scandinavians. The turn of the tide against them in the north and west of England probably persuaded them to concentrate their efforts in Ireland. They were defeated in 917 in the 'grand attack' of Æthelflæd and Edward the Elder; Æthelflæd was 'the principal thorn in the side of the Norse' and 'leader of the anti-Norse coalition'.[58]

As has been suggested,[59] developments in England both of a political and of a settlement nature appear to have played a major, if not the major, part in the foundation of Dublin as a town in the early tenth century after the return to Ireland of the exiled Vikings, their descendants and recruits. It is important to be aware of the English reaction to the Irish-Norse during their exile, for which there is good historical evidence, and especially to acknowledge the defensive action taken by West Saxon and Mercian leaders to protect their settlements and the urban experience to which the exiles would have been exposed at just this time, for which there is archaeological as well as historical documentation.

The 850s and 870s and the rule of Olaf and Ivar marked the high point of the *longphort* phase of the Scandinavian settlement at Dublin. The Vikings soon met with such strong local resistance, especially during the reign of Flann Sinna (879-916), that a period of comparative quiet — the 40 years' rest — ensued during which they turned their attentions to England, Iceland and especially to France. Their enforced exile from Dublin followed a major split among the Dubliners in 893, after which the kings of Brega and Leinster combined against them and destroyed Dublin in 902.[60]

It is not clear whether the Scandinavians were wholly expelled from Dublin, since some may have clung to small islands off the coast.[61] Smyth describes their return to Dublin in 917 as a 'recapture',[62] which presumes that the settlement had continued in existence during the period of exile. Wainwright maintained that 'a mass migration in scale and intensity' of Irish-Norse 'in very great numbers' had gone especially to Lancashire and Cheshire (principally the Wirral region) and that their number included native Irish and Irish-Danes.[63] He thought that these colonists had been in Ireland for long enough to adopt certain Irish methods of place-name nomenclature. Smyth differs on the extent of the Irish-Norse impact and the numbers involved. He doubts that the warriors and traders who were hemmed in behind the stockades of Dublin could have been numerous enough for so large a colonization.[64] Instead he sees the colonists of western Northumbria in the early tenth century as Norwegians or Scottish Norwegians.[65] For him this colonization created a continuous Scandinavian bloc 'from eastern Ireland across central Britain to the Baltic' in which York and Dublin were brought into close proximity, Dublin controlling Norwegian trade with Britain, Ireland, the Orkneys and Shetland, and York dealing with the Danes. He even talks of a 'Scandinavian empire of impressive proportions' and cites archaeological and numismatic evidence in support.[66] While there is no doubt that Smyth is correct in questioning the prominence given by Wainwright to one of the Dublin exiled leaders, Ingimund or Hingamund, who in Smyth's view was the leader of the least important group of exiles,[67] and that the leaders who mattered most were Sitric and Ragnall, the former being the leader under whom many of the refugees of 902 returned to Dublin in 917,[68] he appears to be on less safe ground in citing archaeological and numismatic evidence in support of this argument. York's early tenth-century street layout and defensive embankments resemble closely those of Dublin, but the architectural differences are great and the relative absence of York coins (in comparison with those of Chester) from the Dublin excavations indicates that, however strong the political and dynastic contacts between the two towns may have been, Dublin's trading relations with western parts of England, especially Chester, were much closer. The dominance of Chester coins in Irish hoards of the period 925-75[69] and the high proportion of imported West Saxon pottery (probably brought through, if not produced at, the port of Chester) in Dublin's tenth-century levels pose questions as to the strength of the tie with York, at least in economic terms.

Chester was not without political significance for the exiled Irish-Norse. Even if the most important of the dispossessed Dublin leaders of the exile spent their time in Scotland and the Isle of Man,[70] it is certain that Ingimund's group — accepting that they are 'the least important' — went to the Wirral, where they played an important role for a decade or so. Having been beaten off from Wales,[71] they settled in the Wirral with Æthelflæd's permission. The settlers became so covetous of 'the wealthy city' (of Chester) and the choice lands around it that Æthelflæd had to anticipate their aggression by defending it in 907.[72] Some time between then and 911 they attacked Chester.

Our knowledge of this siege comes from the Fragmentary Annals of Ireland, according to which the Irish-Norse were lured into the city by the defending Anglo-Saxon army which feigned retreat. Many of the Norse were slaughtered and the survivors attempted to undermine the town wall. The attackers had to work under the protection of wattle screens, which were reinforced on the underside with beams to withstand a bombardment of large rocks from the defenders. The assailants next had to put hides on top of the screens to protect themselves from boiling water, which was thrown on them. The Anglo-Saxons finally won by releasing bees on the Norse, who were forced to retreat.[73] Wainwright found it difficult to accept the details of this story because of its legendary flavour.[74] However, apart from the bees, the wattle screens, reinforcing beams and hides were used in many urban contexts at this time, as we know from the Dublin (and other town) excavations. It should also be remembered that the idea of undermining a town fortification in this way is paralleled at Waterford over two centuries later.[75]

This detailed description in an Irish source of an early tenth-century town siege, in which native Irish (who incidentally deserted to the Anglo-Saxons!) and Irish-Norse were heavily involved, must have significance for the fortification of Dublin that was soon to commence, probably at the instigation of some of the participants in the attack on Chester. Wainwright believed that Æthelflæd was remembered in Ireland (she is almost ignored in the West Saxon sources because of the lead she gave against the Norsemen) because Irish writers would have been concerned with the activities of the Scandinavians from Ireland and with 'the success of an English ruler against a common enemy', there being constant contact with Norsemen of Ireland from the beginning of the settlement in the Wirral.[76] While the defection of the Irish at Chester might support this view, it could also mean that the Irish were on friendlier terms with the Norse than is often supposed[77] and that the Fragmentary Annals reflect Irish commercial, dynastic or political interest in the fortunes of the English expedition.

The western Vikings had learnt at first hand the advantages of fortifications and soon applied their hard-won experience to the Irish ports, in which they protected their trading interests. It is possible that the advantage of installing a garrison in a defended town was first seen at Chester, where it may also have dawned on the leaders that they would not have lost Dublin in 902 had it been properly fortified in the West Saxon manner. It is more likely that redefended towns, Chester and York, rather than the more obviously defence-conscious *burhs*, inspired the Norse when they came to embank Dublin. Chester's new defences may have been partly built in stone, as they were built on the decayed Roman walls.[78] Interestingly York's defences in 876 consisted of an earthen bank that completely covered the standing Roman masonry.[79] It was not just at Chester that the Irish-Norse experienced such fortification. While this may have been their first taste, they soon came up against Æthelflæd's system of fortresses or *burhs*, which were built between 910 and 916, as well as her brother's parallel series to the south built at the same time, which included the already existing towns of Hereford, Worcester and Gloucester.[80] Æthelflæd's fortresses at Eddisbury (914) and Runcorn (915) seem to have been built after Ragnall's arrival in northern England in 914 to strengthen the northern frontier of Mercia against the Norsemen in Lancashire and Ireland, 'to awe the Norsemen in Wirral', and to control the lines of communication along the Dee and Mersey that linked Ireland with the Norse in Lancashire and the area occupied by Ragnall's supporters in north-eastern England.[81] The importance of the Mersey as a line of communication is further emphasized by the construction of a fortification at Thelwall and the strengthening of Manchester's defences by Edward the Elder after his sister's death in 918.[82] The fortress at Rhuddlan was also built by King Edward to check the entry of Norse adventurers from Ireland.[83]

These northern and western English defences probably forced the Scandinavians eventually to change their military tactics from raiding to siege warfare and pitched battles. Soon the Scandinavians were defending their own fortresses, or more properly, were defending their own trading settlements in Ireland. The banks at Dublin and possibly Limerick and Waterford, as well as at York, can be seen as a response to this tactical change. The building of banks around these settlements combined the defensive qualities of the *burhs* with the protection that European kings were gradually extending to merchants and towns. Thus the embanking of Dublin fits into a common contemporary European pattern. At Dublin, however, it was introduced by the very people against whom in other countries it had been originated. In this respect the defence of Dublin by the western Vikings seems to parallel the similar response of the Danes who defended Haithabu, Ribe and Århus at about the same time, although within a different embankment system. The obvious contribution, or at least potential, of the Anglo-Saxon *burhs* and towns should not be ignored in our search for the inspiration for Dublin's defences, especially in view of their part in the downfall of the ambitions of the Irish-Norse in north-western England. It is significant that, after Dublin was defended within earthen ramparts, there appear to have been more battles (14 between the Irish and the Dublin Norse) and more attacks on the town itself (11 between 917 and 1014) and fewer raids out of Dublin than in the *longphort* phase up to 902.[84] It would seem that a change in tactics that had been learnt in England and applied to the defence of Dublin soon inspired the Irish to accommodate themselves to siege warfare and battles and, as it were, to beat the Vikings at their own game. This alteration in military tactics and the idea of attacking a fortified town, rather than any perceptible change in the layout, character or role of the Viking settlement at Dublin, may explain why the annalists altered their description of it from *longphort* to *dún* in the tenth century. *Dún* has more military than socio-economic connotations. On the other hand, the rise of Dublin as a wealthy trading centre, with significant amounts of silver and imported luxuries, and its expansion with the growth of international commerce would have meant that it was only a matter of time before the town and its contents were coveted by native rulers and other Vikings, against whom it had to be defended. Annalistic references to exotic items, especially the oriental textiles that were taken in raids on Irish Viking towns, testify to the appeal of such places in the native mentality. It is impossible to decide whether Dublin's defensive embankments were erected as a reaction to the threat to the great wealth derived from increasing international trade, or in anticipation of such a threat as part of a programme of town foundation. Either way, the experience of some of Dublin's leaders in England and their attempts to besiege its fortifications can hardly have gone unheeded. Nevertheless the scale of these banks is very similar to that of the raths within which the native enemy would have been based, in which case it is possible to regard the Dublin banks as an Irish phenomenon, rather as the buildings of Viking Dublin appear to have been. But even if the Scandinavian and especially the English inspiration was more indirect than direct, the coincidence of the construction of the Dublin banks and those of other early towns across Europe, together with the slightly earlier fortification of some English towns, cannot easily be ignored.

The origins of towns in England

Before looking in more detail at the possibility of indigenous contributions to the origins of tenth-century Dublin, it is necessary to look briefly at the archaeological and historical evidence for English town origins, development and character, in order to see Dublin more clearly against a background where late Anglo-Saxon England figures prominently. Despite reservations about urban continuity from the Roman period, especially for the sixth century,[85] there is an almost continuous thread of urban life in England from post-Roman settlements through to seventh- or eighth-century trading settlements such as *Hamwih*[86] and to the towns of the later Anglo-Saxon period. But the 'real beginnings of the Anglo-Saxon town' appear to lie in the commercial rise of London and York and four or five ports, including *Hamwih*, which in terms of their geographical position and chronology can be grouped with Duurstede and Domburg on the continental side of the North Sea — Lopez's 'other Mediterranean' — which are reflective of the same early development of trade.[87] These were 'moving towards urban life . . . [but] were not urban'.[88] In the eighth century London still comprised only 'a series of farmsteads along the Thames'.[89] An indication of the similarity of developments in the North Sea trading area is evident in the term *wic/wik/vik* (cognate with Latin *vicus*) that is used to describe early trading centres all round it.[90] These trading *wics* lasted in England from about 600 to 900 and are seen as having been urban or proto-urban rather than non-urban in character. They were contemporary with the 'inland towns' that dealt more with local than with long-distance trade.[91] The end of this period saw the establishment of 'true towns' throughout southern and eastern England in the reigns of Alfred (871-99) and his son Edward the Elder (899-924). These are of direct relevance to Dublin not only because of their urban status but also because of the nature of their defences, which were erected mainly to counteract Vikings who, at least in part, had come from Ireland. They are part of what could be termed 'an English urban revolution', which was at its zenith during the early tenth-century exile of the Dublin Norse.

The towns of Alfredian Wessex — the *burhs* — represented a planned scheme of national defence and were provided with regular streets within fortifications. They were built in a few years (878-92) before the end of the ninth century. In all, about three dozen towns were built by the West Saxons between 840 and 920,[92] or, to put it another way, there were 50 towns in 930 where there had been 10 in 880.[93] The building of these stronghold settlements was a response to the success of the Great Danish Army of 865 and may be seen as part of the English recovery, which began in the ninth century with Alfred in Wessex and which was extended during the second decade of the tenth century when Edward built a series of forts in the southern English Midlands and, as we have seen, his sister Æthelflæd and her husband Æthelred developed a parallel programme in Mercia.[94] Biddle calls the Wessex *burhs* a watershed in European urban evolution:

> There seems to be no known parallel in contemporary Europe for a deliberate scheme of town foundation on such a scale. . . . Nowhere else north of the Alps at this date, or perhaps for another two centuries, was so extensive an effort of town plantation to be undertaken on royal initiative and on so clearly regulated a basis.

He claims that these towns provided the model for the Mercian *burhs* of the early tenth century and for Edward the Elder's foundations in the Danelaw, with which our Scandinavians were also in contact.[95] The exiled Dublin Vikings would have been exposed to both developments, especially since their threat to north-western England had been partly responsible for the creation of such strongholds. Nevertheless it is possible that the West Saxons derived their ideas for the banks that surrounded these *burhs* from the Scandinavians who fortified Reading as early as 870.[96] The balance of evidence does suggest that the whole idea was of indigenous English derivation. After all, places like Hereford had a deliberately planned subrectangular layout,[97] which appears to have been determined by the location of its ramparts since the eighth or ninth century. Hereford's second bank was a gravel and clay construction of the early ninth century.[98] It is important to realize that not all early tenth-century English towns were deliberately founded. Some, such as Northampton, were of more organic growth and emerged over several centuries rather than as a result of the planned imposition of one period.[99] It is also significant that some of these strongholds occupied the sites of former Roman towns, as at Chester, Chichester, Winchester and Worcester.

Town defences

There are two main components of early medieval towns — the defences and the layout — upon which archaeological excavation can cast considerable light. They are interrelated and they are what gives a town its physical form. Buildings and their methods of construction are related to a broad cultural or regional context; they can be adapted to rural and urban requirements and are not so diagnostic an urban characteristic as street patterns and enclosing embankments or walls. While the evidence for defences is good for English towns, it has to be admitted that archaeologists have been slow to adopt the historical geographer's overview that is necessary to comprehend and compare various town plans. It has also to be said that Irish archaeologists have not previously attempted to project property lines and street layouts inferred from excavations on to maps such as that published by Clarke in 1978.[100] It is necessary to compare what we now know of Dublin's street layout and defensive embankments with the published English town excavations, in order to see to what extent the archaeological evidence coincides with what appears to be a convincing historical suggestion for much influence from that quarter on the origins of tenth-century Dublin.

Turning firstly to the defences, we find that the ramparts of the early tenth-century *burhs* were generally formed of 'dump construction with some wooden strapping and turf revetment' and that they were usually crowned with wooden palisades and occasionally provided with ditches.[101] This general picture and the late replacement of earthen banks by stone walls[102] is consistent with the Dublin evidence excavated at Fishamble Street, where the banks were similarly built in stretches, sharply scarped in front and more gently sloped on the townward side. The scale of the Dublin banks appears to have been smaller than that at some of the English sites such as Lydford, Wallingford and Winchester. The evidence points to a grander scale of construction in England, albeit in similar material and using the same methods of dump construction. Hereford, for example, was defended by a gravel and clay rampart in the ninth century[103] and in the tenth century a substantial clay bank stabilized with turf and branches and a front revetment of vertical posts at 1 m. intervals linked by horizontal timbers.[104] This bank stood 2.50 m. high with a breast-work rising above the surface of the bank, which was revetted on the inside where it incorporated and covered over the earlier defences. It is claimed as part of Æthelflæd's defences of *c.* 914,[105] though Ralegh Radford opts for a construction date of 902.[106] Tamworth (where Sitric of Dublin and York married Æthelstan's sister in 926) appears to have had a pre-tenth-century defensive system of slighter proportions on the line of the later defences.[107] The latter consisted of a 9 m. wide, timber-framed rampart and ditch, which have been regarded as the closest English parallel for a later series in Jutland.[108] If the general method of dump construction in these defences and their reinforcement by the addition of a massive stone wall at the front can be taken as typical of the Wessex *burhs*,[109] they at least provide close parallels to the Dublin banks and their later replacement by a stone wall, even if they are not directly related. In the published excavation literature it is difficult to find evidence that resembles more closely the defences of tenth- and 11th-century Dublin than that at Hereford, both in terms of the physical nature of rampart construction and, even more intriguing, in terms of the replacement of one rampart of dump construction by another, the incorporation of the earlier smaller bank in the body of its larger palisaded successor, and the eventual fronting of an enlarged version of the latter by a stone revetting wall. The fact that, as in Dublin, these English banks encircled their settlements to form true *enceintes*, in contrast to sites in Scandinavia, is significant. The possibility of the borrowing of the banks from the larger native Irish settlements has also to be kept in mind. It would appear that it is the scale of the Dublin banks, rather than their character and function in regard to an urban settlement, that may have been borrowed from native sources. The relative lowness of the earliest bank in Dublin could also be due to its having been designed to a scale demanded by contemporary warfare in Ireland and, perhaps, built by Irish labour or with Irish advice.

It is unfortunate that so little is known archaeologically of Chester's defences,[110] especially since, as we have seen, it figures so prominently in the fortunes of the exiled Irish-Norse of the early tenth century. Thankfully we have a better archaeological understanding of the defences of York, the other English town with which Viking Dublin was closely linked. Despite the differences in architecture and despite the relative absence of coins, both of which are suggestive of an apparent (and geographically logical) lack of trade with Dublin, York's defensive banks and street plan provide relatively close parallels. York had fallen to the Danes in 866 and was defended in 876. After the erection of ninth-century floodbanks comprised of layers of brush-wood along the Fosse, York was provided with an embankment for unloading ships as well as a defensive bank crowned by a stockade, which ran down to meet the river.[111] This bank was of dump construction and incorporated in its elements were brushwood layers[112] that are reminiscent of the early tenth-century embankments at Dublin, which may be of slightly later date and may have been influenced by the York structures. These Anglo-Danish ramparts were of roughly similar height and construction to those excavated in Dublin. The earthen bank with the timber palisade excavated at the Anglian Tower[113] was very similar to the second defensive embankment at Fishamble' Street.

Town layout

The regular Winchester-type layout that characterizes the Wessex and Mercian *burhs* is absent in Dublin, where the natural topography of the chosen site did not lend itself to this kind of street arrangement. It is probable that many English street layouts are much more than mere accommodations of streets to natural features.[114] When properly mapped, they should be used as a vital criterion of comparison between towns. On present evidence, it seems that this element of Dublin's tenth-century character owes little to the grid pattern of Anglo-Saxon towns. Not surprisingly, York presents the most promising English parallel to Dublin's Viking Age street network, since it lacks the gridded layout of the Wessex and Mercian *burhs* and has an irregular layout determined by natural features.[115] Indeed on archaeological evidence it would appear that late ninth- and early tenth-century York was very different from the Anglo-Saxon towns and *burhs* in terms of street layout, though not in the nature of its defences. It was also vastly different from the contemporary northern European town (e.g. Haithabu) in terms of its irregular street plan and the type and scale of its ramparts. Interestingly only Dublin seems to be similar to it in both respects, as well as in respect of the post-and-wattle houses which are a feature of York *c.* 900.[116] It is probable that only after the collapse of Irish-Norse or, more properly, Dublin-Norse interests about the middle of the tenth century, did York and Dublin go their separate ways. Notwithstanding the absence of archaeological evidence for commercial links between the two places in the first half of the tenth century, the political bonds cannot be denied.

The fortunes of the Scandinavian dynasty in Dublin were bound up with ambitions in York, with which there was active political contact from about 919 to 954. In spite of the 'particularly shadowy nature of York's history from 876 to 919'[117] the successes, defeats and final decline of Irish-Norse interests can be traced. The usual pattern was that the senior member of the dynasty ruled at York, while the deputy or junior (usually a brother or son) ruled at Dublin until the York kingship fell vacant. Scandinavian kings with Dublin connexions who ruled in York include Ragnall (918-21) and Sitric (921-7). The latter brought Dublin to the zenith of its military power in 919 when his forces defeated and killed Niall Glúndub, king of Tara, in a battle near Dublin. Godfrid replaced Sitric firstly as king of Dublin when the latter took over York and secondly as king of York when the English king, Æthelstan, banished Sitric (who was his brother-in-law) from the town. Godfrid ruled at York only for a short spell in 927 and was succeeded by his son Olaf, who led the Irish-Norse and their allies (including the king of Scotland) to defeat at the hands of the Anglo-Saxons at *Brunanburh* in 937. Irish-Norse interests went into decline after this decisive defeat, in spite of a flicker of hope that persisted until the expulsion of Eric Bloodaxe in 954. Although Wilson saw the rise of Dublin as dating from this expulsion, after which Dublin became the main Viking base in the West,[118] it would seem from the archaeological evidence that the renewal of interest and population is more likely to have been about the time of the return of the exiled Norse between 914 and 917. This is not to deny that occasional smaller population injections may have followed the defeats of 937 and 954, and may even have continued into the 11th century to the time when members of Harold Godwinesson's family sought refuge in Dublin after the defeat at Hastings in 1066.[119]

Irish-Norse names in north-eastern England, especially in the North and West Ridings of Yorkshire, and the Irish names of some of York's streets underline the strength of the York-Dublin link.[120] Because York appears to have been defended earlier and because Dublin was abandoned and re-founded in the early tenth century, it follows that the direction of the urban influence and inspiration was from York to Dublin rather than the reverse. Like London, York continued to be an important proto-urban centre after the decline of *Hamwih* and the other English *wics*.[121] Not only does York have a longer continuous urban tradition than Dublin, but also it appears to have been defended at an earlier date. The common use of post-and-wattle for buildings and for the reinforcing screens of the town ramparts at York and Dublin probably relates more to a shared northern and western European tradition than to the coincidence of the Norse domination of both places.

Where the Norse at York got their ideas about town defence and house building from is difficult to determine. It seems unlikely that Scandinavia was the source, since its urban development was too late and too different in character. It is possible that the York Scandinavians borrowed their ramparts from their Anglo-Saxon neighbours and that their less rigid street layout was their own original contribution to towns such as York and Dublin, in which they allowed the streets to follow the natural contours of places that were chosen primarily for their ease of defence and proximity to rivers that drained far inland, and to seas that were their passport to trade and to rapid contact with the kinsmen in related overseas settlements.

The task of pinpointing late Anglo-Saxon influences on the form and character of tenth-century Dublin would be a lot easier if the extent of the Scandinavian contribution to the English town was isolated. This is a problem as much for students of the layout and defensive character of York as it is for those of Dublin, especially as York's apparently organic character and ungridded street plan are at variance with those of its more purely Anglo-Saxon contemporaries. Biddle believes that a two-way process was involved, in which the Mercian and West Saxon impact on Viking settlements was probably as important as the reverse.[122] Herteig is undoubtedly correct in reminding us that

> it should [not] be forgotten that the Vikings played an active part in the process of creating towns [in Britain and Ireland and that] the Vikings and the Anglo-Saxons each took a part in the creation of such towns as Lincoln, Stamford, Leicester, Derby and Nottingham, and it is within the bounds of reason that the Vikings had a great deal to say in the creation of Dublin, Waterford, Wexford, Limerick and Cork.[123]

The extent of their say is not in doubt, but the physical nature of their contribution has to be worked out by reference to the archaeological evidence for their settlements, both in their home countries and in their colonies, and to the extent to which they may have allowed a locally recruited labour force to build in its own traditions, using its own materials and keeping to guidelines of a very generalized nature. The guidelines themselves probably reflect a western Norse interpretation of the urban and building traditions of the Franks, Saxons, Irish and others with whom they were in contact. Their own overriding considerations would have centred around military defence, ship protection, access to the sea and, by river, to the hinterland of their projected settlement. The apparent lack of appeal of a gridded town layout to the Vikings of Dublin and York emphasizes that these new townsmen were western Norse and not Danes, who were urbanized at an earlier date and used a grid-system in their own proto-urban settlements. They probably had no urban tradition of their own, other than the emporium at Kaupang and the ninth-century *portus* at Dublin (i.e. the *longphort*). They probably distrusted the military appropriateness of gridded layouts from the experience of their campaigns in England.

The balance of foreign and native traditions

The archaeological evidence, then, suggests that saxonized Norsemen (i.e. the 'returned' Irish-Norse) played the major part in the establishment of tenth-century Dublin as a town. It also suggests that the Danes, those semi-urbanized traders who frequented places such as Haithabu, may have had a much greater say in the character of the ninth-century *longphort* than the Norse majority who could hardly have had much experience of proto-urban life in Norway, where only an emporium the size of Kaupang is known from the ninth century. The triumph of what appears to have been a Danish-derived ruling dynasty in late ninth-century Dublin[124] may be a related demonstration of the disproportionate influence of, and the status enjoyed by, the Danish minority in an essentially Norse settlement. The absence of urban settlements in Scotland, the Scottish Isles, the Isle of Man, the Faroes and Greenland, which were all much more extensively settled than Ireland and northern England, the failure of towns or settlements of *portus*- or even emporium-status to emerge in these places, the emergence of Norse-dominated towns only where they came into contact with urbanized (as at York) or quasi-urbanized (as in Ireland) traditions, and the probable contribution of the Danes to the foundation of Dublin's proto-urban *portus* (the *longphort*) — all these factors qualify the extent, or at least the exclusiveness, of the Norse say in the introduction of towns to Ireland.

Binchy's view that 'the idea of a town, with a corporate personality distinct from that of the ruler, was quite foreign to the Gaelic mind until the Scandinavians set up their "cities" in Dublin, Limerick, Waterford and elsewhere'[125] is probably true as far as the idea of a town was concerned. Lucas's crediting of the Vikings with the establishment of 'the first real civic towns' in Ireland[126] obviously still holds true in the sense that the first consciously established settlements where the primary function was trade and commerce were early tenth-century Dublin, Waterford and Limerick. Recent historical research on the greater Irish monasteries, however, has forced Doherty to the conclusion that 'the major monasteries by the tenth century and for a long time before were ceremonial centres that acted also as political capitals'.[127] These settlements are distinguished from the Viking towns in that 'their main function is religious', even though they otherwise had become 'unequivocally urban communities'.[128] Doherty accepts the great Irish monasteries such as Armagh, Kells, Clonmacnoise, Derry, Clonard, Downpatrick and Kildare

> as urban from the tenth century onwards [because] they clearly have large populations, are divided into districts, have a literate *élite*, some of whom are administrators, are at the centre of large estates, and have

properties in other parts of the country; they have large public buildings and monuments, public open spaces, streets, some of which are paved, and on the outskirts they have a market-place.[129]

This may not satisfy the idea of a town, but it includes elements of which tenth-century Dublin could not boast. Doherty's work highlights two other aspects of tenth-century Ireland. Firstly the Norse and the monastic towns should be seen as part of an overall economic experience in which 'each thrived as a result of the existence of the other' and secondly the trading and commercial aspects of the monastic towns have been underrated, especially in view of the possession by some monastic communities of coastal emporia through which their long-distance contacts (both religious and commercial) were mediated.[130] Binchy had earlier said that 'it would be difficult to exaggerate the formidable impact of these prosperous trading stations, with their local and overseas markets ... upon the primitive economy of their Irish neighbours'.[131] Doherty's coastal emporia are interesting and fit Hodges' fourth class of pre-tenth-century trading settlements in Europe — the river-mouth ports at which trade of an archaic character was transacted, Dalkey Island being cited as an example of the type.[132] Hodges would fit Irish monasteries (of which he singles out Nendrum, Co. Down) into his second group, which also includes Kaupang, and describes these as settlements in which long-distance international trading was controlled by kings or the Church. The role of kings in controlling trade and in establishing towns has been emphasized by Skovgaard-Petersen[133] and by Sawyer, who believes not that Irish kings were slow to become involved in trade but that 'they had little to offer in return that could not be obtained more easily elsewhere' and that Ireland's potential for the export of slaves, cattle and leather was 'first exploited on any scale by the Vikings'.[134] Sawyer's claim that the conversion of Irish Viking strongholds into towns 'may have been partly due to the needs of the Vikings themselves' and to the needs of places like Chester and Bristol for raw materials that could be conveniently shipped by boat from Dublin[135] hardly explains the greater prominence enjoyed by tenth-century Dublin than either of these locations and treats the evolution of Dublin as a town in a local economic context, without reference to what I believe were crucial political and urban developments in England and Ireland.

In spite of all the historical references to Irish monasteries, we must rely mainly on the results of archaeological excavation and survey if we are to estimate the possible contribution of such places to the layout, buildings and defensive ramparts of Viking Dublin. It has to be admitted that archaeology cannot confirm or add very much to what is known from the historical sources, which speak of Armagh with its 'thirds' or sectors for craftsmen, students and traders[136] and describe fires destroying houses and streets in

912, 1112 and 1166.[137] There is little archaeological confirmation as yet for Armagh's suggested urban character. There is no doubt that some of the greater monasteries were organized on a preconceived plan, possibly with their foundation seen as a religious act creating a sacred place. Swan's recent work on the recurrence of founder's tomb, crosses, walls, etc. in the same place at many Irish sites and Herity's identification of the location of many such features on the eastern side of an open space at monasteries are as near as archaeology has brought us to understanding the layout of such places.[138] Apart from hinting that the foundation of a secular place like Dublin may have been attended by a religious ceremony of some sort, there is little to be derived from the layout of native monastic or secular sites that betrays a possible influence on the way we think Dublin was planned. Many of the building methods connected with wooden and post-and-wattle constructions, such as the houses and pathways that we have found in Dublin, probably find their best parallels in native Irish contexts like *tóchars*. Unfortunately the archaeological information is not yet sufficiently collated and the preservation of streets and building remains is insufficient to allow of the measurement of directly attributable indigenous contributions to tenth-century Dublin.

Conclusion

In summary, I feel on reflection that the origins of Dublin, or of what were probably the separate Dublins of the ninth and tenth centuries, are even more involved than a few years ago when the possibility of strong Anglo-Saxon influence on the concept of the town of the early tenth century was suggested.[139] The present conclusions are tentative and possibly conditioned by the excellent preservation of tenth- and 11th-century Dublin, by the absence (to-date) of archaeological evidence for the location and character of the ninth-century settlement, by the excavated and historical evidence for England's remarkable early tenth-century urbanization and, more pertinently, by the unfortunate lack of archaeological detail for the intramural character of Ireland's contemporary monastic and secular sites. It is hoped that the recent welcome advances made in respect of the history of such sites by Doherty and Clarke, and by Swan in aerial survey, will be matched by excavation, so that their proper relationship both to one another and to the Viking towns can be more scientifically measured.

The present study indicates the need to place the origins and character of Viking Dublin in the broader economic and political history of ninth- and tenth-century Ireland, England, Scandinavia and Europe in general. The origins have to be seen against an ascendant economy made manifest in the rise of long-distance and local trade and in the desire of proto-urban and early urban settlers to protect their properties and increased wealth within defensive ramparts. The political reverses suffered by the Irish-Norse in north-western England and the opportunities that political developments opened up for them in the southern half of Ireland played an undoubted part in the refoundation of Dublin in or about 917. The experience by these people of an 'urban revolution' in England during their exile and the necessity to defend settlements within ramparts in a warlike age must also be pertinent to the occupation of Dublin. The idea of establishing a settlement for the purposes of trade, commercial exploitation and (possibly later) the supply of the hinterland was new in tenth-century Ireland and its introduction must be attributed to the Irish-Norse on their return from England. This was a settlement in which an inhabitant could get rich by engaging in international trade or by supplying, servicing and provisioning the merchants and their families who were involved in this trade. The essential contrast with the native monastic site, in which the principal accent was on religion and missionary training, is obvious despite inevitable overlaps. The extent to which the tenth-century town was built on commercial and administrative foundations already laid in the ninth-century *longphort* and whether there was any continuity between the two settlements are important though unascertainable considerations in the present state of knowledge. Clarke parades historical evidence for the existence of native Irish and early Scandinavian proto-towns and suggests that 'Gaelic *and* early Scandinavian Dublin constituted not so much a town as a complex pre-urban core or proto-town'; but he probably claims too much when he says that the 'military base-cum-trading station evolved into a town during the tenth century'.[140] This implication of continuity of settlement from the first Scandinavian settlement at Dublin to the tenth-century town is not so strongly expressed by de Paor. De Paor's description of 'the cluster of bases, or lairs of maritime adventurers [who] formed a small kingdom of farmer-warriors'[141] is probably a very accurate picture of the *longphort* era. There is a lack of physical proof for continuity of settlement from the lowest levels of the many excavations conducted to-date in what could be described as the tenth-century town area, none of which can be said to represent the *longphort*. This and the apparent 15-year break in settlement at Dublin are suggestive of the refoundation of Dublin as a town on a new site based on a preconceived plan to accommodate people in a defended settlement with streets and property divisions, rather than a settlement built on an old site that may not have fizzled out altogether during the absence of the Irish-Norse and may have preserved threads of continuity either of property divisions or of settlement type. Tenth-century Dublin appears to have been a deliberate foundation and not a natural development from a primary core of one kind or another. Indeed it is likely that a town built on an old site would have been hampered by the topographical and psychological constraints of a possibly very different pre-urban core and would have been better built on a new site. It should be emphasized that it is not so much the pre-existence of any native pre-urban core that is significant for the study of the elements that the tenth-century settlement might have acquired locally, but rather the character and layout of the previous Scandinavian *longphort*. The apparent contradiction of the mediation of so much Viking silver into Ireland during the period of the suggested break in the occupation of Dublin only illustrates the difficulties of arguing *ex silentio*.

While agreeing with Doherty's general thesis that native and Viking settlements cannot be separated in the economy of ninth- and tenth-century Ireland and admitting the possibility of a local input for much of the character of the town (i.e. the ramparts, the buildings and the generally indigenous nature of much of our excavated constructional and artefactual evidence), Binchy's view that 'the idea of a town' was introduced to Ireland has to be upheld. If this idea had been introduced directly from somewhere else in an evolved and unchanged state, it would be simpler to find parallels for the totality of tenth-century Dublin among contemporary towns of north-western Europe, in so far as the totality of any town of that time is at present known from archaeology. The fact is that the catalysts in all this, the Vikings, had not much by way of their own urban traditions and, if the Dublin evidence is anything to go by, they were prepared to borrow ideas from anywhere and to adapt them to their own priorities in defence and commercial expansion. No less than the Normans who were descended from them in France, the Norse appear to have been imitators rather than innovators, especially when it came to the establishment of towns. They probably took the best of what they had seen and encountered, and were content to have their town built gradually in local materials and traditions by local forced or hired labourers, to whom they gave only the loosest guidelines. Their most original contribution to Irish urban evolution may have been to allow their streets to follow the natural contours that their defensive embankments enclosed.

It seems likely that on their return to Dublin in 917 the Scandinavians were led by Sitric Cáech, who undertook some works of fortification (*forbaisi*).[142] These works may have been one of the early embankments known from our excavations. The banks became quite substantial, until by 1013 the fortifications were capable of withstanding the siege of Brian Bóruma's army.[143] As late as the 1160s *Dún Duibhlinne* was described as one of the seven Wonders of Ireland,[144] though the impression that Dublin created in the mind of the native commentator was probably due more to the great stone wall that encircled the town, or even to the wealth of the town, than to the *idea* of the town itself, which was then nearly two and a half centuries old.

Norse Dublin

EDMUND CURTIS

The original sources for the history of Norse Dublin are mainly, as one would expect, Irish and Norwegian. The great sagas of Laxárdal, the *Heimskringla*, Burnt Njál and Jarl Rognvald tell much of the Norse doings in Ireland. On the Irish side we have much material in annals and historical tracts; chief among these are the famous history or panegyric of Brian Bóruma called the *Cogadh Gaedhel re Gallaibh*, the *Caithréim Chellacháin Chaisel*, and the chronicles called by O'Donovan Fragments of Irish Annals.

Our title 'Norse Dublin' requires some explanation. Danes (*Danair* or *Dub-Gaill*) and Norwegians (*Lochlannaigh* or *Finn-Gaill*) were mingled in the Scandinavians who invaded our island, but it is the opinion of the great scholar Bugge, and now generally accepted, that the greater part of our invaders (and certainly their rulers) were Norwegian and of the same stock as those who settled in Iceland, Greenland, the Scottish Isles and Man. The Norse being apparently fairer and the Danes darker, the Irish, who had a strong sense of colour, called the former the 'fair foreigners' (*Finn-Gaill*) and the Danes 'dark foreigners' (*Dub-Gaill*); but the name of 'the Danes' is so strongly rooted in Irish popular tradition that it will probably never be displaced.

The Viking settlement

Dublin was first occupied [in 841] by Norse Vikings who landed in the black pool or *linn dubh* in the Liffey and threw up a fort on the high ridge where Dublin Castle later arose. In [or after] 853 [they came] under [the joint rule of] Olaf *inn hvíti* ('the White') and Ivar *inn beinlausi* ('the Boneless'). They gave our capital a name which it has never lost, and which is just as Gaelic as Baile Átha Cliath.

A good many books and learned papers have been written on the Scandinavians in these islands, but the great and comprehensive book remains to be achieved. It is therefore not easy to get a clear picture of what early Dublin as a Norse port-town looked like. Mr. Liam Gogan, in a lecture, quotes the example of Birka in Sweden which has been unearthed. The example would be followed in Dublin, he says. A few miles up the river on a fjord or creek they would build an *oppidum* — an earthen bank surmounted by a stout palisade. The adjacent creeks would give shelter to their ships. Outside the town a mounded area was built for their dead and in some near wood they set up a sanctuary of Thor, Odin or Freyja. (I would add, also, a *thing*-place or place of assembly.) The main citadel of Dublin was on the prominence occupied by the castle and Christ Church. Their 'garths' and villages stretched along the ridge by Kilmainham, Inchicore and Islandbridge to Clondalkin. This was the backbone of Dublinshire and here most of their remains have been found. At Islandbridge between 1845 and 1866, and again in 1933 (in making the war memorial) many interments have been discovered. They include two fine swords, a splendid battle-axe, iron nails and staples, etc.; also the skeleton of a man 6 ft. long with a two-handed two-edged sword lying across his body, no doubt a valiant Viking in his time. But no Norse ship has ever been found in Ireland.

From Ivar the Boneless descended the whole line of Norse kings of Dublin to Sitric who died in 1042. The two between them made our town an important place in the Norse world, a key point for Norse rule in the Hebrides and Man and for their designs on England, and a depot for their rich plunder and the sale of the unhappy slaves they brought back from Britain and other lands.

After the death of Ivar the Boneless in 873 Dublin again fell into Irish hands (Leinster or Ossory), and for 40 years 'there was peace for the men of Erin'. But in 917 Ragnall and Sitric (grandsons, it seems, of Ivar) again occupied Dublin. The high-king Niall Glúndub raised a national host to recover it, but was in 919 defeated and slain at Kilmohavoc, the ford on the Liffey where Islandbridge now is.[1] It was one of the most momentous battles in Irish history and led to a two-and-a-half-century occupation of Dublin and other ports of Ireland by the Norsemen. It was from this time that Dublin became a real town instead of a mere fortress, and one of the places best known to the Vikings in their piratical voyages or summer-farings, during which many a famous sea-king wintered in our pleasant climate by the River Liffey and the Norse sagas must have been almost as well known in Dublin as in Iceland.

Olaf Sitricsson, called Cuarán ('of the Sandals'), ruled Dublin from 945 to 980 and it must have been he who conquered and organized a whole kingdom stretching from Skerries to Wicklow or Arklow and inland to Leixlip and Clondalkin. This kingdom the Norse called *Dyflinnarskíri* (Dublinshire). During the later years, Olaf with his warrior-bands, so superior in mail, heavy sword and axes to the Irish, laid all Meath under tribute 'from the Shannon to the sea'.

The Hiberno-Norse town

In 980 the high-king Máel Sechnaill broke the Norse yoke at the battle of Tara; he defeated Olaf and then took and plundered Dublin, exacting a tribute of 2,000 kine, an indication of the wealth of the Dublin State. Olaf fled oversea and died in pilgrimage to Iona, leaving behind him in Dublin his Irish wife, the Leinster princess Gormlaith, and several sons.

Pure Norse paganism was now on the rapid wane. The Norse felt that the Christian side was the winning one, but were reluctant to abandon the worship of Odin and Thor with whom they associated their grand old pagan life and victories. Hence a victory under the raven banner of Thor might have swung them back to the creed of Valhalla and the valkyries and the heroic traditions of their forefathers. So we read in the saga of Brodar who slew Brian that 'he was God's dastard [a renegade] for he had been a mass-deacon but now worshipped fiends and was of all men most skilled in sorcery' and that 'he left uncut his long black locks which he tucked away into his belt'.

The heroic Máel Sechnaill gave Dublin little rest and continued to break up the Norse terror in the east as Brian was doing in the south. In 989, say the Annals of Tigernach,

> the battle of Dublin was gained over the foreigners of Dublin by Máel Sechnaill son of Domnall, wherein many were slain, and the siege of the fortress afterward for 20 nights, and during it the foreigners drank no water save brine. Wherefore they gave him his award as long as he should be king, and an ounce of gold from every garth to be paid on each Christmas night.[2]

Máel Sechnaill's next and third siege of Dublin was in 995. In this year (he was now high-king) he again took the fort of Dublin by siege, placed its people under tribute, and compelled them to surrender to him the famous insignia of their rulers, the 'ring of Tomar' and the 'sword of Carlus'.[3] The incident shows the decay of pagan religion. The sword of Carlus seems to have been that of the great emperor Charles or Charlemagne whom the Norse greatly admired, or one presented by him to some Scandinavian chief. Thor's (Tomar's) ring is an emblem mentioned in the *Landnámabók* and other Icelandic literature. It was a symbol of office among the priest-kings or rulers whom we find among the heathen Norsemen. It was a ring of silver or gold about 20 ounces in weight which lay upon the altar in the pagan temple except during the ceremonies when the priest wore it upon his arm. Oaths were sworn upon it and it was worn during sacrifices or executions after judgement in the folk *thing*. The wearer was called Thorsman (Thormodr or Thorir) and he would naturally be the chief man or ruler having a sacred as well as an aristocratic character. Hence the Irish annals use Tomar (their version of the name) as the generic name of the Norse rulers of Dublin, and we hear of Tomar's Wood near Drumcondra where, perhaps in some sacred grove, they held their pagan rites.

That Máel Sechnaill was able to wrest from the Dublin Norse the most sacred and essential symbol of Norse religion was perhaps more due to a growing scepticism than cowardly surrender on their part. Having ceased to believe in it they could the more easily give it up. So in our days hereditary keepers of old charms or magic-working objects in parts of the west can be induced to sell them for some small consideration to our National Museum, whereas their grandfathers would have shrunk in horror at the thought.

The battle of Clontarf, fought on Good Friday, 23 April 1014, is the great dramatic moment in the history of Norse Dublin. Sitric Silkbeard, son of Olaf Cuarán and Gormlaith of Leinster, is a notable figure. His personal beauty was unusual and typified in his handsome fair beard; the son of Gormlaith, whom the Norse saga calls the fairest woman of her time, could hardly be otherwise than a fine man. His reign is of remarkable length for a medieval man; he ruled over Dublin from 989 to 1036, nearly fifty years, and was over seventy when he died. His mother being Irish he must have been baptized a Christian. As regards Dublin Sitric was a patriot who objected to Irish rule, though Máel Sechnaill had installed him as a youth in Dublin in 989.

After various efforts to throw off Brian's yoke he lent himself to the great conspiracy of Máel Mórda, king of Leinster, his uncle, and Gormflaith his mother to call in the famous Sigurd, jarl of Orkney, and restore the independence of Leinster, Dublin, and the other Irish kingdoms. Had Sigurd won the battle he might have established a central Norse kingdom of Ireland which Sitric would have liked no better than Brian's, but the death of both Brian and Sigurd solved the question and restored the independence of Irish States, whether Norse or Gaelic.

Instead of their former position of conquerors or rebels the city States of Dublin, Waterford, Cork and Limerick were welded and accepted into the political system of Ireland and got full Irish citizenship. In the Book of Rights, as re-edited under Brian, Dublin is put on the footing of an Irish *mór-thuath* and bound to render tribute and naval service to the high-king and the king of Leinster. The tributes that this little kingdom had to pay show how much richer it was for its size in cattle and other forms of wealth than any other petty State; it had in Fingal some of the richest arable land in Ireland as well as wealth derived from trade and piracy.

Christianity was now generally accepted. Indeed 1014 may be taken as a good round date for the general abandonment of the worship of Odin and Thor in the Norse world generally. The adoption of the word Ostman ('eastmen', as opposed to Ireland which by the Vikings was called Westland) for the Norse settlers in the Irish towns marks the fact that they had now become Irish, and very different men from their fierce Viking forefathers, being normally peaceful traders and mariners and the best, indeed the only, seamen in Ireland.

King Sitric founded about 1030 the church or priory of Holy Trinity (now Christ Church) and gave Dublin its first bishop, Donatus or Dúnán. He struck coins, a thing unknown to Irish kings, and altogether was a considerable potentate. We can imagine that Dublinshire was now a well-populated State full of Ostman farmers and stretching from Skerries to Glencree and westward to the rich salmon fishery at Leixlip. Dublin itself must have been a walled city with the boundaries that the Normans preserved and which up to 1603 were the enclosure of the town: that is to say, east and west from the Dame's Gate at old St. Andrew's Church to the timber bridge at the later Bridgefoot which, called *droichet Dub-Gaill* (the Dane's bridge), remained, though built later in stone, the only bridge over the Liffey till Charles II's reign; and north and south from the Liffey-side to the present grounds of St. Patrick's which, when founded in 1219, was outside the city boundary.

A small town certainly, about half a mile from east to west and less from north to south but with plenty of space outside the walls, especially the green of Dublin which stretched from Islandbridge to the present Coombe, and Hoggen Green, so called in later times, lying south-west of Trinity, on which the Ostmen held their folk-moot or assembly called the *thing* (hence Thing-mount or *Thengmota* of Anglo-Norman records). The river in those days, before draining and reclamation, came up to D'Olier Street, and all between the College and Ringsend was a marsh. Ships had to heave to at the Long Stone or Steine where they cabled their light vessels. This, like Hoggen Green, was sacrificed in Charles II's time to property-grabbers and specu-lators, and is known now only by the curious phenomenon called the Crampton Memorial.

Were Dublin's walls high, and were they of earth or stone? Evidence is almost completely lacking, and it is odd that no stone tower like the imposing structure called Reginald's (Ragnall's) Tower in Waterford survived into Anglo-Norman times. The evidence of Reginald's Tower alone proves that the Ostmen could build stone fortifications. The two sieges that Strongbow and Diarmait, and then the high-king Ruaidrí, had to make of Dublin in 1170-1 prove that the defences at least could not be easily rushed, not to speak of earlier sieges by Máel Sechnaill.

Another piece of evidence as to what the defences of Dublin must have been like is given in Giraldus's description of how Wexford, a much smaller place than Dublin, stood on its defence against the Norman invaders. Fitz Stephen, after landing at Bannow in May 1170, marched with Diarmait to attack Wexford; the townsmen sallied forth but perceiving the Norman army and the novel sight of horsemen with their bright armour, helmets and shields they set fire to the suburbs and retired within their walls. Fitz Stephen, lining the trenches with men in armour and archers commanding the advanced towers, ordered an assault of the walls. The townsmen cast down large stones and beams and a gallant youth, Robert de Barry, struck on the head by a large stone, fell into the ditch. Sixteen years afterwards all his teeth fell out from the effects of the stroke but, what is more strange, new ones took their place! The assault was repulsed, but next day the Ostmen surrendered to Diarmait as their natural prince.

A certain light is thrown on Norse Dublin soon after Clontarf by a contemporary Welsh work called the Life of Gruffydd ap Cynan, written by some Welsh monk. Gruffydd was prince of north Wales or Gwynedd. His father, Cynan ap Iago, being expelled from his principality by rivals in 1039, fled to Dublin, was sheltered by the Ostmen there and married Ragnell (Raghnildr) daughter of the Norse prince Avloed (Olaf), who apparently was a son of Sitric.

Their son Gruffydd was born in Dublin and was fostered at a place called *cwmwd Colomcell* ('the territory of Colum Cille') 3 miles from Swords, where his mother and foster-mother lived. This was the church of Swords (Sord) which the famous St. Columba founded. Finally in 1075 Gruffydd sailed with Ostman aid to Anglesey, but not till 1099 did he recover his kingdom and meanwhile spent a regular Viking life between Dublin, Man and Wales. But from 1100 to his death in 1137, when he ruled as lord of Gwynedd, his fame was widespread and he is renowned in Welsh history as a friend of the poets and musicians. A lover of Irish culture, he introduced the Irish bagpipe into Wales and brought in Irish experts to improve the harp music of his native country. From a grandson of his called Rhiryd who owned Cloghran descended a family called FitzRery who were lords of Cloghran in this district till 1360.

It is worth recording that in 1051, Harold, son of Earl Godwine, sought refuge in Dublin when his father's party was broken up and the whole family expelled. Harold and his brother Leofwine took ship at Bristol and spent the winter in Dublin with Diarmait, king of Leinster, who we must suppose had a house in the town. Next spring Harold sailed back to England and the Godwine family recovered their influence with Edward the Confessor.

This Diarmait was a great man and ruled Leinster and Dublin from 1052 to 1072. His son Murchad began the famous MacMurrough line. One Gofraid ruled Dublin for some years after Diarmait's death, but the history of this time is very obscure; the line of Ivar as represented by Sitric Silkbeard seems to have died out by 1100.[4]

The next great event for Dublin was the visit of Magnus, king of Norway and grandson of Harald Hardrada, who, though a Christian, was a true Viking.

He appeared with a great fleet in 1098 in Scottish waters to restore the Norse empire over Orkney, the Hebrides, Man and Dublin. The *Heimskringla* saga says:

> He was a man easily known; he had a red surcoat over his mail shirt and his hair silky and flaxen fell all over his shoulders. . . . He held much to the fashion of raiment that was common in Westland [Ireland] and both he and his men used to go barelegged in the streets and had short kirtles and overcloaks so that men called him Barelegs or Barefoot.

In short Magnus was the first of those sympathetic foreigners who have loved Ireland, and wore as a token of his affection the Gaelic tunic or skirt and the 'brat' or ample cloak instead of the plaited linen close trousers of Norse and Anglo-Saxons. The reason for this may be that he was in love with a Dublin girl to whom he wrote some verses in Norse which are still preserved in the saga.

This magnificent man had great schemes for beating the Normans out of Wales and allying himself with Welsh and Irish kings against the race that had recently conquered England. He stayed with the high-king Muirchertach Ua Briain in Kincora, and Myrkiartan, as the saga calls him, gave his daughter Bláth-Muman in marriage to Magnus's son Sigurd, but, as the boy was only nine and the girl five, nothing came of it in the end. Magnus himself was slain in an obscure skirmish while on his way back to Norway foraging with only a few men somewhere on the coast of Ulster on 24 August 1103. Though his son Sigurd came to be king of Norway and famous as Sigurd the Crusader or Jerusalem-farer, the glory of the Norse sea-kings was practically over.

It is accepted by historians, as the *Heimskringla* claims, that Magnus in his two sea-farings to these islands restored the Norwegian rule over Orkney, the Hebrides and Man. In the latter island, which, though small, was an important strategic point for Norse activities, the great king Godred Crovan had died in 1095. Magnus captured and perhaps killed Lagmann son of Godred and set up his own infant son Sigurd instead. But after his death in Ulster, Man got a long-reigned king in Godred's other son Olaf (1103-53). Man and Dublin had, since 1072 or so, been a sort of joint kingdom, and it seemed of little importance to these masters of the seas whether it was ruled from the one or the other centre. We hear later of princes of the race of Brian Bóruma attempting to establish a sovereignty there, but without success. Man, of course, was for the most part a Gaelic-speaking island with a Gaelic population, and remained so till Manx died out half a century ago. This little sea-kingdom embraced Dublin, Man and the Hebrides (Innse Gall), but the connexion expired in the 12th century.[5] Magnus is no doubt responsible. In 1102 (say the Annals of Ulster and the *Heimskringla*) the king of Norway was with a big fleet in Man and then, with Muirchertach the high-king, won Dublin and Dublinshire and then spent the winter with Muirchertach (father-in-law to the infant Sigurd) at Kincora. He and the high-king were allies and probably consented to a joint sovereignty over Fingal and Dublin. Muirchertach's greatness ended, however, in 1114 when he became an invalid, dying in 1119; and the O'Brien high-kingship expired for ever.

Some time early in the 12th century Dublin got a new line of rulers instead of the old race of Ivar or Tomar. Her last strong king had been Gofraid who died in 1095. Now there appeared a purely local line, called by the Irish annals Mac Torcaill or sons of Thorkell. Their origin is mysterious; we have merely the name of the founder Torcall. It is possible that they arose under or as a result of the royal visit of Magnus, after whom the Hebrides, Man and Dublinshire ceased their former connexion. According to Bugge, one Thorkell was king of Dublin in 1133. Our annals call them 'kings' (of the foreigners of Dublin) as they do all sorts of petty Irish chiefs, and so does Giraldus Cambrensis, while the Anglo-French poem, the Song of Dermot and the Earl, calls the last of them, Asculf mac Torcaill, 'Sire, lord and defender throughout all the country' (of Dublin).

The Ostmen, a practical race, were now firm Christians. From 1066 onwards they began to send their bishops to be consecrated in Canterbury. They wanted a bishop of their own within the city, rather than a distant one ruling from Glendalough, and possibly one who could speak Norse. Aware of their Teutonic descent, they preferred the Normans to the Irish, for the conquerors of England had a few generations ago in their own duchy been Scandinavian in blood and speech. In short, though the Ostmen had been absorbed into the Irish confederacy of States, they were none too loyal to Ireland. This did not save them when the Normans arrived here, but they did not foresee the consequences of their relations with England. It was only in 1162 that they accepted full unity with the Irish Church and got a pure Irishman for bishop, namely Lorcán Ua Tuathail, but even then they secured that he should reside in the capital and not in far-off Glendalough.

The fall of Norse Dublin came about with the fall of independent Ireland when Diarmait 'na nGall' Mac Murchada brought the Normans in. This Diarmait (II) had made Leinster a very strong kingdom stretching from the Liffey to the Nore and embracing the three Ostman towns of Dublin, Waterford and Wexford. Among the churches which he founded, the priory of All Saints stood where Trinity College stands now, and we may well imagine that Diarmait had a house within the walls. Jarl Asculf mac Torcaill was his vassal, and among other vassals Domnall Mac Gilla Mo Cholmóc, chief of the country from Dublin to Rathdrum, played a remarkable part. He also was a sort of overlord of Dublin and had a street or lane with a house in the city. Mac Gilla Mo Cholmóc's Street near St. Michael's Church is frequently mentioned in early Dublin records.

It was at the end of August, 1170, that Diarmait and his Norman ally Strongbow took Waterford, and on 21 September Dublin fell to them, while Asculf and his chief men fled oversea to enlist Viking help. In the next May (1171), on the death of Diarmait, the high-king Ruaidrí Ua Conchobair prepared a great national levy to expel the Normans. In June Jarl Asculf returned with a thousand Vikings, 'men of iron hearts and iron mail', and landing at the Steine marched against the eastern gate to storm the city. But, valiant as they were, the Norse footmen were no match for their cousins from Normandy, who had won many a battle by shock tactics, light horse charging with lance and sword. Miles de Cogan's attack broke up Asculf's men and they were cut to pieces; Jarl Asculf, taken prisoner, was beheaded in his own hall, defying the conqueror. The later siege by the high-king's vast army failed in September before the sally of the Normans and their Leinster allies, and so Dublin became the capital of the conquerors.[6]

Henry II with his imposing army of 4,000 knights arrived to spend the winter of 1171-2 in Dublin and this city became henceforth the king of England's capital in his lordship of Ireland. His court was pitched on the wide and healthy [space near the] Thingmount of Dublin where College Green now is, and the Irish chiefs who had come in to do him homage, 'made him a royal palace constructed with admirable skill after the fashion of the land', says Giraldus. Henry turned Dublin into a chartered city after the new style in England by giving it the liberties of his city of Bristol,[7] and soon the narrow little Ostman town became a growing city of traders of every race who flocked in from Henry's vast empire.

The Ostman suburb

What was the fate of the old-fashioned Ostmen? One prince of the line of Mac Torcaill survived in Hamund, brother of Asculf, and he was allowed to hold Kinsaley as his demesne for some time by Strongbow's grant; but he was soon either slain or expelled by the conquerors, and his estate went to Christ Church. It was too dangerous a dynasty to encourage, though many individuals with Torcall as part of their name appear holding small pieces of land, or houses, in Oxmantown or Fingal for a century or two. Though the immediate jarls or *mormáers* of Dublin, Waterford and Cork were slain or ousted, an edict of Henry II took the race of the *Houstmanni* under his protection as his lieges. They were too valuable a race to outlaw, for they were the traders, pilots, carriers, mariners and, it appears, the capitalists of Ireland at the time. Probably, never having been quite blended with the native race, they were flattered at being accepted by the conquering Normans and

Saxons with whom they had long been acquainted, and put on equal terms with them. But in the case of the Dublin Ostmen this protection soon proved more apparent than real. Whether they were actually expelled, or preferred to move away from the strangers who now flocked into Dublin we cannot tell, but soon after the conquest they (or those who had not abandoned Ireland, as we are told great numbers of them did) migrated north of the Liffey and founded a new town or unwalled suburb called Ostmantown or Ostmanby, later corruptly known as Oxmantown, with its famous green about Smithfield. Here they would have the protection of the great abbey of St. Mary which had been founded by their ancestors, and here they were allowed to dwell in peace and grow rich. St. Michan's also was the parish church of Oxmantown. Their characteristic names disappear by about 1300, and the later Dubliners got into Oxmantown by intermarriage, bequest, purchase, or other means. But we need not conclude that none of their blood flows in the veins of later Dubliners; surnames were not then fixed, and it is probable that most of these Christeds, Turkills, Wickings, etc., later took English surnames.

I must not prolong this general survey of Norse Dublin. But I may well finish on the interesting question as to how the Norse in Ireland became Irish and what language they spoke. Naturally, in the three centuries from the landing of Olaf and Ivar at the *linn dubh* to the expulsion of the peaceful Ostmen into Oxmantown many changes took place. Olaf Cuarán was so connected with Irish princes (he married the famous Gormlaith) that we must suppose he knew some Irish; otherwise, we must hope that that attractive lady knew some Norse. Certainly his son by her, the famous Sitric Silkbeard, who married Sláine, a daughter of Brian Bóruma, must have been able to converse in his mother's language with his Irish wife.

But already in the tenth century a mixed race of Irish and Norse had grown up; they were known as 'Gall Gaedhil' or 'Norse-Irish', and existed in great numbers in the islands of Scotland and Man and along the coasts of Ireland. They gave their name to a whole region of Scotland (Galloway) and must have been well known in Dublinshire and our eastern coasts. They were pagan, or semi-pagan, or Irish relapsed into heathendom, and were dreaded as pirates and raiders. From a mention of them in a poem of Uraird mac Coisse in the tenth century, it would seem that they spoke Irish but badly, and the expression of 'the *gioc-goc* of a Gall-Gael' meant halting or broken Irish. It is through these Gall-Gaels, who were very numerous in the Hebrides, that a great number of words connected with shipping, the sea and war came into modern Irish. But in that vast sea-world that the Norsemen sailed there must have been a regular *lingua franca* that all seamen knew, and a smattering of Welsh, Anglo-Saxon, Norse and Irish was probably familiar to most Vikings.

After Clontarf it seems that a great many Dublin Norsemen sought refuge in the lakeland and fells of Cumberland, where their place-names and personal names are common, but where they brought in what are called inversion-compounds in place-names; e.g., Aspatria is 'Ash Patrick', but in true Teutonic Norse that would be 'Patrick's Ash'. They had adopted from the Irish the syntax by which the genitive case comes after the word that governs it, as in Latin, a proof that they were deeply influenced by Irish, though keeping up Norse.

But whatever mixed speech, bad Norse or bad Irish, was spoken in the Ostman towns in the 11th century it seems clear that in the period before the coming of the Normans the Norse speech was waning fast. The deeds of Christ Church and the printed *Chartularies of St. Mary's Abbey* throw some light on this. In a list of witnesses to a grant to St. Mary's soon after the Norman conquest, among other Ostman names are 'Polin sun Dunoch' and 'Turkil sun Gillemori'. Here the Norse 'son' is preserved, but in the Gaelic order as if the Ostmen then spoke Norse influenced by the Celtic word-order, for in good Norse these names would have been 'Polin Dunochsson' and 'Turkil Gillemorysson'.

On the other hand, a Christ Church deed of *c.* 1195 mentions the land near Ostmanby of Gillecrist *mac an Suter*, that is Gillecrist (a Norse name) son of the shoemaker. This is pure Irish and looks as if Irish was then the language of Ostmanby and its inhabitants. The surest proof, however, that by the time of the Norman invasion the old Norse of Dublin, Waterford, etc., spoke Irish and seemed Irish is in the numerous complaints made by individuals or communities of them, to the effect that in spite of the charters given by Henry II and other lords they were being treated like the Irish. The native race, when it resisted the invader, was in general treated as *Hibernici*, that is rightless serfs. The Ostmen, however, had been promised legal equality with the newcoming English; but as they were hard to distinguish from their Irish neighbours, the Anglo-Norman lords, to whose interest it was to oust the Irish or turn them into villeins, often claimed them as Irish — my *History of Medieval Ireland* contains many examples. But of these complaints we hear no more when finally, by 1300 or so, the Ostmen survivors died out or blended with the Irish on one hand or the English on the other.

Actual records fail to give us a living and complete picture of Norse Dublin. A remarkable list of pre-Norman benefactors to Christ Church, preserved in the Christ Church deeds though in corrupted form, contains some twenty names of great men of Norse race who ruled Dublin, the Mac Torcaills, etc., as well as the kings of Leinster, who granted lands to Holy Trinity. The records of St. Mary's and of St. Thomas's and other State documents supplement it. All these, if carefully studied and collated, would make almost a map of the little town which surrounded the Norse fortress and Christ Church and its northern suburbs, but no one has yet attempted this.

Fancy, however, not unsupported by facts, enables us to dwell pleasantly on Dublin as it must have been about 1160. We read of Jarl Asculf's garden which survived the conquest, and we know he had a hall, probably where the castle stands now; in some mint there he struck coins. Domnall Mac Gilla Mo Cholmóc had a house and street of his own, and till 1354 at least we read of 'Kilhalmokyslane' to the north-west of Christ Church. In the vaults of Christ Church, according to the Black Book of this priory, the Ostmen stored the wine which they traded into the hinterland, and we may be sure that many a jolly carouse of Vikings and Dublin householders took place there by candlelight, when the great sagas were told. It was the equivalent of the places where, by artificial light, the poets of modern Dublin meet.

Pre-Norman Dublin

JOHN RYAN

In our approach to earliest Dublin we have our choice of three ways, one legendary, one archaeological, one historical. They all bring us to the ford over the Liffey (Aba Lífe, Ruirthech) near its mouth, a ford known from the earliest times as Áth Cliath — 'ford of the wickerwork, wattles or hurdles'. Excavations in the last century[1] showed that the area round Christ Church — Winetavern Street, Fishamble Street, Castle Street, High Street — was in ancient times a bog. This peat foundation may have given a dark colour to the water somewhere near the point where the Poddle joins the larger Liffey stream and thus constituted a *linn dubh* ('black pool') in the river. Both Áth Cliath and Dubhlinn are Gaelic forms, and neither is unique in Ireland. There is an Áth Cliath (Medraige) in the north of Uí Fiachrach Aidne (a territory that corresponds with the diocese of Kilmacduagh) at Clarinbridge near Athenry, and another called Áth Cliath in Chorainn at Ballymote, Co. Sligo. There was a Duiblinn in Ulster, and a Duiblinn in Connacht, apparently on the Suck in Galway. *Áth Cliath* and *Duiblinn* are thus names given to a ford across and a pool in a river by Irish speakers. It may be noted that Baile Átha Cliath as the name for Dublin is found first in the Annals of Ulster in 1368.[2]

Gaelic origins

Where exactly the ford was, and what exactly the construction at, or near, it was, to justify the epithet 'ford of the wattles or hurdles', are questions none too easy to answer. It is natural to suppose that where the ford was there the bridge was built in due course. But where was the first bridge built? Speed's map of 1610 shows the one bridge of that period joining Bridge Street with Church Street.[3] But we know that permission to build a new bridge was granted to the citizens by King John in 1214, at the place 'where it should seem most expedient for the use of the city', and that leave was given at the same time to demolish the old bridge should the citizens desire to do so in order to help to defray expenses. What actually took place then is not recorded.[4] It is obvious that a new bridge may have been built and at a point on the river not quite the same as that on which the older 'bridge of the Ostmen' had stood. Whether this original bridge again had been built at the traditional ford of Áth Cliath is doubtful. According to Haliday, it is to be deduced that the so-called Old Bridge of later times was built in 1428 for the Dominicans, who had a house in Oxmantown, and a school at Usher's Island, south of the river. But it is not clear that this bridge was built at Bridgefoot Street-Queen Street. If de Burgo is right in saying that it was still standing when he wrote[5] it would be at Bridge Street. The suggestion is that after the destruction of Dublin Bridge in 1386, there was no new building, but communication solely by ferry, until the bridge was rebuilt in 1428. Two considerations must here be kept in mind. The bridge would be built well upstream, within the city bounds, so as to allow the river at Wood Quay and Merchants' Quay to be used freely by ships. There are references in the 15th and 16th centuries[6] to fords and shallow places between the bridge of Dublin and the island of Clontarf, at the river mouth, and above all to a ford passing from near Dame's Gate to St. Mary's Abbey. It would appear, then, that there was a well-known and much used ford leading from the Fownes Street-Eustace Street area on the south side to Jervis Street or thereabouts on the north side. This may have been the traditional Áth Cliath.

What is the significance of the *cliath* in Áth Cliath, that is to say, of the wattles of hurdles in the 'ford of the hurdles'? Unfortunately no definition is offered by any ancient source. It is worthy of note that in the 12th century a structure called a *cliath-drochet* ('wattle bridge') was erected on the Shannon at Athlone by Toirrdelbach Ua Conchobair and again by Ruaidrí Ua Conchobair,[7] whilst a similar structure bearing a similar name was flung by Toirrdelbach Ua Conchobair over the Shannon at Áth Liag.[8] I suspect that the difference between an *áth-cliath* and a *cliath-droichet* was not very great in practice. Piles of stones would be placed at short intervals along the ford. On them poles or beams would be laid, and on top of these branches, the whole forming a rude roadway like the *tóchars*[9] or causeways excavated in various bogs. Such a structure might properly be called a *cliath-droichet* when it carried travellers dryshod over the ford; it might be called an *áth-cliath* when it did not. Given the building facilities and the building methods of the day, and taking into account the attentions of hostile forces, I think that the distinction between an *áth-cliath* and a *cliath-droichet* would be mainly theoretical. In passing it may be said that while references to fords in early Irish records are legion, references to bridges are extremely few. Some occur in the literature.[10] In the Latin Lives of the saints, a source which provides us with abundant knowledge of the country and its people, barely one mention of a bridge occurs.[11] It tells of an unfortunate man, who after death was buried in hell, but who in life had done a good deed by constructing a bridge over a dangerous stream, and for that charitable act was granted in eternity some mitigation of punishment. In fact we may say that before the year 1000 the number of bridges in Ireland was negligibly small.

The legend of Áth Cliath is found in the *Dindshenchas* and need not detain us long. Its burden is[12] that owing to Adam's sin a prototype of the Loch Ness monster appeared at Lecc Benn. The beast had four heads and was 140 ft. long. It licked up the Boyne bed till the whole place became a deep valley! At Brug maic ind Oic (Newgrange on the Boyne) it met its end at the hands of some unknown warrior. Its skeleton got tossed into the Irish Sea, and the restless waves carried it to the ford, where it formed a *cliath* or palisade that shall abide till doom. Thereafter the ford was called Áth Cliath.

Duiblind [Dubhlinn] had a like romantic origin.[13] The daughter of Rodub the curly-haired and brave was wife of Énna, son of Nós, who settled in the meadow land of Etar (Howth). She was a wizard, she was a poetess, she was a lady of starlike beauty. Yet Énna cast an eye on another lady, fair and lovely, Aide, daughter of Ochind. Duiblind, daughter of Rodub, grew jealous and one morning sang a spell of the sea. This enraged Ochind, father of the other woman, who suborned a *gilla*, Margin son of Cnucha, to cast a *caer cliss* ('cunning-ball') in her path and destroy her! Thereafter the Liffey pool was called Duiblind in loving memory.

Archaeologically the district round Áth Cliath has yielded some finds of interest. But they do not indicate a settlement of any size or importance. Rather do they suggest a fishing village with huts like the *tegoriolum ubi hospitabam* mentioned by St. Patrick[14] where sailors would find lodgings when they had brought their ships into shelter at nightfall in Dublin Bay.

Historically the earliest reference to Áth Cliath is probably that found in Adomnán's *Life of Colum Cille*.[15] Adomnán died in 704, but the reference is to St. Colum Cille himself, whose death is dated 597. According to the story a strange disease followed a fall of rain from dense and ugly clouds in that part of Ireland which lay between the stream called Ailbene (the Delvin river which enters the sea at Gormanston) and the *vadum Clied* (Áth Cliath on the Liffey). This rain caused ulcers in man and beast, with fatal consequences. Colum Cille sent one of his monks to stop its ravages. Thus in the sixth century Áth Cliath on the Liffey was a place well known to Irishmen.

Strange to relate it entered hardly at all into Irish history before the ninth century, despite its position on a river that marked the boundary between two kingdoms. North of the Liffey lay *Mide*, Meath; south of the Liffey lay *Laigin*, Leinster. A word or two must be said about these boundary States. North of the Liffey was settled a branch of the Ciannachta, a people said to be of Munster origin and found in Éli[16] and in Glenn Geimin, Co. Derry (Ciannachta Glinne Geimin). Their land in the east, from Dromiskin to the Liffey, is said to have been given them in reward for their services to Cormac mac Airt, king of Tara, against the men of Ulster in the battle of Crinna, fought in the second half of the third century A.D. Similarly in Munster the Déisi received lands for the military service given by them to the Eóganachta against the Leinstermen. A subsection of the Ciannachta was the Saitne, settled in the barony of Balrothery, north Co. Dublin. On the western or Meath side was a branch of another ancient people — the Gailenga. This branch was called the Gailenga Becca Breg, and its ruler in pre-Norman times was Ó hAongusa (Ennis). According to the Book of Ballymote and the Book of Lecan, Glasnevin lay in Gailenga territory.[17] Both Ciannachta and Gailenga were subject to the great Uí Néill dynasty of the south, and formed part of the Uí Néill kingdom of Brega, which with the kingdom of Mide, in what is now mainly Westmeath, formed the great Uí Néill (midland) over-kingdom of *Mide*, Meath.

South of the Liffey, the kingdom was Leinster. The subsection was Cualu. Two distinguished septs, the Uí Chellaig Chualann and the Uí Briúin Chualann belonged to this area. The former were of the same descent as the Uí Máil, whose name survives in the place-name of Glen of Imaal, and the Uí Teig, whose lands seem to have been nearer the later city. The Uí Briúin Chualann were connected genealogically with the Uí Dúnlainge, the ruling sept of north Leinster.[18] After 727 the Uí Dúnlainge broke into three groups, of which one, the Uí Dúnchada, had its chief fortress at Liamain, the Newcastle Lyons district of south Co. Dublin. From this sept the place-name Carn Ua nDúnchada, shortened from Carnán Cluana Ua nDúnchada, seems to be derived.[19] It is known to us as Dolphin's Barn. Thus the Uí Dúnchada sub-kingdom reached the Liffey on the west at Islandbridge and the ruling family of Uí Dúnchada, Mac Gilla Mo Cholmóc, had close connexions with the city in medieval times. The River Dodder ran through Cualu. Bruiden Daderga lay in Cualu, an institution still recalled by the road that led to it, Bóthar na bruigne (Bohernabreena). Áth Cliath on the Liffey was also accredited to Cualu, for it was called, commonly, Áth Cliath Chualann.[20] As Cualu was part of Laigin (Leinster), Áth Cliath is also called Áth Cliath Laigen.[21] In other words, though Áth Cliath lay on the boundary between Leinster and Meath, it was regarded always as belonging to Leinster. Indeed, the *Dindshenchas* poem adds to the extent of Cualu by including Howth in it: 'Benn Etair, with its forehead to the flood, the hundred-strong barrier of northern Cualu',[22] and this claim may have been justified, though Howth was reckoned as part of the Meath sub-kingdom of Brega.[23]

One of the five great roads leading from Tara was the Slige Chualann. Did this cross the Liffey at Áth Cliath? Colm Ó Lochlainn, in the very valuable article on the ancient roads of Ireland which he contributed to the MacNeill *Féil-sgríbhinn*, and the late Henry Morris, in an article contributed to the *Journal of the Royal Society of Antiquaries of Ireland* in 1938, argue that it probably did so. I venture, however, to doubt that conclusion. Meath armies marching into Leinster crossed the border normally over the Rye Water somewhere near Leixlip. Then they marched probably by Saggart to

Blessington and Baltinglass. I take it that they followed in this the Slige Chualann, and that the *slige* did not therefore cross the Liffey at Áth Cliath. Had it done so there would, I think, have been major battles at the ford. In fact, an occasional border squabble is all that is recorded to have taken place there.

The Viking settlement

Áth Cliath accordingly was a name of very minor importance until the beginning of the ninth century. The change came with the new and dreadful era in Irish history due to the incursions of the Northmen. As is well known, the opening date of that era is 795. At first the Norse were mere raiders. That the danger which they portended was underestimated is evident from the fact that three high-kings, Donnchad mac Domnaill Mide (770-97), Áed Oirdnide (797-819) and Conchobar mac Donnchada (819-33) never met them in battle. The first king of Ireland to face them in the field was Niall Caille (833-46), soon after his accession in 833. At this date they were still raiders. But Niall was alarmed by the strength and persistency of their incursions and took serious steps to organize the country against them.

Following raids at Howth (Etar) in 821, and at Lusk and the Brega coast in 827, they appeared at the Liffey mouth. The countries of Europe were interdependent in the ninth as well as in the 20th century, and unfortunate developments abroad had unpleasant repercussions here. The last decade of the reign of Louis the Pious (830-40) was marked by violent quarrels between him and his sons, and the situation became worse when Louis died (840). This gave the Northmen their opportunity to wander, more or less at will, in the Frankish empire. Success in France increased their ambition and their boldness elsewhere. In 837 a fleet of 60 ships appeared on the River Liffey. Their crews occupied the rising land beside Áth Cliath and settled there, to all intents and purposes, permanently. In 841 a *longphort* was constructed at the spot. This means that the ships were drawn up on shore, and a fortified wall raised around them on the landward side to keep off attack.[24] From now on the Northmen at Áth Cliath had one foot at least on dry land. The beginning of the City of Dublin is to be placed, therefore, in that year.

It is remarkable how quickly Dublin became the chief focus or rallying point of the Northmen in the country. When the *longphort* was built there in 841 such a rapid rise to eminence was certainly not foreseen. At that time the leading Norse captain in Ireland was Turgéis.[25] His fleet was anchored in Lough Neagh whence he ravaged the north (839). In 844 he had moved to Lough Ree, whence he devastated Mide and Connacht. Next year, 845, he was captured by the king of Mide, Máel Sechnaill I (mac Máele Ruanaid) and executed by drowning in Lough Owel. This Turgéis was the ablest leader of the Northmen in Ireland in his day, but he had nothing to do with Dublin.[26] Other Norse leaders were forthcoming, and the period 845-52 found them active on an unprecedented scale all over the island. The menace was now a national problem of the most serious kind, and was treated as such by Máel Sechnaill mac Máele Ruanaid, who became high-king in 846 and ruled to 862. With Tigernach, king of southern Brega,[27] the high-king attacked, captured and sacked Dublin in 849, the city's first experience of such a misfortune. Matters were complicated by an alliance made between Cináed mac Conaing, king of northern Brega,[28] with the Northmen, the first alliance of its kind in Irish history. It was a scandal that incurred universal condemnation, like the alliance of France with the hated Turk in a later century, and Cináed was tried as a war-criminal and executed.[29] Such a fate he would have met like a man, as the price to be paid by a ruler whose political calculations had gone sadly astray; but the manner of putting him to death was ignominious. He was drowned 'in a dirty streamlet',[30] not in a noble lake nor river nor in the clean if briny sea, and that outrage rankled in the memory of his indignant relatives. Damage to the nation was to them a minor evil; dishonour to the family a major disaster.

When we speak of the Norse in Ireland we must take care not to think of them as a unified force or a number of co-ordinated forces owing submission to a single military or political head. Quite the contrary. Each detachment was accustomed to work on its own, fight for its own hand, seek to further its own fortunes at the expense even of fellow-Northmen. Indeed, an amazing feature of all Scandinavian history during the Viking period is the manner in which raiding leaders and raiding parties preyed on one another. A Viking captain of 20 vessels might attack and destroy a Viking fleet of 10 vessels. There were alliances, coalitions that sometimes brought together fleets of extraordinary strength, quarrels, shattered partnerships, cruel and bloody struggles between the Northmen themselves.[31] In Ireland these disputes among the invaders were as common as they were everywhere else.[32] It can, if my reading of the records is correct, be stated as a historical fact that never from the year 795 to the coming of the Normans in 1170 were all the Northmen of Ireland found working together in the same camp in any cause. Such disunity diminished, but of course did not destroy, their power.

One need go no further than Dublin itself for illustrations. The Norse settlers were plundered badly by Danish raiders in 851. All the wealth which had come to the city in 10 years of industrious robbery on land and sea was lost overnight. Much of this wealth consisted of objects of value taken from the churches, sanctuaries and shrines of Ireland. It was now carried off to the northern countries, the first fruits of an immense spoliation. As an indication of what Ireland lost in this manner we need mention only that Irish objects of the Christian period have been found in over 200 Norse graves of the ninth and tenth centuries.[33]

A new stage in the history of Dublin was reached in 853, when Olaf 'son of the king of Lochlainn' (perhaps nothing more than an important young Norse captain) came to the port with a large fleet and took command of all the foreigners settled there. In other words he was accepted as ruler by all parties. He was a man — rare enough among the Northmen — with political sense of a high order. During the two decades or more of his government (in which he was assisted by Ivar the Boneless),[34] the settlement at Dublin became a stable State, with civil government, and fixed, if still rudimentary, institutions.

To counter the obvious growth of Norse power Máel Sechnaill, the high-king, tried various expedients. He met the rulers of Leth Cuinn at Armagh in 851, but nothing much came of their deliberations. Indeed, the sequel was ironic, for Armagh itself was raided by the Norse in 852. Next Máel Sechnaill tried to come to an understanding with the Viking ruler of Dublin. Nothing was easier. The Norse king travelled to Máel Sechnaill's house near Mullingar, where he was treated as a royal guest. He promised everything, agreed to everything, and then plundered Máel Sechnaill's lands in all directions on his way home![35] This illustrates a point often mentioned in the *Heimskringla* and other sagas in connexion with the Northmen: neither their word nor their bond had any value whatsoever, for in dealings even with one another treachery was a regular weapon.[36]

Within a decade the feeling of horror which Cináed's alliance with the Northmen had aroused was completely outmoded. Cerball, the ablest king that Ossory ever had, took a number of them into his service as mercenaries.[37] He gave a daughter in marriage to a Norse chief, and the lady is reckoned as the ancestress of several distinguished Icelandic families.[38] According to northern sources, also, a granddaughter of Cerball married a son of Olaf of Dublin;[39] while Olaf himself married a daughter of Áed Findliath, then king of Cenél nEógain.[40] The original policy of non-fraternization would thus be breaking down under the strain of daily human contacts.[41] The Norse continued to engage in minor feuds, sometimes from sea bases, sometimes from land settlements, but often now in alliance with Irish rulers against other Norse and other Irish rulers.

After a generation (by 870), the Norse settlement at Áth Cliath had become a small, fairly compact Irish State. It was still the only organized Scandinavian State in the country. Áth Cliath or Dublin was accepted by the Irish rulers as an exotic addition to the varied elements which went to constitute the kingdom of Ireland. They had no wish to drive those Northmen away; they rejoiced, rather, in using them as pawns against one another in the fascinating game of politics. Thus Áed Findliath, when king of Cenél nEógain, used them as a valuable small reinforcement to his own troops.[42] As high-king (862-79) he castigated them so severely in 866 that their strong position in the north was lost for ever.[43] In this we can trace the influence of his queen Land, daughter of Dúnlang of Ossory.[44] By an earlier marriage she had become the mother of Cennétig mac Gáethíne, king of Loígis, who was also famous for anti-Norse activities in the Ireland of his day.[45]

The years 850-70 mark the high-tide of Scandinavian success in continental Europe. It was natural that the Norse of Áth Cliath should follow the progress of their kin in these areas with interest, and should feel the urge to share in their glory. Hence their attack on the Britons of Strathclyde in 870. The Dublin Norse starved the great fortress — Dumbarton — into surrender and returned home with abundant booty. Soon afterwards (873) we find them trying to unite Dublin and York under the same sceptre.[46]

Flann Sinna, son of Máel Sechnaill I, became king of Ireland in 879 and ruled to 916. His rule almost coincides with a so-called 'forty years of rest' from Norse depredations recorded in Irish sources.[47] During this period there was no Norse attack in strength, though there were many waspish and mischievous raids, for the character of the Northmen remained unchanged. Their activity was displayed at this epoch more in England, France and Russia than in Ireland. They reached even Constantinople, where they were soundly trounced by the local fleet.[48] Seamanship in the eastern Roman empire remained far superior in quality to anything which they could achieve. It was different in western Europe, where the Norse on sea were far in advance, not only of England and Ireland, but also of the great Frankish State.

Early in the tenth century Norse power in France collapsed. An arrangement was agreed to by which the French king should let them colonize a strip of territory in the north-west. It was to develop into the duchy of Normandy.[49] In England, too, the opposition of Alfred the Great and his successors led to a serious curtailment of Norse strength. Once again, then, these turned their attention on Ireland. A new era began with the appearance of a large fleet at Loch dá Caech (Waterford harbour) in 914, to be followed by other vessels in 915. Niall Glúndub, son of Áed Findliath, became king of Ireland in 916, and set himself to organize measures of defence. He fought two campaigns, one designed to free Munster from the Norse (917) and the other against Sitric of Dublin (918-19). Both failed. Against Sitric, then Norse ruler of Dublin, he made temporary headway, when he drove him from the city in 918. But Sitric returned with a strong fleet in 919, and a battle was fought at Cell Mo Shámóc near Islandbridge, wherein Niall Glúndub was slain. The result was that the Norse were left in undisputed sway over Dublin; whilst in Waterford they were able to consolidate their position.

From 920 to 937 Norse power in Ireland generally increased. They settled at Inis Sibtonn on the Shannon in 922 and laid the foundations of the City of

Limerick.[50] The Norse of Wexford as a fighting force are mentioned for the first time in 935.[51] Those of Áth Cliath undertook frequent plundering expeditions, more than one (924, 931) directed against the Northmen of Limerick. Meanwhile the Dublin rulers sought to maintain or improve their hold on Danish Northumbria. Sitric Gale, of the Dublin dynasty, became ruler at York in 921. He embraced the Christian faith, and married a sister of King Æthelstan. His successor in Dublin (921) and York (927) was Godfrid, grandson of Ivar. He, however, was expelled by Æthelstan after six months and returned to Dublin, where he died in 934. He was succeeded by his son Olaf Godfridsson. This Olaf advanced his claim to the throne of Northumbria, and was supported by Constantine, son of Áed, king of Scotland, who wanted a buffer State between himself and Æthelstan. Olaf and Constantine united their forces and invaded Northumbria in 937, only to meet a crushing defeat at the hands of Æthelstan.[52] Olaf escaped and returned to Dublin.[53]

From this time onward the kingdom of Dublin begins to decline. The reasons are two: the increasing effectiveness of English resistance in Northumbria and the yet more determined resistance of Irish princes, especially of the redoubtable Muirchertach of the Leather Cloaks (king of Ailech, 938-43). In his effort to hold Northumbria Olaf Cuarán, son of Sitric Gale, became a Christian, but this led to a revolt of the Northumbrian Northmen, still stoutly pagan, against him.[54] The efforts of the Dublin dynasts to maintain themselves at York failed and were practically abandoned after 954.

Donnchad Donn, son of Flann Sinna, king of Ireland (919-44), after 17 years of inactivity, moved against Dublin and burnt the city in 937. Next year, 938, he made a treaty of peace with Muirchertach of the Leather Cloaks (son of Niall Glúndub), now king of Cenél nEógain, and the two besieged Dublin and devastated Norse territory far and wide. When Muirchertach made his famous circuit of Ireland in winter, 941, he spent a night in triumph at Áth Cliath. The Norse did not welcome his coming, but they were wise enough to make the best of a situation that could not be remedied. Supplies in abundance were placed before the northern army — salt bacon, fine wheat, red gold, joints of beef, gorgeous cheeses, and a coloured *brat* (a gala cloak) for every *toíseach*! The Norse king was taken off as a hostage.[55] Two years later (943) Muirchertach was killed in an insignificant skirmish with a Dublin host. The leader of that Norse army was himself slain by the new high-king, Congalach mac Máel Mithig (944-56), in 948. Four years earlier, in 944, Congalach had plundered Dublin and taken great spoils. In the end, however, he was to meet his death at Norse hands, in an ambush near Dublin on his way back from a successful campaign in Leinster. The place of the Norse in Congalach's life was small but important, and their place in all Irish life may be summarized in the same terms.

Domnall ua Néill (son of Muirchertach, son of Niall Glúndub), who succeeded Congalach as high-king (956-80), fought no battle against the Norse as such. In his struggles, however, with the men of Leinster (968, 969) and with the men of Mide (970) he encountered the Norse of Dublin as minor allies of these peoples.

The Hiberno-Norse town

Máel Sechnaill II (son of Domnall, son of Donnchad Donn, son of Flann Sinna) king of Ireland (980-1002, 1014-22) began his career with two resounding victories over the Dublin Northmen. The first was at Tara (980) where Gaill from the Orkneys were numerous on the defeated side.[56] Ragnall, son of Olaf Cuarán, was slain, and Olaf himself went on pilgrimage to Iona, where he died, apparently a Christian.[57] Next year (981) Máel Sechnaill appeared before Dublin and took possession of it after a successful siege.[58] When he marched against Leinster and the Norse of Waterford in 984 the Norse of Dublin, under Glúniarainn, son of Olaf Cuarán, were in his company. Again, however, they proved recalcitrant, so he captured the city and imposed a heavy tribute on the citizens, in 989.[59] They replied by helping Leinster to raid his territory in 990. He entered Dublin again in 995, and took away two famous trophies, the ring of Thor and the sword of Carlus.[60] In 997 Máel Sechnaill and Brian agreed to divide Ireland between them, and the united armies took the hostages of the Dublin State. When Máel Mórda, king of Leinster, refused to submit to Brian, king of Leth Moga, he was supported by the Norse of Dublin. The result was the battle of Glenn Máma (999), in which Brian won a great victory. Sitric of Dublin escaped, but had to return and surrender, as he could find protection nowhere. Immediately after the battle Dublin was entered and sacked.

Brian became king of Ireland in 1002. From that date to 1013 the Norse of Dublin almost disappear from the Irish stage. Their alliance with the Leinstermen against Brian was, however, maintained and was much in evidence at Clontarf. Dublin in 1014 was a small city, which despite frequent plunderings remained wealthy and was thus able to offer inducements to the Norse of many places to come to its help. Sigurd, jarl of the Orkneys, was offered also the crown of Dublin if he came in strength to oppose Brian. Norse accounts say that he was offered the crown to Ireland, but then the same Norse sources[61] speak of Olaf Cuarán as king of Ireland, a ridiculous exaggeration.[62]

Clontarf was a serious, but not an overwhelming, defeat for the Norse of Dublin. Sitric was not deprived of his status of relative independence. He quarrelled with the Leinstermen in 1018 and was defeated by their forces. The same fate befell him in all subsequent encounters with Irish armies. He went to Rome on pilgrimage in 1028, leaving his son Olaf to rule the city in his stead. Olaf was attacked, defeated and taken prisoner by Mathgamain Ó Riagáin, king of south Brega, and held to ransom at an enormous price. Not less than 1,200 cows, 60 ounces of gold, 60 ounces of silver, 120 Welsh horses,[63] and the sword of Carlus (Máel Sechnaill's trophy which he or a successor must have restored during the period of friendliness) was paid to Ó Riagáin. The hostages of Irish race, from Leinster and Leth Cuinn, held by the Norse, were also handed over to him. To this event we are justified in attaching some reflections. Brega was the little border kingdom that had lost a large slice of territory[64] to the Dublin Northmen. Leixlip marked its boundary on the west. South of the Liffey their jurisdiction does not seem to have extended far beyond the city wall, though they had settlements at Dalkey and further down the coast. Dublin was rich enough to pay this ransom easily. If the 1,200 cows were not taken from Fingal farms, they were bought. The city, despite its wealth, was not strong enough to resist unaided a relatively feeble Irish State. Militarily, therefore, it was at the mercy of almost any Irish king. The amount of the ransom demanded and paid caused a gasp of astonishment throughout the country, but it must be remembered that the king of south Brega, had he been accused of extortion, would have had his answer ready — Fingal was part of his ancestral lands, and if the Norse wished to be left in undisturbed possession of it, something unusual might be extracted from them by way of compensation.

Olaf as ruler had experienced a crushing defeat. Sitric, therefore, on his return from Rome, took command once more of the citizens and endeavoured to restore their fortunes. This he did in the old traditional manner. He joined the English in an attack on Wales in 1030,[65] and no doubt brought back to Dublin a considerable share of the plunder. In the following year, 1031, he endeavoured to avenge the defeat of 1029 on south Brega. With his army he proceeded to Ardbraccan where he put to death without mercy 200 people who had taken refuge in the church.[66] Olaf, his son, set out for Rome in 1034, but, unfortunate in peace as in war, he was murdered by the English on the way thither.[67]

Two years later Sitric himself left Dublin for good and retired overseas (1036).[68] It is possible that his departure was occasioned or caused by dynastic strife. At any rate, his place was taken by a Waterford Northman, Echmarcach, son of Ragnall.[69] His reign in Dublin was so undistinguished that it is practically ignored in the records,[70] and it ended in 1052, with his expulsion at the hands of Diarmait mac Máel na mBó, king of Leinster.[71] Echmarcach became king of the Norse in Man and Diarmait became king of the Norse in Dublin, a position which he retained to his death in 1072.[72] He ruled Dublin apparently through his son Murchad, who died in 1070.[73] Thus the independence of Dublin as a Norse State may be said to have ended in

1052. From that year onwards it was an appanage to one or other of the strong Irish kingdoms.

Not that local Norse rulers entirely disappeared. When Diarmait, king of Leinster and of Dublin, died in 1072, the government of the city was taken over by a Northman, Gofraid, son of Olaf, son of Ragnall. But we know from the Annals of Inisfallen that this Gofraid 'came into the house' of Toirrdelbach ua Briain, then king of Munster and the strongest king in Ireland. In other words, he took control of the city as an Ua Briain henchman. In the sequel he did not give satisfaction to Toirrdelbach ua Briain and was banished in 1075.[74] Then Domnall, son of Murchad, son of Diarmait mac Máel na mBó, whose family, as kings of Leinster, always regarded Áth Cliath as part of their kingdom, took possession of the city, but he died rather suddenly, after an illness of three days, within the year.[75] Gofraid, too, died while collecting a fleet strong enough to ensure his return.[76] Toirrdelbach then nominated his son Muirchertach Ua Briain to be king of Dublin.[77] When Toirrdelbach died in 1086 the Leinstermen renewed their claim to suzerainty over the city.[78] This was resisted by Muirchertach Ua Briain and a battle was fought at Howth which Muirchertach won.[79] He thus became Dublin's overlord, and used the Norse as auxiliaries to his army, in an expedition into Leinster and Brega in 1090.[80] Muirchertach's position in Ireland was not, however, as yet assured, and in 1091 a Gofraid Méránach, son of the son of Harald, proclaimed himself king of Dublin. Muirchertach drove him out in 1094[81] and Gofraid died in 1095.[82] In 1100 the fleet of Dublin was dispatched by Muirchertach to help in an expedition against the Cenél Conaill, but it was wrecked off Inishowen.[83] A Dublin battalion was in the army of Muirchertach which advanced to the north against Domnall Mac Lochlainn, in 1103.[84] In 1107 Muirchertach Ua Briain fettered an opposition Ua Briain prince at Dublin. Muirchertach's control over the city seems to have been complete until his health failed in 1114.

Then the old claim of the Leinstermen was renewed and Diarmait mac Enna, king of Leinster, died in Dublin in 1117.[85] Next year Toirrdelbach Ua Conchobair, king of Connacht, whose star was rising on the Irish political horizon, arrived in Dublin (1118).[86] The Norse of the city would form part of his army when he marched to Munster in 1121. For the next 50 years they seem to have retained an open mind in the matter of showing allegiance. They served at various times the O'Connors, the O'Briens, the Mac Murchadas, the Mac Lochlainns, trimming their sails diplomatically to the varying winds that blew.[87] Families of local rulers are occasionally mentioned, the Mac Torcaills,[88] who appear first in 1138, the Mac Ottars[89] from the Orkneys, who made a bid for predominance among the citizens in 1142, with a measure of success, for while Ragnall mac Torcaill was *mórmaor Átha Cliath* in 1146, a Mac Ottar had taken his place and was slain by the Mac Torcaills in 1148.

If we translate *mórmaor* by 'lord mayor' we get a fairly good idea of the role which these Norse leaders filled. When Ruaidrí Ua Conchobair became king of Ireland in 1166 he showed that he considered the allegiance of the Norse worth having by bestowing on them a *tuarastal* of 4,000 cows. Their local head at that time was Ragnall son of Ragnall mac Torcaill.[90] He attended the great assembly presided over by Ruaidrí Ua Conchobair at Athboy in 1167. In 1167 and again in 1169 when Ruaidrí marched against Diarmait Mac Murchada the Dublin Norse were represented in his army.[91] They defended their city against the Normans in 1170, but the attitude of their leader Ascuff (Ascall) son of Ragnall towards Ruaidrí Ua Conchobair and the Irish military chiefs was ambiguous.[92] Ascuff is severely censured by the Four Masters for alleged treachery,[93] and his death at Norman hands in 1171 is recorded without regret. Having passed into Norman hands, the city became the centre of English power in Ireland, and was to remain thus for a long 700 years.

How did the Norse of Dublin react to the Christian faith, whose institutions lay all around them in Ireland, numerous as the hills? Very unfavourably. *Genti* (pagans) is the name by which they were known to Irish chroniclers for nearly two centuries. The word had a nuance of meaning like Vandals or Huns. By all Irish writers the paganism of the Norse was taken as a matter of course to about 975.[94] On the other hand, social intercourse between the two peoples could hardly be avoided, and this led inevitably to marriages, even in the ninth century. I have mentioned the union between the daughter of Áed Findliath, king of Ireland (862-79), and Olaf, king of Dublin. A son of this Olaf married the granddaughter of Cerball of Ossory, and the pair were parents of Helgi, who caused interest later because of the cloudy character of his religious beliefs. An Icelandic source reports of him that 'he was very confused in matters of faith. He put his trust in Christ, and named his homestead after Him, but during stormy weather, in the stress and strain of battle, and generally when things were critical, his prayers were directed to Thor'.[95]

In all the countries where they lived or settled — Norway, Sweden, Denmark, France, England, Ireland — the Northmen proved very difficult to convert. The conversion of Norway may be ascribed to King Olaf, who died in 1030, that of Denmark to King Cnut, who died in 1035, that of the Orkneys to a date after the year 1000, the Norse in Normandy to some extent under their count, Richard, who died in 996.[96]

At Clontarf a few of the Northmen who fought in the battle were certainly Christians, as we learn from casual references.[97] It is likely that the Dublin Norse became Christian in the generation after the battle. They had at this time the example of the great Danish king of England, Cnut, to encourage them. In the Black Book of Christ Church it is stated that Sitric was king of Dublin when the cathedral was founded. He was expelled from the city in

1036 and died in 1042. In the same book the first bishop whose obit is recorded is named Dúnán. He died in 1074. There is reason to think that he was consecrated in Canterbury.[98] Certain it is that his successor, Patrick (Gilla Pátraic), who had been a monk, probably at Worcester, was consecrated in the English ecclesiastical capital. Lanfranc, then archbishop, was a true Norman knight in that he felt an irresistible urge to increase his principality. That for him meant an increase of ecclesiastical jurisdiction, so he induced Patrick to make a formal profession of obedience to the see of Canterbury.

Patrick was drowned, with many others, on his way to England in 1084. Toirrdelbach ua Briain and various Irish bishops assisted at the election of his successor. The choice fell on Donngus Ua hAingliu, a monk of Canterbury, who was duly consecrated by Lanfranc. When he died in 1095 his nephew, Samuel Ua hAingliu, a monk of St. Albans, was elected to succeed him by the Dublin clergy, with the approval of Muirchertach Ua Briain.[99] He was consecrated by St. Anselm at Winchester in 1096. When he died in 1121 he was succeeded — but only after a disputed election and many difficulties — by Gréne or Gregory, a young subdeacon, who was consecrated likewise in Canterbury and ruled the see for 40 years, from 1121 to his death in 1161. His successor was St. Lorcán Ua Tuathail.

To return to the disputed election of 1121. Its underlying cause was the great change in the organization of the Irish Church which had taken place in the early years of the 12th century. The O'Brien kings had raised no objection to the consecration of the early Dublin bishops abroad. Indeed, when the first bishop of Waterford had been appointed in 1096,[100] Muirchertach Ua Briain, his brother Diarmait, and various Irish bishops had joined the clergy of Waterford in requesting St. Anselm to be the consecrating prelate. At this time the situation in Ireland was peculiar, for there was but one metropolitan see, Armagh, in the country, and the chief ecclesiastic in Armagh was not a cleric at all but a lay abbot. This, I think, is the reason why the O'Brien kings turned to Canterbury. It was the nearest metropolitan see and its archbishops were personally men of high distinction. Since 1106, however, Armagh possessed an archbishop who in virtue of his position as successor of St. Patrick was canonical head of the Church in Ireland. In 1111 there had been held the synod of Ráith Bressail, which divided Ireland into 26 dioceses of the type common everywhere in the Church. When, then, the see of Dublin fell vacant in 1121 there was no longer need to have recourse to Canterbury. Within the city of Dublin one section of the clergy accepted the new situation; another section did not. The section that wanted to include Dublin in the new general arrangement of dioceses asked Cellach, archbishop of Armagh, to become apostolic administrator of the see. This he did. The other section, that which desired to continue the connexion with Canterbury, chose Gréne,[101] latinized Gregorius, as their candidate for episcopal orders. His name shows that he was a Northman by race. An objection to his consecration was lodged at Canterbury, but this was overruled. When Gréne returned as bishop, he found Cellach in possession, and being unable to prevail against him returned as guest to his consecrator, Archbishop Ralph of Canterbury. The circumstances under which Cellach returned to Armagh (probably before 1125) and Gréne returned to Dublin are not recorded.

The first church in Dublin was undoubtedly the cathedral of Christ Church. This was provided by Bishop Patrick with a chapter consisting of monks drawn from the abbey of Winchcombe and the priory of Worcester,[102] and was endowed richly with lands by Irish landholders round the city. Bishop Samuel Ua hAingliu did not get on too well with this monastic chapter, despite his own training as a monk of the Benedictine reform at St. Albans. Soon after his consecration in 1096 he founded a new parish and built a new parish church of St. Michan's, a secular church, served by secular priests. The dispute with the chapter became acute, and Bishop Samuel took the extreme step of expelling them from the cathedral. St. Anselm, as metropolitan, ordered him to receive them back, but this he steadfastly refused to do. St. Anselm forbade him also to have his cross carried before him when he journeyed through his diocese — a privilege reserved to archbishops — but Bishop Samuel could not be induced to change his ways. Thus the position of Dublin as a suffragan see of Canterbury was proving highly unsatisfactory to both archbishop and bishop. At the same time Samuel refused to have anything to do with the assembly at Ráith Bressail (1111). His policy was one of glorious isolation.

Christ Church was probably a parish church from the beginning. So was St. Michan's, across the river. In the course of the century and a half between the conversion of the Norse and the coming of the Normans many other parish churches had been built — St. Patrick's, St Brigit's, St. Colum Cille's, St. Mary's, St. Michael's (beside Christ Church), another St. Michael's (le Pole), with a round tower, outside the walls, St. John the Evangelist's, St. Paul's, St. Andrew's. All these continued to exist in medieval times; St. Colum Cille's, however, changed its name to St. Audoen's.

After the expulsion of the Benedictine chapter of Christ Church we know of no regular clergy in Dublin until the foundation of St. Mary's in 1139. This was a daughter-house of Buildwas in Shropshire, itself a daughter-house of Savigny. The Savigniac reform was not Cistercian, but the Savigniac group of houses was incorporated in the Cistercian Order in the years 1147-8. St. Mary's thus became a Cistercian abbey.[103]

Very little is known about the priory of All Saints. It was founded by Diarmait Mac Murchada in thanksgiving for recovery from sickness in *c.* 1162, when St. Lorcán Ua Tuathail was already archbishop. He made a vow, in the presence of many of the clergy, on the eve of 1 November, that if he survived he would erect a religious house in honour of all the saints. How the country would have fared if Diarmait had succumbed to that illness, who can tell? The foundation was for canons regular of St. Augustine, who followed the Arroasian Rule.

Somewhere near the Provost's House stood the Augustinian convent of St. Mary de Hogges (Old Norse *haugr*, 'height'). There was a tradition that the sister of St. Lorcán Ua Tuathail, whom Diarmait Mac Murchada had grossly ill-treated, found refuge in this house. It flourished through the Middle Ages, until its suppression by Henry VIII.

It is naturally difficult to get an idea of what the city and its surroundings looked like at this period. The famous landmarks are enumerated by Haliday.[104] Along the Liffey, to the east towards the Dodder mouth, was a long piece of land called the Steine (Staine). It took its name from a large stone, some 12 to 14 ft. in height, bearing no inscription, erected near the present headquarters of the Civic Guards in College Street. Its purpose, like the hoisting of the flag by modern explorers, was to mark the formal taking possession of the site by the Northmen. On the land called the Steine the priory of All Saints was built. On the Liffey near by was the spot where passengers by boat generally landed. The Steine remained to about 1700, when it was removed to make way for new streets.

Further east, in the region cut by the present Townsend Street, was a hillock called originally Lazars' Hill. The origin of the name is explained in a decree of Pope Innocent III to Archbishop Henry of London. In this decree it is related that lands at Delgany, Kilmacanoge, etc., were granted to maintain a lazar or hospital 'on the sea-shore outside Dublin called Steyn, where pilgrims to the shrine of St. James (at Compostela) awaited an opportunity to embark'. The name became corrupted to Lazy Hill, and later, by an indefensible freak of language — Lousy Hill.[105]

Ringsend was a narrow strip of land jutting forward between Merrion Strand and the Liffey estuary. The Dodder met the Liffey at Lansdowne Road, and a huge area now covered with streets and houses was slobland. Practically all the present railway line, from Westland Row to Bath Avenue, was under water. On the north side, too, Inns Quay, Ormond Quay, Bachelors Walk, were part of the Liffey bed. The straight channel between strong walls, known to us, was the achievement of the Ballast Board — a body that came into existence in 1708.

The eastern gate, or Dame's Gate (whence Dame Street), was not far from the present South Great George's Street. Between it and the Steine lay Hoggen Green. In this green, at the corner of Suffolk Street and Church Lane, was a small conical hill, about 240 ft. in circumference and some 40 ft. high, called the Thingmount. This was the place of assembly of the Norse citizens, corresponding on a small scale with Tara, Uisnech, Carman, Tlachtga among their Irish neighbours. Their system of government, like that of all Scandinavians, was most democratic. Every act of the Northmen, from the election of a king and the making of a law to the trial of a criminal, was governed by the wishes of the people assembled at a *thing*. There were court *things*, house *things* (hustings), district *things*, general *things* (Althing). There, too, public games were celebrated.[106] After the Norman invasion the Thingmount was protected. It was easier to climb than Nelson's Pillar, and citizens enjoyed the fresh air at its summit. It was removed in 1685, and the earth from it used to fill in a laneway called St. Patrick's Well Lane, which ran to the south of Trinity College. The ground here was raised from 8 to 10 ft. and the space between it and St. Stephen's Green also made more level. So the Thingmount in dissolution became the foundation of Nassau Street and the lwer parts of Grafton Street, Dawson Street and Kildare Street.

East of the Thingmount was a rocky hill, surrounded by a field of barren ground, called Hangr Hoeg, which we may translate Gallows Hill. There the gallows remained till about 1700, when the rocky hill was quarried away to provide stone for the growing city. An echo of the height remains in Mount Street.

The general culture of the Norse citizens of Dublin is a subject that requires fuller investigation. It seems to be an historical fact that they produced absolutely no literature. Not a single Dublin writer in prose or poetry is known between the settlement at Áth Cliath in the middle of the ninth century and the coming of the Normans. The same is true of the Northmen all over Ireland. A few runic inscriptions alone bear witness to any knowledge, even rudimentary, of letters. Patrick, the bishop of Dublin who was drowned on his way to England in 1084, has been recognized by Father Gwynn as the author of some Latin poems, but he, of course, belongs to the Irish and continental tradition of classical scholarship.[107]

After the Norman invasion the citizens of Dublin (and the Norse of other towns) sought fraternization, recognition and privileges, because of their distant kinship with the new settlers. At first they achieved some success, as they were taken under the special protection of the Crown. But they were soon swamped by a swarm of colonists, who had little or no Norman blood and no Norman tradition. Nor did they receive much help from the aristocratic leaders, who had won for themselves such princely territories, for these, even when of Norse descent, were so far removed from their northern origins and so latinized that they scorned to recognize any relationship with the old Norse townsfolk. The result was that the city soon became filled with immigrants, predominantly of English stock, who treated the Norse as aliens and drove them ultimately from their homes. They settled north of the river, forming a new quarter called Austmannabyr, Ostmanby, Oxmantown. By

1300 they had lost their identity as Eastmen or Northmen. In Fingal the descendants of the Mac Torcaill dynasty preserved small estates to about that date (Baile meic Torcaill, Ballymakarkill, Ballymacartle). In south Dublin the Harolds in Harold's Country, between Saggart and Dundrum, and the Archbolds in Bray and Little Bray, were more fortunate, for they survived into the later centuries.[108]

The inception of the Dodder water supply

VALENTINE JACKSON

It is now over sixty years since the late Henry Berry wrote the paper entitled 'The water supply of ancient Dublin'.[1] It is safe to say that the history of the origin and early days of the Dodder works, given in this paper, was the first ever published. The material for this history was mainly supplied from the then recently issued first volume of the *Calendar of Ancient Records of Dublin*, edited by Sir J.T. Gilbert. It will be remembered that the cardinal feature of this water supply was the use of water diverted from the River Dodder to augment the flow of the Poddle river at Kimmage.

In the absence of any definite evidence on the matter Berry concluded that these works were initiated by the mandate of 29 April 1244[2] addressed to the sheriff of Dublin by the justiciar and that the diversion of the Dodder was carried out by, and at the cost of, the citizens of Dublin. This assumption of Berry was based on the wording of the mandate.[3] It was supported by the fact that the citizens were in a position to grant a supply of water to Dublin Castle from the conduit of the new works some nineteen months after the issue of the mandate. Berry's opinion on these points has been accepted ever since. However, the present writer has come to the conclusion that on the available evidence Berry's view on this point must be rejected.

Besides the mandate of 1244 there appears to be only one other 13th-century document from which any inference can be drawn as to the origin of the works. This is a Latin manuscript known as the 'Inquisition of 1259'.[4] It was found by Berry in 1902 among the papers relating to the abbey of St. Thomas in the earl of Meath's library at Kilruddery, Bray. It is a report of an inquiry 'concerning transgressions made against the abbot and convent of St. Thomas the Martyr by the mayor and citizens of Dublin'. The inquiry was obviously deemed to be a matter of the first importance. It was held under writ of the king, Henry III, and his son the Lord Edward. The hearing occupied the three weeks following Easter Sunday, 13 April 1259. It was presided over by the justiciar. The inquisitors or jurors numbered 27, apparently drawn from various parts of Co. Dublin. The transgressions complained of concerned different matters, chief of which was the water supply. Berry

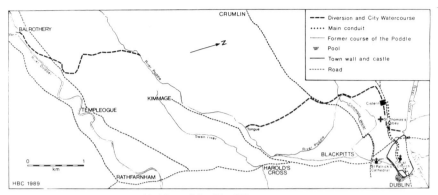

11 Map of the City Watercourse.

with the consent of the earl of Meath read a short paper containing the text of the inquisition at the meeting of the Royal Irish Academy.[5]

The main purpose of the present paper is to subject the wording of this inquisition and the mandate of 1244, conjointly, to a close scrutiny in order to determine to what extent they may be relied upon to support or disprove the assumptions by Berry as to the origin of the works. It will assist the reader if at this point we trace very briefly the layout of this somewhat intricate water supply system (Fig. 11). References to certain sections of it will occur herein from time to time. A short note also on the abbey of St. Thomas the Martyr will not be out of place.

The Dodder-Poddle watercourse

The water supply began by the erection of a weir across the River Dodder at Balrothery, near Firhouse, Co. Dublin. At this point the river runs approximately from west to east. From the upstream side of the dam an open aqueduct was constructed to connect the Dodder with the River Poddle where it flowed through the townland of Kimmage a little over 1 mile to the north-east. The purpose of this aqueduct was to transfer a large proportion of the water in the Dodder to the much smaller Poddle. From Kimmage the combined rivers flowed in the natural bed of the Poddle towards the city passing by Kimmage Road and Harold's Cross.

A little to the city side of the present Sundrive Road and at a point subsequently known as the Tongue Field a branch was taken from the river. This was carried in a north-westerly direction by Rutland Avenue, Dolphin's Barn and the western side of St. James's Walk. Near the present Grand Canal Harbour the channel turned east and passing to the south of James's Street and Thomas Street entered the old city. This channel was called the City Watercourse and through it the city received the Dodder water. From the

Tongue Field the main river continued to Harold's Cross. Near the entrance
to Mount Jerome it divided into two streams. The right-hand, or eastern,
stream continued due north to Blackpitts and New Row leaving Clanbrassil
Street a little to the east. The left-hand stream ran north-west passing near
the present military barracks along Donore Avenue and, after a wide circuit
of the Liberties rejoined the right branch at New Row. From this point the
course of the re-united rivers was east to Patrick Street, through the length
of that street, again east across Bride Street, Little Ship Street, past the
southern and eastern sides of the castle and thence north by Palace Street to
the Liffey at Wellington Quay. In passing through Patrick Street the river ran
in two channels, one on either side of the street. Such, roughly, was the outline
of the Dodder-cum-Poddle water system when completed about the middle
of the 13th century and as it remained with little alteration for over five
centuries.

The abbey of St. Thomas the Martyr was founded by Henry II in 1177 and
placed in the care of Augustinian canons of St. Victor. The canons were given
a grant of the lands of Donore. Some twenty years later Henry's son, John,
made two further grants to the abbey. By these grants the abbey territory was
raised to the status of an independent self-governing barony or manor exempt
from the jurisdiction of the city and, in temporal matters, subject only to the
king. The monastery building, of which no trace remains, occupied the site
between the present Hanbury Lane and South Earl Street. The abbey remained thus until the suppression of the monastery by Henry VIII in 1538
when it was bestowed together with its privileges on Sir William Brabazon
and his heirs (later the earls of Meath). Under the lay control of the Brabazon
line the barony continued as an independent unit for just 300 years before
incorporation in the City of Dublin.

The area of the barony, some 436 statute acres in all, extended from Mount
Jerome in the south, leaving Dolphin's Barn to the west, almost to Thomas
Street and to James's Street in the north and to St. James's Walk in the west.
The stream running north from Mount Jerome to Blackpitts formed the
eastern boundary and separated it from the archbishop's liberty of St.
Sepulchre. From St. James's Walk the area narrowed rapidly ending in a
point at Mount Jerome. The freedom of this district from the control of the
Corporation earned for it in later days the name of the Liberties.

The mandate of 1244 and the inquisition of 1259

The way is now clear for consideration of the two 13th-century documents.
Firstly here is the relevant portion of the mandate of 1244 as translated by
Gilbert:

Maurice FitzGerald, justiciar of Ireland, commands the sheriff of Dublin, without delay, by 12 free and lawful men of his county, to make inquisition, with advice of the mayor and citizens, as to whence water can be best and most conveniently taken from its course and conducted to the king's city of Dublin, for the benefit of the city, and at the cost of the citizens, who have undertaken to pay the amount. By the same 12 men the sheriff is to enquire whether any damage can arise by thus taking and bringing the water. The sheriff, under his seal and the seals of the jurors, is to return the inquisition to the justiciar, so that the damage, if any, may be repaired at the cost of the king . . .[6]

So far the mandate. Here now is a translation of the inquisition of 1259 in so far as it relates to the water supply:

[The jurors] who being sworn say on their oath that it was formerly agreed between the abbot of St. Thomas the Martyr near Dublin and the mayor and commonalty of the same city by mandate of the Lord Maurice FitzGerald that they [the citizens] should take from the running water of the Dodder belonging to the priory as much as would run through the middle of the *mola* [meaning uncertain] of a certain cartwheel and not any more except with the consent of the convent; this in return for a fine of 5 marks of which they had paid 3, and also a yearly rent of 1 mark, which rent the convent has never received. They say also that the aforesaid citizens are bound to make a stone wall on the River Dodder at their own expense around the head [i.e. dam or weir] of the water which has been drawn off; this they have not yet done. And further the said abbot was bound to maintain the said wall in return for the aforesaid mark of annual rent, and for this agreement all contentions between the said abbot and the citizens ought to be allayed and reconciled. And they say that the citizens have already drawn off twice or more than twice as much water as they were entitled to and this to injury of the mills belonging to the said abbot and convent and to the mills belonging to the lord king; and the estimated damage at the rate of multure [miller's fee] of one mill a day each week is 12 pounds in the case of the said abbot and convent and 6 marks in the case of the lord king; and they say that the mayor and the aforesaid citizens sold the aforesaid water to the prior and convent of the Holy Trinity, Dublin, and to the houses of St. John, St. Saviour and St. Francis, but the jurors do not know the amount in money of the sale nor the compensation for the loss thence ensuing.

We now return to the mandate of 1244 in order to study its wording. The first point to note is that the 12 jurors in selecting a source of water supply were not restricted except in so far as they were required to act with the advice of the mayor and citizens. It was proper that the initial step should provide for the consideration of all the available sources. These included the Rivers Camac and Liffey as well as the Dodder. Therefore it is surprising to read in the next breath that the citizens had agreed beforehand to pay the cost of bringing the water to the city. It is evident that this mandate was not quite the initial step, as has been supposed. It is strange that this undertaking should have been given before even the source of the water supply was decided upon. Concerning this undertaking to bear the cost, there arises the question as to how it came about that the city received only one-third of the water taken from the Dodder. Furthermore why was the remaining two-thirds reserved for the use of the barony of St. Thomas, a district outside the control of the citizens? The quantity allowed to the city may have been sufficient for its needs but this is beside the point. These are pertinent questions and must have caused misgivings in others before now. If the views of Berry as to the origin of the works are correct then some arrangements must have been made subsequently with the abbey for this division of the water.

It is now time to consider how the mandate can be reconciled with the agreement made between the citizens and the abbey recited in the inquisition of 1259. By this agreement the citizens were given a supply of Dodder water by the abbey. It should be said here that the River Dodder or any section of it was at no time the property of the abbey. Moreover no portion of the abbey lands was less than 2 miles distant from the river. No date is given for this agreement but it is stated that it was made 'by mandate of the Lord Maurice FitzGerald'. FitzGerald had authority to issue such a mandate only while he held office as justiciar, that is from about 2 September 1232 to October 1245. It will be seen therefore that the agreement had been completed before the water reached the city about the end of 1245. A study of the text of the inquisition makes it unmistakably clear that this agreement with the abbey was the instrument under which the city was being supplied with Dodder water in 1259 and under which it had been supplied from the time the water was first introduced. The key to this problem, if such there be, is the claim that the Dodder water belonged to the abbey. The wording is clear and unequivocal and must be accepted. If, as has been assumed, the city authorities diverted the water at Balrothery then they must have handed the water over to the abbey. This might have been a very generous act but surely one of painful self-sacrifice in view of the urgent need of the city for an improved water supply. Any such idea as this must be dismissed as absurd. There is every probability that the abbey carried out the work at the Dodder but unfortunately no definite proof of this is available.

When the citizens had completed the agreement with the abbey it was essential that they should obtain sanction from a higher authority for the construction of the watercourse to the city. This sanction was conveyed by the mandate of 1244. This order stated that the citizens had already undertaken to pay the cost of the work in reference, no doubt, to the agreement with the abbey. The citizens were required to take their supply from 'the running water of the Dodder belonging to the priory' — a very curious phrase. It appears to be an astute method of defining the section of the River Poddle running from Kimmage to the abbey boundary near Mount Jerome. This portion of the river was outside the abbey lands but the canons could claim that the Dodder water then running through was their property. It could be urged that the portion of the Poddle within the abbey boundary also contained Dodder water, but if this were meant it would be described as the 'watercourse the property of the abbey' and there would be no necessity to use the more elaborate phrase. It will be seen that the 12 jurors appointed by the mandate had after all a very simple task. For a choice of source they were limited to the section of the Poddle lying south of the abbey boundary. As we know they selected the place later known as the Tongue Field a short distance north of the present Sundrive Road. This was chosen because it was the nearest point with an elevation sufficient to enable the water to flow easily to the highest area of the then small city. We already know that this City Watercourse was laid by Dolphin's Barn, the western side of St. James's Walk and by the southern side of James's Street and Thomas Street to the city. From St. James's Walk almost to the city the course was constructed not more than a few yards *outside* the boundary of the abbey. This was the shortest available route from the Tongue to the city; it could only have been shortened by encroaching on the abbey territory and this the abbey would not permit.

The citizens must have known for a considerable time that the new water supply was in the offing. The diversion of the Dodder could not have taken place without their knowledge and, when the agreement was made with the abbey, they knew the section of the Poddle whence the water must be taken and that the matter was settled to all intents and purposes. Hence the assumption implicit in the wording of the mandate that the source of the water was entirely unknown and had still to be explored was not intended to deceive. Nevertheless this piece of judicial pretence, coupled as it was with the call for 12 jurors, did materially help to mislead Berry and those who followed in his wake, not excluding the present writer. This concludes our examination of the mandate of 1244. There are still points in the inquisition which must receive attention.

The apparatus through which the water was delivered to the citizens was, we may presume, placed at the junction of the City Watercourse with the River Poddle (at the Tongue Field). From the meagre description given in the agreement it is not possible to say how the contraption operated. It may have been a primitive form of circular orifice meter. Measuring instruments designed on this principle are not unknown in modern waterworks practice. We are told that the citizens were drawing double or more than double the quantity of water to which they were entitled. It is a pity that this statement was not further expanded. One would like to know what was the exact quantity permitted to the citizens over a given period and how the excess quantity was measured. Further one would like to know how this excess water was drawn off. Did the apparatus not work according to specification, or had it been tampered with by the citizens, or had it been by-passed? In any event the tribunal placed the responsibility on the citizens and severe damages were awarded to the mill-owners for the loss sustained by the undue withdrawal of water by the city.

Under the agreement the citizens were required to pay a fine of 5 marks. This was a substantial sum of money in those days — it is very difficult to say even approximately what this sum represents in terms of present day values, certainly not less than £300. We must assume that the amount was agreed upon as the city's contribution towards the capital cost of the Dodder diversion. Here we have further support for the view that the abbey was responsible for these works. A further pointer in the same direction is the condition that the citizens should pay an annual rent of 1 mark and that they should build a weir on the River Dodder at Balrothery. The annual payment of 1 mark to the abbey was for the maintenance of this weir when constructed. It is strange that the citizens were required to build the weir while the abbey undertook to maintain it. The most plausible explanation is that the water drawn off by the citizens would seriously reduce the quantity available to the mill-owners lower down the river. By erecting a weir on the Dodder the amount of water diverted would be increased, thus restoring the loss to the millers. Therefore it was considered equitable that the citizens should bear the cost of the weir. The decision of the abbey to undertake the maintenance is significant. It could only mean that the other works at the Dodder, including the aqueduct, were at the same time in control of the abbey.

The jurors took exception to the grant by the citizens of piped water supplies to four religious houses. Apparently they considered that these supplies were partly responsible for the high consumption of water. However, they made no ruling on the matter as they did not know at what rate the water was sold. In raising this question the jurors were not on very firm ground. They were unable to accuse the citizens of any breach of contract or breach of faith in granting these four connexions or selling the water supplied thereby. It is possible that these supplies may have increased the amount of water drawn from the Poddle at the Tongue, but it must be remembered that the jurors had already penalized the citizens in respect of excess consumption. The jurors evidently lacked the authority to demand evidence from the parties concerned as to the charges made for the water. We now know that the supply to St. Saviour's was given as free alms in perpetuity[7] and that no mention of any conditions appears in the grant to Holy Trinity.[8] We have no record of grants to the other two houses. These piped supplies were granted several years after the water first came to the city. They were probably an afterthought and not envisaged in the original scheme. The general method of distribution at that time was by means of conduits erected at prominent points in the streets, from which the citizens fetched the water as in the case of the modern village pump. The grant of a piped supply to Dublin Castle made at the end of 1245 was exceptional as the castle was a fortified enclosure. Centuries elapsed before the provision of separate service pipes to individual tenements came into general practice.

It must be admitted that the mayor and citizens of Dublin came very badly out of this inquiry. The court found that they had been drawing at least double the amount of water to which they were entitled; that during the 15 years since the agreement was signed they had paid only 3 marks of the fine of 5 marks agreed upon and that they had not built the weir across the River Dodder at the head water. In other words they had failed to comply with all the terms of the agreement. It must be said that the abbey authorities showed great forbearance in tolerating this gross breach of contract over such a lengthy period. We are left in the dark as to the procedure adopted at the inquisition, but we have taken it for granted that the citizens were afforded the right of filing an answer to the charges of the abbey, and of being represented at the hearing.

We have now concluded the examination of the mandate and the inquisition. There is little need to sum up the result. There can remain no doubt that the Dodder works at Balrothery were the property of the abbey of St. Thomas for a considerable period before the Dodder water supply was laid on to the city and that these works continued to be the property of the abbey until at least 1259. It is also clear that the mandate of 1244 did not initiate these works but referred solely to the City Watercourse. Consequently the view so long accepted as to their origin can no longer be sustained. We have seen that the wording of the mandate is ambiguous and highly uninformative. On the other hand the inquisition of 1259 gives us a detailed and cogent record of transactions and events touching the water supply covering a period of 15 years. For some reason or other, since this document was first discovered by Berry in 1902 it has been neglected; even Berry himself does not appear to have realized its significance. It is high time it was given its proper place in the annals of the period.

The new boundary stream

We have seen that the abbey authorities were in control of the Dodder works for some fifteen years. It is most probable that they were responsible for the actual diversion of the Dodder, but of this there is no direct evidence. It may reasonably be asked why the abbey should have undertaken a work of such magnitude and at a point outside its area of jurisdiction. Fortunately this question can be answered satisfactorily. Some twenty-four years ago the Very Rev. Myles V. Ronan wrote an interesting paper entitled 'The Poddle river and its branches'.[9] At the time this paper was published it was the general belief that the branch of the Poddle flowing through the Liberties was the natural route of that river. Among others, Berry when he wrote his paper in 1892 had no doubts on the matter. Father Ronan proved conclusively that the stream running through the Liberties was an artificial one constructed by the abbey of St. Thomas in the first half of the 13th century and that the natural or ancient course of the Poddle was the stream running due north from Mount Jerome to Blackpitts and New Row, which had for long been cut off. The water which formerly ran through this course had been diverted to the branch running through the Liberties.

It will be remembered that this ancient course had marked the eastern boundary of the abbey territory and separated it from the archbishop's liberty of St. Sepulchre. In constructing the additional watercourse the abbey had several objects in view. Firstly it was required to act as a boundary stream to demark the western and northern limits of the barony in the same manner as the ancient course marked the eastern boundary. But with a difference. While the eastern stream ran on the actual boundary the new stream was carried some yards inside the boundary, being thus wholly inside the abbey lands and not subject to joint user. At that early period a boundary stream was considered the best insurance against encroachment. Secondly the stream was required to operate mills. We know that at a later date there were four mills on the stream. In addition the stream afforded a convenient water supply to any portion of the barony.

When the abbey authorities decided on this work they were faced with certain difficulties, of which they must have been well aware. This new boundary stream, as already stated, was branched from the River Poddle near the southern extremity of the abbey lands, near what is now the gate entrance to Mount Jerome. The catchment basin of the Poddle river is less than 5 square miles in extent. Consequently the dry weather flow at Mount Jerome from this lowland area would be very small and at the end of a dry summer might shrink to a mere trickle. The river therefore could not be divided into two streams of any useful size. Again there was the question of riparian rights on the ancient course. The abbey might be able to curtail the water supply to its own tenants on the left bank of the stream, but could not with impunity impair the supply to the archbishop's tenants on the right bank. The abbey in consequence must have realized that, if the new boundary stream was to materialize, an additional supply of water must be secured. We can only conjecture that it was decided to increase the flow in the River Poddle with water diverted from the River Dodder. To carry out this diversion it would have been necessary to obtain the sanction of the king or his deputy, the justiciar. This would not be difficult to obtain in those early days of conquest and expropriation, more especially if requested by a body which stood so high in royal favour as the abbey of St. Thomas. It is probable that the warrant authorizing the work may have contained a stipulation regarding the future supply to the city. It is also likely that the warrant gave the abbey some measure of control over the section of the Poddle between Kimmage Manor and Mount Jerome. This is mere speculation, but we know that the abbey at a later stage could afford to give a supply of Dodder water to the citizens from this section of the River Poddle. It was the intention, presumably, that the Dodder water should be available by the time the boundary stream was completed.

The first section of the boundary stream to be constructed was that running from the River Poddle at Mount Jerome to the island of Donore. This so-called island was a small portion of the barony near the site of the present church of St. Thérèse, Donore Avenue. This section of the course was put in hand by the abbey *c.* 1230, some twelve years or more before the course was finally completed. It is probable that the first section was primarily made to serve some water requirements at the island. Surplus water delivered at the island could have been discharged through a channel, later known as the Tenter Water which ran from the island to Warrenmount and thence connected with the ancient course at New Row.

Later Maurice FitzGerald, the justiciar, made an agreement with the abbey for a supply of water for the citizens living on the ancient course, which had been deflected by the abbey. The date of this agreement is unknown, but it is obvious that it was made subsequent to September 1232 when FitzGerald assumed office as justiciar. It is probable that the water in the ancient stream was seriously reduced but not completely cut off. Such action would be very high-handed on the part of the abbey.

There is good reason for believing that the boundary course was completed and that the Dodder water had reached the barony of St. Thomas not later than the end of 1243. The paper entitled 'The Poddle river and its branches' already mentioned tells us that the abbey had some mills situated on the ancient course, probably in the neighbourhood of Blackpitts or New Row. By a grant of Archbishop Cumin (*c.* 1210) the canons of St. Patrick's were entitled to tithes from any mills on that stream. In the economy returns of the cathedral there is no mention of revenues from the abbey mills after 1243. From this Father Ronan deduced that the mills had been moved not later than 1243 to the new boundary stream constructed by the abbey. On the new site the mills would not be subject to the payment of tithes to St. Patrick's. Here we may further deduce that the abbey would not have removed these mills until an adequate supply of water was available for their operation and therefore that the Dodder water was already running in the boundary stream. We may take it that when the Dodder water reached the Poddle, or shortly before, the representatives of the abbey and of the city came together to prepare the agreement for the water supply to the city. When this was completed the way was clear for the issue of the mandate to the sheriff of Dublin which, as we know, was issued on 29 April 1244. Some may be inclined to think that the Dodder diversion and the boundary stream were unusual and costly undertakings for a religious community. But the abbey was a well-endowed, wealthy and powerful organization and the abbot, in addition to his titular duties, was responsible for the civil administration of the barony. It is clear that the driving force behind this water supply enterprise was the keen desire of the abbey to preserve its liberties and increase its independence.

Control and maintenance

Before concluding this paper there is another matter to which some attention must be given. We have seen that the abbey was unquestionably in control of the Dodder works at the time the supply was given to the city, and continued so until at least 1259. On the other hand we know from the records of the city assembly roll that by the second half of the 15th century these works had passed to the control of the citizens, where they have remained to the present day. When and why this radical change of control came about is not known. Unfortunately the routine records of the city assembly are not available prior to 1447. It is possible that these might throw some light upon the matter, but in the absence of any information we can only hazard a conjecture. Probably the first step that may have led to the change was the building by the citizens of a weir across the River Dodder at Balrothery, as they were required to do under the agreement with the abbey. The purpose of such a weir was to raise the level of the water on the upstream side, to such a height as would ensure that the required quantity of water would be available for diversion before any water would pass over the cill of the weir and down the river towards Rathfarnham. It is very unlikely that the present substantial and somewhat venerable structure at Balrothery was the one built by the citizens in the 13th century. More probably it is of much later date and may be the last of several weirs which occupied the site at various times down the centuries. We may take it that the early Norman settlers were not fully alive to the havoc that could be wrought by the Dodder in flood. This weir built by the citizens presumably replaced some sort of temporary barrage erected by the abbey and was much higher. Accordingly the quantity of water diverted was considerably increased, to the benefit of both the citizens and the abbey. It would in consequence be necessary to enlarge and strengthen the aqueduct. It might also be necessary to improve the carrying capacity of the River Poddle at some points. These auxiliary works would no doubt have been carried out by the citizens. The building of the weir may have commenced shortly after the inquisition of 1259.

Another matter which must have called for early adjustment was the method of controlling the city water supply. The apparatus prescribed by the agreement with the abbey proved to be very inefficient. The inquisition found that the city was able to draw off more than double the allotted quantity of water. The original apparatus was replaced by a device which became known as the Tongue. The main feature of this was a wedge-shaped pier of stone or masonry erected in the Poddle at the junction with the City Watercourse. This pier partitioned the water in the Poddle into two portions, the smaller passing to the City Watercourse while the remainder flowed down the river to Harold's Cross. The Tongue was a simple arrangement, had no working parts and operated automatically. We have no knowledge of how the water was apportioned in the early centuries, but we do know that in the 18th and 19th centuries the city received one-third of the total quantity of the water in the river, such portion being equivalent to six or seven hundred thousand gallons a day. It is possible that the water was divided in this proportion from the commencement, but the quantity of water was in the earlier days very much less. It may be assumed that the water abstracted from the Dodder was increased from time to time to meet the needs of the growing population, until the maximum quantity was reached in the 18th century. With the installation of the Tongue and the more rigid control of the city water supply there was no further need for the abbey to worry over the methods by which the supply was distributed in the city.

During the progress of the years it is more than likely that the maintenance costs of the watercourse from the Dodder to the Tongue gradually increased. These rising costs might be due to a variety of causes. One of these doubtless would be damage by flood. The River Dodder is liable from time to time to become very unruly. For instance the flood in the autumn of 1931 occasioned damage the repair of which cost the citizens £31,000, although the works at Balrothery escaped damage. It can easily be realized that in the early years of the works, before experience had matured, there was much repairing or rebuilding of the weir. Again the maintenance of the watercourse from the Dodder to the Tongue may have been much more expensive than originally anticipated. There was the danger of deflection of the water by adjoining landowners for irrigation and other purposes. Two such illegal withdrawals remained undetected or were tolerated for so long that they were ultimately legalized and are still in existence.

Another matter which called for attention was the trampling down of the embankment and pollution of the water by cattle, especially in dry weather. The citizens of Dublin were vitally interested in the course of the water from the Dodder to the Tongue, which was under the control of the abbey, and they were naturally anxious that nothing should be left undone to ensure its efficient service. The system of dual control might not have been operating satisfactorily and there might have been demands for a unified control. On the other hand the abbey might not have been unwilling to pass on to the citizens this growing burden, provided always that the rights of the barony in the water supply were recognized and secured. At any rate the citizens were better equipped for this work. We must now leave this speculation and move on to more tangible matters.

In 1491 the city assembly made an order concerning the maintenance of the upper portion of the watercourse.[10] In this order we get the first intimation that the section of the course between the Tongue and the Dodder was definitely in the control of the citizens, and also the inference that it had been so for a very lengthy period. The order was in effect that John Walshe, yeoman, should have custody from that date of the conduit of the water from the head at the Dodder to the Tongue, except when the head was broken by great floods. In such circumstances the mayor and bailiffs of the city should gather a sufficient 'fellowship' of the city and, with all monasteries that had mills on the watercourse, build up the head again at their own cost. Further the keeper should be paid for the duties appertaining to his office as he had been paid in olden times. Further any abbot or other person operating mills upon the water who failed to assist in repairing the head or who neglected to pay the keeper for his duties should have his mill horses impounded by the city until the dues were paid and the head repaired. These regulations might convey the idea that flood damage to the weir was not an unusually rare occurrence.

Despite its resolute character this order by the city assembly did not have an enduring effect on the maintenance problem, for a dispute between the citizens and the abbey of St. Thomas which had been brewing for some years came to a head in 1527. It was finally decided to submit the matter to the arbitration of four prominent men whose appointment had the approval of both parties. The dispute covered a variety of subjects, including the 'ordering of the water that comes from the Dodder' and the custom of levying corn from the mills of the abbey by the keepers of the water. We conclude this inquiry with the award of the arbitrators on the question of the water supply. By the terms of this award the right of the citizens of Dublin to control the head works and the course from there to the Tongue was finally confirmed. Provision was also made that a yearly contribution should be paid by the abbey towards the cost of maintenance. Hereunder we set out the terms of the award which speaks for itself:

> Also we award and juge that the Mayr, Ballivves and Comenys of the sayd cittie of Dublin, and ther successores for ever, shall havv the jurisdiction and ordyrryng of the watyr that comys fro Doddyr unto the forsayd cittie, in as ample and as large maner as they shall devise or havv had in tyme past; the forsayd Abbot of Seynt Thomas Court, and his Covent, and ther successores for ever, aydyng and assistyng the sayd Mayr, Balliffes, and Comenys, and ther successores, all tymes convenyent in as ample and as large maner as the forsayd Abbot of Seynt Mary Abbay and Priour of Cristis Church, and ther successores, shall ayde and assist them to bryng the sayd watyr in his ryght course, as hit hath gon of old tyme, as well unto the sayd Abbot and Covent of Seynt Thomas Court ys myllis as to the cittie; the sayd Abbot and Covent, and ther successores for ever, payng yerly out of all ther myllis, without anny contradiction, unto the keper of the watyr of the cittie for the tyme beyng eyght bussellis of corn, that ys to say, four peckes of whet and four peckes of malte, of such as groys and commys of the profites of the sayd myllys.[11]

Dublin's north-eastern city wall: early reclamation and development at the Poddle-Liffey confluence

NUALA BURKE

The extent of reclaimed land in the Liffey estuary is one of the striking characteristics of the site of Dublin City today. Reclamation undertaken in the 17th and 18th centuries completely changed the configuration of the estuary and development on the reclaimed land gradually linked the two sections of the city, north and south of the Liffey, into one unit. The small area in which reclamation was undertaken in the first decade of the 17th century lay between the north-eastern section of the city wall and the right bank of the Poddle (Fig. 12). The course of the Poddle from its source to Dame Street has been traced by Ronan[1] but not the site and topography of its confluence with the Liffey. Almost all trace of the early topography of this area has long disappeared and the site has been completely transformed by development which has left little surface evidence of former features. Before tracing the reclamation and subsequent development it is therefore necessary to establish the precise location of the north-eastern section of the city wall and its towers together with the other main topographical features of the area. All of these were used as landmarks in describing the boundaries of various holdings which were leased by the city council at the beginning of the 17th century.

Topography of the Poddle-Liffey confluence c. 1600

The documentary evidence on which this reconstruction is based is discussed below. From Dame's Gate a wall 5 ft. thick ran north and west to Isolde's Tower: this wall, 10 ft. high on the inside, varied in height outside from 17 ft. near Dame's Gate to 22 ft. near Isolde's Tower, a difference caused by the sloping strand of the shoreline. West of Isolde's Tower an open quay 9 ft. above the channel at low water veered west-north-west to Fyan's Castle, a square tower of four storeys which stood at the western end of the Blind Quay. Between Fyan's Castle and Dame's Gate there were four towers:

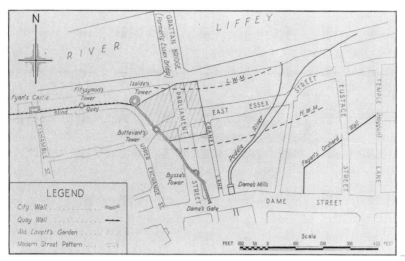

12 Plan of the north-eastern city wall and associated features superimposed on the modern street pattern. The medieval fortifications are drawn to scale.

Case's Tower, a small round tower on the quay 144 ft. east of Fyan's Castle; Isolde's Tower, a round two-storeyed tower at the eastern extremity of the quay, 174 ft. east of Case's Tower; Buttevant Tower, an old square ruinous tower 106 ft. south-east of Isolde's Tower; and Bise's Tower, a semicircular, three-storeyed structure 188 ft. south-east of Buttevant Tower. Dame's Gate was 108 ft. roughly south-east of Bise's Tower. From Dame's Gate a wall extended some 75 ft. east along Dame Street to the Dame's Mills, two watermills on the Poddle; these and a messuage covered with straw were the only recorded buildings on the site outside the city wall. East of the mills the wall of Fagan's orchard veered north-eastwards from Dame Street towards Hog Lane: this wall and lane formed the south-eastern and eastern boundaries of the property.

Ground which was always free from inundation stretched northwards for about 100 ft. from Dame Street. High-water mark lay between Bise's and Buttevant Towers; low-water mark was about 12 ft. north of Isolde's Tower. A fosse outside the city wall was capable of holding a depth of at least 6 ft. of water; its width is not recorded. There was a tendency towards deposition on the shore outside the curved quay wall, which did not benefit from the continual scouring of the channel. The waters of the Poddle issued north of the Dame's Mills in a tail-race which appears to have been uncontrolled prior to the enclosure of the area and which veered north-eastwards as a result of deposition on the left bank near the confluence with the Liffey. Upstream from the confluence there was a small island and near Fyan's Castle there was a ford.

The location of the north-eastern section of the city wall has previously been suggested by sites on the Ordnance Survey maps of Dublin City (1848), namely Fyan's, Case's, Newman's and Izod's (Isolde's) Towers and Dame's Gate.[2] The wall itself has been mapped by John S. Sloane (1882), by Leonard R. Strangways (1906), and by Breandán Ó Ríordáin (1970).[3] Sloane's map illustrates the city walls 'as they probably were about the close of the 17th century';[4] their north-eastern section is shown to be straight and angular, running due east to a tower described as 'Newman's or Buttevant's' and thence due south to Dame's Gate. Strangways illustrates both the site of an angular wall running due east from Fyan's Castle to 'Buttevant's or Newman's Tower' and thence south-westwards to 'Isolde's Tower (Essex Gate)' and that of a 'probable old wall' curving from the northern wall to the eastern, inside the right-angled sector near 'Newman's Tower'. Strangways evidently recognized the significance of the curved street-line of the Blind Quay and considered that the angular section was constructed at a more recent date than the 'probable' inner curved wall, but he does not cite any evidence to support this hypothesis.[5] Ó Ríordáin does not suggest an angular city wall. The sites of the wall and towers indicated by him are closer to those identified by the writer than sites marked by earlier compilers but there are some significant differences. The wall appears to be aligned with the existing quays rather than with the Blind Quay of earlier times (now Lower Exchange Street); the towers are not named; that which corresponds to the Buttevant in the present reconstruction is sited north of the location identified by the writer and the correlation between this tower and the existing streets is not indicated. Ó Ríordáin does not cite the evidence on which his map is based; to the writer it seems to have been based principally on the survey of 1585 which is cited below.

Analysis of municipal records illustrates quite clearly that ground inside the angle postulated by these compilers was actually reclaimed during the 17th and 18th centuries. Therefore, at the end of the 16th century the walls must have been further south.

Discussion of evidence

The city walls were surveyed in 1585 by order of the lord deputy, Sir John Perrot.[6] In the absence of evidence to the contrary, it may be assumed that the city walls were not extended nor were new fortifications constructed during the ensuing two decades;[7] hence, although portions of the walls and some of the towers decayed during that period,[8] this description of 1585 may be taken to indicate the nature and extent of the city wall which formed the south-western boundary of the land which, in the first decade of the 17th century, was leased by the city to private individuals for reclamation. Towers and castles were used as landmarks in delimiting the holdings: the distance from one to the next was measured and a brief description given of each of the buildings and of the intervening sections of the city wall. Measurements and descriptions given in this survey have been used in the present reconstruction of early 17th-century topography. The names of some of the towers remained unchanged for centuries; others changed periodically through the adoption of names of important occupants or lessees; the names used in the present reconstruction are those of the survey of 1585. Since there is no map with this survey it is necessary to correlate this description with such later maps as indicate the site of the wall and towers. Other documentary evidence of later date than this survey also indicates the location of the towers and castles. When evidence from these later sources appears to be contradictory the descriptions given of the buildings in 1585 help to identify the sites. The accuracy of at least part of the survey is attested by an extant lease of a tower and part of the city wall which was granted by the city council to Robert Molesworth in 1704;[9] measurements given both in the text of this lease and on the attached dimensioned lease-map correspond to those given in 1585. According to the lease the tower measured 24 ft. north-south adjoining the city wall: according to the survey of 1585 Bise's semicircular tower was 16 ft. square within the walls and the walls were 4 ft. thick, making a total outer width of 24 ft. The city wall between this tower and Dame's Gate was, according to the lease, $111\frac{1}{2}$ ft. in length and 5 ft. thick; the city wall between Bise's Tower and Dame's Gate was 5 ft. thick and 108 ft. in length in 1585. The correlation is striking. The slight difference in measurements of the length of the wall may be attributed to more efficient surveying of longer distances in the 18th century; or perhaps to taking measurements on different sides of the wall. Further evidence of the accuracy of the survey of 1585 is cited later in this paper.

The city walls are depicted by Speed in the well-known 'map-picture' made in 1610 (Figs. 13, 66).[10] Topographical features suggest that the survey on which this map is based was made before reclamation east of the city began in 1605,[11] for the confluence of the Poddle and the Liffey and a small peninsula are depicted east of the city wall. The name 'Newman's Tower' suggests that the survey was made after 1603, the year in which Newman acquired a lease of Isolde's Tower from the city council.[12] However, although Speed's map can be used in a general way to reconstruct pre-reclamation topography, its accuracy must always be tested by reference to other sources, especially in matters of detail. Between Fyan's Castle and Dame's Gate, for example, only one tower — Newman's — is shown when in fact there were four: the four are described in the survey of 1585 and leases show that they still existed in the first decade of the 17th century.[13]

Speed shows the north-eastern section of the city wall extending north-

146

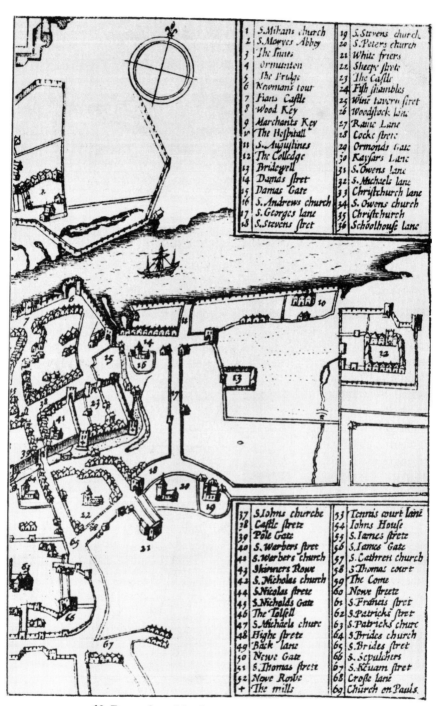

13 Extract from John Speed's map of Dublin, 1610.

north-west from Dame's Gate and projecting northwards into the river at Newman's (Isolde's) Tower. From the other sites identified and located in this paper it is evident that there was a very definite change of alignment and of character in the wall to the east and west of Isolde's (Newman's) Tower, the western portion being a quay wall. The change of alignment is noted by Speed and he shows the wall extending westwards parallel to the river, veering west-south-west. The basic fault in Speed's representation is the apparent extension of fortifications into the channel of the river. If one distinguishes between planimetric and profile elements in Speed's depiction, however, the projection consists only of the quasi-circular base of the tower as shown by Speed. In fact, the dimensions given in the survey of 1585 show that this tower was circular and that it was a particularly strong point of defence since its walls were 9 ft. thick and 30 ft. high. At the beginning of the 17th century Wood Quay and Merchants' Quay did not extend as far northwards as at present and so the north-eastern section of the city wall, terminating in Isolde's Tower, must have projected slightly into the river. Finally, a tendency to emphasize these defensive features may have induced slight distortion in cartographic representation which appears all the greater on a small-scale plan. If Speed's plan is compared with the topographical reconstruction illustrated in Fig. 12 it is seen to give a reasonably correct general impression of the actual early 17th-century topography of the Poddle-Liffey confluence, even though errors can be detected in matters of detail. Bearing in mind that modern small-scale plans of extensive areas necessitate the suppression of detail and that Speed's map-picture is a small-scale plan of the entire city made at an early stage of the development of modern cartographic representation, Speed's map-picture has considerable cartographic merit. Previous compilers probably have been misled by George Semple's interpretation of his excavation which is discussed later, and by neglecting documentary evidence.

In 1720 a survey was made at the request of the city council to establish the extent of ground leased to Jacob Newman and others during the first decade of the 17th century for which leases were soon expiring.[14] The survey was carried out jointly by John Greene, a surveyor appointed by the lessees, and James Ramsay, city surveyor, acting on behalf of the city council. The map compiled by Greene in 1720 (Fig. 14) was copied in 1721 by Ramsay for the city council; a tracing of Ramsay's copy (which itself has not survived) was made in 1755 by Roger Kendrick, who was then city surveyor. Comparison of the two maps has shown that in all essentials Kendrick's map was a true copy.[15]

The ground surveyed by Greene and Ramsay lay immediately north and east of the city wall and towers: therefore, the south-western boundary of this ground should indicate the site of the city wall and towers. The city wall

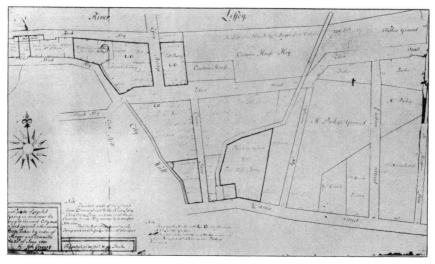

14 Extract from John Greene's plan of the Poddle-Liffey confluence, 1720.

shown by Greene and Ramsay between Dame's Gate and Essex Gate
corresponds to the site of the section of the city wall seen on Purfield's map
(Fig. 15) and will be discussed later in conjunction with that map. The
semicircular tower indicated by Greene and Ramsey on this section of the
wall is misnamed Buttevant for, as already indicated, the tower which stood
on this site was known as Bise's.

Profot's (Proudfoot's) Castle, at the western extremity of the ground
surveyed, was formerly Fyan's Castle. Ground adjoining this castle was
reclaimed by Richard Proudfoot (1605-7) and the castle assumed Proudfoot's
name, although it was inherited by, and later granted in fee farm to, Richard
Barry.[16] According to the survey of 1585 Fyan's Castle, a building '38 foote
sqware one waye, and 20 foote another waye ... the wall fowre foote thicke',
was located at the western end of the Blind Quay (Fig. 12). In a lease recorded
in the assembly rolls of 1455-6 this structure was simply described as the
tower over the fish slip. In 1557 it was described as the tower over the slip
by Fitzsymon's house on Wood Quay when it was leased in fee farm to
Alderman Richard Fyan, from whom it assumed the name Fyan's Castle.[17]

The site of Casey's (Case's) Tower is shown by Greene on the holding of
Jacobs and Page (Fig. 14). This holding projected southwards on to the Blind
Quay along 20 ft. of its frontage and it was 150 ft. east of Profot's
(Proudfoot's) Castle. According to the survey of 1585, from 'Mr. Fians
castell to a smale towre in the pocession of Fitzsymon, of Balmadroght, is
144 foote distant' and Fitzsymon's Tower was '12 foote sqware one waye,
and 14 foote the other waye, the wall 3 foott thick'. These measurements
correspond to dimensions of the site of Case's Tower as illustrated by Greene;

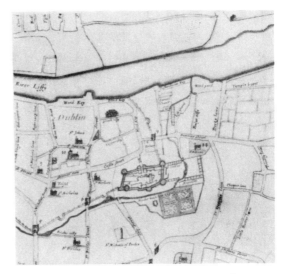

15 Extract from William Purfield's plan of the houses and yards between Essex Street and Dame Street, 1763. North is at the bottom and the intended course of Parliament Street is clearly marked.

16 Extract from Sir Bernard de Gomme's map of the city and suburbs, 1673. The site of the black pool is occupied by the castle garden, south-west of which stands the round tower of the church of St. Michael le Pole.

as in the case of Molesworth's property, the dimensions of the tower are exact, while there is a slight discrepancy in the distance from one tower to the next. Although the succession of lessees cannot now be traced for the second half of the 16th century, Case's Tower must have been that which was called Fitzsymon's in 1585; it had acquired its name from Robert Fitzsymon to whom the tower 'betwix Isot is towre and the Fysshe Slypp' was leased by the city in 1471. In a lease granted to one John Fitzsymon in the 17th year of the reign of Henry VIII, it was described as 'the tower next to Issotts tower that was in term with Robert Fitzsymon'.[18]

The site of Isolde's Tower is marked on the holding of one Denum, which lies at the eastern end of the Blind Quay. At the southern end of this same holding there is a very definite change of alignment in the frontage of the Blind Quay and the holding itself is an irregular shape. From the site of Fitzsymon's (Case's) Tower to the western boundary of Denum's holding, Greene and Ramsay measured 159 ft. Denum's holding had a frontage of $31\frac{1}{2}$ ft., making a total of $190\frac{1}{2}$ ft. from Fitzsymon's (Case's) Tower to the point of change of alignment of the street frontage. In 1585 Isolde's Tower was 174 ft. from Fitzsymon's and 'the said Issoldes towre is a rounde towre,

... 18 foote sqware within the wall, and the wall 9 foote thicke', making a total of 210 ft. from Fitzsymon's to the eastern side of Isolde's Tower. The discrepancy in measurements of the distance from Fitzsymon's to Isolde's Towers is greater than discrepancies in the sections already discussed; nevertheless, it is evident that the site of Isolde's Tower was within this irregular holding of Denum's. Since Isolde's was a round tower its outline was masked by subsequent quasi-rectangular infilling and development and the precise dimensioned site is not definitely marked on any of these maps.

From the corner of Denum's holding to Essex Gate Ramsay and Greene measured 96½ ft. and Essex Gate was then 21 ft. wide.[19] In 1585 Buttevant Tower was 106 ft. from Isolde's Tower and was itself 'an ould sqware ruenus towre, ... the wall 4 foote thicke, ... and 12 foote sqware within the walles'. The Dublin assembly rolls record the fact that one John Greene, a carpenter, was employed in 1674 by the lord mayor and council to take down a 'castle' adjoining Alderman Lovett's house and to make arches and a gate there, now called Essex Gate.[20] Dimensions recorded in 1585 show that Buttevant Tower was 20 ft. wide: clearly, Buttevant Tower was the unnamed castle which was demolished in 1674. In 1585 Buttevant Tower was thought to be 106 ft. from Isolde's Tower. The discrepancy between this and Greene's dimensions suggests that Isolde's Tower may have been about 10 ft. from the frontage of the Blind Quay as mapped in 1720; the Blind Quay had been widened in 1682.[21] Allowance must also be made for inaccuracy in measuring longer distances in 1585, but it should be noted that this is the only case where dimensions given in 1585 are larger than those recorded in 1720.

North of Essex Gate a double line on Greene's map suggests that the city wall, which is clearly marked further south, had previously followed the line of the Blind Quay to Isolde's Tower. Confirmation of this assumption is found in the assembly rolls, where it is recorded that in 1682 the city wall between Essex Gate and Isolde's Tower was demolished in order to widen the Blind Quay. West of Isolde's Tower Greene uses no symbol that might suggest the site of the wall, and the ground that was reclaimed during the 17th century lies immediately north of the Blind Quay. The Blind Quay must therefore have been the quay west of Isolde's Tower that was described in the survey of 1585.

Seventeenth-century topographical features outside the walls can be deduced from Greene's (or Ramsey's) map through correlation with the lease granted by the city council to Jacob Newman in 1605-6. Unfortunately neither the original indenture nor a complete transcription of this lease has survived either among the Corporation records or among records preserved by Newman's heirs. However, the assembly rolls contain a summary of the principal clauses of the lease and a brief description of the property.[22] By this lease Newman acquired parcels of land that lay north and east of Isolde's

Tower and an adjoining tenement, which were then already in his possession. The new leasehold contained:

> firste, from the said tower to thend of the Hog lane, eastwarde, two hundreth fouer score and two yardes; from the loe water marke to thend of the Hog lane in breadth sowthwarde, fyftie eight yardes; from the loe water marke to the myddell of Fagans orchard wall, nowe in the occupacion of the constable of the Castell of Dublin, fortie three yardes; from the Buttevant tower to the corner of Fagans orchard wall, one hundreth fyftie and fouer yardes; from the loe water marke to the Dames mylles sowthward, one hundreth twentye and five yardes; from the loe water marke throughe the smale iland unto the pavement of the Dames street sowthward, one hundreth thirtie and two yardes; the smale peace of grownd lyeing northward of the said tennement and tower, and being of the leingth of the said tennement and tower, and lyeing northward from the same, is in breadth fouer yardes. . . .

The first dimension recorded in this lease is easily checked and correlated. The quay wall measured by Ramsay and Greene from Essex Bridge to Dirty Lane was 724 ft.; the street called Essex Bridge was 24.8 ft. and Berry's holdings west of this street and extending to Isolde's Tower were 96 ft. (59 + 37), making a total of 844.8 ft. The accuracy of this correlation is striking. Since the site of Hog Lane corresponds clearly to Hoggen (alias Dirty) Lane on the maps of Greene and Ramsay, and to Temple Lane on the later maps of Rocque (1756),[23] Scalé (1778),[24] and of the Ordnance Survey (1848), it indicates the site of Isolde's Tower even more clearly than the evidence discussed already.

On its eastern boundary Newman's holding extended southwards from low-water mark for 58 yards along Hog Lane: on Greene's map this corresponds to the combined widths of Essex Street (32 ft.), Butler's ground (90 ½ ft.) and Pooley's ground (62 ft.), a total of 184 ½ ft.[25] Fagan's orchard wall was the south-eastern boundary of Newman's lease; Pooley was a tenant of Newman's,[26] and therefore the eastern boundary of Pooley's holding, as outlined by Greene and Ramsay, should be the site of Fagan's orchard wall. Dimensions given in Newman's lease and cited above from the assembly rolls do not relate clearly to all features of Greene's map. However, the indenture of one of Pooley's leases, granted in 1675,[27] has survived and it can be related to Newman's lease. Dimensions cited in Pooley's lease include a measurement from the orchard wall in the south northwards to low-water mark 148 ft. or thereabouts; Newman's lease records 43 yards as the distance from low-water mark to the middle of Fagan's orchard wall. The two measurements are evidently related since they refer to the same features: the discrepancy here, however, is quite considerable. It probably derives from a difference in the site of low-water mark. The terms of Newman's lease do not indicate clearly whether or not Fagan's orchard was included in the leasehold. If it was not included it probably occupied the ground in lease to Dr. Coghill and to Sir Maurice Eustace in 1720; if it was included in the holding it was probably co-extensive with Pooley's holding, as illustrated in 1720, and one further dimension suggests that this was so. Essex Gate, the site of Buttevant Tower, was 491½ ft. from the north-western corner of Pooley's holding, according to the survey of 1720. According to Newman's lease Buttevant Tower was 154 yards from the corner of Fagan's orchard wall. The discrepancy between the measurements is relatively slight. Pooley's holding, as delimited in 1720, was probably the site of Fagan's orchard.

Newman's lease also contains a measurement taken from low-water mark to the Dame's Mills. The site of these mills is shown by Greene astride the Poddle, east of Dame's Gate. The lease of these premises, granted by the city council to Keane O'Hara in 1704, recites the former lease granted in 1607 to Jacob Newman and also traces the succession from Newman to O'Hara.[28] Newman himself had acquired these mills from one Buyshopp.[29] The site of Dame's Mills is an important one for it can be identified readily on the Ordnance Survey and on the ground, since the location of this section of the Poddle remained unchanged, at least until the first edition of the Ordnance Survey had been published; the river is now completely underground and part of its course has been deflected. From the site of the mills the site of Dame's Gate can be identified with certainty and the site of the city wall extending northwards from this gate can then be reconstructed, based on the evidence discussed in this paper.

The site of the island referred to in Newman's lease may be deduced from Greene's map. The measurement in Newman's lease from the low-water mark through the small island to the pavement of Dame Street southwards 132 yards is immediately preceded by the dimensions related to the Dame's Mills and to other features further east. The small island near low-water mark therefore seems to have been due north from the section of Dame Street between Dame's Gate and the mills. It was probably a small outcrop of rock and may have been part of that which was traditionally known as Standfast Dick.[30] While excavating for the southern abutment of Essex Bridge in 1751 George Semple, architect and overseer, claimed to have struck solid rock:[31] this was probably the island referred to in Newman's lease. The island must have been on or adjacent to the site of Essex Bridge. The configuration of the quays shown by de Gomme (1673) supports this conclusion (Fig. 16).[32] De Gomme shows the north-eastern section of the city wall, which corresponds to the wall described in the survey of 1585 and reconstructed in this paper. From the north-western extremity of the city wall a line which evidently denotes a quay wall extends north-eastwards into the river to a square projection at the western end of the Custom House Quay; the square is on or near the site where Essex Bridge was subsequently erected. The configuration shown by de Gomme marks the extent of reclamation in 1673; irregularity suggests that this was determined by pre-existing topographical features, and if so, the projection was probably determined by the small island referred to in Newman's lease.

The assembly rolls record the building in about 1559 of a wall from Dame's Gate to the mills.[33] Although almost half a century had elapsed before the adjacent property was leased by the city council to Jacob Newman and the wall may have decayed during that period, it nevertheless seems probable that this wall still extended from Dame's Gate to the mills. The mills and a messuage covered with straw were the only recorded buildings on Newman's holding during the first decade of the 17th century.[34] It is true that the lease is not available in full but, had there been other significant buildings, it seems probable that they would have been recorded. Speed shows a row of buildings extending eastwards from Dame's Mills. A grant made in 1612 by James I to Christopher Bise included

> eight thatched houses lying together with their backsides and a garden adjoining without Dame's Gate, extending in breadth between St. Andrew's lands east and St. Nicholas lands west and in length from the street to the King's mill near the Castle, late belonging to the church or chapel of St. Olave or St. Tullockes. . . .[35]

The row of houses shown by Speed should probably have been on the southern side of Dame's Gate, since the king's mill referred to in this grant lay south of Dame Street. Neither site, north or south of Dame Street, was included in the grant made originally to Newman.[36]

The fosse outside the city wall is mentioned in the survey of 1585. Newman's lease was granted provided always that the same be not prejudicial to the watercourse of the castle ditch, which was probably a branch of the Poddle deflected into the moat that surrounded the castle. The course of the other branch of the Poddle is seen on the maps of Greene, Ramsay and de Gomme.

William Purfield's 'Plan of the Houses and Yards between Essex Street and Dame Street' (1763) (Fig. 15) holds the key to identification and reconstruction of the site of the city wall between Dame's Gate and Buttevant Tower. This survey was made for the Wide Streets Commissioners.[37] Purfield's map of this survey shows a maze of lanes, buildings and back-yards. A diagonal line with a semicircular indentation towards the east crosses the street-block from the south-east to the north-west. Analysis of the pattern of landownership, based on evidence recorded in the jury valuations of the Wide Streets Commissioners, revealed that this line was a significant division between the property of Molesworth and that of Keane O'Hara and others.[38] Title to Molesworth's property, traced through extant deeds and the assembly rolls, revealed that Molesworth had inherited that portion of the city wall which lay between Dame's Gate and Buttevant Tower, the tower over Dame's Gate, Buttevant Tower, one other tower (Bise's) which lay between these two, and also the contiguous ground within the city wall (formerly the site of Power's Inns).[39] The eastern boundary of the property should therefore show the alignment of the outside of the city wall and the site of these towers. In fact the site of only one tower can be identified on the map, for Dame's Gate and Buttevant Tower had both been demolished in order to open streets during the 17th century.[40] The site indicated, though unnamed, is evidently that of Bise's Tower. The semicircle (excluding the adjoining square projection) is 24 ft. in diameter. The semicircular tower between Buttevant Tower and Dame's Gate which was described in the survey of 1585 was also 24 ft. in diameter; it was 188 ft. from Buttevant Tower and 108 ft. from Dame's Gate. The tower indicated by Purfield was $175\frac{1}{2}$ ft. from the street frontage of Essex Street and 80 ft. from the street frontage of Dame Street. The percentage difference in both cases is small; the greater discrepancy in the southern portion may be attributed to demolition of part of the city wall when Dame's Gate was demolished towards the end of the 17th century.[41] Dame's Gate must have been near the south-eastern corner of Molesworth's property, adjoining plot no. 8 on Purfield's map, and Buttevant Tower must have been at the northern boundary, adjoining plot no. 30. The site of the city wall between Essex Gate and Dame's Gate is illustrated also by Ramsay and Greene. Since this feature of their map is not dimensioned, it is less valuable than the rest of their survey as a source of evidence for identifying the site of the city wall.

The significant property boundary identified on Purfield's map appears also on the map attached to the deed by which ownership of the property was conveyed by Molesworth to the Wide Streets Commissioners;[42] the conveyance map, a legal document, attests the veracity of Purfield's survey. Nevertheless Purfield's is the more valuable of these two maps, for Purfield superimposed the approved line of Parliament Street on his survey, which itself is drawn accurately to scale. This superimposed street-line marks the precise relationship between the modern street-plan and earlier topography and from this it is possible to establish with certainty the site of Bise's Tower and of related features. Without the evidence of Purfield's survey it would not have been possible, either from the survey of 1585 or from that of Greene and Ramsay, to establish the true site of the city wall between Bise's Tower and Dame's Gate. Change of alignment in the city walls in Dublin was generally marked by a tower or castle. Since there was no such building between Bise's Tower and Dame's Gate, it might be assumed that the wall ran due south or south-east to Dame's Gate. Purfield, however, indicates a definite change of alignment north of Dame's Gate: this point of change was probably protected by a bastion. On Greene's survey a slight change of alignment is indicated at two points between Bise's Tower and Essex Gate: these points seem to indicate structural irregularities observed by Greene and Ramsay and are shown thus on Fig. 12.

The authenticity of the topography illustrated in Fig. 12 has now been demonstrated. The alignment of the city wall in the present reconstruction differs from that shown by earlier compilers: the sites of the towers differ even more. The basic similarity between sites postulated by Sloane, Strangways, and the Ordnance Survey suggests that each used the same source material and not necessarily independently, for the later maps were probably influenced by the earlier. Viewed in this context it is indeed surprising to find Ó Ríordáin publish, without any explanatory comment, a map which evidently rejects the angular site. However, it should be noted also that Ó Ríordáin does not suggest a date or a period of time at which the walls and towers he depicts were the city's fortifications; furthermore, he does not name the towers, and as noted above, there are some significant differences between his map and the present reconstruction. All four compilers seem to have used the survey of 1585 but with different interpretations.

The angular site postulated by the Ordnance Survey, Strangways and Sloane seems to have been influenced by George Semple. While excavating in 1751 Semple claimed not only to have struck solid rock but also to have found the *foundation of Newman's Tower*, which, he said, was built 'very judiciously on solid rock'.[43] This claim has so far remained unchallenged. It was apparently based on Speed's plan, since Newman's Tower is the most northerly point of the eastern fortifications shown by Speed. Indeed, Semple's interpretation of his excavation must have seemed to prove the accuracy of Speed's plan. Previous compilers seem to have accepted Semple's interpretation without query and, using the southern abutment of Essex Bridge as a known and proved fixed point, they have attempted to relate the configuration shown by Speed to existing topography and to traditional sites. What Semple found, however, was more probably the foundation of the original quay wall built by Newman from Isolde's Tower to the island and illustrated on de Gomme's map (Fig. 16). The only tower acquired by Newman from the city council was Isolde's and there is no evidence that he built a tower: on the contrary, according to the terms of his lease, Newman was prohibited from building on the reclaimed land outside the ancient fortifications. The tower named Newman's on Speed's plan must therefore have been Isolde's and the site of this tower has been established above. The modern street frontage of Lower Exchange Street corresponds to that of the Blind Quay, which is shown on Ramsay's map, and Isolde's Tower was situated north-east of the bend in Lower Exchange Street. It has been suggested by the Ordnance Survey (1848) and by Strangways (1906) that Isolde's Tower stood on the site of Essex Gate. The source of this error seems to have been Harris's *History of Dublin*, where he states that 'Isod's tower was demolished in 1675 and on its site was built Essex Gate'.[44] Although the 'castle' which was demolished in 1675 in order to open Essex Gate is not named in the assembly rolls, as indicated above, it must in fact have been Buttevant Tower. The merits of Speed's map-picture have already been noted. The concurrence of previous compilers in delimiting a right-angled north-eastern city wall seems nevertheless to have been derived from Speed for, excluding the site of Newman's Tower, the shape of the north-eastern wall illustrated by Speed was in fact right-angled (Fig. 13).

The late medieval city wall described in this paper was evidently not the original wall of the city, for within it there was some reclaimed land. Modern local topography coupled with the detailed description of 1585 suggests that ground south of Isolde's Tower was reclaimed land and it may be assumed that this earlier reclamation extended south to the line of high-water mark postulated in Fig. 12. An entry in the White Book, however, suggests that the late medieval wall had already been constructed in the 13th century, for a 'tower which is called Butauant, situated upon the bank near Isolda's Gate, together with all their land adjacent . . . extending from the street as far as the new wall, towards the water of Auenlyf' were granted to one William Picot during that century. The tower is mentioned again in an entry which records that Fromund le Brun in 1327 quit claim, in favour of the mayoralty, to all his right in the tower called La Botavant with the adjacent ground. A marginal note referring to this grant — 'Ye ylande without ye Dame's Gate — Buttevante's Towre, certeyne lande adjoyning' — seems to have been added later.[45] It seems probable that the main topographical features west of the Poddle, illustrated in Fig. 12, existed already in the mid-13th century.

Dimensions cited in the survey of 1585 suggest structural similarities in the wall near Newgate and in that between Dame's Gate and Isolde's Tower, and the structural difference between these two sections and the remainder of the walls suggests further that the wall near Newgate and the wall north of Dame's Gate were coeval. Irregularities in the southern section of the city wall may have been caused by decay or by demolition; they also suggest that the southern wall was of different, probably earlier, date than the walls near Newgate and Dame's Gate and place-names support this conclusion. The name Newgate suggests that this gate was part of the most recently constructed portion of the fortifications and, if so, the structural differences in the southern wall may mark the limits of the original walled city. The choice of site for the walls, as delimited in the survey of 1585, seems indeed to have been governed almost entirely by expedience rather than by free choice. Topographical features such as the course of the Poddle, the ridge, and the confluence of the stream which joined the Liffey near Usher's House seem to have determined the extent of the medieval settlement.

Stages of reclamation and development

In 1603 the city council granted to Jacob Newman a lease of Isolde's Tower and an adjoining tenement on the west. Newman had acquired the property in a ruinous state from Alderman John Elliott and had subsequently been at great expense about the enlarging, re-edifying and building up of the said decayed tenement and tower: in recognition of these services to the city the lease granted to Newman in 1603 was for an unusually long term of years, namely 119 years.[46] In the following year the city council granted Newman a piece of waste ground which lay west of his property, extending from the western boundary of the tenement to Fitzsymon's (or Case's) Tower and 36 yards in breadth, and Newman covenanted within the space of four years to build a sufficient wall of lime and stone to keep off the water.[47] In 1605 the city granted to one Richard Proudfoot, a merchant, a least of ground which lay east of Fyan's Castle and north of the quay. Proudfoot was not bound to enclose this ground (evidently this section of the quays was in a good state of repair) but that 'if he build any wall outside the wall of the quay that now is, into the river, that the same be made for height and strength answerable to the wall that now is'.[48] Later that year Newman acquired the ground north and east of his property which was discussed earlier in reconstructing 17th-century topography: this holding extended north to low-water mark and east to Hog Lane. The intention to reclaim this land, of which half at least was overflowed at high tide, is not recorded in the summary of the lease, but clauses included provision that the same be not prejudicial to the watercourse from the said mills, nor to the watercourse from the castle ditch,[49] suggesting that structural changes were imminent.

By 1607 both Newman and Proudfoot had reclaimed land, for in that year the city granted to Alderman Matthew Handcock a lease for a term of 'five score and eighten yeares, uppon soe muche grownde as lyethe voide betwixte the grownde lately gayned by Jacobe Newman and Richard Prudfoote, on Wood Key'; moreover, in 1607 Richard Proudfoot was granted a new lease for a term as long as Newman's for one parcel of void ground lately gained by the said Richard Proudfoot from the Liffey.[50] Newman completed his acquisition of ground outside the city wall in 1609, when the city council granted him a lease of a small arch under Dame's Gate and the ground lying under the said arch.[51]

Inside the city wall a piece of ground, formerly the site of Power's Inns and in possession of the Bise family, was leased in 1608-9 to one Christopher Bise, who also acquired a new lease for a term of 99 years of 'the tower over Dams gate, with the way or staiers uppe therunto, the tower called Butte-vantes tower, and one other tower or flancard uppon the citty wall, scituated betwixte the tower over the Dams gate and Buttevantes tower . . .'.[52] The subsequent development of these holdings of Newman and Bise had a very significant role in the morphogenesis of Dublin.

De Gomme's map (1673) (Fig. 16) illustrates the extent of ground actually reclaimed by Newman and Proudfoot. Proudfoot's ground lay east of Fyan's Castle; the projection into the river west of Fishamble Street marks the site of Fyan's Castle and of Proudfoot's land, which projected into the river further than the castle. The absence of any projection on the Blind Quay, together with the width of the quay as illustrated by de Gomme, indicate a lack of development along this part of the waterfront, of which part was in lease to Handcock and the rest to Newman. In fact, Handcock appears not even to have perfected his lease and Newman to have repaired the old quay wall, as required by the terms of his lease, without extending the quay.[53] The north-eastern projection east of the city wall suggests, as already stated, that Newman built a wall from Isolde's Tower to the island mentioned in his lease, and thence eastward parallel to the channel of the river; the presence of the island, together with a natural tendency towards deposition upstream from the confluence, would have minimized difficulties of reclamation and infilling. Semple's excavation shows that the walls constructed on this site were like the walls of the medieval fortifications. Newman probably built a thick wall of stone and lime on or near low-water mark. A clause in his lease prohibited building outside the city wall and during the ensuing half-century much of Newman's holding remained a garden leased to Alderman Lovett of Blind Quay.[54] The extent of this garden is recorded on Greene's survey; it comprised the four parcels of land marked L.G. on Greene's map, one on either side of Essex Bridge and two outside Essex Gate on the south side of Essex Street.

De Gomme's map illustrates the stage of development reached within the area of the confluence of 1673 (Fig. 16). From the first quarter of the 17th century the main development had taken place on land acquired from Newman by the Crown. In 1620, following a survey made on behalf of the Crown, part of Newman's holding was chosen as a site suitable for a new custom-house and wharf: prior to that time customs had been collected at the crane on Wood Quay at the foot of Winetavern Street.[55] The site now chosen lay west of the mouth of the Poddle but was not contiguous to the city wall.

The choice was probably influenced by two features of the physical environment: namely, the ford in the river near Fyan's Castle, where at low ebb there was but a depth of 3 ft. when the main channel was at least 6 ft. deep; and secondly the island on the northern boundary of Newman's holding, which offered a site on which a wharf would be accessible even at low tide.

By 1621 the new custom-house had been built and from that time, by royal decree, all imports and exports were required to be loaded and unloaded at the new crane and wharf.[56] The only overland approach to the custom-house from the city was by Dame Street and a narrow lane called Custom House or Crane Lane; and so there was much transhipment of goods by small boats from the custom-house wharf to Wood Quay and Merchants' Quay in order to avoid the narrow, congested streets of the old city. Trade seems to have increased consistently during the early decades of the century, for in 1637 the merchants complained that the custom-house wharf had become overcrowded.[57] The Crown then acquired more land to the south and east from Jacob Newman, so that its property extended eastwards to the west bank of the Poddle and southwards about half-way to Dame Street.[58] The wharf was then extended east to the Poddle and a new custom-house was built. By 1673 public buildings on the Crown property included a council chamber, some public offices and accommodation for the Horse Guard.

Meanwhile the wood yard east of the Poddle had been developed by one Pooley, a tenant of Newman's. This venture was also instigated by the merchants who complained that Wood Quay had become overcrowded and Pooley's wood yard was established following a survey made on behalf of the city council in 1637.[59] Pooley's (Sycamore) Alley gave access to this wood yard from Dame Street. To the west of the Crown property Alderman Lovett's garden extended to the city wall, north to the river and south to the site of the council chamber.

Although in 1673 the old city walls still existed, they were somewhat ineffective since by this time so much of the city lay outside the walls.[60] De Gomme's survey was made in order to plan new fortifications for the city, mainly a citadel east of the city, which would control approaches to it by sea.[61] About this time clauses in the leases granted by Bise and Newman, which required that the city walls be kept in repair and prohibited building outside the walls, were no longer enforced. De Gomme's map, therefore, shows Newman's holding on the eve of a new stage of development.

Phillips's map of Dublin, made only 12 years after that of de Gomme, illustrates a new stage of development on Newman's property.[62] Although this map lacks much of the fine detail of de Gomme's, the main features of the new development may be distinguished: the Liffey had been bridged near the custom-house quay; new streets had been laid out; and the city wall north of Dame's Gate has been omitted from the map, suggesting that it had been demolished. Part of it was in fact still standing but was probably masked by buildings.

Although trade and traffic had greatly increased after the Restoration, the only overland approach to the city from the Crown property was still through Crane Lane and Dame Street. In 1673, at the suggestion of the then viceroy, Arthur Capel, the earl of Essex, a new street was opened from Custom House Lane, through Alderman Lovett's garden to the Blind Quay, and Buttevant Tower was demolished in order to open Essex Gate.[63] This new approach to the city, Essex Street, gave more direct access both to the castle and to the waterfront within the city walls and led to redevelopment inside the old walls. Building on Newman's land seems to have begun about this time. In 1675 leases in reversion were granted by the city council to John Crow for Alderman Lovett's garden and to Nevill Pooley for the timber yard. Warehouses and a weigh-house were erected at the southern side of Essex Street.[64] Crow and Pooley were required to keep in repair all the buildings which then existed or would thereafter be built on their holdings, and Essex Street and a passage from the weigh-house to the river were reserved as public highways.

The building of Essex Bridge, ordered in 1676 by the viceroy for the convenience of State and city, was prompted by Humphrey Jervis, alderman and speculator, who in 1674 had acquired the strand of the north bank from the confluence with the Bradogue (almost opposite Fyan's Castle) to the mouth of the Liffey and also some contiguous ground, part of the estate of St. Mary's Abbey.[65] A new bridge was needed in order to link this new development to the south bank and thus to make residential development feasible on Jervis's property. Essex Bridge was built opposite the main thoroughfare on Jervis's holding and a new street opened through Alderman Lovett's garden leading due south from the bridge beside the custom-house quay to Essex Street, probably on the site of the passage from the weigh-house to the river. The formation of this north-south thoroughfare completed the integration of Newman's property into the ground-plan of the city.

Conclusion

The reclamation of this tiny area was to prove influential, out of all proportion to its size, in determining the form and character of subsequent urban development on both north and south banks of the Liffey. This was due to its situation as much as to land-use and tenure. By enclosing the Poddle-Liffey confluence Newman overcame the major physical obstacle to coherent eastward expansion and accretion, and his achievement stimulated plans for more extensive schemes. Already in 1612, Mayor Carroll envisaged extending reclamation east to Ringsend at the mouth of the estuary.[66] This objective was achieved towards the end of the 18th century. The choice of a site for the custom-house and the extension of the Crown property to provide sites for other public buildings and offices also attest the significance of Newman's project. The building of the first custom-house was the first stage of the eastward movement of port facilities and trade, a trend that has continued in Dublin to the present; it also fixed the lowest feasible bridging point on the Liffey until, at the end of the 18th century, the present Custom House was built downstream on the north bank. Centralization of trade at the first custom-house and wharf made the area a major focal point in the city, a role which was emphasized by the building of a replacement for Essex Bridge and the improvement of the north-south axis in the 18th century; this axis, of which Newman's holding was an integral part, influenced the alignment of later planned and co-ordinated development further east.

Many features of the development of this area were also characteristic of the general development of Dublin during the 17th century. The physical environment greatly influenced, if it did not determine, the form of development even when surface evidence of former topography was almost eradicated. Initial development derived from private enterprise and speculation; the demands of a growing economy and increasing trade and commerce prompted expansion. Development was sometimes controlled by conditions of tenure and these were altered in response to demands created by changing circumstances. The significance of changes in tenure introduced by the city council was gradually realized and similar changes were introduced by private landowners. Thus, the reclamation and development of the Poddle-Liffey confluence, both in itself and by its influence, was an important formative element in the morphological development of Dublin.

PART II

Buildings and monuments

The High Street excavations

BREANDÁN Ó RÍORDÁIN

Entries in a number of Irish annals[1] indicate that a *longphort* was established by the Norse at Dublin in the mid-ninth century[2] and the importance of the town which developed there has been noted by several writers.[3] In the 19th and early 20th centuries archaeological material of the Viking and medieval periods was discovered in the course of sewer-laying operations in streets which lay within the bounds of the medieval town.[4] In 1962 redevelopment schemes initiated by the municipal authority, the Corporation of Dublin, resulted in the removal of a number of houses bordering on High Street and Nicholas Street and the National Museum of Ireland was afforded an opportunity of investigating a limited area. In 1967, when a more extensive plot of ground became available at High Street, further excavation was undertaken and continued annually during the period 1967-72. From 1969 to 1973 excavation was also carried out at Winetavern Street[5] and in 1972 investigation of another site was commenced at Christchurch Place, south of the cathedral and lying between it and the bounds of the medieval town wall at Ross Road.[6]

In all of the sites investigated a considerable number of artefacts and structural features were found which ranged in date from the tenth to the early 14th century. Many of the discoveries relate to the Viking period and these include over 50 examples of trial pieces, the majority of which are of bone. This is the largest group of trial pieces recovered from any single centre in Ireland or elsewhere. The geometric and zoomorphic designs carved on the trial pieces (Fig. 17), many of which were found in late tenth-, 11th- and 12th-century levels, bear a close affinity to those which occur on contemporary metal-work and manuscripts such as the Soiscel Molaise,[7] the shrine of the Cathach of Colum Cille,[8] the Kells Crosier,[9] the crosier of the abbots of Clonmacnoise,[10] the shrine of St. Senan's Bell (Clogán Óir),[11] the Southampton Psalter[12] and the *Liber Hymnorum*.[13] In a number of instances the patterns on the trial pieces are carved in the Borre style and in the Hiberno-Viking version of the Ringerike style. Part of a wooden board or panel, which may have formed part of a bench or chest and which has carved interlace and zoomorphic patterns in the Ringerike style, bears comparison with the design on the slab from St. Paul's churchyard, London.[14] Elements

17 a-c. Bone trial piece from High Street, late 11th century. In the centre is an object drawing of the right-hand face and to the right a close-up view of the bottom motif on the left-hand face.

of Urnes style are also present on some of the trial pieces and a finely-incised design in this style occurs on the wooden handle of an iron knife (Fig. 18).

Three objects bearing runic inscriptions were found in the Christchurch Place site: two are of wood, the third is an animal long bone. One example of the inscribed wooden objects which was found in a 12th-century stratum has been examined by Mr. Aslak Liestøl, who has kindly supplied the following report:

> The runic piece (reg. no. E122:361; Fig. 19), which I think is an ordinary spade, was examined by me at the National Museum, Dublin, Saturday, 21 July 1973. The museum had supplied me with a good low-power binocular microscope and good working light. The piece was kept in water and had not been treated in any way.

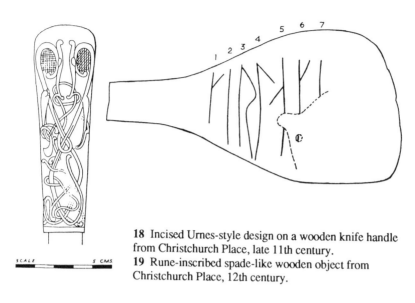

18 Incised Urnes-style design on a wooden knife handle from Christchurch Place, late 11th century.
19 Rune-inscribed spade-like wooden object from Christchurch Place, 12th century.

SCALE   5 CMS

The inscription is partially damaged, probably by wear and tear. There is no indication of recent damage to the runes. A portion of the original surface, containing the lower part of the last two runes, has worn away except for a small trace of rune no. 6. A small portion of rune no. 5 is also missing. The damage does not, however, affect the reading of runes nos. 5 and 6. The same cannot be said about rune no. 7, where less than one-half of a full rune-stem is preserved. The lower end of this line (cut) disappears in a dent. On the other side of the dent there is a fissure in the wood in the same direction as the stem. This is not cut by a sharp instrument but split or torn. There is a possibility that the inscription was longer, and that several runes have been worn away, but I do not think it is likely.

When so little is left of the last rune, there is more than one possible reading.

(1) r. 7 = S which gives *Kirlaks*, probably genitive of *Geirlákr*. *Geirláks*, a man's name, the owner of the spade. This is not a usual type of owner's inscription. Only one example, and a dubious one, is known (*Danmarks Runeindskrifter*, col. 356).

(2) r. 7 = R *KirlakR*, the same name in the nominative. This is a common type of inscription, but the use of palatal *r* (R) in the 11th or 12th century is very unlikely.

(3) r. 7 =   A *Kirlaka*. This will give the usual type of owner's inscription 'N.N. owns' (*á* is third person present tense of *eiga*,
'own'). In this case the nominative of the personal name has
lost its ending *-r*. This is, however, attested in similar contexts, namely, some of the Manx crosses (Andreas II,
Michael II and IV, Maughold I and II).

On the whole the third possibility seems to be the most likely, and there
is no difficulty in explaining the missing twig. There is ample room for
it, and if it was placed only a little lower than the corresponding twig
on rune no. 5, it would have been worn away.

20 Carved wooden head from Christchurch Place, 11th
century. The face is badly damaged, but the 'panache'
illustrates the Dublin version of the Ringerike style.

The other rune-inscribed wooden object is
thought to be part of a small smoothing plane[15]
and it bears inscriptions on each of the long sides.
It was found in an occupation level of the late
11th century, in which many slivers and chips of
wood were present and among which a small but
finely-carved representation of a human head
with decorative features executed in the
Ringerike style was also discovered (Fig. 20).

In the High Street and Christchurch Place sites
in particular a considerable amount of evidence
relating to the craft of comb-making was recovered. The principal raw material was red deer
antler and large quantities of antler waste and
partly finished component pieces of combs
indicative of the existence of comb-making
workshops were found. Most of the discarded antler burrs exhibited natural
ruptures indicating that shed antlers collected in the haunts of the deer were
the main source of supply. Over 600 examples of combs were discovered
and the vast majority are of the single-sided type (Fig. 21).[16] A number of
comb-cases were also found.

Evidence of metal-working, bronze-working in particular, was recovered
from all the sites investigated, but the large numbers of crucibles present in
the Christchurch Place site suggest that this was an area of intensive metal-
working in the 11th and 12th centuries. The occurrence on the same site of
many examples of carved bone trial pieces suggests that these may have been

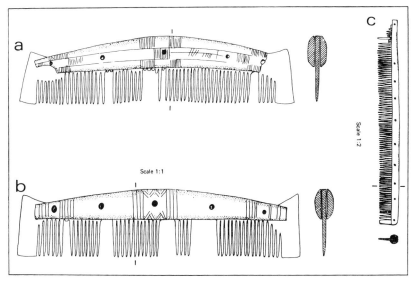

Scale 1:1

Scale 1:2

21 Varieties of comb found in Dublin. KEY: a. class F 1, with bevelled sideplates, from the castle; b. class F 2, with D-shaped sideplates, from High Street; c. class G, an old find possibly from Dublin.

used in some stage of the metal-working process, but definite evidence for this supposition is lacking. It also seems probable that bronze pins were made in the town as the excavations have produced one of the largest collections of bronze pins of the Viking and medieval period yet discovered. Upwards of 800 specimens have been recovered and this figure does not include the large number of simple but well-preserved iron pins. Many of the bronze pins show traces of tinning or silvering and a large proportion are of gilt bronze. Two main groups have been identified: simple stick pins and the more elaborate ringed pins. The writer is indebted to Mr. Thomas Fanning for the following note on bronze ringed pins from sites at High Street and Winetavern Street:

> The bronze ringed pins which total about 150 can be grouped into four distinct classes: spiral-ringed (Fig. 22, no. 1), plain-ringed (Fig. 22, nos. 2, 3), stirrup-ringed (Fig. 22, nos. 4, 5) and kidney-ringed (Fig. 22, no. 6). To-date only one example of the spiral-ringed form has been found, a fact which tends to confirm rather than disprove the pre-Viking associations of this class. Of the remaining forms the stirrup-ringed class is by far the most numerous occurring mainly in the 11th- and 12th-century levels. Another form (Fig. 22, no. 5) is of particular interest as its occurrence on the Dublin sites and its distribution pattern else-

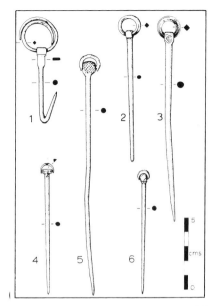

22 Classification of bronze ringed pins.

23 Ship carved on a wooden plank from Christchurch Place, *c*. 1100. At the top is a crude human figure sitting on the yard at the masthead.

where support the known evidence for the Hiberno-Norse involvement in the Viking settlement of the Isle of Man, York, the Western Isles of Scotland and perhaps even Iceland. From a recent study of the ringed-pin series[17] a typological sequence can be postulated based on the development of the ring and head forms and terminating in the small pin with its pin-head and kidney ring cast as one (Fig. 22, no. 6). This sequence has some chronological validity (illustrated here by the numerical sequence in Fig. 22) though one must also assume a certain amount of overlap and continuity. The sequence, as such, is largely supported by the evidence of the associated and stratified specimens from Dublin.

Although weapons were not numerically conspicuous among the finds the examples which came to light included spear-heads and arrow-heads of Viking type; a well-preserved iron sword from a late 11th- to early 12th-century level in the Christchurch Place site bears an inscription reading SINIMIΛINIΛIS on one face of the blade. Material associated with the sword which was found within a house of post-and-wattle construction included sherds of a tripod pitcher of late Saxon type.[18] Apart from the two sketches of Norse-style ships found incised on wooden planks in the Winetavern Street site (Fig. 23)[19] numerous large iron boat nails, a small number of boat models and examples of strakes, ribs, an attachment for a steering oar and a wooden rowlock[20] were also recovered. The existence of trading contacts between the inhabitants of Dublin and Britain, the Netherlands and northern France

24 Close-up view of
post-and-wattle construction.

during the 11th century is exemplified by the finding of coins of Æthelred
and Cnut,[21] of late Saxon wheel-stamped ware of Stamford type and sherds
of Andenne ware,[22] and of vessels, including storage jars and cooking pots,
imported from northern France.

The excavations produced a considerable amount of information about the
types of building in use between the mid-tenth century and the early 14th
century and in a number of instances fairly complete plans of structures were
recovered. The houses and workshops were sub-rectangular in plan and
varied in size from 3.80 m. by 3.20 m. to 8 m. by 6 m. Virtually all of the
structures were of post-and-wattle construction (Fig. 24) and in many examples the doorways were provided with wooden thresholds and with jambs of
squared timber, the outer edges of which had vertical slots to house the ends
of the rods of wattlework which formed the side walls. A few examples of
stave-type structures were found, including one house of which the complete
ground plan was recovered in a habitation level attributable to the mid-11th-
century period. Rectangular in plan, it was 8 m. long and 5 m. wide and its
long axis was oriented east-west. Although only fragments of the walls
survived, sufficient remained to indicate that they had been constructed of a
combination of staves (tree trunks split lengthwise with the curved surfaces
facing outwards) and vertical timber planks. The outer edges of the staves
had been provided with grooves to accommodate the planks which had been
slotted between each pair of staves.[23] The bases of the staves and intervening
planks rested on wooden sill beams or sole plates at ground level (Fig. 25).
Structural evidence was found which showed that the side walls had been
reconstructed and the finding of three superimposed hearths in the central
area of the house suggests that occupation had continued for a fairly lengthy
period of time. Features of particular interest in the house included internal
divisions indicating that one large room containing the centrally placed
stone-edged hearth had been provided with a bench or *pallr* along each of
the side walls. At the western end of the house two small chambers at opposite
sides opened off the central passage. Another small chamber or annexe
abutting the eastern end wall appears to have included a privy, as an

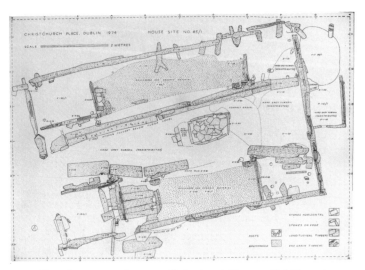

25 Plan of stave-type house at Christchurch Place, mid-11th century.

under-floor wooden culvert formed, in the main, of discarded ship strakes, originally discharged into a cess-pit located within the annexe. The entrance to the house was in the form of a plank-floored vestibule with its opening in the southern side wall.

Upwards of 600 artefacts were found on and in the compressed layers of brushwood and other organic material of the benched areas and in the trodden soil of the central area of the floor of the main chamber and of the smaller chambers at the western end of the house. The principal finds included a number of decorated leather scabbards and the largest example, which was 37 cm. long, bore an inscription which reads + EDRIC ME FECIT. A silver coin of the Sitric series, tentatively dated to the 1040s, was found in one of the benched areas (F 87-1) and other finds — illustrating in microcosm the general range of material from the Dublin sites — included fish-hooks, knives, nails, staples, pointed implements, arrow-heads and small tools of iron, barrel padlocks and keys, fragments of hair-nets, textiles — including small pieces of gold braid — weaving tablets and bone spindle whorls. Many wooden objects were also present: barrel lids, staves, lathe-turned vessels and a wooden shoe last. Evidence of metal-working in the form of crucible fragments, vitreous matter and stone ingot moulds was found and items of bronze included stick pins and ringed pins, a small bell-like object and a bronze spur. Comb-making in the form of antler waste and unfinished tooth plates was in evidence. Single-sided decorated combs and one example of a double-sided comb, which appears to be of whale bone, were found. Potsherds included Andenne ware and sherds of northern French wares and fragments of vessels made of steatite.

The ancient chapter-house of the priory of the Holy Trinity, Dublin

THOMAS DREW

When I first knew anything of Christ Church Cathedral, every trace of its cloistral buildings — if it ever had any, for all popular history of the cathedral has no allusion to such adjuncts — was gone. It was a matter of curious speculation whether they had lain north or south of the church, and yet there were remnants extant of them in my memory which I ought to have recognized as such. I have this apology — that I was then young and inexperienced, and that a more learned ecclesiologist and far greater authority whose mission it specially was later on to investigate the plan of ancient Christ Church, Mr. George E. Street, was no wiser than I. This is what he had to say about the existence of cloisters at Christ Church. It is written in the account of the rebuilding by Mr. Street himself given in a great volume, not accessible to many readers on account of its size and cost, published by Mr. Sutton Sharpe of London:

> The map of the cathedral and its precincts, surveyed in October 1761, is of considerable value as showing the state of the surroundings at that time. The old buildings attached to the cathedral had been in part swept away, and in part applied to new purposes. South of the nave there had doubtless been a cloister. This had been appropriated to the law courts, and on its east side was the exchange — an oblong building, measuring 20 ft. north and south by 40 ft. in length — evidently standing on the site of the chapter-house, and probably retaining its walls. Between this and the south transept was the narrow passage or 'slype' so universal in the large churches of the 12th and 13th centuries.[1] To the south of the chapter-house was another narrow chamber, which in these days had come to be popularly called Hell, probably on account of a grotesque figure preserved there. So early as 1627, the law courts existed here; and rent was paid to the chapter for this incongruous substitute for the buildings which the pious founders had deemed necessary adjuncts to the cathedral. It is interesting to find these arrangements still visible to an eye accustomed to examine the plans and details of cathedral

churches, in the midst of what would appear to the ordinary eye to be the most confused jumble of walls and buildings. . . . The greater part of these walls had been removed before the restoration of the cathedral was begun, &c.

Thus vaguely, and to my mind unsatisfactorily, Street dismissed the hints given by Reading's map: 'to an eye accustomed to examine the plans and details of cathedral churches', it might have revealed more. It might have revealed the priory gateway which was still in existence in my memory, and which Mr. Street removed as not falling in with a preconceived notion or plan of his own. It revealed, what is still to be seen, a built-up doorway in the crypt leading by two or three foot-worn steps, as plainly as anyone accustomed to monastic plans could want to see it, into the west cloister walk. There was another doorway leading by descending steps from the church into the east walk of the cloister which still exists, and which so occurs in the place it is usually found in the plans of a score or two of abbeys — say Westminster for an instance. What it was had never seemed to me open to a minute's misunderstanding of any student of monastic plans, and it was a matter of astonishment to me that Mr. Street should dispose of it in this fashion: 'We found a doorway of singular interest which led *into a building outside the aisle*, and thence by a flight of steps down into the crypt through another archway at a lower level, &c.'.

In the year 1882, when I entered on the care of the cathedral fabric shortly after the restoration, I found the crypt in a bad way (Fig. 26). It was unventilated and pervaded by a kind of choke-damp. Condensed moisture dripped from the vaulting, and umbrellas were much used by damp and depressed visitors. Water burst through the south walls, and the remains of the bishops, in what we call the royal vault, were water-logged. We know now, in after years, that this arose from the blocking up of the great ancient watercourse of the priory by the Corporation in 1881 — the Great Gout, as it is called in old chapter acts — and which gave the foundation for that time-worn tradition of the passage that led to and *under the Liffey* — of course to a convent of nuns, somewhere or other. Such passages have been reported in many places to communicate between monks' and nuns' establishments by a scandalous generation in times after the dissolution of the monasteries. I may say that, in this case, I have found that the course of this 'passage' is traceable all the way to the Liffey, and still opens into it.

In 1882 it was necessary to make an intercepting drain at a low level along the south side of the cathedral, and to divert those waters which formerly flowed away by the Great Gout, into St. Michael's Hill by way of outfall. In the excavation for it I found, as was expected, foundations and remnants of the law courts built on the cloister garth in 1610, but beyond them one of

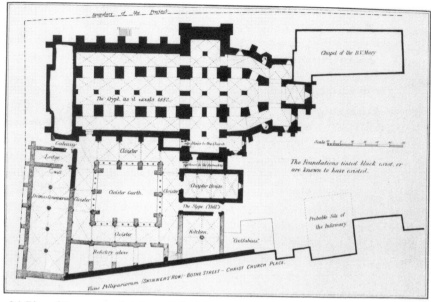

26 Plan of the crypt and cloister garth of Christ Church Cathedral (Holy Trinity Priory).

different masonry, going down to the depth of the underlying peat bog; an ancient wall, and evidence of the western limit of the cloister. There was the additional evidence that the level of the cloister had been nearly as low as that of the crypt floor, and not as had been assumed on that of the upper church.

Following up this clue, the use of the doorway, with its foot-worn steps leading from the crypt into the west walk of the cloisters, was evident; and Mr. Street's restoration as a porch to the church, of what was really the priory gate at a lower level as he found it, was evidently a mistake as a restoration. A study of the leasehold tenements as they existed in 1761, according to Thomas Reading's map — a congerie of booths, stalls, petty tenements and the old law courts — enabled me to lay down a conjectural plan and make this statement in a paper read before the Royal Irish Academy in 1882:

> The cloisters stood on the south side of Christ Church Cathedral, between the nave and present Christchurch Place. The abbey [*sic*] gateway stood exactly under the doorway of the present south porch, but some 8 ft. below it. The chapter-house stood 7 ft. to the south from the south transept. . . . Under the present green sward, between the railings of Christchurch Place and the church, antiquarians may fairly assume the foundations of these buildings lie, and may yet be investigated. It may be a parallel for the discovery of a fragment of old

St. Paul's cloister, lately discovered by Mr. Penrose, and made an object
of great interest in the pretty garden which he has created in the heart
of London, if we should some day uncover some part of our cloisters,
and make them an object of interest in the city garden which I hope to
live to see created in the 'yard' of Christ Church Cathedral.

The realization of this prophecy came about far sooner than I ever hoped,
and with a measure of success which I never anticipated. In the early months
of 1886 — a time of great depression and hardship among the unemployed
poor in Dublin — a considerable sum was collected for a relief fund by a
Mansion House committee. It was easier to collect than to distribute. Public
works of utility could not be at once devised and set agoing to employ labour.
The creation of 'open spaces' and gardens in disused burial grounds was most
desired, but the difficulties of vested interests, negotiations, and palavers,
stepped in. At Christ Church Cathedral, happily, the chapter, moved by His
Grace the Archbishop, Lord Plunket, a man of directness of purpose, swept
aside conventional forms, and welcomed the hungry army of unemployed
into their precincts. It was a good thing for the cathedral and for the poor
dwellers of the neighbourhood that the main part of the Mansion House Relief
Fund had to be spent in digging and removing thousands of tons of rubbish
from 'Christ Church yard'. Other vested interests and consequent delays
would not have opened any other gates to the diggers before the summer
came, and the pinch of necessity was past.

We began our digging in the roadway near the south transept, and in 20
minutes had reached the north-east corner of the chapter-house, where it was
being looked for. It was a revelation of beautiful moulded 13th-century work,
which had actually been opened up in Mr. Street's restoration in laying a
lightning conductor, and unheeded. Further excavation revealed that the
eastern wall of the chapter-house still stood some 7 ft. above its ancient floor,
with the sectional plan extant of a fine triplet eastern window, and the
engaged vaulting shafts of a four-bayed building, the lower part of the
western doorway, the slype, and the door to the calefactory; and the eastern,
southern and western walk of the cloister.

The history of this beautiful building, and the destruction and degradation
of the fragments surviving, might be written as it was excavated, thus. It had
been of the utmost refinement of Early English moulded work at its best
period, and by the most skilled hands. It was evidently the latest display of
skill in master masonry of the mind and hands of those highly-skilled bands
of English workmen, trained in the great school of Wells and Glastonbury,
brought over here 'for the job'. We know not when they came, or who
imported them, for the band of workers which built the nave must have been
a different one from the first one which, under Strongbow and Laurence

O'Toole, built the choir and transepts thirty or forty years before. They could not be their successors by devolution, but a new excursion, bringing with them the latest fashions in early 13th-century architecture. Strange to say, the building tells us that they went away, and we have now a date for the completion of the nave, which Mr. Street was not so fortunate as to have found for him. It will be found in written record in Sweetman's *Calendar of Documents relating to Ireland, 1171-1251*, and for which we are indebted to Dr. Stokes's research:

> 26 September 1234. The king grants to Luke, archbishop, and the prior and canons of the Holy Trinity. In order to lengthen and enlarge their church, they may occupy and close up a street (*chiminum*) lying near it towards the west, provided that in place of the street they carry a road along the neighbouring land of the prior and canons extending to the old street on the other side of that land. This road will give free access to the church. Mandate to the mayor and good men of Dublin to allow this change, notwithstanding that the obstruction be an inconvenience to the city.

So the thoroughfare now known as St. Michael's Hill, formerly as Christ-church Lane, came to be made. Strange to say, the record is written in the building, too. There is no crypt under the western bay of the nave. There is a westernmost arch of the nave arcade of the old work still surviving on the north side, built, it is plain, by different hands and at a different time from the rest of the nave. Its moulding is ruder and its workmanship less masterful. There is no sculpture in its clumsily moulded capitals as in the others. It tells the story that a temporary screen had been maintained for some time at the west end until the king's licence was obtained. When it came the cunning carvers and the best of the mason-men had gone back to their native Somerset, or had otherwise left Christ Church.

Returning to the antecedent work of the chapter-house, there was to be remarked the extraordinary mathematical and even pedantic accuracy with which the moulds were struck, unusual in the more free-hand practice of medieval work generally. Then we observe that they are designed to suit particular scantlings of stones, and not in usual course, the scantlings of stones got out to suit the designer's contours; and, we further observe, these scantlings are mainly uniform; stones 2 ft. x 1 ft. x 1 ft., and soforth; and we read the history of the provision and supply of a foreign sea-borne stone in sized scantlings as we, in these days, get our timber and 'deals' and often adapt our construction to suit them. Mr. Street told us this foreign stone was French Caen stone. We know, from the unhappy condition of decay of the Caen stone, which he employed, compared with that of the excellent weathering qualities of the ancient stone — the experience of seven years as against 700 — and by superficial examination of the two stones, that he was utterly and obstinately wrong. Why, indeed, should the masons of south-western England import stone from a more distant French port when the oolites of Somerset, which they knew well — and whereof Glastonbury and St. Davids and Valle Crucis, and even in later times Great Montacute House were built — could be floated by water from many a quarry to the Bristol Channel, and thence water-borne to the foot of Winetavern Street, Dublin, more readily than Caen stone or than any native stone could have been had for the purpose?

We begin now to see a reason for the well-noted characteristic of Christ Church work — the frequently annulated engaged nook-shafts, when we catch up the fact that a great supply of Purbeck marble shaftlets, with an angle fillet wrought on them, and generally 16½ in. long, had been imported from England in uniform sizes to be worked, with marvellous skill and effect, into the detailed work which a wonderfully dexterous master-mason at Dublin was devising.

Study of what the building can show us, and which is in no written record, tells us that the original plan and general design was one of a masterly mind, beautifully cast and proportioned, original in conception, carried on with an eye to the original plan, from 1190 to 1235, with admirable skill in moulding and details, where the master-mason was a power, but with such abominable execution by the building mason, such jerry building, in fact, such miserable pretence of mortar, and rubbish filling of walls and piers, as, perhaps, has never been seen in any medieval building of a high class. Mr. Precentor Seymour has mentioned how, when a hole was made in the nave piers, the hearting of rubbish gushed out as sand would run in a sand glass. This fine architectural detail, with its bad building, prepares us for such a catastrophe as the fall and ruin of the nave in 1562.

To return now to what the excavated chapter-house can specially tell us of the manner of men that used it, as of those who built it. I have no doubt in my mind in marking the monastic community for whom this noble and refined church and monastery building was imported from England — an architectural exotic — as an uncultured, lazy and indifferent lot, unworthy of what the English invaders and their refined, cultured and travelled ally, St. Laurence O'Toole, archbishop of Dublin, and his Norman successors, Cumin and Luke, had provided for them.

St. Laurence O'Toole changed the old secular community into a branch of the Order of Arroasian canons. When I tell this, most people, and some good antiquaries, ask what are Arroasian canons, and when I reply that I believe they were monks of the reformed Augustinian Order, hailing from Arrouaise in Flanders, people are puzzled to know what brought them to

Dublin. I venture to think, although I have no help from that wonderfully intuitive reader of Irish ecclesiastical history, Professor Stokes, that Laurence O'Toole, the cultured scholar and churchman, far in advance of his countrymen, a lover of architecture, travelled, and with the glory of God and reform of his barbarous surroundings in his foremost thoughts, imported the monks of Arrouaise for the sake of their *music*. It is thus stated in the Life of St. Laurence by Messingham:[2]

> He made regular singers to stand around the altar that they might praise the name of the Lord; and he introduced order to the celebrations, and to their sound — sweet measures [harmonies].[3]

Here is, I think, the record of the first introduction of choral worship of advanced culture into the barbarous Norse-Celtic Church, since maintained throughout 700 years, through good and evil times, with marvellous vitality, and as a model of churches to our day, in the home of its original establishment at Christ Church Cathedral, Dublin. The excavations at the chapter-house continue to give us a hint of what kind of men were the community thus established. I take them to have been both a lazy and an unlettered sort of men. Dr. Todd has noted in his editions of the Book of Obits at a later period, their astonishing ignorance of the Latin tongue.

There was evidence of the remains of a beautiful tesselated floor, and that a stage 3 ft. wide, with a riser made of fine tiles 3 in. thick, had run along the north and south walls and across the west end. At a very early period the monks began to break up the tesselated pavement to make burials. In the place of honour in the centre, at the east end, was found a remarkable coped tomb of black calp stone, with an Early English floriated cross on it.[4] A tantalizing fragment of an illegible inscription remained. Who may have been this important ecclesiastical personage so located? It was none of the bishops of the early period, for their burial-places are matters of record. I have gathered on the authority of Mr. Wakeman, that no longer ago than about 1826 this interment was broken into and a low mitre, ring and ornaments found in it conveyed to the late Father Spratt. A sketch of the mitre was made for me by Mr. Wakeman. In the grave — a stone-built coffin — I found the bones of several burials tumbled in, and a small bronze fibula which had no doubt fastened a vestment; a fragment of gold and filigree work, probably from a mitre, and a quantity of the fish-bone pins used for fastening grave clothes. Is it unreasonable to assign this tomb to the most important personage of the community after the archbishops — namely William fitz Raymond, eldest son of Raymond le Gros, who is said, in later life, to have retired to the cloister, taken orders, and died prior of the Holy Trinity?

On his right hand at the south side lay the Early English effigy of a lady

— of the 'foreign' stone. The careless community had shown it little respect. The features of the face were worn and obliterated by the feet of its members who had taken their seats above it — by chancellors, who in the scheme of evolution were the early predecessors of our perfected Dr. Tisdall. Are we exceeding the bounds of conjecture in naming for the occupant of this much-honoured grave — Basilia, sister of Strongbow, and wife of Raymond le Gros? This grave also had been rifled. Then we observe how the community continued to break up the floor, for we found it all occupied with burials systematically ranged and embedded in a kind of putty of blue clay, doubtless for sanitary considerations. Probably the affiliated 'brothers and sisters of the congregation' of this curiously constituted community paid handsomely for these first-class locations of honour in the chapter-house. The names and the benefactions of many of them are doubtless in the record of the Book of Obits of Christ Church.

It was noted — as a matter of interest for certain dental surgeons who visited the excavations — that the brothers and sisters of the congregation observed the excellent practice of carrying remarkably fine and perfect sets of teeth of their own to their graves with them. It was observed by me too that it was a frequent, if not universal, custom to bury with the deceased a copper token bearing on obverse and reverse an emblem of the Holy Trinity. I exhibit two or three saved from a number; one is still wrapped in a fragment of cloth in which it was found. I have enlarged some of the quaint and beautiful devices, and we have adopted them for marking our books, binding and furniture extensively, and so perpetuate them.

Further, in evidence of the careless laziness characteristic of the community, it was to be read by an attentive eye that from the day the Somerset masons gave up their finished work, one decent bit of workmanlike renewal or repair had never been attempted. Where it was wanted — a patching of coarse mortar or plaster was thought good enough. Notably could be read the occurrence of the burning in 1253. These lazy monks did not take the trouble even to clear out the building after the fire. They left the job for us, and we dug out charred timber and debris of a fire, containing encaustic tiles and some of the original slates and ridge tiles. By the side of the chapter-house adjoining the transept we uncovered a flight of stone steps leading down to the crypt (which is still there); at its foot and in interstices of the masonry more charred remains, which, however, may have been traces of a store of charcoal.

On the other side of the chapter-house was opened up the slype, the passage known as Hell up to the early part of this century, and which was not a novelty. A door opened from it into the calefactory on the south side. Of the latter building three walls, east, west and north, and a portion of a turret stairs were found. The south side was probably open to the weather after the fashion in monastic plans of this type. At the foot of the turret stairs, under a flag, was found a small store of ancient liquor bottles, one still containing liquid. A glass of it was tried upon a too-willing bystander, with the effect that he will probably never desire to try unknown liquors again in his lifetime. Experts at Guinness's Brewery pronounced it to be probably the decomposed remains of a malt liquor.

The further excavations revealed the walls of the cloister walks on the east, west and north sides of the garth. I had before found a wall of the *domus conversorum* on the east side, and identified the priory gateway. Reading's map told the rest of what was to be recovered of the monastery plan.

To finish what may be said about the chapter-house. Good people counselled me to dig deeper at the east end for further finds. 'We had not nearly reached the original ground line', it was said. 'The window sills were not originally but a few inches above the ground.' I heeded them not, as I felt sure enough. I can now call in to witness my predecessor in office, that 'Sir' Peter Lewis, architect and proctor of Christ Church, and chanter likewise, who built up the nave wall after the catastrophe in 1562, and likewise built the bridge of Athlone, and whose effigies and record may be interviewed in the crypt of the Royal Irish Academy to this day. Sir Peter had his own hard times in keeping up Christ Church in its forlorn and dilapidated state, and a plentiful scarcity of money to do it wherewithal. His laments are quaint and pathetic if I had room to quote them. I confine myself to this entry of his, bearing on the east window levels, under the date of 'Fryday last of Aug.': 'Not. this day I made a bargain wth an Englyse boy, a glayssor, for the Chapter-house *that the doggs had brocken*'.[5]

Next in the history of the chapter-house was noted a rough tile floor laid upon the accumulated rubbish at the level of the monks' seats, and serving as the floor when the building was secularized, and subsequently, as we know, used as the merchants' exchange until 1770. We note that even then the secularizers feared to disturb the ancient burials. They covered up the effigy and tomb which we found, and, in the cloister garth itself, those who built the law courts in 1610 had evidently an eye to popular feeling about desecration of graves, for they laid a great cradle of massive oak beams on them, and built their walls on these without digging foundations. As this construction rotted, it is intelligible how these buildings fell into dilapidation, with many settlements and fissures (although solidly built) within a century after their foundation.

The chapter-house, abandoned by the merchants in 1770, was by the dean and chapter of that day filled in with more rubbish. The ends were pulled down to make a picturesque ruined gateway, with a paved carriage drive above the level of the window sills (Fig. 27). What was above ground was finally removed between 1826 and 1831, when awful havoc was being done

27 Christ Church Cathedral from the south-east, *c.* 1791. The larger archway to the left is formed from the remains of the medieval chapter-house, while the smaller slype once gave access to the monastic cloister.

in the cathedral — in the name of restoration — under Bishop and Dean Lindsay, by a barbarous and ignorant architect of the name of Baker. They added their quota of more filled-in rubbish, bringing the cloister site to a level of 5 ft. above the ancient one, and created the dreary desolation of the space which we have known as Christ Church yard.

Are we wiser in our generation in digging up what they buried out of sight? Are the trivial facts I have noted in this paper of value towards our better practical understanding of that great period of our nation's history, of which Christ Church Cathedral is eminently the monument and record; a period — as Mr. Stokes has so charmingly unfolded in his latest book, *Ireland and the Anglo-Norman Church* — when the impulses were stirring which for good and evil laid the social lines of the history of the Ireland we dwell in? Was it worth while to remove many thousands of tons of rubbish, and lay down the lines of the ancient cloister garth again, to patch and preserve the remains of the chapter-house, set a few seats about, and invite the poor and infirm, the little children and the unemployed, to come within the old sanctuary boundary and take what rest and recreation out of it they could? The response from those sorts of our community who throng it daily does not seem doubtful. I feel but too sure of the indulgent verdict of the members of our Society. I do not much trouble myself about those others who cannot enter into our prejudiced views about such things, and who continue to make merry over the digging of a big hole in Christ Church precinct, and the building of a 'Gothic rockery' in it.

The town walls of Dublin

PATRICK HEALY

The City of Dublin, like most important medieval towns, was enclosed by stone walls and protected at intervals with towers and gates. It is not known for certain when these defences were first erected, but if we can accept the evidence of the contemporary account of the Norman invasion in 1170, the city was at that time enclosed by walls, and had at least two gates and the local ruler's hall.

There are many references in documents of the 13th and 14th centuries to the walls, gates and towers of Dublin, but the most important by far, in this respect, is a report written in 1585 for the lord deputy, Sir John Perrot, in which the circuit of the walls is described in extraordinary detail, starting at the Bermingham Tower and finishing at Dame's Gate. In this survey each gate and tower is described in sequence, giving the shape, length, breadth, height and thickness of the walls. It gives the number of storeys and whether they were vaulted or lofted, the number of windows or loop-holes in each storey and the direction in which they were pointing. The length of wall between each tower or gate is also given, with the height and thickness, the depth of the city ditch, and whether or not there was a ramp of earth against the inside of the wall and a stone buttress against the outside. The walled area extended along the Liffey from Parliament Street to St. Augustine Street and in depth as far back as the castle, St. Nicholas Place and Lamb Alley, the greatest length being 800 yards (less than half a mile), the width 400 yards, and the area enclosed 44 acres.

The Poddle river at that time flowed down Patrick Street as far as St. Nicholas's Gate, where it turned eastward along the ditch outside the town walls to Dublin Castle. The wall here was 28 ft. high, 7 ft. thick and had a ramp of earth against the inside 20 ft. high. The Poddle flowed along the southern and eastern sides of the castle and crossed under Dame Street into a small inlet of the Liffey. The wall along the Liffey is said to have been built at the time of the Bruce invasion in 1317 to replace an earlier wall, part of which still stands in Cook Street.

The names of the individual towers, and to some extent those of the gates, changed constantly throughout the centuries, according to the owner, occupier, or use to which they were put. The reconstruction shown on the map

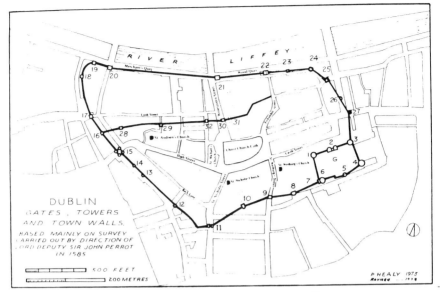

28 Map of the gates, towers and town walls.

KEY: 1. Cork Tower; 2. Castle Gate; 3. Storehouse Tower; 4. Record Tower; 5. Middle Tower; 6. Bermingham Tower; 7. turret; 8. Stanihurst's Tower; 9. Pole Gate; 10. Genevel's Tower; 11. St. Nicholas's Gate; 12. Round Tower; 13. Sedgrave's Tower; 14. Watch Tower; 15. Newgate; 16. Brown's Castle; 17. Gormond's Gate; 18. William Harbard's Tower; 19. William Usher's House; 20. Bridge Gate; 21. Prickett's Tower; 22. Fyan's Castle; 23. Case's Tower; 24. Isolde's Tower; 25. Buttevant Tower; 26. Bise's Tower; 27. Dame's Gate; 28. Fagan's Castle; 29. St. Audoen's Gate; 30. King's Gate; 31. wall located in 1969 excavation; 32. Mac Gilla Mo Cholmóc's Gate.

(Fig. 28) is based mainly on Perrot's survey and the names used by him have generally been adopted. The map of Dublin published by Speed in 1610 shows the general layout of the streets and walls, but it does not attempt to illustrate the details given by Perrot 25 years earlier. Many of the towers omitted by Speed are shown as still existing on detailed plans made more than a century and a half later.

Dublin Castle

The castle stood at the south-eastern corner of the town walls, and was itself enclosed by a curtain wall and ditch. It could thus remain impregnable to an enemy who had gained entry to the city, as happened during the rising of Silken Thomas in 1534. The erection of the castle was started in 1204, but was not completed for many years. It was a rectangular enclosure with a circular tower at each corner and a gateway in the centre of the north wall.

No. 1 Cork Tower: This was at the north-western corner. It fell down in

1624 and was rebuilt in 1629 at the expense of the earl of Cork whose coat of arms it bore. It was demolished during the 18th century.

No. 2 Castle Gate: This was located at the existing entrance in Castle Street. It had two round towers, between which were a gate, portcullis and draw-bridge. The towers were rebuilt in 1617 and were finally demolished during the 18th century. The turret on the Genealogical Office is built on the remains of the western tower. The engraving which appears in J. Derricke's *The Image of Ireland* (1581) shows the lord deputy, Sir Henry Sidney, leaving Dublin Castle (Fig. 29). This includes details of the entrance gateway and of the Cork Tower, as well as a view up Castle Street with Christ Church Cathedral in the background.

No. 3 Storehouse Tower: This was at the north-eastern corner. It had more windows than the other towers, and was sometimes used as a residence by the lord deputy. Lord Sussex in the 16th century removed the roof covering in order to make a platform for cannon. It was also known as the Powder Tower and was demolished in 1711.

No. 4 Record Tower: This tower still stands at the south-eastern corner of the castle. It was also known as the Black Tower and as the Wardrobe Tower. It is a massive circular tower three storeys high with walls 10 ft. thick. The battlements were added in 1819. It was from here that Red Hugh O'Donnell escaped in 1591.

No. 5 Middle Tower: This was a small turret mid-way along the south curtain wall. It was demolished some time before 1766 and a polygonal tower, which still stands, was erected on the site.

No. 6 Bermingham Tower: This stood near the south-western corner of the castle. It was built in the 14th century and was used as a prison and for the storage of records. In 1775 it was damaged by an explosion of gunpowder and was rebuilt two years later on the original sloping base. There are also some remains of the original curtain wall between this and the Middle Tower.

29 Engraving of the departure of the lord deputy, Sir Henry Sidney, from Dublin Castle, 1581.

No. 7 Small Turret: West of the Bermingham Tower and joined to it was this small tower which protected the corner of the castle wall. It stood beside the gateway in Ship Street. According to W. Harris's *History of Dublin* (1766) there was a postern gate named St. Austin's Gate, which gave access from Ship Street to Castle Street. This is not mentioned by Perrot and was probably located where the existing entrance to the Castle Steps now stands.

The outer town wall and gates

No. 8 Stanihurst's Tower: This was 65 yards from the Bermingham Tower; it was round outside the wall and three storeys high. It was named from James Stanihurst, recorder of Dublin, who owned the adjoining property. The remains of this tower and wall, refaced in cut stone, can still be seen on the northern side of Ship Street. An old woodcut used to illustrate Richard Stanihurst's *History of Ireland* (1577) shows the attack on Dublin Castle from Ship Street by Silken Thomas in 1534. Richard was the son of James Stanihurst and must have been very familiar with the view which he illustrates.

No. 9 Pole Gate: This gate was in Werburgh Street near the corner of Ship Street. It was 56 yards from Stanihurst's Tower, the wall between them still surviving behind Pappin's yard in Ship Street. The Pole Gate was a square tower, the first storey vaulted with a portcullis for the gate, and it was so named from a pool which formed here in the River Poddle. The tower was let to various tenants: to Thomas Bellew in 1491 at an annual rent of 8*d.* in silver; to Nicholas Yonge in 1600; and to the Corporation of Barber Surgeons in 1661 at £5 yearly, reserving the portcullis room for the city in time of danger.

No. 10 Genevel's Tower: From the Pole Gate the wall skirted the southern side of Darby Square for 62 yards as far as a three-storied tower, round outside the wall and square within. This was Genevel's Tower, so named from the adjoining Genevel's Inns, the property of Sir Henry Genevel whose wife Maud Lacey died in Dublin in 1302. The tower was occupied in 1585 by Mr. Parkins and in 1603 it was let to Richard Durninge at 2*s.* per annum. It was located just inside the Corporation gate in Ross Road.

No. 11 St. Nicholas's Gate: From Genevel's Tower to St. Nicholas's Gate was 84 yards, the line of wall cutting across Ross Road to the southern end of Nicholas Street at St. Nicholas Place where the gate was situated. This gate was three storeys high, and had two round towers outside the walls and two square ones within, with a portcullis for the gate. In 1466 William Meyler, cutler and keeper of the town clock, was granted as his wages the toll of wood at the Pole Gate and St. Nicholas's Gate, or as much as comes to the sum of 13*s.* 4*d.* yearly. According to the Corporation rental of 1763

Robert Rochford was paying £4 a year for a building over St. Nicholas's Gate. It was on this gateway that the head of Luke O'Toole of Castlekevin, lord of Fertire, was impaled by the Parliamentarians.

No. 12 Round Tower: From St. Nicholas's Gate to the Round Tower was 104 yards, the wall being on the line of the old wall which now separates St. Joseph's Night Shelter from Powers Square. The tower was only 16 ft. high and was filled with earth. In 1585 it was held by Sir William Sarsfield. Its position is marked on a deed map of 1780 showing that it was located on the site behind 10 John Dillon Street. Part of the wall here was 16 ft. high with ground 9 ft. high within, and part was 16 ft. high with a bank of soil 15 ft. thick of equal height.

No. 13 Sedgrave's Tower: From the Round Tower to Sedgrave's Tower was 113 yards, the ditch outside the wall being 19 ft. deep. The tower was two storeys high with stairs into it from the wall. It was occupied in 1585 by Christopher Sedgrave. It was usually known as the Hanging Tower because it leaned outwards over the city ditch.

No. 14 Watch Tower: From Sedgrave's Tower to the Watch Tower was only 30 yards and both towers were located on the northern side of Lamb Alley. The Watch Tower was 26 ft. high with stairs inside leading to the top, and it was so called because a sentry stood there watching over Newgate Jail. In 1618 Alderman Thadee Duffe was given a lease at an annual rent of 2*s.* Irish.

No. 15 Newgate: From the Watch Tower to Newgate was 40 yards, the wall following the northern side of Lamb Alley, where a considerable portion still stands to the original height and thickness. According to Perrot's survey there was no ramp here against the inside of the wall, but houses were built against the wall. Newgate had a circular tower at each corner, with a gate and portcullis in between. Lettings of the cellars and towers were made: in 1189 to Henry Mausanure; in 1199 to Roger de Limminstr; and during the following century to Ranulph de Salle, Roger de Asshebourne and Ralph de Leycaster.

In 1485, under a grant of Richard III, the city jail was established in Newgate. Five years later it was ordained by the assembly that 2*s.* in silver were to be paid each year to the keeper of every gate in the walls of the city, except Newgate which the jailer of the city for the time being should keep.

No. 16 Brown's Castle: About 60 yards from Newgate was Brown's Castle, four storeys high and named from Sir Richard Brown who was elected mayor in 1614, 1615 and 1620. It stood about the middle of the vacant site between Upper Bridge Street and St. Augustine Street. This tower is described in many early documents as the tower at the corner of the old wall, i.e. the earlier wall which lay along the southern side of Cook Street. During the 13th century it was granted first to John Garget and later to Roger de

30 Brown's Castle, 1792. The predecessor of this tower stood at the north-western angle of the Hiberno-Norse defences, commanding the approach to the bridge from the south.

Asshebourne. In 1492 it was held by Reynold Talbot and in 1585 by Nicholas FitzSimons.

A drawing of this tower made in 1792 was published by Grose (Fig. 30), who repeats the rather ambiguous statement made by Harris that 'it was within the verge of the Marshalsea of the Four Courts, commonly called the Black Dog'. This has led many to identify Brown's Castle incorrectly with the Black Dog prison, which actually stood 20 yards to the east of it.

No. 17 Gormond's Gate: The next was Gormond's Gate, 47 yards from Brown's Castle. It stood in the street named Wormwood Gate, near the corner of St. Augustine Street, and was two storeys high, vaulted and had a portcullis for the gate. It was built some time before 1280 and appears to have been named from William Gudmund, who was living near by in 1233. It was granted in 1556 to Peter Carrick, in 1573 to William Barrene, and in 1582 to Nicholas Ball. In 1593 the Corporation of Smiths and Goldsmiths got a lease for 61 years, which was renewed in 1640 and 1653.

In 1571 it was agreed that two privies were to be built, one east of Mr. Fyan's new tower and the other over the millstream outside Gormond's Gate. This explains very clearly the origin of the name of the street outside Gormond's Gate, which is still known as Mullinahack (the Shitty Mill). During the 17th century the name of the gate became corrupted to Ormond's Gate and subsequently to Wormwood Gate.

No. 18 William Harbard's Tower: From Gormond's Gate to the tower held by William Harbard was 103 yards. This tower was two storeys high with the upper storey vaulted. Its location was at the rear of the Brazen Head Hotel in Bridge Street. It was held in 1584 by Thomas Cheyvers, in 1585 by

William Harbard, in 1598 by the widow Harbard, and in 1605 by Christopher Cosgrave.

No. 19 William Usher's House: From this tower to Usher's House was 47 yards, the latter being at or near the north-western corner of the town wall, where it met the Liffey. In 1284 William de Nottingham was granted a stone tower near Ostman's Bridge and joining the tower beyond Ostman's Gate. In 1310 Geoffrey de Morton was given permission to build a tower at the town end of the great bridge of Dublin and another at the corner of the town wall to the west of the said bridge, and between them to build an embattled house. He built this house in such a way as to prevent access to the city wall and the house was ordered to be unroofed. In 1317 John de Grauntsete got permission to restore the roof, reserving a passage to the wall for the citizens.

No. 20 Bridge Gate or Ostman's Gate: From Usher's House to Bridge Gate was 35 yards. This gate defended the bridge across the Liffey at Bridge Street and was two storeys high, with the lower storey vaulted. First mentioned in 1200, it was granted to Ralph le Hore about 1236, to William de Nottingham in 1284, and was rebuilt in 1310 by Geoffrey de Morton. In 1595 Bridge Gate was in danger of falling and an order for it to be repaired at Usher's expense was issued. This caused a dispute which was resolved by each party depositing £500 and appointing a representative to act on an arbitration board. The gate was rebuilt in 1598 when a slab bearing the arms of Queen Elizabeth and the date was placed upon it. A public clock was erected in 1573.

No. 21 Prickett's Tower: From Bridge Gate along Merchants' Quay to Prickett's Tower was 281 yards. There appears to have been no continuous wall here, but the quay was 9 ft. high from the channel to the pavement. A tower is mentioned here 'on the bank outside and opposite the King's Gate' in the 13th century, when it was granted to John le Warre. In 1585 it was occupied by Mr. Prickett. This tower was located at the bottom of Winetavern Street; it was 34 ft. high, with a turret on the top.

No. 22 Fyan's Castle: This was 119 yards along Wood Quay from Prickett's Tower. It was four storeys high and was situated at the bottom of Fishamble Street. It is first mentioned in 1305 and was granted to John Marcus in 1455. In 1557 the castle was granted to Richard Fyan, alderman, at 18*d.* a year, and in 1614 it was purchased by Richard Barry. In 1605 Richard Proudfoote had reclaimed some land east and north of Fyan's Castle, which was granted to him by the city. The castle was later known as Proudfoote's Castle.

No. 23 Case's Tower: This was a small round tower two storeys high and was 48 yards from Fyan's Castle. It was situated on Essex Quay nearly opposite St. Michael & John's Church. It was granted in 1471 to Robert FitzSymon on condition that he repair it with stone and lime, and roof it with oak and slates. It was still held by this family in 1585. A few years later, in 1604, it is referred to as Case's Tower.

No. 24 Isolde's Tower: This was also a round tower 40 ft. high and was situated in Lower Exchange Street, then known as Blind Quay, and 58 yards from Case's Tower. It was granted in 1558 to the Corporation of Bakers and in 1602 to Jacob Newman, with permission to sue the bakers for causing the ruin of the tower.

No. 25 Buttevant Tower: This is described as an old square ruinous tower with one vault. It was so named from the French, meaning 'forward tower', and was 35 yards from Isolde's Tower. It was granted in the 13th century to William Picot. In 1563 it was held by John Money, bellman; in 1574 by Robert Byce; and in 1662 by John Byce. In 1675 a new gateway was required towards the east, and this was accomplished by demolishing Buttevant Tower and erecting the new gate on the site. This was called Essex Gate and was located in the short thoroughfare of that name beside Parliament Street.

No. 26 Bise's Tower: This was a three-storied half-round tower, 63 yards from Buttevant Tower and so named because it adjoined Mr. Bise's house, to whom it was granted in 1574. It was held by Christopher Bise in 1608 and John Bise in 1639. Its situation was in the middle of Parliament Street, about two-thirds of the way up, and it was demolished in 1763 when that street was laid out.

No. 27 Dame's Gate: From Bise's Tower to Dame's Gate was 36 yards. The latter was located at the top of Dame Street, opposite the entry into Palace Street. It was named from the adjoining church of St. Mary del Dam, and before the Reformation a statue of the Blessed Virgin stood in a niche over the gate. It had two towers and a portcullis, and was one of the narrowest entries into the city. The tower was let to various tenants: in 1459 to William Grace, goldsmith; in 1469 to John Roche, tailor; and in 1543 to Richard FitzSimon. In 1574 it was let to Robert Bise, along with Buttevant Tower and the tower in between, and held by this family down to later than 1662. The gateway was demolished in 1698. From Dame's Gate the town wall joined the castle at the Storehouse Tower. This completes the circuit of the outer wall of the city, but there were also a number of gateways in the inner north wall along Cook Street.

The inner town wall and gates

No. 28 Fagan's Castle: From Brown's Castle (no. 16) the earlier wall ran eastward to a gate named Fagan's Castle, which stood in Page's Court. This passage led from Cornmarket to Cook Street, and both passage and castle were still standing in 1788, but not a trace now survives.

No. 29 St. Audoen's Gate: The next gate to Fagan's Castle was St.

Audoen's, the only surviving gateway of the city. A part of the wall also remains along the southern side of Cook Street. In 1552 the country butchers were directed to sell their meat under the tower next to St. Audoen's Church. The tower was let in 1602 to the master of the tanners, who continued to meet there down to the middle of the 18th century. It was later occupied by the publishers of the *Freeman's Journal* from 1764 to 1782. The Corporation in 1880 condemned the tower, and would have demolished it, had it not been for the public outcry that was raised over this suggestion. It was subsequently restored, but without much regard for the original design.

No. 30 King's Gate: Near the top of Winetavern Street stood King's Gate, which is marked on Speed's map of 1610. It was later known as Winetavern Gate and is referred to in 1701 as Winetavern Gate House. From King's Gate the town wall continued to the east where it has recently been exposed during excavations carried out by the National Museum.

The portion that was excavated in 1969-73 was 5 ft. thick and 6 ft. high above the foundations. The inner face was very roughly built with little mortar, but the outer face was of the finest rubble masonry built in courses, and had close mortared joints that would give no finger hold to a person trying to climb over the wall from the outside. The wall had been built on the old stony beach and in several places platforms of flagstones survived, upon which the mortar had been mixed.

Although this inner wall is not mentioned in Perrot's survey of 1585 it must, even at that time, have served as a second line of defence. Since there was no continuous wall along the quays an enemy with ships at his command could have effected an entry here at full tide, in which event the presence of the inner wall would have confined him to that quarter of the city.

No. 32 Mac Gilla Mo Cholmóc's Gate: Further to the west was another gate which stood at the bottom of Mac Gilla Mo Cholmóc's Street, now St. Michael's Close. This is mentioned in a 12th-century deed, but no further information about it is available.

Maintenance and repair

The maintenance and repair of the walls were a constant source of trouble to the city fathers. During the 15th century annual royal grants were made for the defence of the city, but subsequent funds appear to have come from the city coffers. Consequently repairs were put off from year to year until some emergency would force the city council into action. There was also endless trouble with postern gates, cut through the walls by those whose premises adjoined the town wall, and these were regularly ordered to be stopped up or fitted with iron gratings. The filling of the city ditch was another source of annoyance, the near-by tenants depositing the filth from their dwellings and the butchers the offals from their slaughterhouses into the ditch. In addition those who lived outside continually encroached on the ditch, especially the inhabitants of Francis Street.

In 1536 the king was requested to supply six falcons (small cannon), one for each of the city gates. In 1580 it was directed that all houses, cottages, walls and gardens built within 20 yards of the city wall were to be demolished. In 1598, after their victory at the Yellow Ford, the power of the Ulster chieftains threatened even this stronghold of the Pale. The civil regulations for the defence of Dublin give a vivid picture of the anxiety of the citizens and are a fitting extract with which to close this paper. Thirty-four night watchmen were to patrol within the walls. All the postern gates of the city were to be stopped up with lime and stone. Two men by night and two men by day were to guard each gate. If an alarm sounded the wicket gate was to be opened to let in the women and children, but no man of the suburbs was to be admitted:

1598, November 8. At a meeting this day of the Mayor and aldermen it was resolved, for the more safety of this city, that the several gates shall be shut every night at five of the clock, and the wickets stand open till six, and then the keys to be brought to the Mayor. And, for the better warning to be given to all men to take knowledge hereof, the Mayor is to make proclamation and will all Saint Audoens bells to knoll, to begin half an hour later and hold till six, by which those that have charge of the keys may the better keep their time of bringing the same to the Mayor, etc.

It was likewise agreed that twenty-four faithful and sufficient men should be hired by the several wards within the city to watch the walls and gates in the form following, videlicet: at either gate two, whereof one to be placed at the top of the gate, at the castle of the Crane one man; upon the tower in Mr. Stanihursts background one man; upon the tower at Jenevylls Inns, one man; upon the wall betwixt Saint Nicholas gate and New gate in three several places most convenient, three men; uppon the tower in John Cars background, one man; uppon the tower in the Widow Habards background, one man; and the little new tower in Mr. Ushers background, one man; which men, being furnished with armour and weapons, shall begin the watch every night at six, and continue till six in the morning.

Seventeenth-century plans of Dublin Castle

J . B . M A G U I R E

The mandate for the building of Dublin Castle was issued in 1204.[1] Having commenced life as a medieval fortress, it retained its appearance until the latter part of the 17th century. In its former state it bore no resemblance to the castle with which we are familiar today, and the layout of buildings within its walls was also totally different.

From the time the ancient structures disappeared, many of the historians who made a study of the castle tried to discover where the various buildings were located. Written accounts told them what accommodation existed, but without maps or drawings for guidance the accounts were nearly always misinterpreted and this invariably led to wrong conclusions about siting. Among the mysteries which occupied historians from time to time were the location of the Great Hall of Henry III,[2] the position of the postern gate in the east curtain wall,[3] and the site of the ancient chapel.[4]

The scarcity of reliable graphic evidence dating from earlier than the 18th century was responsible for this lack of knowledge. Gilbert in his *History of the Viceroys of Ireland* states: 'No precise particulars have been transmitted to us of the architectural design or arrangements of the castle of Dublin, but several entries respecting it, are scattered through official records'.[5]

Speed's map of Dublin (1610) was used for reference by some (Fig. 13), but this was worse than useless as far as the castle was concerned because it was totally inaccurate and led many astray.[6] Of the accurate maps which became available the most widely known was Thomas Phillips's survey of the castle, 1685 (Fig. 31).[7] This showed the walls and towers but unfortunately omitted the buildings within. The survey appears to have been carefully made but the angle of the east curtain wall is slightly inaccurate: this was discovered when the face of the wall was exposed during the rebuilding of the Cross Block between 1961 and 1964.

Another, lesser known, plan is the one in the possession of the National Library of Ireland (Fig. 32).[8] Although it is roughly drawn and not to scale, it is very valuable because it names the principal buildings: the 'Deputies house' lies along the south wall and the 'Dep. kitchin yeard' adjoins; midway

194

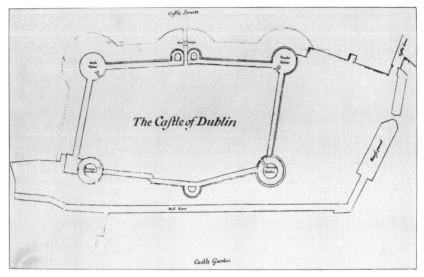

31 Thomas Phillips's plan of Dublin Castle, 1685.

along the west wall is the 'Hall', in the corners of which are the four courts of justice: Exchequer, Pleas, Chancery, and King's Bench. The prison and former prison lie next to the hall and adjacent to these; along the northern boundary is a building containing the offices of the remembrancer, the master of the rolls, and the auditor. The 'drawe bridge' is shown across the 'northe ditche' and to the left of this, inside the northern boundary, is the 'Counsel chamber'; also indicated is 'A great Court where the Artillery lies'.

The person who drew the map, however, made no attempt to show the form of the buildings accurately, and its value was further diminished by the fact that, until recently, it was undated.[9] Fortunately this latter point can now be settled, for by comparing the map with the text of the letter below (dated 1606) one can see that the facts contained in both tally completely, and I am satisfied that this plan is the 'plot' referred to in the last paragraph of the letter:

> The hall now in use in the Castle of Dublin is very fit but it is suggested to be inconvenient for greater respects. The same stands convenient from the Deputy's house without impediment, where there may be one gate broken down in the wall at the west end and a bridge framed to pass over the Castle ditch, by which plot may be avoided all inconveniences, for if the door at the east end of the same hall leading into the Castle be shut up, it makes a safety from any sudden surprisal of the rest of the Castle.

Or if there shall be a wall made at the east end to sever the hall from the rest of the Castle and thereby to include the several offices belonging to the courts adjoining to the hall, the same wall will divide his Majesty's house and the rest of the Castle from the hall, so as thereby no inconvenience in the kind of treason can ensue to impeach the State. But if one house lately built upon the entry of the passage now intending towards the new bridge does not hinder this proceeding, then this plot may be allowed whereby his Majesty may save the sum of 1,200L. now demanded. For I can direct how these works may be finished for 400L. so as the passage at the entry may be procured. . . .

Doubting that your lordship may not well understand my meaning, I have requested Mr. Wattson to demonstrate the same by a plot, for that he knows the situation of the Castle.[10]

In spite of its limitations the map does solve one mystery: it indicates very clearly the location of the Great Hall. It shows it, not as most people thought, on the site of the present St. Patrick's Hall, but at right-angles to the western curtain wall and more or less midway between the towers. The 'Deputies house' and the 'Counsel chamber' refer to the two buildings erected by Sir Henry Sidney, as the following report of 1570 shows:

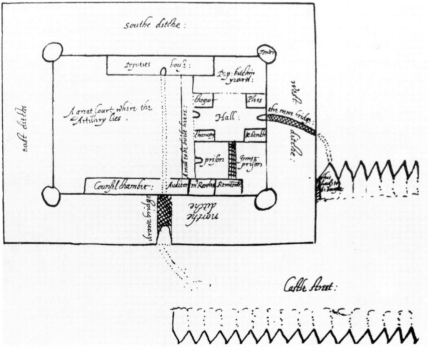

32 Wattson's plan of Dublin Castle, 1606.

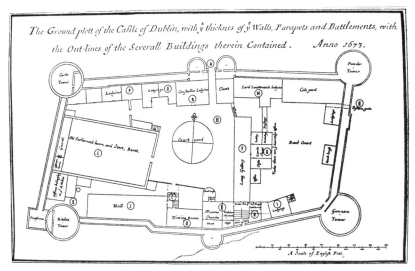

33 Anonymous plan of Dublin Castle, 1673.

By the Lord Deputy and Counsaill.

Henry Sidney,

Wheras ther haith ben erected of late within hir majestie's castell of Dublyn, certen lodging and outher fair and necessarie roulmes, boeth for a convenient plaice for the lord deputie's howse, and a fit seate for the placing and receiving of any gouvernour heraftir, as for the bettir and more commodious resorte and assembly of the counsaill. . . . [11]

The store of knowledge relating to the layout of the castle can now be supplemented, because another map, dated 1673, has come to light (Fig. 33). It is part of the manuscript collection of the earl of Dartmouth, housed at present in the Staffordshire Record Office. Another portion of the same collection, now in the Maritime Museum, Greenwich, contains three maps of Dublin and its harbour, also dated 1673, which are associated with the survey made in that year by Sir Bernard de Gomme, engineer-in-chief to Charles II. George Legge, later earl of Dartmouth, was a naval officer who then held the office of Lieutenant-general of the Ordnance. A letter to him, dated 1673, refers to this map of the castle.[12] The map helps to clear up most of the remaining mysteries. It shows the castle in its fully developed state, 11 years before the disastrous fire which was the direct cause of its metamorphosis.

To bring the layout more immediately alive it is best studied with the contemporary account of Robert Ware, who gives us what is, in effect, a guided tour of the entire castle complex.[13] For this purpose he is using the 'authentic records and the manuscript collections of Sir James Ware, Knt', his father (1678). Without the map, Ware's description is nearly impossible to follow,[14] but both documents together complement each other to a remarkable degree. I have inserted letters to make it easier to locate the buildings described.

> As you enter . . . [the castle] . . . you may be pleased to take notice that ye Constable of ye Castle holds ye Tower on each side of ye Castle gate [A] for ye custody of his Ma'ties prisoners. This Castle was built (att least the most part thereof) in the time of *Henry Loundres, Archbishop of Dublin* his government. It is furnished with great ordnances planted on the platformes of the severall Towers thereof.
>
> Thus you see this Cittadel well fortifyed against all emergencies being as commodious for its own defence, as it is convenient to succour the Cittie; though it was somewhat stronger when it was encompassed and fortifyed by the flowing of ye sea round about it.
>
> Let us now look upon it as it is the Kings Court and Pallace as you make your entrance into the Court [B], you may behould the beautifull forme of a fair building, unto which you ascend by a noble stayrcase [C] lately erected in the time of the Duke of *Ormond's* government under our Royall Soveraigne *Charles* the second since his most happy restauration.
>
> The next thing considerable is the dineing room [D] lately re-edifyed and raised to a stately height, together with all ye upper parts of ye building proportionably thereunto by the Earl of *Essex*.
>
> The next part of the Pallace contiguous hereunto is the chamber of presence, the Lobbies, and the chambers [E] thereunto appertaineing which, being an ancient structure, is thought to want reparation or rebuilding . . .
>
> From this building towards the Gate, extends itself a statelie structure on your left hand as you pass from the Gate to the Pallace door, erected in the time of the Lord Deputy *Falkland*, borne upon Pillars in the nature of a *Piazza*, a stately long Gallerie [F] and many other places [G] of conveniences for the chief Governour and his family.
>
> Contiguous unto this structure is another ancient piece of building,

wherein upon the ground is a Chappell, over which is a stately drawing-room [H] built in the time of *Sir Henry Sydney* his government whose armes are placed thereon.

Hereunto on the place of an old decayed building was lately raised a stately and convenient structure, contained within these walls by the Earl of *Essex*, whereon are fixed the Kings armes, and underneath his own coat of armes, in memory of his name; in this appartment [I] are the Lord Lieutenants private lodgings and the rooms thereunto apper-taineing, much more noble and convenient than formerly they have bene.

I have now described the front with such other buildings as are contiguous thereunto on the left hand of your Entrance into the Pallace; and on the right hand are the Hall [J], on the ground, the kitchen and other places belonging to the offices below staires, reaching as farre as *Berminghams* Tower [K].

Now hereunto on the right hand was an ancient structure [L] built after the forme of a Church, raised upon severall stately pillars in the lower part whereof was kept his Maiesties store, but the powder by God's admired providence was removed thence by order of that circumspect Governor of *Ireland* the lord *Roberts* a very short time before the fire which hapned in the time of Lord *Berkley* his government, the occasion and originall thereof is yet unknown, destroyed the said storehouse and upper loft of that famous building wherein was anciently kept his Maiesties Courts of Justice, and also were held both houses of Parliament, untill the wisedome of the State thought fitt to free the Castle from so great a concourse of people as usually frequented that great assembly, and to hold the last Parliament att *Chichester* house. The roof and lofts of this building being burned as aforesaid the most part of the Walls with the Arches were demolished in the time of the Earl of *Essex*, his Lieutenancy and the stones thereof disposed of by him towards the building of Saint Andrews Church.

This great structure [L] though built in the forme of a Church was anciently called the Hall of the Castle and had Iles thereunto belonging covered with lead, untill ye time of King Edward ye 4th who caused the same to be sold by the Treasurer of Ireland for repair of the said structure
. . .

I . . . shall therefore desire the reader to turne his face with mee to that side of the buildings, which are on the same side with the great Gate; where hee may behold, on the right hand as hee goes out of ye Pallace, the place of the Council chamber [**M**], and what other roomes belonged thereunto, of late converted into an appartment for the Lodging of such persons of the Chief Governours household as are consigned thereunto. And on the other side of the Gate hee may place his eye on the Constables Lodgings [**N**], very much beautified and reduced to the better accommodation of modern contrivance in the time of the Duke of *Ormond's* first Government after his Maiesties happy restauration, as also the appartment built of brick [**O**] in the time of the Earl of *Strafford*, for the accommodation of Sir George *Radcliff*, Bart. . . .

Next to this appartment are other more ancient brick buildings [**P**] in the same range under the Castle wall which were built in the time of King *James*, and are now within a Portall adioyneing to *Cork* Tower.

There were untill of late two sally ports or posterne Gates lying open; the one towards *Sheep Street*, the other towards ye Castle-yard, but that towards *Sheep Street* was closed up by order of the *Duke of Ormond*, upon occasion of the conspiracie of *Warren* and Jephson, who designed to make their treasonable entrance into the Castle by the surprize of that Port, since which time it hath bene stopt against all passage out or in to the Castle, the other Posterne Gate [**Q**] is still open, but secured by a constant Guard, which will permit you to descend thence into the Stable yard, where you may take delight in seeing the great horse ridden and managed by the rules of the best horsemanship, and of martiall skill, there also you may behold large statelie stables of an elegant contrivance built in ye time of ye Earl of *Strafford* as also a place designed for a mint, and other offices for the forgeing of Armes and other uses appertaineing to the stores there, also were built in the time of that vast minded Governour, a great store house for the keeping of all furniture belonging to Warre, the Office for the Ordnance is now kept at the issueing out of the said last mentioned postern Gate; and I have now no more to say concerneing the Castle in this place, or what appertains thereunto, then that there passeth through the Stable yard a full stream of water, issueing out of the Castle gardens which plentifully serves to all uses belonging unto the horse there kept, and to the severall artificers, and persons who minister to publique uses in that place.

There are additional marginal notes with the above text: opposite the reference to 'a stately long Gallerie' [**F**] is 'This Gallery built anno 1624'; where he mentions the chapel, Ware has the note 'The Chappel built by Sir

Henry Sydney anno 1567';[15] referring to apartment [I] he has a note saying
'The late addition that was built by Arthur Earl of Essex anno 1674', and
opposite the reference to the Hall [L] is 'A description of ye late storehouse
in ye Castle of Dublin which was burned in 1671'.

The building [E] which Ware refers to as an ancient structure, and which
the 'Clock house' adjoins on the map (Fig. 33), is part of the 'Deputies house'
(Fig. 32) built by Sidney. His 1570 report, already quoted, continues: 'We
have therfor thought fytt, that as well for the keaping of the said howse, and
roulmes newly erected, . . . as for the tending and keaping of the clocke
within the said castell, whiche requireth daily attendance to be tempred and
kept in frame, to appoint sume honest, carefull, and diligent person to take
that chardge in hand'.[16] The man who was given the job, George Arglass of
Dublin, was paid 16*d.* a day for the work.[17]

This reference to the buildings erected by Sidney brings to mind another
mystery connected with the castle. It concerns a Latin epigram, which was
carved in stone and mounted over one of the gateways. It was composed to
honour the erection of these buildings, and in particular the man responsible
for them:

> Nostro autem tempore, dum Henricus Sidneius, satrapas dignitatis
> plenissimus, vicarium principis munus in insula sustinebat, ampla &
> praeclara aedificia in castello exstructa erant. In hanc commemorabilem
> aedificationem nos iam olim hoc epigramma fecimus.

> Gesta libri referunt multorum clara virorum,
> Laudis & in Chartis stigmata fixa manent.
> Verum Sidnaei laudes haec saxa loquuntur,
> Nec iacet in solis gloria tanta libris.
> Si libri pereant, homines remanere valebunt,
> Si pereant homines, ligna manere queunt.
> Lignaque si pereant, non ergo saxa peribunt,
> Saxaque si pereant tempore, tempus erit.
> Si pereat tempus, minime consumitur aevum,
> Quod cum principio, sed sine fine manet.
> Dum libri florent; homines dum vivere possunt;
> Dum quoque, cum lignis, saxa manere valent;
> Dum remanet tempus, dum denique permanet aevum,
> Laus tua, Sidnaei, digna perire nequit.[18]

It was also the subject of a letter from Thomas Wentworth to the earl of
Leicester in 1633:

I confess I made a Fault against your noble Grandfather, by pulling down an Old Gate within this Castle, wherein was set an Inscription of his in Verses, but I did so far contemplate him again in his Grandchild as to give him the best Reparation I could, by setting up the very same Stone, carefully taken down, over the new one, which one Day your Lordship may chance to read, and remember both him and me by that Token.[19]

The mystery is where the gateway was located and what became of the stones eventually. According to Thomas Dineley they were still in position in the 1680s: 'Dublin Castle was first founded by John Comyn Archbishop of Dublin, and since beautified by Sr Henry Sydney then Lord Lieutenant Anno 1575 under Queen Elizabeth as appears by Inscripcon'.[20]

This is virtually the last glimpse of the castle in medieval form, so it is, perhaps, an appropriate note on which to end. As it is extremely doubtful whether we shall ever uncover the actual carved inscription, we must remain grateful for having the verses recorded in a book. It is only when we examine the epigram itself, however, that the irony of it all becomes apparent:

Books record the famous deeds of many men,
And marks of praise stay fixed in documents.
These stones do truly tell of Sidney's praise,
For such glory is not enshrined in books alone.
If books perish, people can remain,
Should people perish, timber can endure.
If timber perishes, stone will not therefore perish,
And should stone perish in time, time itself will be.
If time perishes, eternity will hardly be consumed,
Because it exists with a beginning, but without an end.
While books are flourishing; while people live;
While stone, with timber, is strong enough to last;
While time remains, and finally eternity endures,
Your worthy praise, O Sidney, cannot pass away.

The medieval sculpture of Christ Church Cathedral, Dublin

ROGER STALLEY

The invasion of Ireland by the Anglo-Norman armies in 1169-70 is not normally regarded as an event of any importance in the history of English art. Such an attitude is understandable, for Irish works in the Middle Ages rarely made any substantial contribution to artistic developments elsewhere. But the military activities of 1169-70 did have important results from an English point of view, since they greatly extended the 'geography' of English art and architecture. Following the Anglo-Norman conquest, Irish churches increasingly looked to England for ideas, and native styles were gradually supplanted by imported techniques. Very few of the standard histories of English architecture or sculpture devote much attention to this process, and a page or two describing the occasional Irish cathedral is normally deemed sufficient. Yet this does little justice to the Anglo-Norman achievement in Ireland, where, in just over a century, an immense amount of building was carried out. Most of this was English in style and ought to be considered within the context of English developments. Indeed, in some cases Irish evidence can considerably extend an understanding of specifically English problems: no study of West Country architecture, for example, would be complete without a parallel study of contemporary Irish work.

The transition from native to English styles can be seen in all types of architecture. It is particularly obvious in the cathedrals, several of which were totally rebuilt in the century after the conquest. The explanation for this interest in cathedral building lies in the Anglo-Normans' interpretation of the role and function of a cathedral in society. They had grander notions than the Irish of what a cathedral church should look like, and thus there was often a correlation between programmes of building and the appointment of Anglo-Norman bishops. By about 1230 at least ten of the Irish sees were occupied by Anglo-Norman ecclesiastics and remained in English hands for the rest of the century. In six of these sees — Dublin, Kildare, Ossory, Ferns, Meath, and Waterford — a major reconstruction of the cathedral took place soon after the appointment of the first Anglo-Norman (Fig. 34). In contrast, of 15 sees consistently held by Irishmen in the period, only two — Cashel and

34 Map of the diocesan structure of Ireland in the 13th century (after J.A. Watt).

Killaloe — had cathedrals which were rebuilt on a substantial scale, and both of these were in areas increasingly subject to Anglo-Norman influence.[1] This pattern of building illustrates the very different view held by the invaders of the importance of a cathedral. It coincides with their attempt to strengthen the diocesan structure of religious life in Ireland and, as in England after 1066, it shows that they were fully aware of the propaganda value of splendid new buildings. In both countries large and elaborate cathedrals provided visual symbols of the new régime.

The architectural changes, however, were not so abrupt as those in England after 1066. The conquest of Ireland was not a coherent and efficiently organized campaign directed by the Crown, and large areas, particularly in the west, remained outside Anglo-Norman control.[2] Even in areas of heavy settlement, the appointment of Anglo-Norman ecclesiastics was not as speedy or systematic as it had been in England.[3] Consequently, the transition from native to imported styles was relatively slow. Very little cathedral building was carried out by the Anglo-Normans in the first 30 years after the invasion, and the eastern limb of Christ Church, Dublin, is the only obvious example. The full effect of the invasion, therefore, was not felt until the early years of the 13th century, and this meant that there was a long period of overlap, probably as long as 50 years. While churches on the east coast reflected the latest techniques imported from England, further west churches continued to be erected in traditional Hiberno-Romanesque. A good example of this is Tuam Cathedral, head of the archdiocese covering the north-west of Ireland. In 1184 the Annals of Loch Cé record that the 'great church' of Tuam fell 'both roof and stone'.[4] Parts of the building reconstructed after this disaster remain and they include a highly elaborate chancel arch, carved in typical Hiberno-Romanesque fashion, with complex chevron arches and capitals carved in exceptionally shallow relief.[5] While Irish masons were cutting stone for this arch, over a hundred miles away in Dublin masons recruited from England were preparing to build the new choir for the cathedral in a very different style.

The problem of the overlap has not received much consideration from writers on Irish architecture, although it was briefly mentioned by Leask.[6] There has been a tendency to assume that almost all Hiberno-Romanesque buildings must date from before 1170. The chancel arch at Tuam, for example, has been variously assigned to *c.* 1170 and *c.* 1152,[7] despite the documentary evidence to the contrary. The generally slow spread of Anglo-Norman settlement in the west would in any case lead one to expect the long retention of traditional styles, and this is borne out by what documentary evidence survives. The choir of the Augustinian church of Ballintober is firmly dated to 1216-25,[8] and the inside jambs of the east windows have carving fully in the spirit of Hiberno-Romanesque. This includes masks cut in very shallow relief at capital level, with dragons leering at them each side.[9]

Another factor which must be remembered in assessing the impact of the invasion, is the degree of English influence before 1170. For over 40 years before the conquest Irish Romanesque sculptors had been aware of English methods. This contact is strikingly illustrated by the west doorway of St. Cronan at Roscrea, where the placing of a figure in a gable above the main arch closely corresponds to the arrangement at the Somerset church of Lullington.[10] Elements of the decoration of Cormac's Chapel at Cashel have also been traced to England,[11] and one should not forget the English origin of chevron, which proved so popular in Ireland. However, these imported ideas were absorbed into a distinctively Irish style, and although an occasional English mason might have found his way to Ireland before the conquest, Hiberno-Romanesque is obviously the product of native masons. The crucial change effected by the invasion, therefore, was not so much the arrival of English ideas but rather the arrival of groups of English craftsmen.

At the close of the 12th century, the presence in Dublin of English tradesmen and craftsmen of all kinds is well attested by a surviving list of citizens. This contains over 1,600 names, and in many cases the specific trade of the individual is mentioned. It provides an instructive cross-section of Dublin society, referring for example to goldsmiths, bakers, millers, fishermen, tanners, weavers, cordwainers, saddlers, smiths, butchers, vintners, etc. Eleven carpenters are mentioned as well as a certain Robert, *cementarius*. As Robert was undoubtedly English, this is the first clearly documented reference to an English mason in Ireland. The mention of only one mason at first sight seems strange, for there must have been many more in Dublin at the time. However, as the list mentions professions only occasionally, numerous masons may be included among the unidentified citizens.[12] There are three further rolls of names dating to the 13th century. These are much shorter and include just one reference to a mason, a certain Nicholas of Coventry, mentioned in a list of 1225-50.[13]

The late Romanesque sculpture

When one turns from documents to buildings, the first evidence for the work of such immigrant masons is to be found at Christ Church Cathedral. In fact, the choir and transepts are among the earliest surviving ecclesiastical work of the Anglo-Normans in Ireland, thus forming a landmark in the history of Irish architecture.[14] In view of the importance of the building, its modern state is rather depressing. At first glance it appears to be largely Victorian, and the exterior contains almost no medieval stonework at all. The condition of the fabric in the 19th century was so disastrous that a very substantial restoration proved essential. Inside the cathedral, rather more medieval masonry survives. The transepts are basically original, and one arch survives on each side from the 12th-century choir. The rest of the choir was demolished as long ago as the 14th century, though George Edmund Street tried to recreate it with a somewhat fanciful elevation.[15]

Judging from the surviving section, the late 12th-century design was undistinguished. It had a three-stage elevation with passages at both triforium and clerestory level. Pointed and round arches are mixed in a disconcerting way, and the arch of the triforium touches the base of the clerestory, giving

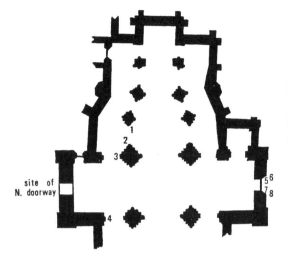

35 Christ Church Cathedral: plan of the choir and transepts showing the position of Romanesque capitals. KEY: 1. shepherd and two sheep; 2. fruit-pickers; 3. dragons and human busts; 4. entertainers; 5. men fighting monster beasts; 6. two birds; 7. two men with animals; 8. unidentified figure subject.

a very cramped appearance. The style is obviously English in character, although compared to contemporary work like that at Wells Cathedral it appears strikingly backward. There is little doubt that the building was carried out by masons brought from the Bristol Channel and Severn Valley area. Indeed, some of the stone was imported from the same region, from the quarry at Dundry just outside Bristol.[16] As long ago as 1882 Street gave a detailed list of all the architectural features which corresponded to those found in the west of England. As a result of his analysis, he concluded that 'the architecture of Glastonbury and Wells had an extraordinary influence not only in the south of England and in Wales, but equally throughout the Irish Pale and even beyond its circuit'.[17] But, curiously, Street did not discuss the sculpture of Christ Church in any detail. In the earliest parts of the building, in the somewhat dismal remnants of the late Romanesque choir and transepts, can be found several fine pieces of carving which include a number of historiated capitals. Since there is a relative dearth of such sculpture in England in the later 12th century, the Christ Church sculpture deserves to be better known. Moreover, its style provides an intriguing contrast with the work of contemporary Irish sculptors.

Capitals with animal or figure scenes represent only a small proportion of the total in the cathedral and they were restricted to the north transept and the north side of the choir (Fig. 35). Most of the remainder consist merely of foliage designs. Probably the earliest surviving capitals are those on the north side of the one remaining bay of the 12th-century choir. The arch of this bay has an inner order of chevron, resting on triple shafts, and the capitals form a continuous frieze stretching across all three shafts. The eastern capital depicts a shepherd and two sheep, one of which twists its neck to eat some

36 Christ Church Cathedral: choir, north arcade, capital with shepherds.

37 Christ Church Cathedral: choir, north arcade, capital with fruit-pickers.

leaves (Fig. 36). Opposite on the western capital is a more elaborate scene with fruit-pickers, who are collecting large succulent berries from branches above (Fig. 37). There are four fruit-pickers altogether, and one of them carries an oval basket with pointed ends, not unlike the fruit basket on the famous 'thieves' capital in the south transept at Wells Cathedral.[18] This similarity may reflect no more than contemporary fashions in fruit baskets, but it is significant that the capitals of Wells also depict a series of scenes from daily life, though not exactly the same scenes as those at Christ Church. Fruit-pickers had also appeared elsewhere in English Romanesque sculpture, on a capital at Castor (Northamptonshire) dated to 1124[19] and on another at Leominster (Herefordshire) dated to *c.* 1150.[20]

The style of these two Christ Church capitals points directly to Wells Cathedral. Unfortunately, they are both very worn, which renders precise comparison difficult. But the style of the figures does display a general similarity with that on the capitals of the north porch of Wells, depicting the martyrdom of St. Edmund. In the scene of the wolf presenting the head of St. Edmund to the saint's former retainers, some hints of the Christ Church style can be detected — the general proportions of the figures, the arrangement of drapery in clear, rounded pleats, and above all the sense of movement. The way St. Edmund's follower almost kneels to receive the saint's head recalls the kneeling poses of the Dublin fruit-pickers. A further similarity is the way the figures are perched somewhat precariously on the necking of the capital, leaning outwards at an angle. On the basis of the simpler type of foliage at Christ Church, it is tempting to regard the capitals there as somewhat earlier than those at Wells.

Not far from the fruit-pickers is one of the finest of the Dublin capitals, depicting dragons and human busts (Fig. 38). It is situated on the south side of the arch leading from the north transept into the north choir aisle. It rests

208

38 Christ Church Cathedral: north transept, capital with dragons and busts.

39 Wells Cathedral: south transept, east triforium, corbel with human bust.

on twin shafts and here the division of the shafts is continued into the capital above, which is neatly divided into two separate parts. Instead of the effect of a frieze, therefore, one gets the impression of two distinct capitals. Altogether there are four dragons entwining themselves around two human busts who peer out below the bodies of the monsters at the angles. The tail of each dragon is twisted around that of its neighbour, before being fastened to a hook. One claw of each beast grips the head of the unfortunate human bust, and the other is locked together with the neighbouring dragon. The heads of the dragons turn away to devour some neighbouring fruit, while the human busts wrench their arms backwards and clutch the wings of the dragons. The composition is complex and skilfully organized. If seen from an angle, a bust forms the centre of the composition framed by the beasts, but if studied frontally two symmetrically placed dragons are the dominant theme.

Fortunately, this capital is well preserved with far less sign of wear. An old drawing in the cathedral shows that the adjoining arch was partially blocked for a long period,[21] and the capital was probably walled up before its discovery in the restoration of 1871-8. Parts of the capital are deeply undercut, with relief as deep as $2-2\frac{1}{2}$ in.

The theme of two beasts either facing or turning away from each other is, of course, common in Romanesque art. The motif was especially popular in France where it sometimes appears associated with human busts as well. At Vézelay, for example, there is a capital (nave, north arcade, eighth pier from the east) on which four birds are depicted, each pair surrounding two men and biting the skull of one of them. Such compositions must have been very common in the pattern books of 12th-century masons. In England the best parallels for the Christ Church sculpture are again to be found at Wells. In the north triforium of the nave (eighth pier from the west) is a corbel with two affronted dragons whose heads are turned away to eat some neighbouring leaves, while their claws are fixed to the skull of a grotesque mask. The composition is not so tightly organized as at Christ Church; nor are there any human busts. But in the south transept at Wells, on another corbel at triforium level (east side, second pier from the north), can be found a bust remarkably close to those on the Christ Church capital, with arms wrenched back, diagonal folds over the shoulders, and deeply furrowed brows (Fig. 39). Thus both components of the Dublin capital can be traced at Wells. Once again the English sculpture looks rather later, particularly the corbel in the nave where the looser composition, unconstrained by any architectural form, lacks the specifically 'Romanesque' characteristics of the Christ Church carving.

On the western side of the north transept, on the north respond of the arch leading to the nave aisle, is a very battered capital which retains sufficient detail to show its original quality. Like the neighbouring dragon capital, it surmounts a pair of shafts, but here the division is not continued into the capital itself, and instead we are presented with a frieze of figures (Fig. 40). Unfortunately the capital is broken at the left corner, destroying two of the figures, but five more survive roughly intact. The scene depicted appears to be a troupe of entertainers. Three of them were once playing musical instruments, and at the right corner the viol of the leading musician is still clearly visible. The figure behind might have been clanging cymbals, and the gesture of the third musician leaves little doubt that he was playing some form of pipe. In front of the musicians is a jester, attired in an overall costume, and together with a figure beyond, he is apparently performing a trick of some sort.

There appears to be no exactly similar subject elsewhere in English Romanesque sculpture. As another scene taken from daily life it fits the Christ Church sequence well, and it is the type of subject which would not have been out of place at Wells. Perhaps the closest parallels are the capitals in the

40 Christ Church Cathedral: north transept, capital with entertainers.

41 Christ Church Cathedral: doorway in south transept, capital with two birds.

crypt of Conrad's choir at Canterbury *c*. 1120, where strange conjuring tricks and weird animals playing musical instruments are depicted.[22] One such capital shows a goat playing a pipe, and opposite him a creature with ram's horns performing on a viol.[23] The way these two instruments are held enables us to reconstruct a picture of the instruments on the Dublin capital. The idea of musical animals was popular in Romanesque art, but it is hard to find any parallel scene with human performers. A man playing a fiddle can be found on an early 13th-century capital at Hawkchurch in Devon and many Beatus initials in Romanesque psalters contain the musicians of King David seated amongst leafy scrolls, as in the Winchcombe Psalter at Trinity College, Dublin.[24] Thus, even if the immediate antecedents of the Christ Church capital remain unclear, the composition itself is no surprise.

The style of the entertainers' capital is slightly different from the fruit-pickers and the shepherd with his flock. The figures are taller in proportion, they move more elegantly and they avoid the crouching poses seen in the previous capitals. All wear long flowing garments, with a belt at the waist, and the repeated vertical folds provide a strong linear emphasis. On two of the figures, the drapery is daringly blown open to reveal a bare leg behind, and one of these figures — that playing a pipe — has a mysterious band or rope stretching across its thighs. The swaying poses of the figures and the long flowing folds of the garments recall the style of the north porch of the Lady Chapel at Glastonbury (1184-6).[25] Two mothers from the scene of the Holy Innocents are not unlike the Christ Church figures, although their drapery is more bulky and the pleats less regular. But any attempt to discover the origin of the Christ Church drapery style tends only to expose the problems involved. So little late 12th-century figure sculpture has survived in England, that inevitably too great an importance is attached to the chance survivors. A style involving tall elegant figures with regular rounded drapery folds might have been more widespread than one imagines, for a similar technique can be seen on the late Romanesque cross from Kelloe in Co. Durham.[26] It would be foolhardy to suggest any direct link between Kelloe and Dublin, and this general similarity merely reflects the gradual breakdown of sharp distinctions between regional schools at the end of the 12th century.

The north transept of Christ Church once had an elaborate doorway which was moved to the south transept during alterations to the cathedral in 1831.[27] Although extensively restored, it still contains some of the original Romanesque stonework. The doorway has two major orders of chevron arches, with a plain roll moulding between and there are four extremely worn capitals.[28] On the eastern side one of the capitals illustrates a battle between two human beings and two monster birds. On the right a tall figure clothed in drapery similar to that of the entertainers grapples with one of the beasts, clutching it by the neck. The head of the beast has unfortunately long since been broken off. Just to the left was another monster, but this has been completely destroyed. At the extreme left a warrior with a shield prepares to do battle. Possibly, he once held a spear or a sword. The scene is therefore yet another example of the familiar Romanesque subject of man versus beast, and once again an interesting parallel can be found in the Bristol Channel area, this time in the abbey of St. Augustine, Bristol. Amongst the fine early 13th-century carvings there in the Elder Lady Chapel is a scene which recalls the one at Christ Church. In a spandrel on the south side are the remnants of a human figure clutching the necks of two enormous birds with his out-stretched hands. The arrangement of the scene, with the two monsters either side of a human being, is obviously different from that at Christ Church, but the theme of the carving is similar. The work at Bristol was carried out in the years around 1220 and at least one of the sculptors came from Wells. The letter which Abbot David wrote to the dean of Wells asking for the loan of his sculptor 'L' to carve the pillars of the Lady Chapel is well known.[29] It provides a rare glimpse of the circumstances in which a skilled mason might move from one site to another.

Adjacent to this battle scene at Christ Church is a capital with two bloated looking birds (Fig. 41). They twist their heads to an extraordinary degree, their necks moving not only along the face of the capital but also back into its depth. When first carved it must have been a sculpture of considerable force and tension.

On the western jambs of the doorway are two further capitals with scenes that are hard to interpret. Both are badly damaged. One shows two figures apparently riding animals whose heads were joined at the angles (Fig. 42). Close examination, however, suggests that the right figure may not necessarily be riding, but could be standing behind the beast with one arm around its stomach. As for the left figure, the most distinctive feature is his extravagant hair, with long tresses blowing in the wind and in considerable danger of being caught in some neighbouring foliage. Could this perhaps depict Absolom, his hair caught in the branches, and Joab about to slay him?[30] Unfortunately, the sculpture is too worn to permit any definitive judgement and the fact that religious subjects are not found elsewhere in the carvings of the cathedral reduces the likelihood of such an interpretation.

The carving of the left figure may well be related to contemporary designs illustrating Samson and the lion. An ivory draughtsman, made in the second half of the 12th century and now in Hanover, shows Samson with an equally bizarre hair style.[31] Some authorities believe the ivory comes from England and this type of design might have been common in the pattern books of West Country artists. The Samson carved on the tympanum at Stretton Sugwas (Herefordshire) *c.* 1150 has equally long hair, although on this occasion arranged neatly down the back.[32] Perhaps a drawing originally worked out

212

42 Christ Church Cathedral: doorway in south transept, capital with unidentified scene.

43 Christ Church Cathedral: capital with monster head stored in the crypt.

for Samson was taken over by the Christ Church sculptor and used by him without any specific reference to the Biblical figure.

The final capital on the doorway is too battered to allow for much speculation over its subject-matter. Four figures can be discerned with drapery similar to that of the entertainers. At the angle one of the figures appears to be kneeling while another, evidently standing on one leg, stretches out an arm.[33]

Further 12th-century fragments have recently come to light in the crypt where they were stored after the 1871-8 restoration. These include a splendid monster-head capital, with its mouth carved so that it seems to be swallowing the shaft below (Fig. 43).[34] The pierced eyes are deeply undercut and consequently they appear to be protruding right out of the face. Regrettably the nose is smashed, but nevertheless it remains a bold and startling piece of sculpture.[35] The capital follows a type common in the west of England during the 12th century and fine examples can be observed at Malmesbury Abbey.[36] Such capitals are also found in manuscripts, especially amongst the architecture of canonical tables.[37] At least one such capital had appeared in Ireland before the Anglo-Norman invasion, at Cormac's Chapel, Cashel, dated to 1127-34.[38] It lies in the north-east corner of the nave, and it is distinguished by a curious twist of the jaws. This must also be related to English West Country examples, for a similar treatment appears on a capital at Elkstone, Gloucestershire.[39] The style of the Christ Church version, with its vigorous cutting of the stone, comes closest to the work of Malmesbury where the sculptural ornament is equally bold in design.

Human heads on capitals, though not in the act of swallowing shafts, are a common theme in Hiberno-Romanesque, and it is interesting to compare the Irish examples with the Christ Church fragment. In Ireland these heads were sometimes placed on the angles of twin shafts as at Kilteel (Kildare), where they are given a distinctly Irish flavour by abundant interlace woven into the moustache, beard, and hair (Fig. 44).[40] Although the Irish heads are firmly modelled, the sculptors did not cut so deeply into the stone. They produced an effect of complex and meticulous surface ornament, rather than the dramatic contrast of light and shade so evident in the Christ Church head. The fact that both Irish and English sculptors were using a similar theme helps to stress the stylistic individuality of both schools of Romanesque. Kilteel is not many miles from Dublin, and although its carving predates the invasion, it demonstrates very clearly how the imported masons at Christ Church brought to Ireland a quite different version of Romanesque sculpture.

A second remarkable fragment, discovered in the crypt, is a piece which once formed the keystone of an arch (Fig. 45).[41] A human face is carved in the centre and, with a stroke of real ingenuity on the part of the sculptor, it is made to bite one of the mouldings of the arch itself. The design appears to be unique. Faces biting leaves and scrolls are common enough, but nowhere else does a human head bite an architectural moulding in this way. A clue to its origin is again provided by Malmesbury Abbey, where there are grotesque masks which bite the apex of the nave arches.[42] But in none of them is the actual moulding detached before it passes into the mouth. This latter trick is, however, the type of thing one might expect from the masons who built the north porch at Wells, for there mouldings are treated with a novel freedom, crossing over each other in a way which is more generally associated with

44 Kilteel: chancel arch, capital with heads.

45 Christ Church Cathedral: keystone with human head stored in the crypt.

French *Flamboyant* or German *Sondergotik*. Moreover, the horizontal cornices of the Wells porch are bitten by beasts at each end, a technique also found in the Elder Lady Chapel at Bristol. Thus the design of the biting head of Christ Church also seems to fit into the context of the West Country school.

The style of the face on the keystone is quite unlike the monster head previously discussed. Its eyes are unpierced and the bottom eyelid is distinguished by a gentle double curve. The treatment of the hair with a central parting and clearly defined locks is close to the corbel in the south transept at Wells (Fig. 39), already cited in connexion with the Christ Church capital of dragons and busts. Indeed, the busts on this latter capital, although tiny in scale, have similar eyelids with a pronounced curve.

When cleaned recently, traces of what may be original paint were discovered, red on the forehead and blue in the cracks of the beard. The natural colour of the stone was also revealed, a golden yellow typical of that quarried at Dundry. When first built these golden yellow dressings must have formed a pleasant contrast with the whitewash which, no doubt, covered the rough stonework of the intervening walls.

A further fragment from the crypt is a badly damaged figure capital which was originally located in the north transept.[43] Once there were at least four figures arranged along the necking, but traces of only two and a half survive. They are dressed in three-quarter-length tunics, with gentle, vertical folds. This drapery style recalls that of the entertainers, but it lacks the swaying movement and these figures consequently remain stiff and upright. In view of its battered state no opinion as to its subject can be surmised.

Although only 11 pieces of sculpture have been discussed, it is clear that there is a considerable divergence of style among them. They were either the work of one versatile mason or, more likely, the product of several different hands. The largest single group is that carried out by the sculptor of the entertainers, whose work, as we have seen, implies a knowledge of Glastonbury. With a distinctive style of drapery and a delight in swaying movement, he was also responsible for at least two of the capitals of the north transept doorway. The technique employed by the sculptor of the choir capitals is somewhat different, with stockier figures arranged in a more compressed fashion. The best parallels for this style seem to be at Wells. Different again are the figures on the final fragment from the crypt, where the individuals are more rigid in their poses. It is hard to know whether any of these three masons was also responsible for the magnificent capital of dragons and busts in the north transept. Its composition is so much tighter than the other capitals, that perhaps one has to envisage a fourth craftsman. And even this leaves out of account the monster-head capital and the keystone in the crypt which do not fit easily into any of the above categories. The keystone might, however, belong to the master of the dragons and busts, since the faces depicted on both are related to the same corbel in the south transept at Wells. The presence of several highly skilled masons would suggest an excess of talent at the cathedral, although they may not have stayed in Dublin for long. The fact that figure sculpture was employed only in the lower parts of the north transept and north arcade of the choir might imply that these masons paid only a brief visit to Dublin when this part of the cathedral was under construction.

Despite the extensive damage which almost all the Christ Church sculpture has suffered, its original quality is not in doubt. In many cases limbs of individual figures were completely detached from the stone behind, indicating sculptors with confidence and experience. Indeed, the quality of the sculpture forms a curious contrast to the accompanying architecture, for the choir and transepts, even when intact, were massive and clumsy, with none of the delicacy found in the contemporary work at Wells and Glastonbury. This is all the more curious since the themes and styles of the Christ Church carvings are so undeniably associated with these two churches. While none of the sculptural parallels cited is sufficient to suggest the same mason at work in both places, one at least feels that the Dublin craftsmen were trained in the same environment. But one must admit that the relationships between Christ Church and specific buildings in the Bristol Channel area are not precise, and if the Dublin masons did also work at Wells or Glastonbury it must either have been in a subordinate capacity or else after some intervening lapse of time.

The work of the most skilled masons was obviously not restricted to the historiated capitals, and it is therefore important to glance briefly at some of the other ornamental stonework. Amongst the quantity of stiff leaf foliage, there is a considerable variety of style, even within the transepts alone. Here the earliest capitals seem to be those in the south transept. Apart from a solitary trumpet scallop, those at ground level tend to have plants with long coarse stems and rather sparse leaves. Occasionally, the stems curl and intertwine, rather poor versions of a type which also appears in the north porch of St. Mary Redcliffe, Bristol, *c.* 1200. At ground level in the north transept the quality is higher, and there is one very clearly organized capital in the arch leading to the nave aisle. This has several nicely grouped berries, and a distinctive leaf formation, in which one triple leaf is laid upon another (Fig. 46). In a small doorway, opening east from the north transept, are two foliage capitals, unlike any found elsewhere in the cathedral. They have no necking, which gives the impression that the shaft itself is bursting into leaf (Fig. 47).[44] A similar technique is found on the turrets of the Lady Chapel at Glastonbury, and a close relationship with the abbey is confirmed by the presence of an ornament which has been aptly described as an ice cream whirl — a twisted piece of foliage with a curl at the top. It is almost certainly derived from the acanthus foliage used in contemporary manuscripts. At Glastonbury it can be seen on a capital in the choir (south aisle, second window from the crossing) and on the north doorway of the Lady Chapel, where some of the figure sculpture, as already noted, has links with Dublin.

At clerestory and triforium level in the transepts, the foliage is very different from that below and far more homogeneous. A few set types are used repeatedly. Many general similarities for them can be found in England *c.* 1200 where they fit comfortably into the evolution of stiff leaf, but it is hard to trace any exact parallels. A few of the Christ Church examples have well-developed crockets or bunches of foliage at the top, shooting out above acanthus leaves. In the West Country some of the finest acanthus capitals are to be seen at Abbey Dore, but these have little similarity with those in Dublin. The edges of the Christ Church acanthus are stressed with a series of lines which form a continuous curving pattern below crockets above. A similar arrangement occurs on one of the capitals at St. Cuthbert's, Wells (fourth pier from the west), although here some of the knobs of foliage are replaced by grotesque heads. Better parallels for Christ Church are the capitals in the north porch of St. Mary's, Shrewsbury. Bunches of foliage at the angle are treated in a similar way and they are linked by similar lines curving below (Fig. 48). Also appearing at St. Mary's is a short leaf which droops across the stem of its neighbour as in one of the Christ Church capitals (south transept, east triforium) (Fig. 49). The abaci profiles are, moreover, almost identical in both places. Shrewsbury also provides a parallel for one of the most unusual Christ Church ornaments. This consists of a series of small, plain, upright leaves arranged vertically around the moulding of an arch (Fig. 50). Fragments were found by Street in the choir of Christ Church, and two other known examples appear on the south doorway at Shrewsbury and at the near-by church of Edstaston. This link between Dublin and Shrewsbury is not as strange as might at first appear. Both were drawing ideas and presumably masons from the same sources in the Bristol Channel area, with which Shrewsbury had easy communication along the River Severn.

Before leaving the subject of stiff leaf foliage, it is important to note that on the whole there are relatively few precise parallels between the foliage capitals of Christ Church and the huge quantities of such capitals found at Wells and Glastonbury. Similarities tend to be only of a general nature.

An analysis of other details — the various types of chevron used, the presence of Greek key ornament,[45] the base and abaci mouldings,[46] the use of triple shafts, the lack of a necking on many capitals, and the design of piers with chamfer and chamfer stops — further confirms the links between Christ Church and the Bristol Channel area.[47] A telling detail is the chamfer stop employed on the piers. At the base these consist of plain knobs of masonry projecting upwards, and at the top the chamfer is finished off either with a

46 Christ Church
Cathedral: north transept,
capital.

47 Christ Church Cathedral: north
transept doorway, capital.

48 St. Mary's, Shrewsbury: north porch,
capital.

sprig of foliage or some other ornamental device. At Christ Church the
technique was used in the choir, transepts, and that part of the crypt lying
under the nave. In the west of England their appearance confirms the
importance of the Bristol Channel as a network of communication, for their
distribution includes such buildings as Llandaff Cathedral, Margam Abbey
(chapter-house), Llanthony Abbey (east bay of the nave), Abbey Dore
(transepts), Deerhurst, Glastonbury (choir), and the Elder Lady Chapel at
Bristol. The chevron used at Christ Church fits this pattern equally well, but
as six different types were employed in the cathedral, any distribution map

218

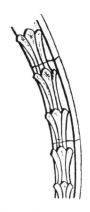

49 Christ Church Cathedral: south transept, east triforium, capitals.

50 Christ Church Cathedral: ornament decorating arches in the choir.

would be complex. It is worth observing, however, that four of the Dublin types were also used at Glastonbury.

In general, therefore, the ornament of Christ Church confirms the conclusion reached with regard to the figure sculpture, but it does not add any further information about the exact origin of the masons. One particular problem is the lack of contemporary buildings in Bristol, which makes it difficult to assess what role the city played in the development of the West Country school. As a port it was the focal point of communication throughout the length of the Severn and its estuary, and it was from the quays of Bristol that Dundry stone was exported to such places as Llandaff[48] and Dublin.[49] Outside Bristol other key buildings are also missing. These include the new church of Winchcombe completed under Abbot Robert III (1194-1221),[50] and the early 13th-century choir of Evesham Abbey.[51] Without a knowledge of such buildings any picture of the West Country school is obviously incomplete.

A further problem in studying English West Country architecture of the Transitional period is the lack of firmly attested dates, and these difficulties equally beset Christ Church. Traditional accounts have put the start of the Romanesque work at *c.* 1172,[52] and these no doubt influenced Leask in proposing a date of *c.* 1175-90.[53] An earlier suggestion of Street that the work must have been carried out under Archbishop Cumin (1181-1212), has been largely ignored.[54] Both stylistic and historical evidence, however, tend to support Street's conclusion.

The stylistic comparisons with English buildings are particularly helpful in trying to date the work at Christ Church. Glastonbury Abbey was destroyed by a great fire in 1184 and the new Lady Chapel there was consecrated in 1186.[55] The links that Christ Church displays with Glastonbury thus imply a date of 1184-1200 for the choir and transepts. Wells Cathedral is not documented with the same precision, but a convincing case has been made for a starting date of *c*. 1180,[56] which fits the Christ Church evidence well. The corbel in the south transept at Wells, which has affinities with the Christ Church sculpture, can thus be dated *c*. 1190 (Fig. 39). The other related work at Wells, the north porch sculpture and the corbel in the nave, must be somewhat later if one assumes that building moved steadily from east to west. This again coincides with the Christ Church evidence, for it was observed above that stylistically the Dublin sculpture appears to be earlier than most of that at Wells. These dates for Wells therefore support a building period of 1186-1200 at Christ Church.

The links between Christ Church and the Bristol area suggest that whoever took the initiative in organizing work on the new choir had a good knowledge of architecture there. Many citizens of Dublin came from the Bristol neighbourhood and so too did Archbishop Cumin. He came from a Somerset family[57] and shortly before he was appointed archbishop of Dublin in 1181 he acted as custodian of the revenues of Glastonbury on behalf of the Crown.[58] When Cumin arrived in Dublin the canons of Christ Church were still largely Irish,[59] and it is quite possible that the archbishop himself suggested how masons might be recruited.

If Cumin did commence work on the new choir, it is likely that he did so several years after his appointment as archbishop. Apparently, he did not make his first visit to Ireland until late in 1184[60] and a likely time for the start of work is two years later in 1186. In that year a major church council was held in Dublin, which passed a series of reforms, seeking to bring Irish ecclesiastical practices into line with those in England.[61] It would have been appropriate for Cumin to give visual expression to this reforming zeal by reconstructing his cathedral in an English style.[62] The period 1186-1200 is thus the most likely date for the Romanesque work at Christ Church, a date which the style of the sculpture helps to confirm.[63]

Although the Christ Church masons imported new themes and new sculptural techniques, they do not seem to have had much influence in Ireland. There is no sign of them working elsewhere, and only in Connacht is there any remotely similar carving. In the nave of the Cistercian abbey at Boyle, and in the choir of Ballintober, are a few capitals of *c*. 1220 with animal designs carved with a boldness not normally found in Irish Romanesque.[64] Perhaps this is a distant reflection of Christ Church, particularly as one Dublin mason certainly worked at Boyle.[65] By the early 13th century, however, when English masons were arriving in greater numbers, this essentially Romanesque approach to capital carving was being replaced by universal stiff leaf. Consequently, the figural capitals of Christ Church are almost unique in Ireland, isolated examples of a purely English style.

The early Gothic sculpture

The nave of Christ Church was built a few years after the eastern limb and the quality of its design fully compensates for the disappointing Romanesque architecture. It is a sophisticated essay in Early English, important for its neat integration of triforium and clerestory. The main arcade, relatively low in proportion, has massive piers surrounded by an elaborate cluster of shafts. Unfortunately, only the north arcade survives from the Middle Ages, the south being a replica constructed by Street. Sculptural ornament on the medieval section is sparse and, apart from an occasional corbel head, it is restricted to the capitals.[66] Those above the level of the main string course are stereotyped, either plainly moulded or carved with simple foliage, but those on the shafts of the main piers are more complex and enterprising. They are decorated with well-developed forms of stiff leaf and on a few of them this is combined with projecting human heads. On the second pier from the east two such heads are to be found, and on the third pier there are seven, one for every major capital (Fig. 51). Two further heads appear in the most westerly bay, but these are not combined with foliage in quite the same manner. One on the west respond acts as a corbel below the rib of the aisle vault, and the other is situated on the fifth pier, placed rather awkwardly at the top of one of the minor shafts in place of a capital. These heads, appearing intermittently, do much to relieve the monotony of continuous bands of stiff leaf. They are carved boldly and precisely, competent in technique but not particularly beautiful. Several are characterized by their long wavy hair, and a few have some distinguishing form of headgear. Two wear crowns, one has a tight-fitting cap, and another wears a cowl or some other close-fitting hood.

The date of these carvings obviously coincides with the building of the whole nave. A campaign lasting from *c.* 1212 to *c.* 1235 has for long been accepted by both Leask in 1955 and myself in 1971.[67] But it is now clear that there is no positive evidence for a starting date of *c.* 1212. The only certain date for building operations is 1234 when the cathedral chapter sought royal permission to block a lane in order to lengthen and widen the church.[68] This request has always been associated with the final western bay of the nave which is clearly an addition. It displays minor variations of style, and this is the only part of the church under which the crypt does not extend.[69] The first five bays were therefore complete by 1234. If one assumes a building campaign lasting at least ten years, it implies a start of *c.* 1220 for work on the nave. This in fact was the year that St. Patrick's, a collegiate church near by, was raised to the status of a cathedral, becoming a rival to Christ Church.[70] A large church was begun almost immediately and this may have acted as a spur to the authorities of the older cathedral. But it is equally possible that

51 Christ Church Cathedral: nave, third pier from the east, capitals.

work began a few years before. About 1216 a certain Philip de Portbich granted land to Christ Church, 'plus 10 shillings and 10 sheep towards the building of the church; also one cow and one heifer, and during his life a sheep at the Nativity of St. John the Baptist'.[71] In the same year Milo le Bret granted the canons commonage of his wood at Maynclare and allowed them to take timber from there 'sufficient for building or repairing their church, or houses, and for all necessary occasions'.[72] Neither grant actually proves that building was going on, but they at least suggest that activity was envisaged in the immediate future. The evidence thus implies that the first five bays of the nave were built c. 1216-30, with the final bay being added in 1234-6.

During this period foliage capitals with projecting human heads were not uncommon in the west of England. The idea is normally assumed to have started at Wells where they first appear in the transept, perhaps about 1190. They were copied in south Wales at Haverfordwest, and it has been argued that they spread thence to Dublin.[73] But in terms of style the Christ Church heads relate to neither Wells nor Haverfordwest. The capitals at Haverford-west, though obviously derived from Wells, are crude and provincial, and they date from after 1223, too late to act as prototypes for Christ Church.[74] The faces at Wells moreover bear little resemblance to the physiognomy of those in Dublin,[75] and for the origin of the Dublin masons one has to look elsewhere.

There are in Worcestershire two churches with capitals so close to those at Christ Church that one has little hesitation in ascribing them to the same workshop. The first of these is St. Andrew's, Droitwich. The church has a complicated building history and large parts of it were rebuilt in the 14th century.[76] The remaining 13th-century work includes a small transept on the

52 St. Andrew's, Droitwich: north transept, capitals.

53 St. Faith's, Overbury: chancel, capital.

north where there are several head capitals. They are largely concentrated on the south-east pier which forms the east respond of the arch leading into the choir. Here there is a continuous frieze of capitals, decorated with early forms of stiff leaf and a row of nine human heads (Fig. 52). The heads are all badly worn and one appears to be a later replacement. But the condition of the eight genuine heads is still sufficiently good to detect resemblances to those at Christ Church. Facial characteristics are similar and the same long wavy hair appears. One of the Droitwich heads has a skull cap as at Christ Church, another wears a cowl, but there are no examples of crowns. The arrangement of the heads, in particular the way they are fitted into the general context of the capital, is also close to Christ Church. It is equally interesting to notice the employment of fillets on the shafts in both places, a feature which is rare at Wells. But the abaci on the shafts at Droitwich are polygonal, whereas those at Christ Church are round. However, on the nook shafts of the two north windows the abaci have been changed to a round form, and this shows that the Droitwich transept was under construction when the transition from square and polygonal abaci to round ones was taking place, a change usually ascribed somewhat vaguely to *c.* 1200.[77] Unfortunately, there is no documentary evidence to confirm such a date for the work at Droitwich.[78] Apart from the heads on the south-east pier, remains of four further heads are visible on the capitals of the north windows. All, however, are damaged and worn.

The other Worcestershire church with head capitals is St. Faith's, Overbury, a village church lying at the foot of Bredon Hill, about 6 miles north-east of Tewkesbury. The building contains a delightful early Gothic chancel, vaulted in two bays.[79] The central respond on the south side has a well-preserved capital with two boldly projecting heads (Fig. 53). Here the similarities with Christ Church are even more clear cut. If the left head at Overbury is compared with one at Dublin (Fig. 51), striking resemblances are immediately apparent, the long wavy hair, a rather mean narrow mouth, and the same cutting of the eyes. Even the neighbouring foliage is becoming closer to Christ Church. In view of these links, there is little doubt that the same mason worked at both Overbury and Dublin. The corresponding capital on the north side of the chancel has only one head, grimacing violently like some of those at Droitwich. The face is surrounded by a tight shroud, reminiscent of one at Christ Church (second pier from the east). As well as the capitals at Overbury, there are two carved keystones in the vault. One depicts a head enclosed by a circular serpentine body, and the other has a crowned head with the familiar wavy hair, once again recalling some of the faces in Dublin. Nor are the parallels restricted to sculpture. The shafts and soffit rolls of the little Worcestershire church abound in fillets, though even these cannot match the profusion of such features at Christ Church. Some of the precise forms, the abaci profiles, for example, are simpler but this is to be expected in a village church. The chancel at Overbury looks somewhat later in date than the transept at Droitwich. If Droitwich is tentatively assigned to *c.* 1190-*c.* 1210, a date of *c.* 1210-20 might be given to Overbury.[80] Such a chronology would best fit the evidence of Christ Church, for the stylistic parallels show that there cannot be any substantial time-lag between the carving at Overbury and Dublin. Further pieces of carving which may be associated with this sculptor can be found on two capitals under the tower arch at Kinlet (Shropshire).[81] The south capital is decorated with three crowned heads, reminiscent of those at Christ Church, with each face having the same rather morose countenance. As in the Worcestershire examples, the abaci profiles and foliage details are not so elaborate as those in Dublin.

The circumstances which brought this Worcestershire mason to Ireland remain a mystery. The manor and advowson of Overbury belonged to the cathedral church of Worcester,[82] and it is possible that the mason was recruited via the cathedral workshops. During the period there was considerable communication between Dublin and Worcester. Christ Church possessed a relic of St. Wulfstan,[83] the Anglo-Saxon bishop of Worcester, and Archbishop Cumin was one of those instrumental in getting him canonized. Recent excavations beside Christ Church have produced a pewter ampulla inscribed 'In honore Santi Vulstani' which once held a portion of healing water from the saint's shrine.[84] It appears that the cult of St. Wulfstan enjoyed some degree of popularity in Dublin at the time. Moreover, the

224

54 Map of the distribution of head capitals in Ireland.

Dublin city roll compiled towards the end of the 12th century contains the names of no fewer than 29 people who had originated from Worcester,[85] so the presence of a mason from the same region a few years later should occasion no surprise. Clearly, the artistic links between Christ Church and Worcestershire are important. Not only the sculpture of the cathedral nave but also the architecture appear to have their roots in this district.[86]

The arrival of this Worcestershire workshop in Dublin was to have considerable implications for early Gothic sculpture in Ireland. The idea of capitals with human heads reaching out amidst foliage proved popular in the south of the country, and there is no doubt that Christ Church was the source of the idea (Fig. 54). They were used with particular sensitivity by a sculptor whom I have nicknamed the 'Gowran master' active in Co. Kilkenny in the third quarter of the 13th century.[87] Apart from his work at Gowran, he also carved head capitals in three churches in the town of Kilkenny, in the cathedral of St. Canice (tomb recess in the north transept), in St. John's Priory, and in the Franciscan friary. His style is characterized by faces with thick lips, and a distinctive cutting of the eyes with sharply curved upper eyelids. His foliage tends to be stereotyped, often taking the form of rosettes. Cruder versions of the theme appear at Cashel Cathedral (nave and transepts) and near by in the Augustinian priory of Athassel (one loose capital, and a capital below the rood screen).[88] Further west in Co. Cork an example can be seen in the west window at Ballybeg, and some very worn heads can still be distinguished on the capitals of the Gothic nave at Mona Incha (Tipperary). It is a fascinating exercise to trace the spread of this motif — from Wells to Worcestershire, thence to Dublin, and finally to this group of buildings in the south of Ireland. It indicates that in this one respect Christ Church played an important role in the dissemination of an English theme, although in architectural matters it seems to have exercised almost no influence. The nave was too ambitious and sophisticated a design to be of much use as a model for church builders in Ireland who were largely concerned with buildings on a smaller scale. But a sculptural idea like the head capitals could be copied and used however small the church.

Conclusion

When discussing the capitals at Wells, the late Arthur Gardner argued that the little men and creatures looking out from the leaves have 'a charm and fanciful imagination combined with that touch of caricature which serves to lift them out of the rut of commonplace craftsmanship into the region of inspired art'.[89] It would be hard to argue that the Christ Church sculpture ever reached the same heights. Perhaps some of the late Romanesque capitals did once have the vivacity of Wells, but their damaged condition now leaves that to the imagination. Even so there is no sign of the sense of humour which makes the Wells sculpture so attractive. Nor can the Christ Church carvings be regarded as particularly original. For the most part styles and themes were brought wholesale from England. Instead their interest is of a more general historical nature. First, they provide a very precise illustration of the way English ideas infiltrated into Ireland after the Anglo-Norman invasion. Secondly, they enhance an appreciation of the English West Country school, revealing the extent and importance of its influence in Ireland. Finally, they provide further examples of the travels of medieval masons, for which there is so much documentary and stylistic evidence in the 13th century.

In 1220, at about the time that work was beginning on the nave of Christ Church, Richard Poore, bishop of Sarum, decided to move his cathedral and he laid out 'spacious foundations by the advice of famous architects whom he had invited from distant parts'.[90] Although there is no documentary evidence, we can conclude that the authorities at Christ Church followed the same procedure, summoning craftsmen 'from distant parts'. For such major projects local men were not suitable, and certainly this was the case in Ireland where the local masons might belong to another race. It is symptomatic of this attitude that no Anglo-Norman patron ever appears to have employed a mason trained in traditional Hiberno-Romanesque techniques. No doubt English Gothic ideas eventually would have found their way to Ireland just as English Romanesque themes had before, but the sculpture in Dublin indicates the way this process was hastened by the conquest. The carvings of Christ Church are, therefore, one small illustration of the way an alien culture was implanted in Ireland during the century after the invasion of 1169-70.[91]

The monuments of the pre-Reformation archbishops of Dublin

H.J. LAWLOR

The earliest archbishop of Dublin of whom it can be said with certainty that a monument was erected to his memory is St. Laurence O'Toole. St. Laurence was consecrated for the see of Dublin on the death of Gréne, the first archbishop, by Gelasius, archbishop of Armagh, assisted by the bishops of Kildare and Ferns, in 1162.[1] In 1180 he left Ireland on a mission to Henry II, who was then in Normandy. On his journey he fell ill of a fever, and on 14 November he died in the church of St. Mary at Eu, in the *département* of Seine-Inférieure.[2] He was buried 'in the middle of the church'; but five years later his body was translated to the crypt, and buried before the altar of St. Leodegarius (17 April 1186). He was canonized on 11 December 1225, by Pope Honorius III.[3] Subsequently the body was again translated to a tomb before the high altar of the church, the head and right arm being preserved apart as relics (10 May 1226).[4] The resting-place of St. Laurence is now pointed out in the crypt of the church of Notre-Dame-et-Saint-Laurent at Eu, and over it is a monument, of which by the kindness of Père Guignaut, *curé-doyen* of Eu, I have obtained a representation.[5] It was injured in the revolution of 1789, and only the recumbent effigy of the archbishop is original. He is represented as holding a pastoral staff with both hands. The staff is broken, but it has been restored from a cast in the museum at Versailles. There is no inscription. The monument, like the church to which it belongs, is said to date from the 13th century. It was, therefore, probably erected on the occasion of his canonization, half a century after his death. Whether it gives, or was intended to give, a correct representation of the personal appearance of the archbishop I do not venture to offer an opinion.[6]

The 13th-century archbishops

St. Laurence was followed by three archbishops of English birth, all of whom were buried in Christ Church Cathedral — John Cumin, 1181-1212; Henry of London, 1213-28; and Luke, 1228-55. Of their tombs and that of a later archbishop we have some information in an important note in the *Liber Niger* of Christ Church.[7] John Cumin and Luke, we are told, were buried in a stone tomb on the south side of the church, and Archbishop Henry on the other side of the chancel in a wooden tomb opposite the former (*mere ex opposito*), while Archbishop John of St. Paul (1349-62) was buried under a marble stone with a brass figure, which lay on the second step of the high altar.

This note was probably written not long after the death of John of St. Paul. It seems to give a full list of the archbishops who were known to the writer to have been buried in Christ Church. Now there is in the cathedral at present only one monument of an early archbishop. It is in the so-called chapel of St. Laurence on the south side of the choir. It has suffered considerably from the ravages of time; but there remains the recumbent effigy, in marble,[8] of an archbishop fully vested. He wears a low mitre. The pall, though considerably defaced, is quite distinct: it seems to be shorter than those found in monuments of the 13th and 14th centuries, to be described later on. The cross-staff, which has no *infula*, is on the archbishop's left, but it is held by his right hand, the right forearm lying across the figure. The inscription, if there was one, is no longer legible.[9] The effigy is of life-size, the extreme measurements of the stone on which it is carved being about 6 ft. 6 in. by 2 ft. at the head and 1 ft. 6 in. at the foot. Does it belong to one of the tombs mentioned in the *Liber Niger*? Certainly not to that of John of St. Paul, whose grave was under one of the steps of the altar, and was covered with a brass. Not, again, to that of Henry of London, which was a wooden structure. But it agrees with the description given of the tomb of John Cumin and Luke.[10] With that tomb, therefore, we may with tolerable security identify it. Which, then, of the two archbishops who rested under it does the effigy represent? That question cannot, of course, be answered with certainty. But where two eminent persons were buried in one grave, the probability is high that the figure that lies over them is of the earlier rather than of the later. Hence we conclude that, in all likelihood, the Christ Church effigy represents John Cumin, the first English archbishop of Dublin, and the founder of St. Patrick's Cathedral. This was the belief of Sir James Ware,[11] and in the opinion of the present writer it may be accepted with little misgiving.

But I must add that it is commonly held that the effigy represents not Cumin, but Laurence O'Toole. Street calls it 'the effigy of St. Laurence', but deems it unnecessary to give any authority for so describing it.[12] He probably accepted, without question, the tradition current among the officials of the cathedral. This tradition, however, seems to be of recent origin. It was evidently unknown both to Ware and to his editor, Walter Harris. Moreover, in the note quoted above from the *Liber Niger* there is no reference to a monument to St. Laurence. This is the more remarkable inasmuch as the writer dilates upon the benefactions of St. Laurence to the cathedral. The fact is that, as we have seen, Laurence O'Toole was buried at Eu, and it may be doubted whether in the 12th or 13th century a monument would be erected to the memory of a prominent personage, as is often done nowadays, elsewhere than in his place of sepulture.[13] All that Christ Church ever possessed of St. Laurence was some relics.[14] These would, of course, be placed, not in a tomb, but either in the high altar or in the altar of the chapel of St. Laurence. The legend that his heart was buried in Christ Church seems to have no historical foundation, and it is at least extremely difficult to reconcile with the elaborate account of the disposal of his remains which may be read in his Life.[15] It is true that our monument is in what is known as St. Laurence's Chapel. But this chapel was built when the cathedral was restored in the seventies of the last century, and there is grave doubt whether it is on the site of the ancient chapel, whose name it has usurped.[16] There is thus no evidence that there was ever a monument of St. Laurence, and all the probabilities are against the supposition.

The tomb of Henry of London has long since disappeared. It was not to be expected that a wooden structure would last for many centuries.[17] Whether there was a representation of the archbishop upon it we do not know. There is a 14th-century portrait of Henry of London preserved in the muniments of the City of Waterford.[18] It is of considerable interest, and may be a drawing (with some modifications, e.g. in the canopy) of the effigy on the lost monument in Christ Church. In it the archbishop is represented as holding a cross, attired with an *infula*, in his left hand.

We must now pass from Christ Church to St. Patrick's. We there find in the chapel, commonly known as St. Peter's, in the north choir aisle, the recumbent effigy of an archbishop. It measures at present about 7 ft. 2 in. by 2 ft. 6 in. The archbishop is vested, and holds his cross in his left hand, the right hand being raised in benediction. The upper part of the cross has been lost, but the *infula* remains. The mitre is low, the pall long, reaching to the lower edge of the chasuble. The feet of the effigy rest on an animal, apparently a dog. The inscription on the modern base of the monument informs us that it is a memorial of Fulk de Sandford, the immediate successor of Luke, who held the see of Dublin from 1256 to his death in May 1271. Is this statement correct?

We have no ancient inscription by which we may check it. But the archiepiscopal vestments are of the 13th century; and it is stated by Ware that Fulk was buried in the Lady Chapel of St. Patrick's Cathedral. Further, it is almost certain that no other archbishop, with the exception of Fulk's brother John, who was his second successor, was buried in St. Patrick's in the same century. As we have seen, John, Henry, and Luke rest in Christ Church. Fulk was succeeded, after a long interregnum, occupied by litigation between the chapters of the two cathedrals, by John de Derlington in 1279. He ruled the diocese for a little over four years, during which he apparently never visited it. He died in or near London, on 29 March 1284,[19] and was buried in the monastery of Black Friars. John de Sandford followed (1284-94). He died in England, but he was buried in St. Patrick's Cathedral, in his brother's tomb.[20] The next archbishop was William of Hotham (1296-8), who, after a short episcopate, died at Dijon, on 27 August 1298, and was buried in Black Friars, London.[21] The last archbishop of the century was Richard de Ferings, who succeeded in the summer of 1299. He died on 17 October 1306, apparently in or not far from Rome, where his death was known to the *Curia* three days later.[22] We may take it, therefore, as certain that the 13th-century effigy in St. Patrick's represents one of the de Sandfords. And, arguing as we did before in the case of John Cumin and Luke, we may assign it to Fulk, the elder of the brothers, rather than to John, the younger. If Ware's statement about the burial-place of the de Sandfords is to be trusted, this effigy must have been originally placed in the Lady Chapel. But it was apparently unknown both to Ware and to Harris. Possibly in the 17th century it lay hidden under the ruins of a portion of the church. It was subsequently, no doubt at the restoration of 1864, fixed to one of the walls of the baptistery. Thence it was brought to its present position in 1902.

I have now passed in review the eight archbishops of Dublin of the 13th century, and have stated all that I can discover about the places of their death and burial. It is not likely that any of their monuments, other than the two which I have mentioned, will ever be found. Monuments to John de Derlington and William of Hotham may have been set up at Black Friars, London, but, if so, they must have been destroyed long ago. It is highly improbable that Richard de Ferings, one of the crowd of bishops at the papal *Curia*, was honoured with a memorial at Rome. Of the rest enough has been said.

Four monumental brasses

From 1307 to 1310 the temporalities of the see were held by Richard de Haverings, who was provided to the archbishopric, but was never consecrated. He was followed by nine archbishops, whose pontificates covered a period of nearly 140 years, the last of them dying in 1449. Of their monuments, three still exist, while of a fourth we have accurate information. It may be well to speak of these four first, deferring for the moment discussion of another, of which we have less satisfactory knowledge. All four were brasses, and they form an interesting series.

The earliest of them was the monument of John of St. Paul (1349-62). It is lost, but of its existence up to a comparatively recent date there is no doubt.

The *Liber Niger*, as we have seen, tells us that he was buried in Christ Church under a marble stone with a brass figure, on the second step of the high altar. Ware gives an almost identical description of the monument. But he had examined it for himself; for he quotes the inscription, which, according to him, ran as follows:

Ego Johannes de S. Paulo quondam archiepiscopus Dubliniae credo quod redemptor meus vivit et in novissimo die de terra surrecturus sum et iterum circundabor pelle mea et in carne mea videbo deum salvatorem meum.[23]

Ware's *De Praesulibus Hiberniae* saw the light in 1665. About fifteen years later Thomas Dineley visited Ireland (1680-1), and in his diary there is a drawing of a monument — apparently a brass — of an archbishop (Fig. 55).[24] Dineley gives no explanation of the

55 Thomas Dineley's drawing of the monument of John of St. Paul.

drawing in his text, but from its position in the diary we gather that it was in Christ Church.

Now, round the figure there was an inscription, the whole of which he was evidently unable to read. He has copied so much as was legible. Down the sinister side he found the words: '. . . quondam archiepiscopus dublinie . . .', the dots indicating, we may suppose, illegible letters. Nearly half the space (the lower part) is left blank. Up the dexter side he found 'in carne mea videbo deum saluatorem meum', followed by a considerable blank space. It is obvious, when we compare this with the inscription which I have copied from Ware, that the subject of Dineley's picture was John of St. Paul's monument. We conclude that the monument was still *in situ* up to the last years of the 17th century. Indeed, I think we may bring it further down. Harris, in his edition of Ware's *Bishops*, translates Ware's account of the monument without comment.[25] If it had been destroyed before he wrote (1764), he would surely have said so. Possibly, however, some significance should be attached to his free translation of Ware's 'ubi haec verba legimus inscripta' as 'on which *were* these words inscribed'. Was it no longer possible to read them? It is not unlikely that the brass suffered some injury in the troublous period which followed 1641. Ware's statement was originally published in the *De Praesulibus Lageniae*, in 1628; and he may not have thought it necessary to alter it in 1665, even though the inscription was not then intact. But if by that year parts of the inscription had become defaced we can better understand Dineley's imperfect reproduction of it, and the peculiar turn of Harris's sentence.

It would be very unwise to press the details of Dineley's drawings, for they are not always accurate. But in this case he cannot be wrong in figuring the archbishop as holding his cross in his left hand, while raising his right hand in the act of blessing. The cross is represented without an *infula*. Probably the inscription ran round three sides of the brass, the space at the top, which might have been used for the inscription, being filled with ornament or left blank. It will be noticed that above the canopy there are two heraldic shields, which have been left blank by Dineley. They probably bore the arms either of the St. Paul family[26] or of the see of Dublin. This monument is interesting as being not only the first brass we have come across in our investigation, but also the earliest known inscribed monument to an archbishop of Dublin.

The earliest inscribed monument now in existence is also a brass. It is that of Robert Waldeby (1390-5). Waldeby was a remarkable man in many ways, but not least because of the number of bishoprics which he successively held within a short space of time. He began with the see of Aire, in Gascony, in 1386[27] from which he was promoted to Dublin in November 1390.[28] Thence he was translated to Chichester, in 1395.[29] In the following year he became archbishop of York.[30] He died on 6 January 1398, and was buried in Westminster Abbey. And there his monument remains to this day, as Ware correctly says, 'almost in the middle of St. Edmund's Chapel'. It is attached to a slab of Purbeck marble, measuring 9 ft. 6 in. by 4 ft., which rests on a solid structure, so that the base is 17 in. above the floor. Its worn condition, however, suggests that it was originally level with the pavement.

Neither Ware nor his editor, Harris, was inspired with sufficient interest in this monument to take the trouble to look at it. Ware tells us truly 'that the epitaph is mutilated'.[31] Accordingly, he makes use of a faulty transcript of it by Dr. Thomas Stubbs, 'whose *History of the Archbishops of York* is extant in the Cotton Library'.[32] The result is that he gives us a wrong date for Waldeby's death: 29 May 1397. Harris makes mistakes of his own. He tells us that 'this epitaph is not now legible'.[33] He also throws doubt on the position of the monument, because Stubbs puts it 'in the Chappel of St. Thomas the Martyr'.[34] A visit to the abbey would have made everything clear; for, though half the inscription is gone, the more important parts of it are preserved. It ran round the brass, beginning at the top left-hand corner. The strips of brass above the head of the archbishop and next to his right hand, on which are engraved the beginning and the end of the inscription, remain: and these

56 Brass of Robert Waldeby in Westminster Abbey.

57 Brass of Thomas Cranley in New College, Oxford.

portions are legible, as is proved by a rubbing, which I owe to the kindness of Mr. David Weller, dean's verger at Westminster Abbey. The other strips have been removed from the stone.

I give the inscription in full, relying on Ware's transcript of Stubbs for the middle part. It is in verse, the end of each line being marked on the brass by an ornament. To make the lines scan, the letters k (l. 9) and C (l. 10) must be taken as monosyllables. In other words, we must pronounce the name of the letter in each case, not the word (*Kalendas* or *centum*) for which it stands.

> hic fuit exp*er*tus in quouis iure Rob*er*tus
> De Waldeby dic*tus* [nunc est sub marmore strictus
> sacrae scripturae doctor fuit et geniturae
> ingenuus medicus et plebis semper amicus
> consultor regis optabat prospera legis
> ecclesiae choris fuit unus bis quoque honoris
> praesul adurensis post archos dubliniensis
> hinc Cicestrensis tandem] primas eboren*sis*
> Quarto . k . ianui[35] mig*r*auit cursib*us* anni.
> Sepini[36] . milleni . ter C nonies[37] quo*que* . deni:
> vos precor orate q*ue* sint sibi dona beate:
> Cum *sanct*is vite requiescat et hic sine lite:

Mr. Weller informs me that the brass is in too bad a state to be photographed. I must be content, therefore, to give a photographic reproduction from Macklin's *Brasses of England* (Fig. 56). The archbishop, as usual, raises his right hand in blessing, and holds his cross, without *infula*, in the left. Waldeby was the tutor of Richard II in his youth, which explains the fact that the arms of the king are above the finial of the canopy. There were two other shields, placed as in John of St. Paul's brass; but of these only the matrices remain. They probably bore the arms of Waldeby, or of the see of York; or perhaps both.

The monument of Waldeby's second successor, Thomas Cranley (1397-1417), is a very beautiful brass (Fig. 57), in the chapel of New College, Oxford, of which he was warden for some years,[38] before his elevation to the episcopate. Again the archbishop has his right hand raised, and holds his cross with the left. The cross is in this case a crucifix; but of the figure upon it only the arms remain. There are two shields; but here they are below the canopy, not, as in the Waldeby brass, above it. Both of them bear the arms of Cranley — a leopard's head between three ducal crowns.[39] Ware knew nothing of this monument. Harris had apparently seen it, for he prints copies of its two inscriptions, which were certainly not borrowed from Anthony Wood,[40] who also transcribed them. One of the inscriptions is beneath the archbishop's feet. It is engraved in two columns. Harris, not noticing this, read it as though each line of the inscription contained two consecutive verses. Consequently, he printed the verses in the order 1, 5, 2, 6, 3, 7, 4, 8.[41] He naturally dubbed the resulting effusion 'barbarous'; but he had the courage to add a metrical translation of it. As his errors of transcription are not confined to the order of the lines, it may be well to give a correct copy. In the first two lines of each quatrain the rhyme is between the first and second part of each verse, separated from one another by a point.

> Incedens siste . locus aspice quid tenet iste
> Pontificis *gratum* . deuelyn corp*us* tumulatum
> Tr*a*nsfuga qu*a*m carnis . d*u*m vita vices vari*a*uit
> Mors carnis viuis . sub humo lect*um* sibi str*a*uit
>
> Annis bis denis . pat*er* alm*us* Alu*m*pn*us* egenis
> Sedit sac*r*atus . fungens vice pontificatus
> Spirit*us* eripit'[42] . n*on* arte valens reuocari
> Queso piis precib*us* . sibi v*e*stris Auxiliari

The second inscription is marginal. It was apparently intact when Harris wrote (1764), but now only a fragment — about a quarter of the whole — is left. Though the inscription was metrical, it is clear from the existing portion that the ends of the verses were not marked, as they are, for example, in the Waldeby brass. For the lost parts we have the evidence of the independent transcripts of Wood and Harris. It ran thus:

[Flori pontificum Thome Cranley deus istum
          Annuit optatum funeris esse locum
Talem nutrivit locus is quem postea rexit
Quo sibi quesivit requiem cum lumina flexit
M C iunge quater I duples V numera ter
          Invenies annum quo] ruit iste pater
Aldelmi festo cursu migrauit honesto
Qui circumstatis [precibus sibi subveniatis]

The festival of St. Aldhelm here referred to is his deposition (25 May).[43] The ribbon of brass on which the inscription was engraved measured about 8 ft. 6 in. by 3 ft. 4 in.

The last of the line of archbishops with which we are for the moment concerned is Richard Talbot, the immediate successor of Cranley (1417-49). His mutilated monument still exists, though it is only a few years since we became aware of the fact. Ware tells us that he died on 15 August 1449, and was buried in St. Patrick's Cathedral 'under a marble monument adorned with his portraiture cut in brass'.[44] He proceeds to give a copy of the epitaph. Harris, in 1764, added some further particulars. He informs us that his tomb was 'before the steps of the altar', and that he was represented with 'a mitre on his head, and a pastoral staff in his hand, some fragments of which yet remain'.[45] This proves that in Harris's time the monument was *in situ*, and that a considerable portion of the brass was still in its place, though he implies that the inscription could no longer be read.[46] And, indeed, as late as 1820 Mason writes: 'Archbishop Talbot's gravestone is before the steps ascending to the altar'.[47] But, as he does not describe the monument, it may be inferred that by that time the brass had disappeared, and only the stone was left. In the closing years of the 19th century there seemed to be no trace of it. Now, in the interval between the publication of Ware's *De Praesulibus Hiberniae* and that of Harris's edition of his work, Thomas Dineley made his tour through Ireland, and in his diary he described the monument. His statement that it was then 'in the body of the quire even with the pavement of St. Patrick's' enables us to fix its position with almost complete precision. He gives no hint that it was mutilated; and he has left us a drawing of it (Fig. 58),[48] which proves, at the least, that the mutilations were not serious. The drawing includes the inscription; and, oddly enough, it is there reproduced more completely than in another copy, which he inserts in the text of the diary. He implies that he actually saw the inscription, and that it was, with the possible exception of a few words, legible.

236

58 Thomas Dineley's drawing of the monument of Richard Talbot.

59 Albon Leveret's drawing of the brass of Richard Talbot.

Now, when the portion of Dineley's diary which contains this drawing was recovered and became known in Dublin, about ten years ago, it was perceived that a stone which had long lain in the churchyard of the cathedral, and which was obviously the matrix of a brass, is in fact the matrix of the brass which Dineley describes. It is Talbot's monument, denuded of its adornment. It measures 7 ft. 2 in. by 4 ft. 4 in. It is now in the cathedral.

The recovery of the concluding portion of Dineley's diary, and the consequent 'invention' of Talbot's monument, were due to a former dean's vicar of St. Patrick's, the Rev. Horace Monroe. The present succentor of the cathedral, the Rev. J.L. Robinson, has carried the matter a step further. In the office of Ulster King of Arms there is a volume which bears the title *Monumenta Eblanae*. It contains a collection of drawings of monuments in the Dublin churches. Most of them are of monuments erected in the 17th century, and some seem to be designs prepared before the monuments were constructed. A few are sketches of medieval tombs. Mr. G.D. Burtchaell, Athlone Pursuivant, tells me that the drawings were probably made by Albon Leveret, who was Athlone Pursuivant from 1618 to 1650. Now, when looking through this book, Mr. Robinson noticed that one of the sketches, which has neither title nor note of any kind, bears a striking resemblance to Dineley's picture of the Talbot brass. It is clear that it is another and much more accurate representation of the same monument (Fig. 59).

It may be well to test the accuracy of the drawings in one particular, which has some historical interest. Dineley has a group of six small figures on the archbishop's right, and a smaller group — apparently of three or four — on the left. Those on the right are represented as speaking, though the words which they use do not appear in the drawing. Doubtless, they were offering a prayer for the repose of the archbishop's soul — *cuius animae propitietur deus,* or the like. Leveret makes the smaller group consist of exactly four persons. This is undoubtedly correct. The groups evidently represent respectively the minor canons and the boy choristers, the foundation of which by Talbot was mentioned in the inscription. The choristers on Talbot's foundation have always been six in number. It is known that from 1493, at the latest, there have been four minor canons,[49] though the charter of foundation mentions six.[50] Leveret's drawing proves that if the college ever had six members, the number had been reduced to four in Talbot's lifetime. Now Dineley places the larger group to the archbishop's right and the smaller to the left, thus representing the choristers as praying, while the four priests remained silent. Leveret reverses the arrangement; and he is obviously right. When we turn to the stone we find that in another matter of detail both drawings are astray. The matrix of the brass on which the minor canons were engraved is greater, in both height and width, than that reserved for the 'children of the choir'.[51] In both pictures the figures are of about the same height, and the group of six takes up more room laterally than the group of four. Neither draughtsman perceived that the six were children and the four men.

In one respect there is a striking difference between the Talbot brass and all the monuments which we have hitherto considered, with the exception of that of Laurence O'Toole. Talbot carries, not the cross-staff of an archbishop, but a crozier. What may be the explanation of this I cannot guess. But it must be in some way connected with another curious fact. If the drawings are to be trusted, Talbot is not arrayed in the full archiepiscopal habit. He alone among the archbishops is represented in his effigy without the pall. The only parallel known to me is the stone figure of Archbishop Walter de Gray (*d.*1255) in York Minster. Here also there is no pall, and a crozier is held in the left hand. The inscription may be given from Ware:

Talbot Richardus latet hic sub marmore pressus
    Archi fuit praesul huius sedis reverendae
Parvos canonicos qui fundavitque choristas
    Anno milleno C quater quater X quoque nono
Quindeno augusti mensis mundo valedixit
    Omnipotens dominus cui propicietur in aevum.

Five 14th-century archbishops

We have some knowledge of another monument of an unnamed archbishop. But before discussing it, I must make some remarks about the five archbishops of the period now under consideration who have not yet been mentioned. They are the following: John Lech (1311-13), Alexander Bicknor (1317-49), Thomas Minot (1363-75), Robert Wikeford (1375-90) and Richard Northalis (1395-7).

According to Ware, Lech 'was buried at Westminster in the middle of the presbytery'.[52] This statement is so precise that we must suppose that Ware had authority for it, in spite of the fact that there is no monument to Lech in the abbey, and that Dr. E.J.L. Scott, Keeper of the Muniments, who has kindly examined the records, can find no reference to his burial. We may conclude that he had no monument in Ireland. Indeed, a prelate who had resided in his diocese for barely two years would not be likely to be so honoured.

Alexander Bicknor, on the other hand, held the see of Dublin for a long period, and he was the most prominent archbishop in the 14th century. If he died in his diocese it is difficult to believe that no monument commemorated him. That he died in Dublin is probable; for it appears that he was in the city, and engaged in fierce controversy with the archbishop of Armagh, a few months before his death.[53] Ware says he was buried in St. Patrick's, but he qualifies his statement with the words, 'I think'.[54] Little stress can be laid on this testimony. It is clear that it was not based on definite documentary evidence. Ware's hesitating remark is most easily explained on the supposition that there was in the cathedral a monument connected with Bicknor either by mere tradition or by Ware's unsupported judgement. Mason, writing in 1820, is more dogmatic. 'Archbishop Alexander de Bicknor', he writes, 'was buried near Archbishop Talbot'.[55] But at the most that only proves that near Talbot's tomb was another, which Mason believed to be Bicknor's. If there had been a monument with an inscription which justified the assertion, Ware would have known and read it, and Mason himself would have recorded it. It is probable, however, that in 1820 there was a second defaced monument close to Talbot's, which has since disappeared. The existence of such a monument, if it were already mutilated at the beginning of the 17th century, would amply account for Ware's halting opinion.

Thomas Minot was a great benefactor of St. Patrick's; but it is improbable, though not impossible, that he had a monument there, for Ware informs us that he died in London.[56] Of the place of sepulture of Robert Wikeford nothing seems to be known. Ware says that Richard Northalis died in Dublin;[57] and Harris adds that he was buried in 'his own cathedral'.[58] On what authority Harris based this statement, or whether by 'his own cathedral' is meant Christ Church or St. Patrick's, I do not know. But Northalis was archbishop only a little over a year.

If there is in existence an anonymous monument to an archbishop of Dublin, or a record of the former existence of such a monument, other than Talbot's, before 1450, it must, of course, be assigned to one of these five.

60 Thomas Dineley's drawing of the matrix of the brass of Alexander Bicknor (?).

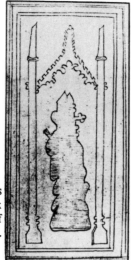

61 Albon Leveret's drawing of the matrix of the brass of Alexander Bicknor (?).

What has been said may suffice to show that the most likely of them to have been so commemorated is Alexander Bicknor, because of his prominence and his long episcopate. Robert Wikeford may, perhaps, be placed next, inasmuch as we know too little about him to assess his claim. The others may be set aside with more or less probability.

Now in Dineley's diary there is a picture of what seems to be the matrix of a brass (Fig. 60).[59] Dineley gives no description of it. But its position in the diary suggests, if it does not prove, that it was a sepulchral monument, and that Dineley saw it in St. Patrick's Cathedral. Fortunately, there is another and better representation of it in the volume in Ulster's Office, already referred to — *Monumenta Eblanae*. Its very presence in that volume assures us that it was a monument in a Dublin church. The drawing itself makes us more certain than Dineley's did that it was the matrix of a brass (Fig. 61). Moreover, the brass was quite clearly the effigy of an archbishop. There is no doubt about the mitre, nor about the archiepiscopal cross, the top of which is quite distinct, and very little doubt about the right hand raised in blessing. This drawing also confirms our inference that the monument was in St. Patrick's, for it is on the back of the sheet, on the front of which is the representation of the Talbot brass, described above. In short, here is a brass, commemorating an archbishop, which was in existence in the time of Charles I, though defaced, and which was almost certainly in St. Patrick's Cathedral. We may conjecture that the stone on which it had rested was in Mason's day in the choir of St. Patrick's close to Talbot's 'gravestone'. And we may claim to have shown that Mason had a prima facie case for assigning it to Alexander Bicknor, as Ware seems to have done before him.

Let us consider it from a different point of view. In the earliest of the brasses which we have examined, those of John of St. Paul and Robert Waldeby, the inscription ran round the edge; in the later ones, those of Cranley and Talbot, there is an inscription beneath the feet of the effigy. In this matrix there was no room for an inscription in the latter position; but there is a groove round the figure which was obviously intended to hold a strip of brass. On it may well have been engraved an inscription. Again, in the four monuments we notice an increasing elaboration in the canopy over the figure. John of St. Paul stands under a pediment, the sides of which are straight, and adorned with crockets, the point where they meet being surmounted by a finial. In the Waldeby brass an ogee takes the place of the straight edges. In the Cranley and Talbot brasses we find a triple ogee, while the details of the shafts remind us that we are well on in the Perpendicular period of architecture. In all its distinguishing features our matrix resembles John of St. Paul's monument, the earliest of the four; but it seems to represent a brass of a simpler and therefore, as we may believe, an earlier style. In brief, if we assume that the brass, to which it corresponds, was earlier than the other four, we can trace a regular development as we pass from it, through St. Paul, Waldeby and Cranley, to Talbot. If, on the other hand, we put it second in the series, the development is somewhat disturbed; if we bring it further down, it must be regarded as a retrogression to an earlier type. Thus again we reach the conclusion that it is much more likely to have commemorated Bicknor than any other of the five archbishops.

I am aware, of course, that the dating of brasses is no easy matter, apart from the inscriptions. And I cannot claim to have any knowledge either of brasses or of architectural detail. Yet it seems, if we take a wider range, that the features of our matrix give us reason to believe that it belongs to the time when Bicknor's monument, if he had one, was constructed. The earliest existing brass in England belongs to the year 1277, though there are a few records or matrices of brasses of earlier date.[60] Architectural canopies begin to appear early in the reign of Edward II (1307-27). The earliest existing canopy in England is dated c. 1320; the earliest matrix of a canopy apparently c. 1310.[61] It is hardly likely, therefore, that a brass, such as our matrix held, adorned the tomb of Lech in 1313, even if we suppose that his body was brought to Dublin for burial. And the earliest type of canopy is of the kind exemplified in the drawings of our matrix. After describing the famous Queen Eleanor crosses, in which 'on each side of the carved figures rise slender shafts supporting a graceful pediment, of which the upper sides are straight, in the form of a triangle, ornamented with a row of crockets, and terminating in a bunch of foliage of considerable size', while 'the lower arch is curved and pointed, with pierced cusps', Mr. Macklin proceeds to say that 'the same form of canopy is found in early brasses, though only one example now remains, surrounding the figure of Joan de Cobham, Cobham, Kent, in *c*. 1320'.[62] This is exactly what we find in the drawings of the matrix under consideration, and in Dineley's drawing of the brass of John of St. Paul. The period in which this form of brass was used is said to have closed about 1325. But later examples are found in 1337 and 1347.[63] It was soon abandoned, however, in favour of the ogee, which has been found as early as 1324.[64] Triple canopies are found as early as 1333,[65] but they appear to have been rare until after the middle of the 14th century. Again, in the earliest period the inscriptions were composed of letters, each of which had a matrix of its own: it was not till the middle of the 14th century that they began to be engraved on a band of metal surrounding the effigy,[66] and, if we may judge from Mr. Macklin's pictures, the marginal inscription soon went out of fashion in favour of one placed below the figure.[67] The form of the canopy, considered in connexion with the presumed position of the inscription, points, therefore, to a date not far removed from 1350, and so brings us back once more to Bicknor. These indications of date seem to put out of court not only Lech, but also the later archbishops who died between 1375 and 1397.[68]

There is one difficulty in the way of our conclusion which ought not to be passed over in silence. We have assumed that the canopy of the brass had straight edges. But it may be asked, can we trust the drawings in such a matter as this? Dineley, for example, represents the canopy over John of St. Paul with straight edges. But we can scarcely believe that, in this particular, his picture is correct; for St. Paul died after the period of straight edges was over.

In reply to such criticism as this, it is to be remarked, in the first place, that it was not uncommon for a brass to be laid down several years before the death of the person whom it was intended to commemorate.[69] All we know about the date of St. Paul's brass is that it was not earlier than 1350, the date of his entry into the see of Dublin. And we cannot affirm that in that year a straight-edged canopy would have been an anachronism. The number of existing specimens of brasses dating from the first half of the 14th century is scarcely great enough to warrant a dogmatic assertion on such a point. Dineley's drawing may not, after all, be so inaccurate as the objection assumes.

But let us grant that he was so careless as to represent an ogee by two right lines. It must be remembered that in the foregoing argument reliance was placed, not on Dineley, but on the more careful draughtsman of the *Monumenta Eblanae*. If it is possible that the acute angle of Dineley's drawing of the St. Paul canopy represents an ogee arch, no such possibility exists in the case of the obtuse angle of the sketch of the anonymous matrix in the *Monumenta*. If the choice here lies between straight edges and an ogee, the former alternative is to be preferred.

And, lastly, the nature of the question at issue must be understood. We are

62 T.J. Westropp's drawing of the monument of Michael Tregury, 1898.

not seeking, from the architectural details of the matrix, taken by themselves, to fix its date within a year or two. On other grounds we can affirm that, if it does not commemorate Bicknor, it must commemorate either Minot, or much more probably Wikeford. We have to determine whether it belongs to the first half of the 14th century or to its closing years. I find it very difficult to believe, making every allowance for inaccuracy, that the pictures in our hands are drawings of a brass laid down within the period represented by the Waldeby monument in Westminster Abbey and those of Sir Nicholas Burnell at Acton Burnell, and Lady Cobham at Cobham.[70] But I must leave the final decision to experts.

In such an investigation as this it would obviously be more satisfactory to deal with the stone itself than with drawings of it. I do not despair of its recovery. It was not improbably discarded at the same time, and for the same reason, as the Talbot matrix, which seems to have been beside it; and, like it, it may have been conveyed without injury from the cathedral to the churchyard. There a diligent searcher, armed with a pickaxe and a spade, may one day find it.

The last pre-Reformation archbishops

After Talbot we have few archbishops to deal with. He was succeeded by Michael Tregury (1449-71). Tregury's tomb (Fig. 62) was still over his grave, 'in his beloved metropolitan church of St. Patrick, at the corner of the altar of St. Stephen, the proto-martyr', in 1665.[71] The fine stone slab which covered it was saved from destruction by Dean Swift about 1720,[72] when it was found among the ruins of St. Stephen's Chapel. After occupying various positions in the cathedral, it was restored to the original site by the present archbishop of Dublin when he was dean of St. Patrick's. The slab measures 7 ft. 2 in. by 4 ft. On it Tregury is represented in the act of blessing. He holds his cross (the head of which is a crucifix) in his left hand. It is attired with an *infula*. He wears a rather high ornamented mitre and a short pall. Above his right hand is the emblem of St. Michael, reminiscent, no doubt, of the vow by which the archbishop was bound personally or by deputy to visit 'with a decent oblation' St. Michael's Mount in Cornwall.[73] It will be remembered that he was a Cornishman, and that his name was Michael. There is a shield on the upper part of the stone. It bears the Tregury arms (three choughs) impaling those of the see of Dublin. This is, perhaps, the earliest instance of a coat in which the family arms of an archbishop of Dublin are on the same shield with those of his see. Round the edge runs this inscription:

Iesus est salvator meus. obiit mcccclxxi die Decembris xxi
Praesul metropolis Michael hic Dubliniensis
Marmore tumbatus pro me christum flagitetis.[74]

The next archbishop, John Walton (1472-84), resigned the see some years before his death. When and where he died is not known. There is no record of a monument to his memory. He was succeeded by Walter FitzSimons (1484-1511). There is a description of his funeral obsequies in the *Liber Albus* of Christ Church, in which it is stated that he was buried before the image of St. Patrick in the nave of St. Patrick's Cathedral.[75] There is no mention of a monument.

Archbishop William Rokeby (1512-21) died on 29 November 1521, and was buried in St. Patrick's. So Ware tells us,[76] and we may accept his statement, for it was probably based on the register of William Hassard, prior of Holy Trinity. That register was certainly known to Ware, and it is not unlikely that it contained an account of the archbishop's funeral. It proves, at any rate, that he died in Dublin; for it states that on the last day of his life he handed over the archiepiscopal cross to the custody of Prior Hassard.[77]

Now, a week before his death Rokeby made a will, some extracts from which may be found in Anthony Wood's *Athenae Oxonienses*.[78] It is dated 22 November 1521, and was proved in York on 4 February 1522. There is a copy of it in the register of Thomas Wolsey, fo. 155. It makes the following provisions, amongst others:

1. That his heart and bowels were to be buried in the church of Halifax, of which he had been vicar, within the choir.

2. That his body was to be buried in the new chapel at Sandal, and that a tomb of stone was to be erected there, with the inscription: 'Ego Willielmus Dublin archiepiscopus, quondam rector istius ecclesiae, credo quod redemptor meus vivit, etc. — qui obiit, etc. Cuius animae propitietur deus'.

3. That a chapel was to be built 'in all convenient haste' on the south side of the church at Halifax, 'after the discretion of mine executors and church masters', and in it a tomb placed with his image, and the inscription: 'Hic iacet cor[79] Willielmi Rokeby nuper Dublin archiepiscopi et vicarii perpetui istius ecclesiae, qui credo, etc.'.[80] This inscription seems to be modelled on that of the monument of John of St. Paul, who, like Rokeby, was a Yorkshire man.[81] Rokeby seems to have intended, though he does not expressly say so,

that his heart should first be buried in the church, and that it should be removed to the chapel when it was built.

There is no doubt that the first of these directions was carried out. Ware writes, with some inaccuracy of statement it is true, that 'his heart was conveyed into England, and deposited in the monument of his ancestors'.[82] Anthony Wood, who knew Halifax Church, informs us that 'his heart was buried in the chancel of the church at Halifax, and thereon was laid a stone with the figure only of an heart engraven thereon'. No vestige of this stone remains.

The third provision of the will was also to some extent fulfilled. To quote Anthony Wood again:

> On the north side[83] of the Church was also founded a chappel wherein was a monument built for him, with an inscription put thereon. Which being since partly defaced you shall have that part which lately[84] remained thereon. Orate pro anima Willielmi Rokeby, iur. can. profess. ac etiam Episcopi Medensis et deinde Archiepiscopus Dublin. capelle fundatoris istius. Qui obiit [die xxviii°][85] Novembris an. Dom. mcccccxxi.

It will be noticed that this differs materially from the inscription composed by Rokeby. In particular, it does not appear to have included the words *hic iacet*. The monument was subsequently destroyed.

The Rev. Dr. A.E. Burn, the present vicar of Halifax, has been so good as to tell me that, notwithstanding the inference which the change in the form of the inscription and the silence of Anthony Wood suggest, Rokeby's heart was actually removed from the church to the chapel. Whether it is still there is uncertain. There is a tradition that the box which contained it was several times removed. The chapel, which has recently been restored, is now filled with stained glass windows in memory of members of the Waterhouse family, whose vault is beneath it. Nevertheless, it is still known as the Rokeby Chapel. It is at present used for daily prayers.

Was the second direction of Rokeby's will obeyed? Anthony Wood did not know, as he had never seen the new chapel of Sandal. Harris and other writers give a negative answer to the question.[86] Some of them may have confused Sandal Parva, or Kirk Sandal,[87] near Doncaster, which is the place mentioned in the will, with the better known Sandal Magna, near Wakefield. But, however it came about, they are wrong.

About the time when Dineley, from whose diary we have received so much help in our inquiry, was making his tour of Ireland (1680) an 'industrious antiquary', James Torre by name, was engaged in examining the churches of Yorkshire. His notes are (or were) preserved in the Prerogative Office of the see of York. They contain a full account of what he saw in St. Oswald's Church, Sandal Parva.[88] Through the kindness of the Rev. Thomas Todd, rector of Kirk Sandal, I have been able to correct and supplement the information which he gives, and to bring it up to date.

On the north side of the choir of St. Oswald's Church there is a chapel dedicated to St. Nicholas.[89] It opens into the choir through an arch, under which is a handsome wooden screen, and into the north aisle through another arch, under which there is a second screen, of more elaborate work, but less well preserved, and it is now used as an organ chamber. The five lights of the east window — which is blocked up by a 'hideous monument' to the memory of Sir Thomas Rokeby, who died on 26 November 1699 — were once filled with painted glass, of which fragments are preserved in a window, of four lights, in the north wall.[90] In 1680 there were seen among them 'a picture of St. Peter, standing with a book in one hand and two keys in the other, and this broken inscription: ". . . istius capelle fundatoris qui obiit Novembris die xxviii 1521"'. The picture of St. Peter has disappeared, but most of the lettering can still be read, in spite of the industry of a spider, which has obliterated a small portion.[91] There is no doubt, therefore, that this is the 'new chapel' of Archbishop Rokeby's will, and that it was founded by the archbishop himself. That it was not completed till after his appointment to the archbishopric, in 1512, is shown by the fact that the arms of the see of Dublin and of the Rokebys, surmounted by a mitre, are carved in stone on the exterior, above the east window. His purpose in founding it is fairly clear. The branch of the Rokeby family from which the archbishop was descended had lived at Synocliffe[92] Grange, in the parish of Ecclesfield, since the beginning of the 15th century. But it seems that when William Rokeby was presented to the living of Kirk Sandal, in 1487,[93] his father, John Rokeby, migrated to that parish. It is certain, at any rate, that in his will (dated 1505) he describes himself as 'of Kirk Sandal', and expresses a desire to be buried in St. Oswald's Church.[94] His descendants lived at Sandal Grove up to the 18th century. Probably, then, William Rokeby founded the chapel of St. Nicholas to serve as the burial-place of his father and other members of the family.

It is interesting to observe that there is a local tradition that the screens and roof of the chapel are of Irish workmanship. This tradition may be correct. Hunter, it is true, does not mention it; but he tells us that they 'are of some foreign wood, probably Irish oak';[95] and we have seen that the chapel was completed after the founder had formed an Irish connexion by his consecration as archbishop of Dublin. There are fine carvings in the roof, among them four bosses representing the Evangelists. The bosses of the present roof of the choir of St. Patrick's Cathedral also represent the evangelical symbols. Now, the late Sir Thomas Drew, under whose supervision the choir was

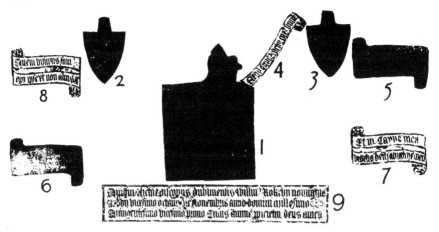

63 Diagram of the brasses and matrices on the Rokeby monument.

restored, in 1900, penned the following sentence when his work was nearing completion: 'Within a few months the choir of St. Patrick's may be looked for as a surviving gem of 13th-century architecture, with no feature or moulding varying from its original building'.[96] We have, therefore, ground for supposing that in the matter of the bosses Sir Thomas followed a tradition which spanned the interval between 1787, when the ancient roof was removed, and the end of the last century. If so, it is probable that the design of the Kirk Sandal bosses was borrowed from Rokeby's own cathedral, and the local belief that the roof and screens of the chapel of St. Nicholas were the work of Irish wood-carvers is confirmed.

The chapel of St. Nicholas presents a strange contrast to the church of St. Oswald, of which, in theory, it is a subordinate part. 'In the fabric of the church itself', wrote Hunter, in 1828, 'there is nothing to admire, nothing on which to remark; but the archbishop's chapel, which is attached to it, is of singular beauty'. The exterior shows that it is actually more lofty than the choir, and the curious lean-to roof of the latter (evidently a modern improvement) leaves the impression that the choir is a mere annexe of the chapel.

Against the north wall of the chapel, behind the organ, stands the archbishop's monument. In design it is an altar tomb, surmounted by a stone canopy. It is of no great size. Its entire height, including the canopy, is 7 ft. 3 in.,[97] the horizontal altar slab, which is 2 ft. 7 in. above the ground, being 5 ft. 11 in. in length.

On the front of the altar tomb are four shields in quatrefoils, on which were emblazoned arms. Three of these escutcheons were still in existence in 1828, though they have now disappeared. The other was removed before 1680. On the first (whether reckoned from the east or from the west is not clear) were the arms of Rokeby;[98] on the second the same, impaling a griffin (or, as

Hunter has it, a lion) rampant ermine; on the fourth the same, impaling Barry of 6 argent and azure (Hunter says, 'impaling three bars'), a chief parted per pale, on the sinister side a chaplet.

The vertical slab, fixed against the north wall, was adorned with nine brazen plates, of five of which only the matrices remain. A diagram showing their relative positions will make the description clearer (Fig. 63). We may take the matrices in the order in which they are numbered in the diagram.

1. 'A little image of the archbishop', only about 13 in. high. The brass was already 'out' in 1680. There remains now only a portion of the matrix; but enough is left to show that Rokeby was represented as wearing a mitre, and holding his cross in his left hand.

2. A shield, bearing the arms of the see of Dublin.[99] The brass was in position in 1828, but is now gone. The marks of the nails which held it in its place remain.

3. A vacant matrix of a shield, not mentioned by Torre. If it differed from no. 2, it may have contained the Rokeby arms.

4. A scroll issuing from the archbishop's left hand,[100] bearing the inscription:

Credo quod redemptor me' vivit.

5. Vacant matrix. In it was probably the brass, seen by Torre in 1680, but now gone, which had the inscription (in two lines):

Et in nouissimo die de terra surrecturus sum.

6. Vacant matrix, not mentioned by Torre. It probably had (in two lines) the clause of the text, *Credo quod redemptor* (Job xix, 25-7), which cannot have been omitted:

Et iterum circumdabor pelle mea.

7. A brass with the inscription:

Et in Carne mea
videbo deum saluatorem meum.

8. A brass with the inscription:

Quem visurus sum
ego ipse et non alius.[101]

9. A brass inscribed thus:

Qui fui Archiepiscopus dublinensis Willelmus Rokeby nominatus
Ac obii vicesimo octavo die Novembris anno domini millesimo
Quingentesimo vicesimo primo Cuius anime propicietur deus amen.

A comparison of these inscriptions with the text of Rokeby's will, quoted above, shows that the direction which he gave as to his monument in the new chapel of Sandal was carried out almost to the letter. The most remarkable deviation from the legend, as he penned it, is the omission of the words *quondam rector istius ecclesie*, and it was probably due to failure of space. In all essentials the inscription agrees with what he wrote.

But was his body buried in the chapel? The answer comes from what Torre called 'a loose stone on the ground'. It now lies north and south under the pedals of the organ, and is reported to be much broken. When Torre examined the chapel there was attached to it an inscribed brass, which is now fixed to the east wall beside the monument of Thomas Rokeby, already mentioned. It displays a metrical epitaph, the last four lines of which are a paraphrase of the inscriptions on the monument. The letters, it may be remarked, unlike those on the other brasses, are incised. The epitaph runs thus:

> Heccine qui transis Gulielmi presulis ossa
> Sub pede fossa jacent tu precor adde preces
> Qualis erat tibi tumba notat constructa sacelli
> Ad latus integrum: palma relicta sua est
> Credo meus quod vivit Ait in carne redemptor
> Quem visurus ero carnis in effigie
> Sic fatus lachrimans animam tibi christe locauit
> Ihesu verus amor hanc tuearis Amen.

It is evident that pains were taken at Kirk Sandal to do all that Archbishop Rokeby desired. In particular, this versified epitaph gives absolute proof that St. Oswald's Church was the final resting-place of his body. Thus we learn the curious fact that Rokeby's remains were interred at four different places: his body, first in St. Patrick's Cathedral, then in the chapel of St. Nicholas, in St. Oswald's Church, Kirk Sandal; his heart, first, in the parish church, and then in the Rokeby Chapel, at Halifax. He had at least three monuments, of which one only remains.

Rokeby's successor was Hugh Inge (1523-8). The Obits of Christ Church inform us that he died on 3 August 1528, and, according to Ware,[102] he was buried in St. Patrick's. There is there, however, no monument, and the position of his grave is unknown. But not far away he has a memorial in stone, to which it may be not improper to refer, as it is perhaps not known to all.

On the west side of the palace of St. Sepulchre's, within a few yards of Marsh's Library, there is a doorway, now partly built up and converted into a window, the flattened arch of which proclaims it to be some four centuries old. It is 8 ft. 6 in. in height and 4 ft. 11 in. in width. Above it is a stone built into the wall, measuring 2 ft. 3 in. by 1 ft. 8 in. and above that another stone, measuring 3 ft. 10 ½ in. by 2 ft. 3 in. Both stones are inscribed, the inscription in the lower one being in relief, and much more elaborate than that of the upper one, which is incised. When I first saw these stones they were covered with a thick lime-wash, and it was impossible to read the inscriptions. The wash being partially removed, I was able to decipher the greater part of the inscriptions.

On the lower stone is carved a shield, supported by angels, which has the arms of the see of Dublin impaling another device, which apparently represents a tree. On the four edges of the slab there is a projecting ribbon of stone, chamfered in its inner side, which forms a frame round the shield. On the ribbon, along the upper edge, we read:

VIRTVS: NOBILITA

To the right of this is an interlaced ornament, which, no doubt, was matched by a similar ornament on the left, some remains of which seem to be visible. On the chamfer below it, and above the shield, is the date 1523 in Arabic figures.

It is evident that this stone was placed in the wall by an archbishop of Dublin, and the date leaves no room for doubt that the archbishop was Inge, to whom the pall was granted on 16 March 1523.[103] It is reasonable to infer that he constructed the doorway, or, as Ware has it, restored the palace, near the beginning of his short archiepiscopate. The only difficulty is that the Inge arms are or a chevron vert, with additional charges in some families of the name. But the fact is that the Inges of Shepton Mallet, in Somerset, of which the archbishop was a native,[104] and the neighbouring village of Croscombe were not armigeri: they appear to have been farmers and tradespeople. It may be assumed, therefore, that Hugh Inge took arms when he was promoted to the episcopate.[105]

This doorway was probably not the main entrance to the palace, but a way of access to the archbishop's garden, in which, two centuries later, Marsh's Library was built. The upper stone is a memorial to a later archbishop, to whom likewise, in spite of the veneration in which he was held, no sepulchral monument has ever been raised. Its plain but mutilated inscription runs thus:

WILL[ELMUS] DUBLI[NE]NS[IS][106]
[I]LLAPS: [RE]STA[V]RAVIT[107]
    A[NNO] 1723.

Thus we learn that Archbishop William King (1703-29), as his predecessor had done exactly 200 years before, restored the ancient palace of St.

Sepulchre's, or at least the western part of it. The last pre-Reformation archbishop was the unfortunate John Alen, who succeeded Inge in 1529, and was murdered at Artane on 28 July 1534. There is no record and no probability that he had a monument.

Conclusion

For the text of the closing paragraphs of this paper I take a remark which may be attributed to an English scholar, whose learning and accuracy are well known. In 1908 a committee of the Upper House of the Convocation of Canterbury, of which the late Dr. John Wordsworth, bishop of Salisbury, was convener, drew up a report on 'The Ornaments of the Church and its Ministers', from which I extract the following statement (p. 22):

> When used by an archbishop the cross-staff is not properly a substitute for but an addition to the crozier, and it is carried before him, not by him. It is, however, found sometimes represented in the hands of an archbishop on monumental effigies and seals. Thus, it may be seen on brasses of Robert de Waldeby, York, d.1398, in Westminster Abbey, and Thomas Cranley, Dublin, d.1417, at New College, Oxford, in both of which it is in the left hand. On some German brasses one hand holds the cross-staff and the other the crozier.
>
> We have not noticed both cross and crozier on English effigies or seals, but John Sharp, archbishop of St. Andrew's (1661-79), is represented holding both; and Arthur Ross, his successor (1684-8, d.1704), holds the cross of St. Andrew in his left hand and a crozier in his right [on seals].

This statement implies that representations of archbishops holding their crosses are rare in England, and in early times, so far as existing memorials show, unknown in Scotland. And it is remarkable that the two English specimens which are mentioned are monuments to Dublin archbishops — of whom one died in office, while the other resigned his see, and was promoted to York, only a couple of years before his death.

The correctness of the implication can easily be tested. In Canterbury Cathedral there are 14 monuments to pre-Reformation archbishops, seven of which have effigies. In one of these the archbishop (Walter Reynolds, d.1327) has neither pall, cross, nor crozier; in another (John Pecham, d.1292), he wears the pall, but neither cross nor crozier appears. In the remaining five the figure is vested with the pall, the hands are in the attitude of prayer, and the cross lies on the right (John Stratford, d.1348; John Morton, d.1500; William Warham, d.1532) or the left shoulder (William Courtenay, d.1396;

Henry Chichele, *d*.1443). In no single case is the cross-staff held in the hand. In York Minster there are 11 monuments, but only two have effigies of the archbishops. One (William Greenfield, *d*.1315) wears the pall and carries the cross in his left hand; the other (Walter de Gray, *d*.1255) has neither pall nor cross, and carries a crozier in his left hand. Thus, nine monumental figures of English archbishops yield only one instance of the cross-staff being held in the hand.[108]

On the other hand, we have noted no fewer than 10 sepulchral effigies of archbishops of Dublin, existing or depicted in drawings — or 11 if we may include the representation of Henry of London. In all but two of these the archbishop holds his cross-staff. In every case it is on the left of the figure, though in one it is grasped by the right hand. The two exceptions are St. Laurence O'Toole, whose tomb was designed, not by Irish, but by Norman artists, and Richard Talbot, who, for some unexplained reason, is not vested as an archbishop. The contrast between the customs of Dublin and those of Canterbury and York is remarkable. It may be rash to conclude that the habit of representing an archbishop in effigy as carrying his cross is peculiarly characteristic of Dublin, for I know nothing of the monuments of the archbishops of Armagh, Cashel and Tuam; but it has at least been shown that it is a tradition rather Irish than English.

Another contrast may be pointed out. Two-thirds of the archiepiscopal monuments at Canterbury and York are without effigies — 16 out of 25. The proportion cannot have been nearly so great in Dublin. For of the 25 archbishops before the Reformation 10 are known to have had monuments with figures and two to have been buried in the tombs of preceding archbishops. Of the remainder, it is highly probable that many had no monuments, at any rate in Dublin. The monuments without figures must, therefore, have been less than half of the whole number. We have actually found no record of a monument of an archbishop of Dublin which had not an effigy, in stone or in brass.

The market cross of Dublin

H . S . C R A W F O R D

The market cross or High Cross of Dublin stood in ancient times at the junction of Skinners' Row (now Christchurch Place), High Street, Christchurch Lane (now Winetavern Street), and Nicholas Street; or, in other words, opposite to the bridge which now connects Christ Church Cathedral with the Synod Hall. Its position is plainly indicated on Speed's map of 1610 (Fig. 66) and is noticed in Harris's *History of Dublin*.[1] The streets at this point are not over wide, and as traffic increased the monument must have been greatly in the way, and this probably led to its removal.

The illustrations of the cross which accompany these notes were kindly given me by Mr. Thomas Mason, of Dame Street, Dublin (Fig. 64); and as I cannot find that any pictures of it have been published or even exist, I think it well to place these on record. They are prints from wet plate negatives of an early type, such as may have been taken 40 to 50 years ago, and represent drawings or sketches of the cross. Mr. Mason obtained the negatives at a sale held at the Apothecaries' Hall in consequence of a change of management which took place there some years back. It has been suggested to me that the negatives have been copied from originals in a book entitled *Monumenta Eblanae*, and now preserved in Ulster's Office; but Mr. Burtchaell assures me that the cross is not amongst the structures there illustrated.

The drawings were signed at foot: 'Ja^s. Simon, F.R.S., delin^t. Rev^d. J^s. Turner, pin^x., Oct., 1794'. James Simon was a Dublin merchant, who carried on business at 26 Great Strand Street up to 1801. He was the author of a work on Irish coins, printed in 1749 by S. Powell, Fleet Street, under the title of *Essays towards an Historical Account of Irish Coins and of the Currency*

64 James Simon's drawing of the High Cross, 1794.

of Foreign Monies in Ireland. The Rev. James Turner seems to be unknown.

In the drawings the monument is shown as consisting of a square shaft crowned by an orb and cross, and set on a circular base or plinth, which in its turn surmounts a set of three octagonal steps. The orb is decorated with a branching pattern; and the shaft with figures and scenes in panels under Gothic canopies, somewhat resembling those on the crosses in the market-place at Duleek and elsewhere in Meath. The scenes occupying the panels are so summarily indicated that it is impossible to say with certainty what they represent. One of the panels in the second row from the top appears to contain a Crucifixion, another a Descent from the Cross, and the rest of the upper carvings may be scenes from the Passion. Two of the third row seem to be armorial bearings, and the others perhaps figures of saints. All the panels at the bottom of the shaft contain rectangular tablets, which may have borne emblems and inscriptions.

Unfortunately the scale is not given, but there are several circumstances which show — if the drawings may be trusted — that the monument was a large one. It is, for example, unlikely that the steps were less than 5 or 6 in. in height, and as the cross is drawn about thirty-six times as high, it must have been from 16 to 18 ft. in all. Similarly, the shaft must have been at least 11 to 12 in. square (its breadth is represented as nearly equal to the height of three steps), and this indicates a total height of 15 ft. or more. It is interesting to notice that one side is shown darker than the others, perhaps to indicate the north; that the small cross on the top is placed diagonally as regards the shaft; and that though the drawings evidently represent opposite sides of the cross, the shadows fall in the same direction. The latter effect could only occur at an interval of 12 hours on a long summer day.

The market cross was of considerable importance in former times, as it was the custom to read from its steps public proclamations, papal bulls, sentences of excommunication, and other documents of importance. During the Commonwealth even banns of marriage were published at the cross under a special act of parliament. Here also were performed public penances, the penitents being seated on the highest step of the cross on market days, clothed in white sheets and bearing placards announcing their offences.

Notes and Bibliographies

NOTES TO INTRODUCTION

1. Gabler, H.W. with Steppe, W. and Melchior, C., (eds.), *James Joyce, Ulysses: the Corrected Text* (1986), pp. 189, 190.

2. Smyth, A.P., *Scandinavian York and Dublin: the History and Archaeology of Two Related Viking Kingdoms*, 2 vols. (1975-9).

3. 'Pale' and 'pele' (or peel) probably go back to the same Latin root, *palus*, meaning 'stake' and by extension 'defensive enclosure'. For a regional comparison exclusive of Yorkshire see Ellis, S.G., *The Pale and the Far North: Government and Society in Two Early Tudor Borderlands* (1988).

4. Chap. 26 has been included in this collection partly in order to illustrate this important point.

5. From 1361 to 1394 the exchequer was at Carlow, which was nearer to the geographical centre of a colonial territory that was steadily shrinking in size.

6. The year of Poynings' parliament at Drogheda, which provided for the vetting of Irish parliamentary legislation by the English king and his council. Dublin's nearest rivals as the venue for parliaments, great councils and other afforced councils were Kilkenny (13.8%), Naas (9.4%) and Drogheda (7.5%). Moreover, after the first Dublin parliament in 1279, there is no long gap in the sequence, whereas Kilkenny drops out of the list after the 1425 parliament and Drogheda's involvement begins only in 1412 with an afforced council, followed by a parliament in 1440.

7. Cf. Reid, R.R., *The King's Council in the North* (1921), pp. 2-3: 'York . . . is the natural centre of the whole region. . . . A market town, a port, and a cathedral city, it was until the 19th century the capital of northern England, the focus of all its activities, social, political, ecclesiastical, and economic, a city second in importance to London only'; Russell, J.C., *Medieval Regions and their Cities* (1972), pp. 126-7, table 15 and fig. 6.

8. Printed in Mac Niocaill, G., *Na Buirgéisí XII-XV Aois*, vol. 1 (1964), pp. 103-6; calendared in *Anc. Rec. Dublin*, vol. 1, p. 32.

9. *Anc. Rec. Dublin*, vol. 1, p. 33.

10. On the Lambert Simnel episode see now Bennett, M., *Lambert Simnel and the Battle of Stoke* (1987); Martin, F.X., 'The crowning of a king at Dublin, 24 May 1487', *Hermathena*, no. 144 (1988).

11. *Anc. Rec. Dublin*, vol. 1, p. 33.

12. For the key to chapter numbers see the list of contents.

13. As far as Dublin is concerned the first public libraries date from 1884, while the National Library of Ireland was opened officially in 1890.

14. On 'the sharply contrasting splendour and squalor' of Dublin and 'a sullen hatred of the

ascendancy' in the early 19th century see D'Arcy, F., 'An age of distress and reform, 1800-1860', in Cosgrove, A., (ed.), *Dublin through the Ages* (1988), pp. 93-112. In the middle decades of the century, when 'social life and entertainment in the more fortunate circles went on despite the troubles below', nearly half of the city's population occupied a single-room, slum accommodation: *ibid.*, p. 102.

15. Crosthwaite, *Obits; Reg. All Saints, Dublin*. For standardized references see the list of abbreviations and conventions. The ascendancy viewpoint is apparent in a comment by the Rev. Richard Butler on the feudal system, which was 'eminently fitted . . . to discipline a rude people by the introduction of notions of right and of law, and by familiarizing them with legal forms and ceremonies': *Reg. All Saints, Dublin*, p. xiv.

16. Gilbert, J.T., *A History of the City of Dublin*, 3 vols. (1854-9, reprinted 1978). The format of this work is topographical, though it contains no maps other than Speed's.

17. *Hist. & Mun. Doc. Ire.*

18. *Chartul. St. Mary's, Dublin; Reg. St. Thomas, Dublin*. On the distinction, not very precise in practice, between a cartulary and a register see Davis, G.R.C., *Medieval Cartularies of Great Britain: a Short Catalogue* (1958), pp. xi-xiii.

19. *Anc. Rec. Dublin*. The contents of vol. 1 include two miscellaneous assemblages of documents that still survive in the city's archives. These are the White Book (*Liber Albus*), which contains copies of charters and statutes, land grants, agreements, writs and wills; and the Chain Book, which contains a calendar, acts passed by the city assembly, customs of the market-places and the annual fair, and a general custumal known as the Laws and Usages.

20. Gilbert, J.T., (ed.), *Crede Mihi: the Most Ancient Register Book of the Archbishops of Dublin before the Reformation* (1897).

21. Berry, H.F., (ed.), *Register of Wills and Inventories of the Diocese of Dublin in the Time of Archbishops Tregury and Walton, 1457-1483* . . . (1898). This was an extra volume in the Royal Society of Antiquaries of Ireland series.

22. Berry, H.F., 'History of the religious guild of St. Anne, in St. Audoen's Church, Dublin, 1430-1740, taken from its records in the Haliday Collection, R.I.A.', *R.I.A. Proc.*, vol. 25 (1904-5), sect. C; Twiss, H.F., 'Some ancient deeds of the parishes of St. Catherine and St. James, Dublin, 1296-1743' and 'Some ancient deeds of the parish of St. Werburgh, Dublin, 1243-1676', both in *R.I.A. Proc.*, vol. 35 (1918-20), sect. C.

23. Robinson, J.L., 'On the ancient deeds of the parish of St. John, Dublin, preserved in the library of Trinity College', *R.I.A. Proc.*, vol. 33 (1916-17), sect. C.

24. Mills, J., (ed.), *Account Roll of the Priory of the Holy Trinity, Dublin, 1337-1346* (1891). This was an extra volume in the Royal Society of Antiquaries of Ireland series.

25. Cal. Christ Church deeds.

26. Lawlor, H.J., 'A calendar of the *Liber Niger* and *Liber Albus* of Christ Church, Dublin', *R.I.A. Proc.*, vol. 27 (1907-9), sect. C. Many years later some of the texts in the *Liber Niger* were printed in full: Gwynn, A., 'Some unpublished texts from the Black Book of Christ Church, Dublin', *Anal. Hib.*, vol. 16 (1946).

27. Daly, M.E., *Dublin: the Deposed Capital, 1860-1914* (1984). The phrase 'nationalist and Catholic monolith', as applied to Dublin Corporation from the 1880s, comes from the same author's 'A tale of two cities, 1860-1920', in Cosgrove, A., (ed.), *Dublin through the Ages* (1988), p. 113.

28. Analysed in Breen, T.C., 'Stray Finds of Early Christian and Medieval Date from the

Greater Dublin Area in the National Museum of Ireland' (University College, Dublin, M.A. thesis, 1980). Ironically the population of the city, as distinct from its suburbs, was actually falling during the 1850s, 1860s and 1880s: Daly, *Deposed Capital*, p. 3, table I.

29. Wilde, W.R., 'On the Scandinavian antiquities lately discovered at Islandbridge, near Dublin', *R.I.A. Proc.*, vol. 10 (1866-9); Coffey, G. and Armstrong, E.C.R., 'Scandinavian objects found at Islandbridge and Kilmainham', *R.I.A. Proc.*, vol. 28 (1910), sect. C; Bøe, J., 'Grave finds from Kilmainham and Islandbridge', in Shetelig, H., (ed.), *Viking Antiquities in Great Britain and Ireland*, pt. III, *Norse Antiquities in Ireland* (1940), pp. 11-65; Briggs, C.S., 'A neglected Viking burial with beads from Kilmainham, Dublin, discovered in 1847', *Medieval Archaeology*, 29 (1985).

30. Frazer, W., 'Description of a great sepulchral mound at Aylesbury Road, near Donnybrook, in the county of Dublin, containing human and animal remains, as well as some objects of antiquarian interest, referable to the tenth or 11th centuries' and 'The Aylesbury Road sepulchral mound: description of certain human remains, articles of bronze and other objects obtained there', both in *R.I.A. Proc.*, vol. 16 (1879-86); Hall, R.A., 'A Viking Age grave at Donnybrook, Co. Dublin', *Medieval Archaeology*, vol. 22 (1978).

31. Sloane, J.S., 'A map of the walls of the city of Dublin, compiled from the few authorities that exist, to illustrate the antiquarian rambles', *Irish Builder*, vol. 24 (1882), p. 191, with an editorial note at p. 190. This map was drawn in 1881.

32. Strangways, L.R., 'A map of the walls of Dublin from all available authorities', *Ireland*, vol. 6 (1906), p. 30 and in a volume entitled *Dublin Main Drainage Scheme Souvenir Handbook* (1906), facing p. 10. This map was first reproduced in a school magazine in 1903. For both maps in context see Clarke, H.B., 'The mapping of medieval Dublin: a case-study in thematic cartography', in *Comparative Urban Origins*, pp. 626-9 and figs. 23.3, 23.4.

33. McCready, C.T., *Dublin Street Names, Dated and Explained* (1892, reprinted 1975).

34. Sir Thomas Drew was the consulting architect to both Christ Church and St. Patrick's Cathedral. Born in Belfast as the son of a precentor of Down Cathedral, he died in Dublin in 1910.

35. On the contemporary background see, for example, Daly, 'A tale of two cities', which highlights the stark contrasts that arose from the process whereby 'throughout the late 19th century the rich gradually migrated to the suburbs leaving the city centre as a largely working-class ghetto': *ibid.*, p. 113. On pre-independence Dublin see also O'Brien, J.V., *'Dear Dirty Dublin': a City in Distress, 1899-1916* (1982); Daly, *Deposed Capital*.

36. At that time the Rev. Elliott was rector of St. Catherine's Church in Dublin. He died in 1910.

37. Having retired as Assistant Deputy Keeper of the Public Records of Ireland in 1912, H.F. Berry (Twiss) died in England in 1932 as the last survivor of the original staff of the Public Record Office appointed at or immediately after its formation in 1868.

38. The author published numerous papers and notes on Irish art and archaeology. He died in 1927.

39. The author held the office of precentor in St. Patrick's Cathedral from 1902 until his appointment as dean in 1924: Lawlor, H.J., *The Fasti of St. Patrick's, Dublin* (1930), p. 59. Having retired as dean after 10 years, he died in 1938.

40. Technically the Irish Free State came into existence one year later on 6 December 1922.

41. Cf. Hopkinson, M., *Green against Green: the Irish Civil War* (1988), p. 122: 'In the end, however, the only policy followed was a demonstration of Republican intransigence and protest. The attack culminated with the explosion of two mines, *laid beforehand* by the Four Courts men in the archives department of the building, which was then being used as their munitions centre. A Provisional Government report commented that the second explosion caused a column of smoke to rise 200 ft. into the air. Most of the contents of the Public Record Office were destroyed by the explosion' (italics mine). For a general account of what survives see Griffith, M., 'A short guide to the Public Record Office of Ireland', *I.H.S.*, vol. 8 (1952-3).

42. *Reg. Kilmainham; Reg. St. John, Dublin*. A fragment of the latter (B.L., Add. MS. 4797, fo. 8) was printed independently in Mac Niocaill, G., 'An unpublished fragment of the register of the hospital of St. John the Baptist, Dublin', *R.S.A.I. Jn.*, vol. 92 (1962).

43. White, N.B., (ed.), *The 'Dignitas Decani' of St. Patrick's Cathedral, Dublin* (1957); Bernard, J.H., 'Calendar of documents contained in the chartulary commonly called *Dignitas Decani* of St. Patrick's Cathedral', *R.I.A. Proc.*, vol. 25 (1904-5), sect. C.

44. *Alen's Reg.* This was an extra volume in the Royal Society of Antiquaries of Ireland series. There is a less comprehensive trial run from the ascendancy period: Stokes, G.T., 'Calendar of the *Liber Niger Alani*', *R.S.A.I. Jn.*, vols. 23 (1893), 27 (1897). See also Lawlor, H.J., 'Note on the register of Archbishop Alan', *Hermathena*, no. 33 (1907). It is important to distinguish this, the *Liber Niger Alani*, from the *Liber Niger* (Black Book) cited above, n. 26.

45. Smyly, J., 'Old (Latin) deeds in the library of Trinity College', *Hermathena*, nos. 66 (1945), 67 (1946), 69 (1947), 70 (1947), 71 (1948).

46. Mac Niocaill, G., 'The charters of John, Lord of Ireland, to the see of Dublin', *Reportorium Novum*, vol. 3 (1961-4); Sheehy, M.P., 'The *Registrum Novum*, a manuscript of Holy Trinity Cathedral: the medieval charters', *Reportorium Novum*, vols. 3 (1961-4), 4 (1965-71). For texts associated with the religious life of medieval Dublin see Hand, G.J., 'The psalter of Christ Church, Dublin', *Reportorium Novum*, vol. 1 (1955-6); Hawkes, W., 'The liturgy in Dublin, 1200-1500: manuscript sources', *Reportorium Novum*, vol. 2 (1957-60).

47. Mac Niocaill, *Na Buirgéisí*, vol. 1, pp. 2-59, 75-106.

48. Lydon, J.F., (ed.), 'Survey of the memoranda rolls of the Irish exchequer, 1294-1509', *Anal. Hib.*, vol. 23 (1966).

49. Wheeler, R.E.M., 'Proceedings at meetings of the Royal Archaeological Institute: the summer meeting at Dublin', *Archaeological Journal*, vol. 88 (1931), facing p. 335. For the context and a reproduction see Clarke, 'Mapping of medieval Dublin', p. 629 and fig. 23.5.

50. Fanning, R., *Independent Ireland* (1983), p. vii.

51. Change in the *avant-garde* world of music and poetry can be traced back to the late 1950s: O'Connor, H., 'Sounds and voices: aspects of contemporary Irish music and poetry', in Bramsbäck, B. and Croghan, M., (eds.), *Anglo-Irish and Irish Literature: Aspects of Language and Culture*, vol. 2 (1988), pp. 211-17.

52. The author, W.G. Strickland, was for many years Registrar and in 1915-16 Acting Director of the National Gallery of Ireland. He died in 1928.

53. The elder brother of Eóin MacNeill, the author was a largely self-taught scholar who spent most of his long life as a civil service pensioner. He died aged 95 in 1958.

54. Professor of Modern Irish History (1944-79) and Director of Archives (1975-9) at University College, Dublin. He died in 1988. The year 1938 also saw the launching of *Irish Historical Studies*, of which Edwards was the founding joint-editor with T.W. Moody. Coupled with the establishment of the Irish Committee of Historical Sciences in March of that year, this was an enterprise that denoted the increasing maturity of historical writing in independent Ireland. Less than a year earlier the 1937 constitution had been adopted, whereby 'the Irish nation hereby affirms its inalienable, indefeasible, and sovereign right . . . to develop its life, political, economic and cultural, in accordance with its own genius and traditions' (art. 1) .

55. Tait, J., *The Medieval English Borough: Studies on its Origins and Constitutional History* (1936).

56. The author, T.K. Moylan, was a playwright in the comic, stage-Irish mould of the mid-20th century.

57. The author, Edmund Curtis, was Erasmus Smith Professor of Modern History (1914-39) and Lecky Professor of History (1939-43) at Trinity College, Dublin.

58. So wrote the author of this essay and of *The Reformation in Dublin, 1536-1558* (1926). M.V. Ronan was the parish priest of St. Michan's Church in Halston Street, one of the oldest post-penal Catholic churches in Dublin. He died in 1959.

59. The author, Brian Mac Giolla Phádraig, was an active member of the Old Dublin Society. He died aged 90 in 1978.

60. The author, Benedict O'Sullivan, O.P., entered the Dominican Order at Tallaght in 1914 and was assigned to many places in Ireland as well as acting as Vicar Provincial in Australia in the early 1930s. He died at Waterford in 1970.

61. The author, John Ryan, S.J., was Professor of Early (including Medieval) Irish History at University College, Dublin, from 1942 to 1964. He died in 1973.

62. Oftedal, M., 'Scandinavian place-names in Ireland', in Almqvist, B. and Greene, D., (eds.), *Proceedings of the Seventh Viking Congress* (1976), p. 131.

63. The author, A.E.J. Went, came as an Englishman to Ireland in 1936 and eventually became Chief Inspector of Fisheries. He was also a major collector of coins and medals, and a founder member of the Numismatic Society of Ireland. He died in 1980.

64. For a recent, and shocking, evocation of institutional and quasi-theocratic Ireland in the 1950s see Doyle, P., *The God Squad* (1988).

65. Professor of Medieval History at University College, Dublin, from 1949 to 1962. He died aged 91 in 1983.

66. Gwynn, A., 'The origins of the see of Dublin', *I.E.R.*, vol. 57 (1941).

67. Duke of Normandy from 1035 and king of England from 1066 until his death in 1087.

68. The author served in the City Engineer's Department of Dublin Corporation. He died on 16 October 1952, having read this paper to the Old Dublin Society in the previous January.

69. The author, G.J. Hand, formerly of the Faculty of Law at University College, Dublin, has since 1980 been Barber Professor of Jurisprudence at the University of Birmingham.

70. Michael Dolley spent most of his working career in the Department of Modern History at The Queen's University, Belfast. He died in 1983.

71. The author, A.J. Otway-Ruthven, was Lecky Professor of History at Trinity College, Dublin, from 1951 to 1980. She died in 1989.

72. Also a number of archbishops of Armagh, whose seat was effectively either at Drogheda or at Termonfeckin in Co. Louth.

73. Almqvist, B. and Greene, D., (eds.), *Proceedings of the Seventh Viking Congress* (1976). The first meeting in Ireland of the Bureau of the *Comité international des sciences historiques* was held at Dublin in July 1971.

74. James, E., (ed.), *Visigothic Spain: New Approaches* (1980); Clarke, H.B. and Brennan, M., (eds.), *Columbanus and Merovingian Monasticism* (1981); *Comparative Urban Origins*.

75. Ní Chatháin, P. and Richter, M., (eds.), *Ireland and Europe: the Early Church* (1984); *Ireland and Christendom: the Bible and the Missions* (1987).

76. Lydon, J.F., (ed.), 'A 15th-century building account from Dublin', *Irish Economic and Social History*, vol. 9 (1982).

77. Clarke, H.B., *Dublin c. 840 to c. 1540: the Medieval Town in the Modern City* (1978); Andrews, J.H., 'The oldest map of Dublin', *R.I.A. Proc.*, vol. 83 (1983), sect. C. An illustrated version of the 1978 map had already been brought out: Walsh, P.J., *Dublin c. 840 to c. 1540: the Years of Medieval Growth* (1977, reprinted 1988). For the context see Clarke, 'Mapping of medieval Dublin', pp. 633-9, where it is also suggested that 'an historian's knowledge and understanding of a medieval town are intimately associated with, and conditioned by, the stage that has been reached in the historical cartography of that town' (p. 640).

78. For a list and location map of the excavations of the National Museum and of the Office of Public Works see the inside cover of the Royal Irish Academy series cited in the following note. The earliest excavation (no. 9) is misdated to 1960-1, while those of the Dublin Archaeological Research Team on the site of the church of St. Michael le Pole and of the Office of Public Works on the site of the Four Courts extension are not shown.

79. Mitchell, G.F., *Archaeology and Environment in Early Dublin* (1987); Lang, J.T., *Viking Age Decorated Wood: a Study of its Ornament and Style* (1988); Wallace, P.F., (ed.), *Miscellanea 1* (1988). These definitive archaeological reports are being issued in three series: A — building and topography; B — artefacts; C — environmental evidence.

80. Bradley, J., (ed.), *Viking Dublin Exposed: the Wood Quay Saga* (1984); Heffernan, T.F., *Wood Quay: the Clash over Dublin's Viking Past* (1988). The Friends of Medieval Dublin were founded in April 1976. Deficiencies in the organization of local government were another cause of the long-term failure to formulate and implement desirable and realistic policies in the historic city centre: Bannon, M.J., 'The capital of the new State', in Cosgrove, A., (ed.), *Dublin through the Ages* (1988), pp. 143-9.

81. Much more material than is generally realized was lost: Clarke, H.B., 'The historian and Wood Quay', in Bradley, J., (ed.), *Viking Dublin Exposed: the Wood Quay Saga* (1984), p. 152 and n. 33; Heffernan, *Wood Quay*, pp. 27-8, 46-7, 89-90, 94, 98, 120-1, 126.

82. The author, Patrick Healy, is highly experienced in the fields of archaeological excavation and survey. That same year (1973) the National Museum mounted an exhibition in order to illustrate the results of the excavations it had conducted to-date: Nat. Mus. Ire., *Viking and Medieval Dublin, National Museum Excavations, 1962-1973: Catalogue of Exhibition* (1973).

83. The author, Nuala Burke, was a freelance conservationist, who went on to propound an absurd and totally indefensible thesis focused on a mythical Fluvial Epoch: *Dublin's*

Wood Quay (1977), pp. 11-26. She died in 1986.

84. For the context see Clarke, 'Mapping of medieval Dublin', pp. 633-7 and figs. 23.8, 23.9.

85. See further Gilligan, H.A., *A History of the Port of Dublin* (1988). Capel Street and Parliament Street would become the city's main thoroughfare, with the Linen Hall near one end and the Exchange (now the City Hall) at the other. The present north-south axis represented by O'Connell Street and Grafton Street dates only from the 19th century: Daly, 'A tale of two cities', pp. 123-4.

86. The author is an architect with the Department of Education.

87. The author, Breandán Ó Ríordáin, was Director of the National Museum of Ireland from 1979 to 1988.

88. The author, H.B. Clarke, lectures in Medieval History at University College, Dublin, and has been chairman of The Friends of Medieval Dublin since 1986.

89. Swan, L., 'Enclosed ecclesiastical sites and their relevance to settlement patterns of the first millennium A.D.', in Reeves-Smyth, T. and Hamond, F., (eds.), *Landscape Archaeology in Ireland* (1983), pp. 269-94; 'Monastic proto-towns in early medieval Ireland: the evidence of aerial photography, plan analysis and survey', in *Comparative Urban Origins*, pp. 77-102.

90. The author, Roger Stalley, lectures in the History of Art at Trinity College, Dublin.

91. The author, Anngret Simms, lectures in Geography at University College, Dublin.

92. Material in square brackets inside direct quotations from primary sources is usually the author's own.

93. McCarthy, J., *Joyce's Dublin: a Walking Guide to 'Ulysses'* (1986), p. 6.

NOTES TO CHAPTER 1

[Translated from 'Frühe Entwicklungsstufen der europäischen Seehandelsstädte auf dem Hintergrund ethnischer Überlagerungen, dargestellt am Beispiel von Dublin in Irland', *Lübecker Schriften zur Archäologie und Kulturgeschichte*, vol. 5 (1981), pp. 113-26. The initial translation by B. Simms has been revised by the editor and the English text, under a new title, incorporates a number of modifications to the German original. The comparative dimension is now more fully developed in *Comparative Urban Origins*. Of particular relevance to this essay are the following: Wallace, P.F., 'The archaeology of Viking Dublin' and 'The archaeology of Anglo-Norman Dublin', *ibid.*, pp. 103-45, 379-410; Fehring, G., 'The archaeology of early Lübeck: the relation between the Slavic and German settlement sites', *ibid.*, pp. 267-87.]

1. Vogel, W., 'Handelsverkehr, Städtewesen und Staatenbildung in Nordeuropa im früheren Mittelalter', *Zeitschrift der Gesellschaften für Erdkunde zu Berlin*, vol. 66 (1931).

2. Jankuhn, H., *Typen und Funktionen vor- und frühwikingerzeitlicher Handelsplätze im Ostseegebiet* (1971); 'Frühe Städte im Nord- und Ostseeraum (700-1100 n. Chr.)', in *Topografia urbana e vita cittadina nell' alto medioevo in Occidente*, Settimane di studio del Centro italiano di studi sull'alto medioevo (1974), pp. 153-201; 'Zusammenfassende Schlussbemerkungen', in Jankuhn, H., Schlesinger, W. and Steuer, H., (eds.), *Vor- und*

Frühformen der europäischen Stadt im Mittelalter, vol. 2, 2nd edn. (1975), pp. 305-22; 'New beginnings in northern Europe and Scandinavia', in Barley, M.W., (ed.), *European Towns: their Archaeology and Early History* (1977), pp. 355-72.

3. Jankuhn, H., Schlesinger, W. and Steuer, H., (eds.), *Vor- und Frühformen der europäischen Stadt im Mittelalter*, 2 vols., 2nd edn. (1975). [Vol. 1 contains essays in English by P.V. Addyman on Southampton and M. Biddle on Winchester; vol. 2 contains an essay in English by C. Blindheim on Kaupang.]

4. Delaney, T.G., 'The archaeology of the Irish town', in Barley, M.W., (ed.), *European Towns: their Archaeology and Early History* (1977), pp. 47-64.

5. Haliday, C., *The Scandinavian Kingdom of Dublin*, 2nd edn. (1884, reprinted 1969).

6. Ó Ríordáin, B., 'Excavations at High Street and Winetavern Street, Dublin', *Medieval Archaeology*, vol. 15 (1971); see also above, pp. 165-72; Wallace, P.F., 'The growth of 13th-century Dublin', in *Dublin Arts Festival 1976* (1976), pp. 22-4; 'Recent discoveries at Wood Quay', *Bulletin of the Group for the Study of Irish Historic Settlement*, no. 5 (1978). [For the chronological sequence and location of the excavations see above, p. 260, n. 78.]

7. [For further information on the Wood Quay controversy see Bradley, J., (ed.), *Viking Dublin Exposed: the Wood Quay Saga* (1984).]

8. Aalen, F.H.A., *Man and the Landscape in Ireland* (1978), p. 273.

9. Binchy, D.A., 'Secular institutions', in Dillon, M., (ed.), *Early Irish Society* (1954), pp. 55-6.

10. Andrews, J.H., 'The ethnic factor in Irish historical geography', unpublished lecture to the Conference of Irish University Geographers (1974).

11. De Paor, L., 'The Viking towns of Ireland', in Almqvist, B. and Greene, D., (eds.), *Proceedings of the Seventh Viking Congress* (1976), pp. 29-30.

12. Haughton, J.P. *et al.*, (eds.), *Atlas of Ireland* (1979), p. 43.

13. Jankuhn, 'Zusammenfassende Schlussbemerkungen', p. 317.

14. See above, pp. 55-65.

15. De Paor, L., 'The age of the Viking wars', in Moody, T.W. and Martin, F.X., (eds.), *The Course of Irish History*, 2nd edn. (1984), p. 93.

16. Gilbert, J.T., *A History of the City of Dublin*, 3 vols. (1854-9, reprinted 1978); Haliday, *Scandinavian Kingdom*.

17. Wheeler, R.E.M., 'Proceedings at meetings of the Royal Archaeological Institute: the summer meeting at Dublin', *Archaeological Journal*, vol. 88 (1931), facing p. 335.

18. Little, G.A., *Dublin before the Vikings: an Adventure in Discovery* (1957).

19. See above, pp. 110-27.

20. See above, pp. 142-61, 183-92.

21. Smyth, A.P., *Scandinavian York and Dublin: the History and Archaeology of Two Related Viking Kingdoms*, 2 vols. (1975-9).

22. Butlin, R.A., (ed.), *The Development of the Irish Town* (1977).

23. Walsh, P.J., *Dublin c. 840 to c. 1540: the Years of Medieval Growth* (1977); Clarke, H.B., *Dublin c. 840 to c. 1540: the Medieval Town in the Modern City* (1978).

24. Clarke, H.B. and Simms, A., 'Early Dublin, 790-1170' and 'Medieval Dublin, 1170-1542', in *N.H.I.*, vol. 9, pp. 36-7, 104-6.

25. See above, pp. 55-65; Simms, A., 'Medieval Dublin: a topographical analysis', *Irish Geography*, vol. 12 (1979).

26. Ellmers, D., 'Hafentechnik und ihre Bedeutung für die Siedlungsgenese', *Berichte zur deutschen Landeskunde*, vol. 52 (1978), p. 178.

27. Ó Lochlainn, C., 'Roadways in ancient Ireland', in *Féil-sgríbhinn Eóin Mhic Néill*, pp. 465-74 and map following p. 593.

28. *Geological Survey of Ireland, Drift Edition* (1915), sheet 18.

29. See above, pp. 157-60.

30. Ó Corráin, D., *Ireland before the Normans* (1972), pp. 67-8.

31. Norman, E.R. and St. Joseph, J.K.S., *The Early Development of Irish Society: the Evidence of Aerial Photography* (1969), pp. 90-121; Swan, D.L., 'The Recognition and Recovery of Ecclesiastical Enclosures by Aerial Observation and Air Photography', unpublished M.A. thesis, University College, Dublin, 3 vols. (1971); ['Monastic proto-towns in early medieval Ireland: the evidence of aerial photography, plan analysis and survey', in *Comparative Urban Origins*, pp. 77-102].

32. See above, pp. 63-4.

33. Burke, N.T., 'An early modern Dublin suburb: the estate of Francis Aungier, earl of Longford', *Irish Geography*, vol. 6 (1969-73) .

34. Henry, F., *Irish Art during the Viking Invasions (800- 1020 A.D.)* (1967), pp. 35-6; see also above, pp. 63-4.

35. See above, pp. 64, 69.

36. See above, p. 59.

37. Jennings, B., (ed.), *The 'Acta Sanctorum Hiberniae' of John Colgan* (1948), p. 147.

38. See above, p. 60.

39. *A.U.*, vol. 1, pp. 338-9.

40. See above, pp. 114-19; Sawyer, P.H., 'The Vikings and the Irish Sea', in Moore, D., (ed.), *The Irish Sea Province in Archaeology and History* (1970), pp. 88, 90.

41. Wallace, 'Recent discoveries at Wood Quay', p. 24; [cf. 'Archaeology of Viking Dublin', pp. 114-17].

42. Smyth, A.P., *Scandinavian Kings in the British Isles, 850-880* (1977), pp. 154-68; Graham-Campbell, J., 'The Viking Age silver hoards of Ireland', in Almqvist, B. and Greene, D., (eds.), *Proceedings of the Seventh Viking Congress* (1976), pp. 39-74.

43. Ó Ríordáin, 'Excavations at High Street and Winetavern Street', pp. 73, 77.

44. Wallace, 'Recent discoveries at Wood Quay', p. 24; [cf. 'Archaeology of Viking Dublin', p. 136].

45. See above, pp. 165, 168-70, 172.

46. Henry, *Irish Art, passim*; [Ó Floinn, R., 'Viking and Romanesque influences, 1000 A.D. - 1169 A.D.', in Ryan, M., (ed.), *Treasures of Ireland: Irish Art, 3000 B.C. - 1500 A.D.* (1983), pp. 58-69; Graham Campbell, J., 'From Scandinavia to the Irish Sea: Viking art reviewed', in Ryan, M., (ed.), *Ireland and Insular Art, A.D. 500-1200* (1987), pp. 150-1; O'Meadhra, U., 'Irish, Insular, Saxon and Scandinavian elements in the motif-pieces from Ireland', *ibid.*, pp. 159-65; Lang, J.T., *Viking Age Decorated Wood: a Study of its Ornament and Style* (1988)].

47. See above, pp. 122-4 and in companion volume, pp. 37-61.

48. De Paor, 'Viking towns of Ireland', p. 32.

49. Foote, P. and Wilson, D.M., *The Viking Achievement: the Society and Culture of Early Medieval Scandinavia* (1970), pp. 207, 211.

50. Steuer, H., 'Die Entstehung der Städte in Mitteleuropa', in Blaszczyk, W., *Die Anfänge der polnischen Städte im Lichte der archäologischen Bodenforschung* (1977), p. 14.

51. De Paor, 'Viking towns of Ireland', p. 33.

52. Lucas, A.T., 'Irish-Norse relations: time for a reappraisal?', *Cork Hist. Soc. Jn.*, vol. 71 (1966).

53. *Alen's Reg.*, p. 29.

54. *Anc. Rec. Dublin*, vol. 1, p. 7.

55. *Alen's Reg.*, p. 83.

56. *Ibid.*, p. 203.

57. Clarke, *Medieval Town in the Modern City*.

58. Simms, 'Medieval Dublin: a topographical analysis'.

59. Webb, J.J., *The Guilds of Dublin* (1929, reprinted 1970), p. 70.

60. [The Royal Irish Academy has undertaken the publication of the definitive excavation reports, which will appear in separate fascicles: see above, p. 260, n. 79.]

61. This contribution is a revised version of a lecture on the same topic delivered in Lübeck on 22 January 1980 at the invitation of the Gesellschaft zur Beförderung gemeinnütziger Tätigkeit. I am indebted to the Alexander-von-Humboldt Stiftung for their research grant, which enabled me to complete this work, and to Professor K. Fehn for receiving me as a guest at the Historisch-Geographischen Seminar in Bonn.

NOTES TO CHAPTER 2

[Reprinted from *R.S.A.I. Jn.*, vol. 107 (1977), pp. 29-51. On cartographical aspects of medieval Dublin see also Clarke, H.B., *Dublin c. 840 to c. 1540: the Medieval Town in the Modern City* (1978); 'The mapping of medieval Dublin: a case-study in thematic cartography', in *Comparative Urban Origins*, pp. 617-43; Simms, A., 'Medieval Dublin: a topographical analysis', *Irish Geography*, vol. 12 (1979). Speed's map is expertly analysed in Andrews, J.H., 'The oldest map of Dublin', *R.I.A. Proc.*, vol. 83 (1983), sect. C. For an archaeological response see above, pp. 70-97.]

1. Wainwright, F.T., *Archaeology and Place-names and History: an Essay on Problems of Co-ordination* (1962).

2. Nat. Mus. Ire., *Viking and Medieval Dublin, National Museum Excavations, 1962-1973: Catalogue of Exhibition* (1973), p. 6.

3. Gilbert, J.T., *A History of the City of Dublin*, 3 vols. (1854-9, reprinted 1978); Haliday, C., *The Scandinavian Kingdom of Dublin*, 2nd edn. (1884, reprinted 1969).

4. Wheeler, R.E.M., 'Proceedings at meetings of the Royal Archaeological Institute: the summer meeting at Dublin', *Archaeological Journal*, vol. 88 (1931), facing p. 335.

5. Speed, J., *The Theatre of the Empire of Great Britaine . . .* (1611), following p.141.

6. Little, G.A., *Dublin before the Vikings: an Adventure in Discovery* (1957).

7. Pool, R. and Cash, J., *Views of the Most Remarkable Public Buildings, Monuments and Other Edifices in the City of Dublin* (1780), facing p. 1; Little, *Dublin before the Vikings*, facing p.133.

8. Schledermann, H., 'The idea of the town: typology, definitions and approaches to the study of the medieval town in northern Europe', *World Archaeology*, vol. 2 (1970-1); Ennen, E., *The Medieval Town*, trans. N. Fryde (1979), pp. 37-93; [Clarke, H.B. and Simms, A., 'Towards a comparative history of urban origins', in *Comparative Urban Origins*, pp. 669-714 and the references given there].

9. Dillon, M., 'The Irish language', in Dillon, M., (ed.), *Early Irish Society* (1954), pp. 12-16.

10. Hensel, W., 'The origins of western and eastern Slav towns', *World Archaeology*, vol. 1 (1969-70); [Herrmann, J., 'Hinterland, trade and craftworking of the early trading stations of the north-western Slavs', in *Comparative Urban Origins*, pp. 249-66; Leciejewicz, L., 'Polish archaeology and the medieval history of Polish towns', *ibid.*, pp. 335-51] .

11. Leciejewicz, L., 'Medieval archaeology in Poland: current problems and research methods', *Medieval Archaeology*, vol. 20 (1976), fig. 2.

12. Jazdzewski, K., 'La formation de la civilisation urbaine polonaise du haut moyen âge à la lumière des recherches récentes', in Francastel, P., (ed.), *Les origines des villes polonaises* (1960), pp. 84, 88-96, 100-1; plates I-IV; Lalik, T., 'Recherches sur les origines des villes en Pologne', *Acta Poloniae Historica*, vol. 2 (1960); [Zbierski, A., 'The development of the Gdansk area from the ninth to the 13th century', in *Comparative Urban Origins*, pp. 289-334].

13. Leciejewicz, L., 'Early medieval socio-topographical transformations in west Slavonic urban settlements in the light of archaeology', *Acta Poloniae Historica*, vol. 34 (1976), fig. 9; [Fehring, G., 'The archaeology of early Lübeck: the relation between the Slavic and German settlement sites', in *Comparative Urban Origins*, pp. 269-72 and fig. 11.3].

14. Mrusek, H.J., 'Zur städtebaulichen Entwicklung Magdeburgs im hohen Mittelalter', *Wissenschaftliche Zeitschrift der Martin-Luther-Universitäts*, vol. 5 (1955-6); Smith, C.T., *An Historical Geography of Western Europe before 1800* (1967), pp. 319-21.

15. *Geological Survey of Ireland, Drift Edition* (1915), sheet 18.

16. Byrne, F.J., *Irish Kings and High-kings* (1973), p. 150.

17. *Chron. Scot.*, pp. 6-7.

18. *A.U.*, vol. 1, pp. 238-9: 'Robbadhad sochaidi di Chiannacht illan mora oc tinntud'.

19. McCready, C.T., *Dublin Street Names, Dated and Explained* (1892, reprinted 1975), pp. 27, 83.

20. *Anc. Rec. Dublin*, vol. 1, p. 193.

21. Carroll, F., 'The ancient name of the Poddle', *D.H.R.*, vol. 13 (1952-4), p. 155; D.H., 'Observations on the Irish statutes, chiefly the more ancient', *Anthologia Hibernica*, vol. 1 (1793), p. 274.

22. O'Curry, E., (ed.), *The Battle of Magh Leana, together with the Courtship of Momera* (1855), p. 107 and n.

23. Ó Lochlainn, C., 'Roadways in ancient Ireland', in *Féil-sgríbhinn Eóin Mhic Néill*, pp. 465-74 and map following p. 593.

24. *A.F.M.*, vol. 1, pp. 102-5; Ó Corráin, D., *Ireland before the Normans* (1972), pp. 67-8.

25. Hull, V., 'The Exile of Conall Corc', *Publications of the Modern Language Association of America*, vol. 56 (1941), pp. 940, 942; Dillon, M., *The Cycles of the Kings* (1946), p. 35.

26. Meyer, K., (ed.), *The Triads of Ireland* (1906), pp. 6-7.

27. *A.U.*, vol. 2, pp. 532-3; see also above, p. 110.

28. Nat. Mus. Ire., *Viking and Medieval Dublin*, p. 7 and plate 5.

29. Little, *Dublin before the Vikings*, pp. 57-65.

30. *Stat. Ire., Hen. VI*, pp. 402-3.

31. Stokes, W., (ed.), 'The prose tales in the Rennes Dindshenchas', *Revue celtique*, vol. 15 (1894), pp. 328-9.

32. O'Brien, M.A., *Corpus Genealogiarum Hiberniae*, vol. 1 (1962), p. 3: 'Fut falnastar ní áiled / Áth Cliath cabraid, / cosmail comlaid óir / úa Luirc Labraid'.

33. Anderson, A.O. and M.O., (eds.), *Adomnan's Life of Columba* (1961), pp. 332-3: ' . . . usque ad vadum Clied' .

34. Little, *Dublin before the Vikings*, pp. 116-17.

35. *Anc. Rec. Dublin*, vol. 3, pp. 55-6; Donnelly, N., *A Short History of Some Dublin Parishes*, vol. 2 (1909-11), pp. 202-3.

36. White, N.J.D., (ed.), '*Libri Sancti Patricii*: the Latin writings of St. Patrick', *R.I.A. Proc.*, vol. 25 (1905), sect. C, p. 240: '. . . ut uenirem ad tegoriolum ubi hospitabam'.

37. Byrne, *Kings and High-kings*, p. 150.

38. Stokes, 'Prose tales', pp. 328, 455.

39. Byrne, *Kings and High-kings*, pp. 152-3.

40. Mac Niocaill, G., *Ireland before the Vikings* (1972), pp. 112-13.

41. Byrne, *Kings and High-kings*, pp. 150-1.

42. *Ibid.*, p. 132.

43. Dillon, M., (ed.), *Lebor na Cert: the Book of Rights* (1962), pp. 4-5, 10-11. [On the role of non-commercial exchange see Doherty, C., 'Exchange and trade in early medieval Ireland', *R.S.A.I. Jn.*, vol. 110 (1980).]

44. *Bk. Leinster*, vol. 1, p. 212: '. . . is ess immar Ess nDuthaite / ocus dún immar Dublind'.

45. Jennings, B., (ed.), *The 'Acta Sanctorum Hiberniae' of John Colgan* (1948), p. 147: '... et ad ciuitatem maritimam, quae Dun Dubhlinne seu Ath Cliath appellatur, prospero cursu appulit'.

46. Grosjean, P., 'Gloria postuma S. Martini Turonensis apud Scottos et Britannos', *Anal. Bolland.*, vol. 55 (1937).

47. Reeves, W., *Memoir of the Church of St. Duilech* . . . (1859); [Clarke, H.B., 'The historian and Wood Quay', in Bradley, J., (ed.), *Viking Dublin Exposed: the Wood Quay Saga* (1984), p. 152 and n. 37].

48. Haworth, R., Letter to *The Irish Times*, 10 October 1977.

49. Hughes, J.L.J., 'Main Street, Dublin', *D.H.R.*, vol. 3 (1940-1), pp. 76-7.

50. Little, *Dublin before the Vikings*, p. 127.

51. Proudfoot, V.B., 'Clachans in Ireland', *Gwerin*, vol. 2 (1958-9), p. 112.

52. Camblin, G., *The Town in Ulster* (1951), pp. 5-6.

53. Hughes, K., *The Church in Early Irish Society* (1966), pp. 71, 76; Swan, D.L., 'The

Recognition and Recovery of Ecclesiastical Enclosures by Aerial Observation and Air Photography', unpublished M.A. thesis, University College, Dublin, vol. 1 (1971), p. 45.

54. Drew, T., 'Surroundings of the cathedral church of St. Patrick de Insula, Dublin', *R.S.A.I. Jn.*, vol. 21 (1890-1), facing p. 428.

55. Little, *Dublin before the Vikings*, p. 110; Hughes, *Church in Early Irish Society*, p. 68.

56. Stokes, W., (ed.), *The Martyrology of Oengus the Culdee* (1905), pp. li-lii, 12-13.

57. Little, *Dublin before the Vikings*, pp. 109-10.

58. Ó Danachair, C., 'The holy wells of County Dublin', *Reportorium Novum*, vol. 2 (1957-60), pp. 79, 80, 233.

59. Norman, E.R. and St. Joseph, J.K.S., *The Early Development of Irish Society: the Evidence of Aerial Photography* (1969), pp. 90-121; Swan, 'Ecclesiastical Enclosures', vol. 1, p. 40.

60. Swan, 'Ecclesiastical Enclosures', vol. 2, pp. 13, 25. [These measurements place the Dublin enclosure well within Swan's biggest size category of over 140 m.: Swan, L., 'Enclosed ecclesiastical sites and their relevance to settlement patterns of the first millennium A.D.', in Reeves-Smyth, T. and Hamond, F., (eds.), *Landscape Archaeology in Ireland* (1983), p. 274 and fig. 4.]

61. Ronan, M.V., 'Lazar houses of St. Lawrence and St. Stephen in medieval Dublin', in *Féil-sgríbhinn Eóin Mhic Néill*, pp. 483-4; [cf. Craig, M., *Dublin 1660-1860* (1952), p. 40].

62. Ronan, M.V., 'Cross-in-circle stones of St. Patrick's Cathedral', *R.S.A.I. Jn.*, vol. 71 (1941); Ó hÉailidhe, P., 'Early Christian grave slabs in the Dublin region', *R.S.A.I. Jn.*, vol. 103 (1973).

63. Donnelly, *Dublin Parishes*, vol. 2, p. 134.

64. Ryan, J., 'The early Irish Church and the see of Peter', in *Med. Studies presented to A. Gwynn*, pp. 3-18.

65. Ryan, J., *Irish Monasticism: Origins and Early Development* (1931), pp. 288-9.

66. Hennig, J., 'The place of the archdiocese of Dublin in the hagiographical tradition of the Continent', *Reportorium Novum*, vol. 1 (1955-6).

67. O'Donovan, J., (trans.), Todd, J.H. and Reeves, W., (eds.), *The Martyrology of Donegal: a Calendar of the Saints of Ireland* (1864), pp. 184-5: 'Rumoldus, epscop Duibhlinne, da ngoirther Ath Cliath'.

68. *A.F.M.*, vol. 1, pp. 264-5, 392-3; Kelly, M., (ed.), *Calendar of Irish Saints, the Martyrology of Tallagh* (1857), p. xv; O'Donovan, Todd and Reeves, *Martyrology of Donegal*, pp. 46-7; Stokes, W., (ed.), *The Martyrology of Gorman* (1895), pp. 34-5.

69. Hughes, *Church in Early Irish Society*, p. 65.

70. Cf. Henry, F., *Irish Art during the Viking Invasions (800-1020 A.D.)* (1967), pp. 35-6.

71. Hadcock, R.N., *Map of Monastic Ireland*, 2nd edn. (1964); Gwynn & Hadcock, *Med. Relig. Houses*, pp. 31, 40, 44, 45, 384, 385, 394, 403.

72. McCready, *Dublin Street Names*, p.10.

73. *Anc. Rec. Dublin*, vol. 1, pp. 157, 193, 493.

74. Swan, 'Ecclesiastical Enclosures', vol. 1, pp. 48, 49-50.

75. Meyer, *Triads of Ireland*, pp. 6-7: 'belach Duiblinne .i. Átha Clíath'.

76. O'Donovan, J., (ed.), *Leabhar na gCeart, or the Book of Rights* (1847), pp. 14-15: 'ges do dul re sluagh malle / Luan tar belach nDuibhlindi'.

77. Cf. Norman and St. Joseph, *Early Development of Irish Society*, pp. 96-7, 114.

78. Henry, *Irish Art*, pp. 39-43 and fig. 2. [On the evidence for Kildare and Clonmacnoise see Doherty, C., 'The monastic town in early medieval Ireland', in *Comparative Urban Origins*, pp. 60-7.]

79. Swan, 'Ecclesiastical Enclosures', vol. 1, p. 18; vol. 3, plates 14-16; ['Monastic proto-towns in early medieval Ireland: the evidence of aerial photography, plan analysis and survey', in *Comparative Urban Origins*, plate 4.V] .

80. Burke, N.T., 'An early modern Dublin suburb: the estate of Francis Aungier, earl of Longford', *Irish Geography*, vol. 6 (1969-73).

81. Lucas, A.T., 'Irish-Norse relations: time for a reappraisal?', *Cork Hist. Soc. Jn.*, vol. 71 (1966), pp. 63-5.

82. *C.G.G.*, pp. 12-13: ' . . . in Dublind Atha Cliath'.

83. Dillon, 'Irish language', p. 19.

84. Henry, *Irish Art*, p. 24.

85. Ó Corráin, *Ireland before the Normans*, pp. 91-2.

86. *C.G.G.*, pp. 16-17: 'Tanic iarsin longes adbul mor in desciurt Atha Cliath'.

87. Plummer, C., (ed.), *Vitae Sanctorum Hiberniae . . .*, vol. 1 (1910), p. 249: 'Et ipse sanctus Garbanus prope ciuitatem Ath Cliath habitabat, que est in aquilonali Laginensium plaga, super fretum maris possita. Et illud scotice dicitur Duibh Linn, quod sonat latine nigra terma . . .'.

88. Smyth, A.P., *Scandinavian York and Dublin: the History and Archaeology of Two Related Viking Kingdoms*, vol. 1 (1975), pp. 86, 88.

89. Biddle, M., 'Towns', in Wilson, D.M., (ed.), *The Archaeology of Anglo-Saxon England* (1976), pp. 123-4; Selkirk, A. and W., 'York', *Current Archaeology*, no. 58 (1977).

90. *C.G.G.*, p. 251: ' . . . ocus ro lensat lucht tighe Taidhg í Ceallaigh iad gur marbsat a ccinn droichit Atha Cliath iad .i. droichett Dubgaill'; Haliday, *Scandinavian Kingdom*, pp. 219-20.

91. *A.F.M.*, vol. 2, pp. 994-5.

92. *C.G.G.*, pp. 34-5: ' . . . gur gabsat ar eiccin i nDuibhlinn Atha Cliath, ocus do ronsat forbaisi ann'.

93. *Ibid.*, pp. 150-1.

94. Foote, P. and Wilson, D.M., *The Viking Achievement: the Society and Culture of Early Medieval Scandinavia* (1970), pp. 207, 211.

95. *A.F.M.*, vol. 2, pp. 722-5; *Chron. Scot.*, pp. 232-3.

96. Dolley, M., 'Some Irish evidence for the date of the *Crux* coins of Æthelred II', in Clemoes, P., (ed.), *Anglo-Saxon England*, vol. 2 (1973), pp. 147-8.

97. Dolley, R.H.M., *Viking Coins of the Danelaw and of Dublin* (1965), pp. 10-11, 26-8; *The Hiberno-Norse Coins in the British Museum* (1966).

98. Haliday, *Scandinavian Kingdom*, pp. 151-2, 154, 162-6, 179-80.

99. Smyth, *Scandinavian York and Dublin*, vol. 1, pp. 9, 41, 44-6, 52-5.

100. Henry, *Irish Art*, pp. 23-4.

101. Graham, B.J., 'The towns of medieval Ireland', in Butlin, R.A., (ed.), *The*

Development of the Irish Town (1977), p. 28.

102. Cf. Smyth, *Scandinavian York and Dublin*, vol. 1, p. 41.

103. Sawyer, P.H., 'The Vikings and the Irish Sea', in Moore, D., (ed.), *The Irish Sea Province in Archaeology and History* (1970), pp. 88-9; Smyth, *Scandinavian York and Dublin*, vol. 1, pp. 60-8.

104. Cf. de Paor, L., 'The Viking towns of Ireland', in Almqvist, B. and Greene, D., (eds.), *Proceedings of the Seventh Viking Congress* (1976), p. 30.

105. Biddle, 'Towns', pp. 120, 137.

106. I am indebted to Professor F.J. Byrne, Mr. Charles Doherty and Dr. George Eogan for critical comments and suggestions that have improved this paper without necessarily committing them to the views expressed. This brief study has arisen out of the activities of The Friends of Medieval Dublin, two of whose members, Mr. Patrick Healy and Mr. Peter Walsh, have given freely of their extensive knowledge and limited time.

NOTES TO CHAPTER 3

[A revised version of an article with the same title published in Scott, B.G., (ed.), *Studies on Early Ireland: Essays in Honour of M.V. Duignan* (1982), pp. 129-43, which this supersedes. For an up-to-date bibliography see the same author's 'Dublin 840-1300: an archaeological bibliography', in Wallace, P.F., (ed.), *Miscellanea 1* (1988), pp. 1-6.]

1. Clarke, H.B., 'The bloodied eagle: the Vikings and the development of Dublin, 841-1014', *Irish Sword*, forthcoming.

2. *Ann. Inisf.*, pp. 192-3.

3. Wilson, D.M., 'Scandinavian settlement in the north and west of the British Isles: an archaeological point of view', *R. Hist. Soc. Trans.*, 5th series, vol. 26 (1976), p. 106.

4. See above, p. 68.

5. Smyth, A.P., *Scandinavian York and Dublin: the History and Archaeology of Two Related Viking Kingdoms*, vol. 1 (1975), p. 41.

6. Herteig, A.E., 'Archaeological contributions to the history of urban communities: the Continent and Scandinavia', in Herteig, A.E., Lidén, H.-E. and Blindheim, C., (eds.), *Archaeological Contributions to the Early History of Urban Communities in Norway* (1975), p. 12.

7. Wainwright, F.T., *Scandinavian England*, ed. H.P.R. Finberg (1975), p. 159.

8. Ó Corráin, D., *Ireland before the Normans* (1972), p. 90.

9. De Paor, L., 'The Viking towns of Ireland', in Almqvist, B. and Greene, D., (eds.), *Proceedings of the Seventh Viking Congress* (1976), p. 30.

10. See above, pp. 65-6, 68.

11. O'Daly, M. and Ó Fiannachta, P., *Contributions to a Dictionary of the Irish Language — L* (1966), p. 202.

12. *A.U.*, vol. 1, pp. 338-9; *A.F.M.*, vol. 1, pp. 454-5; *C.G.G.*, pp. 12-13.

13. Ó Corráin, *Ireland before the Normans*, pp. 81-2, 89-90.

14. See above, p. 114.

15. Sawyer, P.H., 'The Vikings and the Irish Sea', in Moore, D., (ed.), *The Irish Sea Province in Archaeology and History* (1970), p. 86.

16. Sawyer, P.H., '*Wics*, kings and Vikings', in Andersson, T. and Sandred, K.I., (eds.), *The Vikings: Proceedings of the Symposium of the Faculty of Arts of Uppsala University, June 6-9, 1977* (1978), pp. 23-7.

17. Smyth, A.P., *Scandinavian Kings in the British Isles, 850-880* (1977), pp. 154-68.

18. Lucas, A.T., 'Irish-Norse relations: time for a reappraisal?', *Cork Hist. Soc. Jn.*, vol. 71 (1966), p. 64.

19. Wamers, E., 'Some ecclesiastical and secular Insular metal-work found in Norwegian Viking graves', *Peritia*, vol. 2 (1983).

20. Arbman, H., *Birka, Sveriges äldsta handelsstad* (1939); *Birka*, vol. 1 (1940); Blindheim, C., 'A collection of Celtic(?) bronze objects found at Kaupang (Skiringssal), Vestfold, Norway', in Almqvist, B. and Greene, D., (eds.), *Proceedings of the Seventh Viking Congress* (1976), pp. 9-27; Graham-Campbell, J.A., *Viking Artefacts: a Select Catalogue* (1980).

21. De Paor, M. and L., *Early Christian Ireland* (1958), p. 134.

22. Doherty, C., 'Exchange and trade in early medieval Ireland', *R.S.A.I. Jn.*, vol. 110 (1980), pp. 80-2.

23. Oftedal, M., 'Scandinavian place-names in Ireland', in Almqvist, B. and Greene, D., (eds.), *Proceedings of the Seventh Viking Congress* (1976), pp. 125-33.

24. Greene, D., 'The influence of Scandinavian on Irish', in Almqvist, B. and Greene, D., (eds.), *Proceedings of the Seventh Viking Congress* (1976), pp. 75-82; 'The evidence of language and place-names in Ireland', in Andersson, T. and Sandred, K.I., (eds.), *The Vikings: Proceedings of the Symposium of the Faculty of Arts of Uppsala University, June 6-9, 1977* (1978), pp. 119-23.

25. Ó Corráin, *Ireland before the Normans*, pp. 37-42.

26. Lucas, A.T., 'The plundering and burning of churches, seventh to 16th century', in Rynne, E., (ed.), *North Munster Studies: Essays in Commemoration of Monsignor Michael Moloney* (1967), pp. 213-14.

27. Lucas, 'Irish-Norse relations', pp. 67, 74-5.

28. Sawyer, P.H., 'The Vikings and Ireland', in Whitelock, D., McKitterick, R. and Dumville, D., (eds.), *Ireland in Early Medieval Europe: Studies in Memory of Kathleen Hughes* (1982), pp. 345-61.

29. Hodges, R., 'Ports of trade in early medieval Europe', *Norwegian Archaeological Review*, vol. 11 (1978), p. 97, citing Polanyi, K., 'Ports of trade in early societies', *Journal of Economic History*, vol. 23 (1963), p. 30.

30. Ó Corráin, D., 'Aspects of early Irish history', in Scott, B.G., (ed.), *Perspectives in Irish Archaeology* (1974), pp. 64-6; Doherty, 'Exchange and trade', p. 69.

31. See above, p. 65.

32. Clarke, H.B. and Simms, A., 'Towards a comparative history of urban origins', in *Comparative Urban Origins*, pp. 674-6.

33. Ennen, E., *The Medieval Town*, trans. N. Fryde (1979), p. 2.

34. Cited *ibid.*

35. Reynolds, S., *An Introduction to the History of English Medieval Towns* (1977), p. 16.

36. Heighway, C.M., (ed.), *The Erosion of History: Archaeology and Planning in Towns*

(1972), pp. 3, 8-10.

37. Biddle, M., 'Towns', in Wilson, D.M., (ed.), *The Archaeology of Anglo-Saxon England* (1976), p. 100.

38. Doherty, C., 'The monastic town in early medieval Ireland', in *Comparative Urban Origins*, p. 68.

39. Clarke, 'Bloodied eagle'.

40. Ennen, *Medieval Town*, p. 3.

41. Whitehouse, R., 'The urban revolution in western Asia', in Collins, D., (ed.), *The Origins of Europe* (1975), p. 180.

42. Herteig, 'Archaeological contributions to the history of urban communities', p. 11.

43. Brown, P., *The World of Late Antiquity* (1971), *passim.*

44. Ennen, *Medieval Town*, p. 37.

45. Lopez, R.S., *The Commercial Revolution of the Middle Ages, 950-1350* (1971), p. 20.

46. Herteig, 'Archaeological contributions to the history of urban communities', p. 19.

47. Jankuhn, H., 'New beginnings in northern Europe and Scandinavia', in Barley, M.W., (ed.), *European Towns: their Archaeology and Early History* (1977), p. 369.

48. *Ibid.*, pp. 355-71.

49. Herteig, 'Archaeological contributions to the history of urban communities', p. 14.

50. Hensel, W., 'The origins of western and eastern European Slav towns', in Barley, M.W., (ed.), *European Towns: their Archaeology and Early History* (1977), pp. 373-90.

51. Wilson, D.M., 'Defence in the Viking Age', in Sieveking, G. de G., Longworth, I.H. and Wilson, K.E., (eds.), *Problems in Economic and Social Archaeology* (1976), p. 442; Herrmann, J., 'Research into the early history of the town in the territory of the German Democratic Republic', in Barley, M.W., (ed.), *European Towns: their Archaeology and Early History* (1977), pp. 243-59.

52. Reynolds, *English Medieval Towns*, p. 18.

53. Wilson, 'Defence in the Viking Age', p. 439.

54. De Paor, 'Viking towns of Ireland', p. 32.

55. Smyth, *Scandinavian York and Dublin*, vol. 1, p. 64.

56. Sawyer, 'Vikings and the Irish Sea', p. 89; Ó Corráin, *Ireland before the Normans*, p. 106.

57. Smyth, *Scandinavian York and Dublin*, vol. 1, p. 68.

58. Wainwright, *Scandinavian England*, p. 305.

59. Wallace, 'Origins of Dublin'.

60. Ó Corráin, *Ireland before the Normans*, p. 95.

61. De Paor, 'Viking towns of Ireland', p. 31.

62. Smyth, *Scandinavian York and Dublin*, vol. 1, pp. 107-8.

63. Wainwright, *Scandinavian England*, pp. 116, 154-6, 209, 214, 216, 316; *Frag. Ann.*, pp. 170-1.

64. Smyth, *Scandinavian York and Dublin*, vol. 1, p. 79.

65. *Ibid.*, pp. 62, 82, 84, 86.

66. *Ibid.*, p. 86.

67. *Ibid.*, p. 61.

68. *Ibid.*, p. 79.

69. Dolley, R.H.M., 'The mint of Chester', *Journal of the Chester and North Wales Architectural, Archaeological and Historical Society*, vol. 42 (1955), p. 20.

70. Smyth, *Scandinavian York and Dublin*, vol. 1, p. 61.

71. Wainwright, *Scandinavian England*, pp. 84-5.

72. *Frag. Ann.*, pp. 168-9.

73. *Ibid.*, pp. 172-3.

74. Wainwright, *Scandinavian England*, pp. 80-1.

75. Giraldus, *Expugnatio*, pp. 66-7, 301.

76. Wainwright, *Scandinavian England*, pp. 77-87, 131-61.

77. Lucas, 'Irish-Norse relations'.

78. Biddle, 'Towns', p. 135.

79. Ralegh Radford, C.A., 'The pre-conquest boroughs of England, ninth to 11th centuries', *Proceedings of the British Academy*, vol. 64 (1978), p. 146.

80. Wainwright, *Scandinavian England*, pp. 310-11.

81. *Ibid.*, pp. 89-91, 313.

82. Smyth, *Scandinavian York and Dublin*, vol. 1, pp. 76-7.

83. Wainwright, *Scandinavian England*, pp. 160-1.

84. Clarke, 'Bloodied eagle'.

85. Whitehouse, D., 'Towns and trade', in Collins, D., (ed.), *The Origins of Europe* (1975), p. 309; Hill, D.M., 'Continuity from Roman to medieval Britain', in Barley, M.W., (ed.), *European Towns: their Archaeology and Early History* (1977), p. 293.

86. Biddle, 'Towns', p. 112; Hodges, R., 'Trade and urban origins in Dark Age England: an archaeological critique of the evidence', *Berichten van de Rijksdienst voor het Oudheidkundig Bodemonderzoek*, vol. 27 (1977), pp. 191-7.

87. Biddle, 'Towns', p. 118.

88. *Ibid.*, p. 120.

89. Hodges, 'Trade and urban origins', p. 193.

90. Reynolds, *English Medieval Towns*, p. 19.

91. *Ibid.*, pp. 24-7.

92. Hill, 'Continuity from Roman to medieval Britain', p. 299.

93. Biddle, 'Towns', p. 137.

94. Wainwright, *Scandinavian England*, p. 88.

95. Biddle, 'Towns', pp. 125, 134.

96. Wilson, 'Defence in the Viking Age', p. 439.

97. Biddle, 'Towns', p. 122.

98. Rahtz, P.A., 'Hereford', *Current Archaeology*, no. 9 (1968), p. 244.

99. Williams, J.H., *Saxon and Medieval Northampton* (1982), pp. 27-8.

100. Clarke, H.B., *Dublin c. 840 to c. 1540: the Medieval Town in the Modern City* (1978).

101. Biddle, 'Towns', pp. 128-9.

102. Ralegh Radford, 'Pre-conquest boroughs of England', pp. 138-41.

103. Rahtz, 'Hereford', p. 244.

104. Shoesmith, R., 'Hereford', *Current Archaeology*, no. 33 (1972), p. 257; Rahtz, P.A., 'The archaeology of west Mercian towns', in Dornier, A., (ed.), *Mercian Studies* (1977), p. 117.

105. *Ibid.*

106. Ralegh Radford, 'Pre-conquest boroughs of England', pp. 133, 135.

107. Selkirk, A. and W., 'Tamworth', *Current Archaeology*, no. 29 (1971), pp. 164-5; Rahtz, 'Archaeology of west Mercian towns', pp. 111, 114.

108. Ralegh Radford, 'Pre-conquest boroughs of England', p. 144.

109. Biddle, 'Towns', p. 135.

110. Rahtz, 'Archaeology of west Mercian towns', p. 116.

111. Radley, J., 'Economic aspects of Anglo-Danish York', *Medieval Archaeology*, vol. 15 (1971), figs. 5, 6.

112. Richardson, K.M., 'Excavations in Hungate, York', *Archaeological Journal*, vol. 116 (1959), pp. 59-61 and plate Va.

113. Webster, L.E. and Cherry, J., 'Medieval Britain in 1971', *Medieval Archaeology*, vol. 16 (1972), pp. 165, 167.

114. Biddle, 'Towns', pp. 107, 109, 113, 120-2, 125-6, 129-31, 135, 137.

115. Hall, R.A., 'The topography of Anglo-Scandinavian York', in Hall, R.A., (ed.), *Viking Age York and the North* (1978), p. 36.

116. Hall, R.A., 'Markets of the Danelaw', in Roesdahl, E. *et. al.*, (eds.), *The Vikings in England* (1981), p. 96.

117. Hall, R.A., *The Viking Kingdom of York* (1976), p. 17.

118. Wilson, 'Scandinavian settlement in the north and west of the British Isles', pp. 110-11.

119. Hudson, B., 'The family of Harold Godwinsson and the Irish Sea province', *R.S.A.I. Jn.*, vol. 109 (1979).

120. Smith, A.H., 'Some aspects of Irish influence in Yorkshire', *Revue celtique*, vol. 46 (1927).

121. Biddle, 'Towns', pp. 116-18.

122. *Ibid.*, p. 124.

123. Herteig, 'Archaeological contributions to the history of urban communities', p. 18.

124. Smyth, *Scandinavian York and Dublin*, vol. 1, pp. 16-17, 27-9; *Scandinavian Kings in the British Isles*, chaps. 1, 2.

125. Binchy, D.A., 'The passing of the old order', in Ó Cuív, B., (ed.), *The Impact of the Scandinavian Invasions on the Celtic-speaking Peoples, c. 800-1100 A.D.* (1975), p. 122.

126. Lucas, 'Irish-Norse relations', p. 74.

127. Doherty, 'Monastic town', p. 68.

128. Delaney, T.G., 'The archaeology of the Irish town', in Barley, M.W., (ed.), *European Towns: their Archaeology and Early History* (1977), p. 48.

129. Doherty, 'Monastic town', p. 68.

130. *Ibid.*; 'Exchange and trade', p. 71.
131. Binchy, 'Passing of the old order', p. 122.
132. Hodges, 'Ports of trade', p. 100.
133. Skovgaard-Petersen, I., 'The historical context of the first towns in northern and eastern Europe', in Bekker-Nielsen, H., Foote, P.G. and Olsen, O., (eds.), *Proceedings of the Eighth Viking Congress* (1981), pp. 9-18.
134. Sawyer, P.H., 'Kings and merchants', in Sawyer, P.H. and Wood, I.N., (eds.), *Early Medieval Kingship* (1977), p. 157.
135. *Ibid.*
136. Henry, F., *Irish Art during the Viking Invasions (800-1020 A.D.)* (1967), pp. 39-43 and fig. 2.
137. *A.U.*, vol. 1, pp. 424-5; vol. 2, pp. 86-7, 150-3.
138. Swan, L., 'Monastic proto-towns in early medieval Ireland: the evidence of aerial photography, plan analysis and survey', in *Comparative Urban Origins*, pp. 77-102; Herity, M., 'The layout of Irish Early Christian monasteries', in Ní Chatháin, P. and Richter, M., (eds.), *Ireland and Europe: the Early Church* (1984), pp. 105-16.
139. Wallace, 'Origins of Dublin'.
140. See above, p. 68.
141. De Paor, 'Viking towns of Ireland', p. 31.
142. *C.G.G.*, pp. 34-5.
143. *Ibid.*, pp. 150-1; see also above, p. 67.
144. *Bk. Leinster*, vol. 1, p. 212.

NOTES TO CHAPTER 4

[Reprinted from *D.H.R.*, vol. 4 (1941-2), pp. 96-108. The most substantial work on this subject is now Smyth, A.P., *Scandinavian York and Dublin: the History and Archaeology of Two Related Viking Kingdoms*, 2 vols. (1975-9), on which see the review article by Page, R.I., 'A tale of two cities', *Peritia*, vol. 1 (1982). For detailed maps of Viking raids, wars and settlements see those of Byrne, F.J. and Doherty, C. in *N.H.I.*, vol. 9, pp. 20-3, 99-100. For a genealogical table and king-list see *ibid.*, pp. 139, 208-10. Other relevant publications are as follows: Stacpoole, G., 'Gormflaith and the Northmen of Dublin', *D.H.R.*, vol. 20 (1964-5); Lucas, A.T., 'Irish-Norse relations: time for a reappraisal?', *Cork. Hist. Soc. Jn.*, vol. 71 (1966); Hall, R.G., 'A Viking Age grave at Donnybrook, Co. Dublin', *Medieval Archaeology*, vol. 22 (1978). The archaeology of this period is outlined in Wallace, P.F., 'The archaeology of Viking Dublin', in *Comparative Urban Origins*, pp. 103-45; see also above, pp. 70-97.]

1. The name Kilmohavoc comes from the Irish *Cell Mo Shámóc* and occurs in Anglo-Irish medieval records. Cell Mo Shámóc has no connexion with the name of the mountain Kilmashogue, though an absurd legend has got started that the above battle was fought on the summit of this mountain and an old Bronze Age grave-site there is now called Niall's Cairn!

2. Garth, in the Irish text *garrdha*, is the Norse word *garðr* meaning a homestead with some ground attached to it, the residence of a free Norseman. That the Dubliners should

be reduced to drinking brine is odd, seeing that they must have had the Poddle close at hand as well as the Liffey, which may be peaty and poor drinking but certainly is not salt. However, the Irish may have cut them off from both. [In fact the lowest reaches of the Poddle south and east of the ridge were probably subject to tidal influences: see above, pp. 56-7.]

3. These pagan relics, however, some time later got back into the hands of their original owners, for in 1029 'Olaf, son of Sitric, king of the foreigners, was taken by Mathgamain ua Riagain, king of Brega, and only released on condition of rendering 1,200 cows and six score Welsh horses, three score ounces of gold and the same of white silver and the sword of Carlus': *A.U.*, vol. 1, pp. 560-1. According to the editor of these annals the sword of Carlus was that of Carlus, son of Olaf the White, slain in battle at Killineery in 868. I prefer, however, the Charlemagne explanation.

4. We call this Diarmait (slain in 1072) 'Diarmait I', and his famous descendant who brought Strongbow over 'Diarmait II', king of Leinster (Diarmait Mac Murchada). In 1074 Lanfranc, archbishop of Canterbury, addressed a letter to Gofraid [*Gothricus*] 'glorious king of Ireland', and another to Toirrdelbach ua Briain the high-king as 'magnificent king of Ireland', recommending Patrick to them as bishop of Dublin. [For the text of these letters see Clover, H. and Gibson, M., (eds.), *The Letters of Lanfranc Archbishop of Canterbury* (1979), nos. 9, 10.] To place this Gofraid is not easy, as there were more than one of the name claiming Dublin then. But there was a famous man of the name, Gofraid Méránach or Godred Crovan, who appears in 1068, and in the Manx annals is said to have been king of Man from 1079 to 1095. His son Olaf ruled from 1103 to 1153. Godred Crovan, these annals say, '*subdued Dublin and the greater part of Leinster* and held the Scots in such subjection that no one who built a vessel dared put in more than three bolts'. It was probably to him that Lanfranc's letter went. [The Gofraid who received the letter is now thought to have been Gofraid mac Amlaíb meic Ragnaill: *N.H.I.*, vol. 9, p. 139, no. 20a.]

5. Sumerled, a famous sea-king, ancestor of the *Clann Somhairle* or MacDonalds, whom we may call a Gaelic-speaking Norseman, who was descended on his mother's side from Sigurd, jarl of Orkney (who fell at Clontarf), was the rival of King Godred [II Olafsson] who succeeded in Man in 1153. He married a sister of this Godred, and finally wrested from him the northern part of this petty kingdom, i.e. the Hebrides and Argyll, while Godred kept Man. Sumerled died in 1164. The Manx Chronicle says: 'The kingdom of the Isles was ruined from the time when the sons of Sumerled got possession of it'.

6. This order of the events of the siege of Dublin by Ruaidrí Ua Conchobair, contrary to the view of Orpen, is worked out in O'Doherty, J.F., 'St. Laurence O'Toole and the Anglo-Norman invasion', *I.E.R.*, vol. 50 (1937), pp. 465-72; and I agree with it.

7. [Henry II's brief charter of 1171-2, confirmed by the Lord John in 1185, made Dublin in effect a colonial outpost of Bristol. The liberties of Bristol were presumably to be enjoyed by those English burgesses who chose to settle in Dublin. It was John's charter of 1192 that endowed the town of Dublin with a municipal identity on the standard Western model. Cf. Mac Niocaill, G., 'The colonial town in Irish documents', in *Comparative Urban Origins*, pp. 373-4. For the Latin text of these charters see Mac Niocaill, G., *Na Buirgéisí XII-XV Aois*, vol. 1 (1964), pp. 75-81. There is an excellent analysis of the process of enfranchisement at Cork in O'Brien, A.F., 'The development of the privileges, liberties and immunities of medieval Cork and the growth of an urban autonomy *c*. 1189 to 1500', *Cork Hist. Soc. Jn.*, vol. 90 (1985).]

NOTES TO CHAPTER 5

[Reprinted from *R.S.A.I. Jn.*, vol. 79 (1949), pp. 64-83. The most striking developments in our understanding of pre-Norman Dublin since 1949 have been in the fields of archaeology and numismatics. For the archaeology see, for example: Ó Ríordáin, B., 'Excavations at High Street and Winetavern Street, Dublin', *Medieval Archaeology*, vol. 15 (1971); Reynolds, M., 'Irish combs from the ninth to the 13th century', in Clarke, H.B., (ed.), *Focus on Medieval Dublin*, Dublin Arts Festival (1978), pp. 15-20; Wallace, P.F., 'Anglo-Norman Dublin: continuity and change', in Ó Corráin, D., (ed.), *Irish Antiquity: Essays and Studies presented to Professor M.J. O'Kelly* (1981), pp. 247-67; Murray, H., *Viking and Early Medieval Buildings in Dublin* (1983); Wallace, P.F., 'The archaeology of Viking Dublin', in *Comparative Urban Origins*, pp. 103-45; see also above, pp. 70-97. For the numismatics see, for example: O'Sullivan, W., *The Earliest Irish Coinage* (1961); Dolley, R.H.M., *Viking Coins of the Danelaw and of Dublin* (1965); *The Hiberno-Norse Coins in the British Museum* (1966); see also companion volume, pp. 135-44.]

1. Haliday, C., *The Scandinavian Kingdom of Dublin*, 2nd edn. (1884, reprinted 1969), p. 208 ff.

2. *A.U.*, vol. 2, pp. 532-3: 'o baile Atha Cliath co baile Atha Luain'. Cf. *A.U., s.a.* 1369: 'ag Gallaib Atha Cliath' ; 1412: 'd'elogh a hAth Cliath'; 1473: 'co baile Atha Cliath'. Thus Baile Átha Cliath is hardly found in Irish mouths until about 1500, if even then. The Four Masters consistently use Áth Cliath, without the Baile.

3. Hogan, E., *Onomasticon Goedelicum, Locorum et Tribuum Hiberniae et Scotiae . . .* (1910), *s.v.* drochat dubgaill, says, quoting Gilbert, J.T., *A History of the City of Dublin*, vol. 1 (1854, reprinted 1978), p. 319, that the only bridge in Dublin between *c.* 1000 and 1670 was the Old Bridge that led from Bridgefoot Street to Oxmantown.

4. Haliday, *Scandinavian Kingdom*, p. 216 ff.

5. De Burgo, T., *Hibernia Dominicana sive Historia Provinciae Hiberniae Ordinis Praedicatorum . . .* (1762), p. 193.

6. Haliday, *Scandinavian Kingdom*, p. 205.

7. *A.F.M., s.a.* 1155, 1159.

8. *Ibid., s.a.* 1140.

9. *A.U., s.a.* 1001. A *tóchar* was made across the Shannon at Athlone by Máel Sechnaill II and Cathal, king of Connacht.

10. Cf. *drochet* in Windisch, E., *Irische Texte mit Wörterbuch* (1880), p. 503; *Frag. Ann.*, pp. 154-5. The Munster forces came to Droichet Lethglinne on their way to fight the battle of Belach Mugna in 908. Celléne *drochtech* was abbot of Iona, 726-52, but does the epithet *drochtech* here mean 'bridge-builder'?

11. Plummer, C., (ed.), *Vitae Sanctorum Hiberniae . . .*, vol. 2 (1910), p. 288. Cf. *ibid.*, vol. 1, p. civ, n. 4; Rees, W.J., (ed.), *Lives of the Cambro-British Saints . . .* (1853), pp. 68-9. All references to bridges in Plummer, C., (ed.), *Bethada Náem nÉrenn: Lives of Irish Saints . . .*, 2 vols. (1922, reprinted 1968), e.g. Droichet Atha (Drogheda), are late.

12. Gwynn, E., (ed.), *The Metrical Dindshenchas*, vol. 3 (1913), p. 100.

13. *Ibid.*, p. 94.

14. White, N.J.D., (ed.), '*Libri Sancti Patricii*: the Latin writings of St. Patrick', *R.I.A. Proc.*, vol. 25 (1905), sect. C, p. 240.

15. Anderson, A.O. and M.O., (eds.), *Adomnan's Life of Columba* (1961), pp. 332-3.

16. In this territory lay Dúrlas Eile (Thurles) and Buirgheas Cloinne Céin (Borrisokane).

17. *Bk. Ballymote*, p. 222, col. c; *Bk. Lec.*, p. 44, l. 22.

18. *Bk. Lec.*, p. 86ᵛ and cognate texts.

19. Hogan, *Onomasticon, s.v.* Cell Moshamóg and Uí Dúnchada.

20. Cf. Stokes, W., 'The prose tales in the Rennes Dindshenchas', *Revue celtique*, vol. 16 (1895), p. 284.

21. Dillon, M., (ed.), *Lebor na Cert: the Book of Rights* (1962), p. 16 f.

22. Gwynn, *Metrical Dindshenchas*, vol. 3, p. 104: 'Etar étan ri dílind, / in clár cetach tuath-Cualand'.

23. Hogan, *Onomasticon, s.v.*

24. A *longphort* was constructed at Annagassan, Co. Louth, in the same year. The term *longphort* was later extended to mean any fortified base. Hence Longford, an inland town, many miles away from the sea and from ships.

25. The name I take to be from the Norse Thorgestr, the intervening forms being Thorgest, Thorgess, Torgeis. But it may be derived from Thorgeirr or Thorgils.

26. The editor of the English translation of the *Heimskringla* (1932) [E. Monsen] is thus doubly at fault, when he places the death of Turgéis in 836 and says of him: 'Torgils or Turgesius subdued the Irish by his conquest of Dublin' (p. 42). [The standard translation of the *Heimskringla* is now that of S. Laing, revised by J. Simpson and P. Foote, 2 pts. in 3 vols. (1961-4).]

27. The chief fortress of this family was at Loch Gabor, Lagore: *A.U.*, *s.a.* 785, 805, 825, etc.

28. This territory is called generally Ciannachta Breg, from the branch of the Ciannachta there settled. They had come under the control of the Síl nÁedo Sláine section of the southern Uí Néill. In a poem by Fland Manistrech, Cináed appears in the list of Síl nÁedo Sláine kings: *Bk. Leinster*, vol. 4, pp. 811-13. Cnoghbha (Knowth), near the Boyne, is mentioned as a prominent fortress of the family: *A.U.*, vol. 1, pp. 436-7: *ri Cnoghbhai*.

29. His execution took place with the approval of the good of Ireland and the successor of St. Patrick in particular: *A.U.*, *s.a.* 851; *Chron. Scot.*, *s.a.* 851; *Frag. Ann.*, pp. 90-1.

30. 'Ro baidhead é tre comhairle Maoilseachlainn i sruthán shalach': *Frag. Ann.*, pp. 90-1. *A.U.* and *Chron. Scot.* say that he was drowned in a lake, but *Chron. Scot.* and *A.F.M.* give the place as the Ainghe, the Nanny Water in Meath about 3 miles south of Drogheda.

31. Laing, *Heimskringla*, pt. 2, pp. 44-6, 51-2, 54, 57-9, etc.; Pálsson, H. and Edwards, P., (trans.), *Orkneyinga Saga: the History of the Earls of Orkney* (1978), pp. 122-3, 125, 132, 138-9, etc.

32. *A.U.*, *s.a.* 851, 852, 857, 867, 875, 877, 893, 914, etc.

33. Mahr, A., *Saorstat Éireann Official Handbook* (1932), p. 213.

34. *Frag. Ann.*, pp. 96-7. [For a genealogical table and king-list of the house of Ivar see *N.H.I.*, vol. 9, pp. 139, 208-9.]

35. *Ibid.*

36. Laing, *Heimskringla*, pt. 1, pp. 13-14; pt. 2, pp. 116-17, 121, etc.; Pálsson and Edwards, *Orkneyinga Saga*, pp. 36-7, 85-6, 192-3, etc.

37. *Frag. Ann.*, pp. 98-105.

38. Pálsson, H. and Edwards, P., (trans.), *The Book of Settlements: Landnámabók* (1972), p. 137 [the *Sturlubók* version]; Haliday, *Scandinavian Kingdom*, p. 100 ff.; *C.G.G.*, p. 300 — a list of descendants in tabular form. These northern genealogies cannot be regarded as reliable. It is, however, significant that Cerball has such a prominent place in Norse tradition. In the *Landnámabók* (p. 16) he is made king of Dublin and in the *Orkneyinga Saga* (p. 38) he is made father of Eithne, wife of Hlodvir, who became jarl of the Orkneys in 978.

39. Kendrick, T.D., *A History of the Vikings* (1930, reprinted 1968), p. 282.

40. *Frag. Ann.*, pp. 112-13. For the dynastic family in Dublin see Bugge, A., *Contributions to the History of the Norsemen in Ireland*, vol. 1 (1900), pp. 13-14.

41. Marriage alliances between Irish and Norse dynastic families were later common; cf. Haliday, *Scandinavian Kingdom*, p. 77 ff.

42. *A.U.*, *s.a.* 861, 862.

43. *Ibid.*, *s.a.* 866.

44. *Frag. Ann.*, pp. 118-19: 'Innisit dno h-éoluigh gurob í a bhean as móo ro greis Aod i cceann na Lochlannach'.

45. *Ibid.*, pp. 118-19, 122-5, 128-33; *A.F.M.*, *s.a.* 860, 864, etc.

46. Haliday, *Scandinavian Kingdom*, p. 44 ff.; Kendrick, *History of the Vikings*, p. 281; Hodgkin, R.H., *A History of the Anglo-Saxons*, 3rd edn., vol. 2 (1952), p. 490.

47. *C.G.G.*, pp. 26-7: 'Bai, imorro, arali cumsana deraib Erend fri re .xl. bliadan can inred Gall'.

48. Kendrick, *History of the Vikings*, p. 149.

49. *Ibid.*, p. 222 ff.

50. *C.G.G.*, pp. 48-9; *Ann. Inisf.*, *s.a.* 922; *Chron. Scot.*, *s.a.* 921 (*recte* 922).

51. *Chron. Scot.*, *s.a.* 934; *A.F.M.*, *s.a.* 933.

52. The battle of *Brunanburh*, near the Humber, in 937. Cf. Kendrick, *History of the Vikings*, p. 252; *A.U.*, *s.a.* 937; *C.G.G.*, p. 279 f.

53. *A.U.*, *s.a.* 938.

54. Kendrick, *History of the Vikings*, p. 255; *C.G.G.*, pp. 281-6.

55. O'Donovan, J., (ed.), *The Circuit of Ireland by Muirchertach mac Neill, Prince of Aileach* (1841), pp. 32, 34.

56. *A.U.*, vol. 1, pp. 490-1: 'for Gallaibh Atho Cliath 7 na n-indsedh'.

57. *Chron. Scot.*, pp. 226-7: Olaf died 'after holiness and penance'; *A.F.M.*, vol. 2, pp. 712-13: 'after penance and a good life'.

58. *Chron. Scot.* and *A.F.M.* put this event in 980. The siege lasted three days; the victory was complete and the spoil taken (2,000 cows, etc.) immense.

59. *Chron. Scot.*, *s.a.* 987; *Ann. Tig.*, vol. 17, p. 346; *A.F.M.*, *s.a.* 988. The siege lasted 20 days and succeeded through the cutting off of the defenders' fresh water supply. Among the conditions imposed was the payment to Máel Sechnaill of an ounce of gold from every garden [garth] in Dublin each Christmas night 'for ever'.

60. *Chron. Scot.*, *s.a.* 993; *Ann. Tig.*, vol. 17, p. 350; *A.F.M.*, *s.a.* 994. The *fail óir* (ring of gold) had religious significance. It was kept in temples and oaths were sworn on it. Moore changes this ring to a collar: 'When Malachy wore the collar of gold'.

61. Pálsson and Edwards, *Orkneyinga Saga*, p. 39.

62. For the battle of Clontarf see Ryan, J., 'The battle of Clontarf', *R.S.A.I. Jn.*, vol. 68 (1938).

63. Wales seems to have been ahead of Ireland then in the production of high-class bloodstock!

64. From the Liffey or Howth to the Delvin river, that part of Co. Dublin which lies between the city and the Meath border. It came to be called Fine Gall, Fingal.

65. *Ann. Tig.*, vol. 17, p. 370.

66. *A.U.*, *s.a.* 1031; *Ann. Tig.*, vol. 17, p. 372; *A.F.M.*, *s.a.* 1031.

67. *A.U.*, *s.a.* 1034; *Chron. Scot.*, *s.a.* 1032; *Ann. Tig.*, vol. 17, p. 374; *A.F.M.*, *s.a.* 1034.

68. *Ann. Tig.*, vol. 17, p. 376: 'Sitriuc mac Amlaim do dul assa righi tar muir'.

69. *Ibid.*: '7 Eachmarcach 'sa righi'.

70. *Ann. Tig.*, vol. 17, pp. 383-4, suggest that the throne of Dublin was taken from him for a while by Ivar, son of Harald.

71. *Ibid.*, pp. 392-3; *A.F.M.*, *s.a.* 1052. Haliday's view (*Scandinavian Kingdom*, p. 92) that Diarmait 'assumed the kingship of the foreigners in right of his descent from these kings' is untenable. Diarmait was not descended from the Dublin or other Norse kings, and *Ann. Tig.* say definitely: 'Mac Mail na mbó do gabail righi Átha cliath ar écin' (by force).

72. The Norse of Dublin formed part of his army: *A.U.*, vol. 2, pp. 24-5: 'ár Gall 7 Laighen ime'.

73. *Ann. Tig.*, vol. 17, p. 409; *A.F.M.*, *s.a.* 1070. Murchad was king of Dublin 'under his father'. He was buried in Áth Cliath: *A.U.*, *s.a.* 1070.

74. *Ann. Inisf.*, *s.a.* 1075.

75. *Ibid.*; *A.L.C.*, *s.a.* 1075.

76. *Ann. Inisf.*, *s.a.* 1075; *Chron. Scot.*, *s.a.* 1072.

77. *Ann. Inisf.*, pp. 232-3: 'Ríge Átha Cliath do gabail do Muirchertach mc. Thairdelbaich Hui Briain'; *A.F.M.*, *s.a.* 1075 (where the translation of the Irish annal is omitted); *Chron. Scot.*, *s.a.* 1076; *Ann. Clon.*, *s.a.* 1074.

78. The Leinstermen helped the Norse in a battle against Máel Sechlainn Ó Máel Sechlainn, king of Mide, at Dublin in 1086: *Chron. Scot.*, *s.a.* 1082; *Ann. Tig.*, vol. 17, p. 418; *A.U.*, *s.a.* 1086; *A.F.M.*, *s.a.* 1086.

79. *Ann. Inisf.*, *s.a.* 1087; *Chron. Scot.*, *s.a.* 1083; *Ann. Tig.*, vol. 17, p. 419; *A.F.M.*, *s.a.* 1087. The Leinster army was led by the king, and the princes slain show that the control of Dublin was regarded by the Leinstermen as a matter of great importance.

80. *Ann. Tig.*, vol. 18, p. 13; *A.F.M.*, *s.a.* 1090.

81. *Ann. Inisf.*, *s.a.* 1094.

82. *Ibid.*, *s.a.* 1095; *A.L.C.*, *s.a.* 1095.

83. *A.U.*, *s.a.* 1100; *Ann. Tig.*, vol. 18, p. 21; *A.L.C.*, *s.a.* 1100; *A.F.M.*, *s.a.* 1100: 'Loinges Atha Cliath'.

84. *Ann. Inisf.*, *s.a.* 1103; *A.F.M.*, *s.a.* 1103: 'Ar Gall Atha Cliath', etc. [On the political role of this king see now Candon, A., 'Muirchertach Ua Briain, politics and naval activity in the Irish Sea, 1075 to 1119', in Mac Niocaill, G. and Wallace, P.F., (eds.), *Keimelia: Studies in Medieval Archaeology and History in Memory of Tom Delaney* (1988), pp. 397-415.]

85. *Chron. Scot.*, *s.a.* 1113; *Ann. Tig.*, vol. 18, p. 38; *A.F.M.*, *s.a.* 1117.

86. *Chron. Scot.*, *s.a.* 1114; *Ann. Tig.*, vol. 18, p. 39; *A.F.M.*, *s.a.* 1118; *A.L.C.*, *s.a.* 1118: 'go tuc . . . gialla Gall bhudhéin'.

87. Cf. *Ann. Tig.*, *s.a.* 1146; *A.F.M.*, *s.a.* 1149 (Mac Lochlainn), 1150 (O'Brien), 1156 (Mac Murchada), 1162 (Mac Lochlainn), 1166 (O'Connor).

88. *A.F.M.*, *s.a.* 1138.

89. *Ibid.*, *s.a.* 1142.

90. *Ibid.*, *s.a.* 1166, 1167; *Ann. Tig.*, vol. 18, pp. 267-8, 271-2.

91. *Ann. Tig.*, vol. 18, p. 274: '7 Gaill léo'; *A.F.M.*, *s.a.* 1169: '7 Goill Atha Cliath'.

92. *Ann. Tig.*, vol. 18, p. 279; *A.F.M.*, *s.a.* 1170.

93. His return with a few ships, after he had made good his escape, and his bearing towards the Normans after his defeat at their hands show a lack of understanding with the Irish leaders rather than treachery towards them. Cf. Giraldus, *Expugnatio*, pp.76-9.

94. *A.U.*, vol. 1, pp. 488-9: 'Ferdalach airchinnech Rechrann a gentilibus occisus est'.

95. Cf. Pálsson and Edwards, *Landnámabók*, p. 97.

96. Kendrick, *History of the Vikings*, p. 40, dates the beginning of general conversion among the leaders to A.D. 950. Isolated cases of conversion had been taking place since the Scandinavians first came into contact with Christian Europe. But the people remained unmoved by such events. Swegn I Forkbeard, king of Denmark (986-1014), the father of Cnut, was as heathen as any of his ancestors.

97. Cf. Ryan, 'Battle of Clontarf', p. 44. Jarl Sigurd of the Orkneys is to be numbered among the Christians. The manner of his conversion is noteworthy: Pálsson and Edwards, *Orkneyinga Saga*, p. 39. King Olaf Tryggvason, with five ships, met Jarl Sigurd with three ships, in South Ronaldsay (*c.* 995). Olaf invited the jarl on to his ship and when they met he addressed him thus: 'I want you and all your subjects to be baptized. If you refuse, I'll have you killed on the spot, and I swear that I'll ravage every island with fire and steel'. The jarl left the decision in Olaf's hands. He had him baptized and took his son as a hostage to ensure that the jarl would persevere in well-doing.

98. Gwynn, A., 'The origins of the see of Dublin', *I.E.R.*, vol. 57 (1941), pp. 108-10. For a detailed study of ecclesiastical events in Dublin before the coming of the Normans see the series of articles by Gwynn: 'Ireland and Rome in the 11th century', *I.E.R.*, vol. 57 (1941); 'Lanfranc and the Irish Church', *I.E.R.*, vols. 57-8 (1941); 'Pope Gregory VII and the Irish Church', *I.E.R.*, vol. 58 (1941); 'St. Anselm and the Irish Church', *I.E.R.*, vol. 59 (1942); 'Bishop Samuel of Dublin', *I.E.R.*, vol. 60 (1942).

99. As the Ua hAingliu (O'Hanly) family belonged to Cenél Dobtha, in northern Roscommon, the appearance of two of its members as bishops of Dublin is surprising. The explanation may lie in their proximity to Lough Ree and their activity on the Shannon. They commanded Ua Conchobair's ships on the great river and made settlements in Tipperary and Limerick, where their descendants are still fairly numerous: O'Daly, J. and O'Donovan, J., (eds.), 'Inauguration of Cathal Crobhdhearg O'Conor, king of Connaught', *R.S.A.I. Jn.*, vol. 2 (1852-3), pp. 344-5. One of them was killed by O'Grady of Clare in 1137: *Ann. Tig.*, vol. 18, p. 156. It may well be that the family from which the bishops sprang had settled in Limerick and intermarried with the city population (Samuel = Sumerled?). From Limerick uncle and nephew would have sailed to join English Benedictine monasteries.

100. Máel Ísu Ua hAinmere, who had also been a monk at Winchester; cf. Gwynn, A., 'The

origins of the diocese of Waterford', *I.E.R.*, vol. 59 (1942).

101. Perhaps the Norse Grane; cf. Laing, *Heimskringla*, pt. 2, p. 184.

102. Gwynn, 'Pope Gregory and the Irish Church', p. 101.

103. Gwynn, A., 'The origins of St. Mary's Abbey, Dublin', *R.S.A.I. Jn.*, vol. 79 (1949), p. 110.

104. Haliday, *Scandinavian Kingdom*, pp. 143-99.

105. Its position appears clearly on the survey map of 1673: *ibid.*, p. 228.

106. As at the Irish *óenach* and the Anglo-Saxon *gemot*. On the democratic spirit of the Northmen see Olrik, A., *Viking Civilization* (1930), p. 17 ff.

107. Gwynn, 'Lanfranc and the Irish Church', pp. 4-8.

108. Cf. Curtis, E., 'The English and Ostmen in Ireland', *E.H.R.*, vol. 23 (1908).

NOTES TO CHAPTER 6

[Reprinted from *D.H.R.*, vol. 15 (1958-9), pp. 33-41. The main conduit serving the townspeople is shown on the large-scale map in Clarke, H.B., *Dublin c. 840 to c. 1540: the Medieval Town in the Modern City* (1978). I should like to take this opportunity to correct an error on this map: the watercourse through the precincts of St. Thomas's Abbey should be deleted and be replaced by a channel from the cistern to St. Catherine's Church, running behind the houses in Thomas Street. This artificial channel, known as the Glib river or water, is shown correctly in Andrews, J.H., 'The oldest map of Dublin', *R.I.A. Proc.*, vol. 83 (1983), sect. C, p. 212, fig. 1. On the lesser watercourses of medieval Dublin see also: O'Brennan, L.M., 'Little rivers of Dublin', *D.H.R.*, vol. 3, no. 1 (1940); Jackson, V., 'The Glib water and Colman's brook', *D.H.R.*, vol. 11 (1949-50); Goodbody, O.C., 'The neighbourhood of the Glib river', *D.H.R.*, vol. 16 (1960-1); Fitzgerald, A.D., 'Down the old Poddle', in Gillespie, E., (ed.), *The Liberties of Dublin* (1973), pp. 24-32.]

1. Berry, H.F., 'The water supply of ancient Dublin', *R.S.A.I. Jn.*, vol. 21 (1890-1).

2. *Anc. Rec. Dublin*, vol. 1, p. 92.

3. *Cal. Pat. Rolls, 1232-47*, p. 467 [a later mandate of 18 November 1245].

4. Printed in Berry, H.F., 'Notes on an unpublished manuscript inquisition (A.D. 1258), relating to the Dublin city watercourse, from the muniments of the earl of Meath', *R.I.A. Proc.*, vol. 24 (1902-4), sect. C, pp. 40-1. [The text as printed is dated 43 Henry III = 1258-9.]

5. [*Ibid.*, pp. 39-46.]

6. [*Anc. Rec. Dublin*, vol. 1, p. 92.]

7. *Ibid.*, pp. 101-2.

8. *Ibid.*, pp. 86-7.

9. Ronan, M.V., 'The Poddle river and its branches', *R.S.A.I. Jn.*, vol. 57 (1927).

10. *Anc. Rec. Dublin*, vol. 1, pp. 372-3.

11. *Ibid.*, p. 185. [The author gives an abridged version in modern English.]

NOTES TO CHAPTER 7

[Reprinted from *R.I.A. Proc.*, vol. 74 (1974), sect. C, pp. 113-32. For John Speed's map see further Andrews, J.H., 'The oldest map of Dublin', *R.I.A. Proc.*, vol. 83 (1983), sect. C. There is a valuable catalogue of local maps in Clark, M., *The Book of Maps of the Dublin City Surveyors, 1695-1827* (1983). On the historical background to the process of reclamation here described see Lennon, C., *Richard Stanihurst the Dubliner, 1547-1618* (1981).]

1. Ronan, M.V., 'The Poddle river and its branches', *R.S.A.I. Jn.*, vol. 57 (1927); 'The Poddle river (1803-1829)', *R.S.A.I. Jn.*, vol. 78 (1948).

2. Ordnance Survey of Dublin City (1847-8), 5 ft. scale, revised edn. (1864-97), sheets 20, 21; 25 in. scale, revised edn. (1910-11), sheet 18 XI.

3. Sloane, J.S., 'A map of the walls of the city of Dublin, compiled from the few authorities that exist, to illustrate the antiquarian rambles', *Irish Builder*, vol. 24 (1882), p. 191; Strangways, L.R., 'A map of the walls of Dublin from all available authorities', *Ireland*, vol. 6 (1906), p. 30; as frontispiece in *Dublin Main Drainage Scheme Souvenir Handbook* (1906); and as frontispiece in Cosgrave, E.M. and Strangways, L.R., *Dictionary of Dublin*, 2nd edn. (1907); Ó Ríordáin, B., 'Dublin: gates, towers and town walls', *Current Archaeology*, no. 22 (1970), p. 312; and *Medieval Archaeology*, vol. 16 (1972), p. 74.

4. Anonymous note, 'The walls of Dublin', *Irish Builder*, vol. 24 (1882), p. 190.

5. Cosgrave and Strangways, *Dictionary of Dublin*, pp. 67-9.

6. *Anc. Rec. Dublin*, vol. 2, pp. 551-7; summarized in *Cal. S.P. Ire., 1574-85*, pp. 1590-2.

7. Entrenchment within the existing city walls is suggested by an edict of 25 October 1597, by which the mayor and council directed that all postern gates be closed with lime and stone. Evidence that this edict was actually enforced is found in Berry, H.F., 'Minute book of the Corporation of Dublin, known as the Friday Book, 1597-1611', *R.I.A. Proc.*, vol. 30 (1912-13), sect. C, pp. 492-500.

8. Original indenture of Corporation lease to Jacob Newman of Isolde's Tower and the adjoining tenement, 20 January 1603: P.R.O.I., Dublin Corporation records (at present largely unsorted). Some of the expired leases, including this one of Newman, bear no catalogue number; others bear 19th-century catalogue numbers but only part of this catalogue has survived. In the following references catalogue numbers are cited for those leases which bear them. Cf. *Anc. Rec. Dublin*, vol. 2, pp. 418, 435.

9. P.R.O.I., original indenture of Corporation lease no. 20, to Robert Molesworth of the tower over Dame's Gate, Buttevant Tower and ground in Fishamble Street, 1704.

10. Published as inset on the map of 'The Countie of Leinster' to illustrate 'The Fourth Book containing the Kingdom of Ireland' in Speed, J., *The Theatre of the Empire of Great Britaine . . .* (1611), following p. 141.

11. *Anc. Rec. Dublin*, vol. 2, pp. 418, 435, 445, 457-8, 481, 486.

12. P.R.O.I., Newman's lease of Isolde's Tower, 1603.

13. P.R.O.I., indentures of Corporation leases: lease of Isolde's Tower, 1603; lease no. 49, to Jacob Newman of a small piece of void ground near Case's Tower, 18 January 1604; lease to Richard Proudfoot of Dublin, merchant, of one parcel of void ground situated on Wood Quay, 1607; lease no. 135, to John Bysse for the tower of Dame's Gate . . . one other tower or flancard standing upon the wall situate between Dame's Gate and Buttevant Tower, 1639; lease no. 20, to Robert Molesworth of the tower over Dame's Gate, Buttevant Tower and ground in Fishamble Street, 1704 (in which other leases are

recited). Cf. *Anc. Rec. Dublin*, vol. 2, *passim*.

14. *Anc. Rec. Dublin*, vol. 7, pp. 159, 219-20, 349.

15. Greene's map is reproduced from a microfilm copy in the N.L.I. The original was in the possession of Mr. D. O'Hara, Annaghmore, Collooney, Co. Sligo, but has not been in his possession since 1969. Kendrick's tracing of Ramsay's map is among the Corporation maps in the P.R.O.I. Historic sites marked by Greene were not all copied by Kendrick, but the essential details of the topography of 1720 were all faithfully copied, except the street-widths.

16. *Anc. Rec. Dublin*, vol. 2, pp. 445, 486; vol. 3, p. 49. Gilbert interprets the name Profot somewhat differently, claiming that it was derived from 'George Proudfoot, merchant, cousin to James Barry, first earl of Santry, who inherited it [i.e. the castle] from his father, Alderman Richard Barry, merchant and sheriff of Dublin': Gilbert, J.T., *A History of the City of Dublin*, vol. 1 (1854, reprinted 1978), p. 375. George Proudfoot's connexion with the castle seems rather tenuous and derivation from Richard Proudfoot's name seems more probable.

17. *Anc. Rec. Dublin*, vol. 1, pp. 290, 469.

18. *Ibid.*, p. 347; P.R.O.I., original indenture of lease to John Fitzsymon, merchant, of 'the tower next to Issotts tower that was in term with Robert Fitzsymon . . . 4th April, 17th Henry VIII'. Sloane (1882) suggests that Fitzsymon's and Case's Towers were two separate and distinct buildings. Strangways (1906) follows this interpretation but names only one building, 'Casse's'. Dimensions given in the survey of 1585 and by Greene and Ramsay in 1720 disprove the interpretation of these two authors.

19. Both dimensions are marked on Greene's survey. The width of Essex Gate is not marked on Ramsay's tracing but the location of Isolde's Tower, which is suggested by Ramsay near the boundary of Denum's holding, seems more accurate than that suggested by Greene.

20. *Anc. Rec. Dublin*, vol. 5, p. 30.

21. *Ibid.*, p. 222.

22. *Ibid.*, vol. 2, pp. 457-8. Among the O'Hara Papers (N.L.I., microfilm n. 2670, p. 1576) there are several documents which refer to Newman and his leasehold. These include a genealogical abstract, 18th-century copies of letters patent and abstracts of leases of several houses and plots of ground in Dublin. A copy of a patent of 16 May 1608, granted to James Hamilton, by which premises were granted in trust for Jacob Newman, includes a brief description of the leasehold near Dame's Gate on which there was a 'messuage covered with straw'.

23. *An Exact Survey of the City and Suburbs of Dublin . . . by John Rocque, 1756*. Copies in the N.L.I. and in T.C.D. [See now Andrews, J.H., *Two Maps of 18th-century Dublin and its Surroundings* (1977).]

24. *An Accurate Survey of the City and Suburbs of Dublin by Mr. Rocque with Additions and Improvements by Mr. Bernard Scalé to 1773*. Copies in the N.L.I. and in T.C.D.

25. In this case the discrepancy between measurements taken in 1605 and in 1720 was probably due to more extended reclamation than that sanctioned by Newman's lease: *Anc. Rec. Dublin*, vol. 3, p. 337; vol. 4, p. 87; vol. 5, p. 85.

26. *Ibid.*, vol. 4, p. 87; vol. 5, p. 85.

27. P.R.O.I., indenture and counterpart of Corporation lease no. 12, to Nevill Pooley, of 'ground near the Custom House, 3rd Fri. after the Feast of St. Michael the Archangel,

1675'.

28. Dublin, City Hall, Muniment Room, indenture of Corporation lease MA 7, to Keane O'Hara of the mill-pond and tenements called Dame's Mills, 21 July 1704.

29. P.R.O.I., indenture of Corporation lease to Jacob Newman of two watermills without the Dame's Gate called the Dame's Mills, together with the mill-pond, 25 January 1605.

30. *Commons' Jn. Ire.*, vol. 9, pt. 1, appendix, p. ccix.

31. Semple, G., *A Treatise on Building in Water* (1776), p. 52.

32. De Gomme, B., 'The city and suburbs of Dublin from Kilmainham to Ringsend ... 15th November, 1673 A.D.': Greenwich, National Maritime Museum, Dartmouth Collection, no. 11.

33. *Anc. Rec. Dublin*, vol. 2, p. 4.

34. O'Hara Papers, copies of letters patent.

35. *Cal. Pat. Rolls Ire., Jas I*, p. 9.

36. *Anc. Rec. Dublin*, vol. 2, p. 458.

37. Dublin, City Hall, Minutes of the Wide Streets Commissioners, vol. 1, p. 24 (20 March 1759).

38. Molesworth's property comprised the lots numbered 1-10 inclusive and 30-34 inclusive, as shown on Purfield's survey, while Keane O'Hara's comprised lots numbered 11-29 inclusive: Minutes of the Wide Streets Commissioners, vol. 1, p. 24 (12 March 1759).

39. P.R.O.I., indenture of Corporation lease no. 67, to 'Robert Byse of Dublin, gent., of the tower over Dame's Gate with appurtenances ... the tower commonly called Buttevant's tower ... [the city] wall between Dame's Gate and Buttevant's tower ... 16th year of the reign of Elizabeth'; indenture of Corporation lease no. 135, to 'John Byse for the tower over Dame's Gate ... 1639'; indenture of Corporation lease no. 20, to Robert Molesworth, 1704. Cf. *Anc. Rec. Dublin*, vol. 2, pp. 512, 514.

40. *Anc. Rec. Dublin*, vol. 5, p. 30; vol. 6, p. 222.

41. *Ibid.*, vol. 6, p. 222.

42. P.R.O.I., deed of conveyance no. 21, from Lord and Lady Molesworth to the commissioners of the new street, 12 March 1763.

43. Semple, *Building in Water*, p. 52.

44. Harris, W., *The History and Antiquities of the City of Dublin* (1766), p. 62.

45. *Anc. Rec. Dublin*, vol. 1, pp. 95, 115, n. 4.

46. *Ibid.*, vol. 2, pp. 457-8.

47. P.R.O.I., indenture of Corporation lease no. 49, to 'Jacob Newman, of a small piece of void ground near Casse's tower, 18 Jany 1604'.

48. P.R.O.I., indenture of Corporation lease to 'Richard Proudfoot of Dublin, merchant, of one parcel of void ground situated on Wood Quay, First Friday after the feast of St. Michael Archangel, 1607'.

49. *Anc. Rec. Dublin*, vol. 2, p. 458.

50. *Ibid.*, pp. 481-2, 486.

51. *Ibid.*, p. 518.

52. *Ibid.*, pp. 512, 514.

53. The only record of municipal property actually held by Matthew Handcock is a deed of ground near Gormond's Gate: P.R.O.I. Comparison of de Gomme's, Phillips's and Greene's maps shows that these holdings, which were assigned to Handcock and Newman during the first decade of the 17th century, were not reclaimed until the end of the 17th or the beginning of the 18th century.

54. *Anc. Rec. Dublin*, vol. 5, pp. 85-6.

55. *Ibid.*, vol. 3, p. 547; vol. 4, p. 456; vol. 5, pp. 52, 92, 430.

56. *Ibid.*, vol. 3, pp. 546-50.

57. *Ibid.*, pp. 329-30.

58. *Ibid.*; O'Hara Papers.

59. *Anc. Rec. Dublin*, vol. 3, pp. 337-8.

60. De Gomme's survey, 1673.

61. B.L., Add. MS. 16370; microfilm copy in the N.L.I., n. 779, p. 505, and published in *Anc. Rec. Dublin*, vol. 5, pp. 566-73; Greenwich, National Maritime Museum, Dartmouth Collection, nos. 11, 12.

62. B.L., K. Top. LIII, 10, an undated, unsigned survey which is thought by the writer to be the original survey made by Phillips, of which B.L., K. Top. LIII, 9 and 11 are contemporary manuscript copies. Another manuscript copy is included in N.L.I., MS. 2557.

63. *Anc. Rec. Dublin*, vol. 5, p. 30; *P.R.I. Rep. D.K. 17*, appendix III, p. 27.

64. *Anc. Rec. Dublin*, vol. 5, pp. 85-6; P.R.O.I., indenture and counterpart of Corporation lease no. 12, to Nevill Pooley, of 'ground near the Custom House, 3rd Fri. after the Feast of St. Michael the Archangel, 1675'; Corporation lease to 'John Crow of houses, garden, orchard and other appurtenances now or late in the tenure . . . of Alderman Lovett or his undertenants, the said garden lying on the north and south sides of Essex Street, 1675' (attested copy used in evidence at the King's Bench trial at the Bar, Michaelmas term, 1827).

65. *Anc. Rec. Dublin*, vol. 5, p. 58; vol. 6, pp. 582-605.

66. *Ibid.*, vol. 3, p. 33.

NOTES TO CHAPTER 8

[Reprinted from Almqvist, B. and Greene, D., (eds.), *Proceedings of the Seventh Viking Congress* (1976), pp. 135-40. The house remains discovered on the High Street site are among those analysed in Murray, H., *Viking and Early Medieval Buildings in Dublin* (1983).]

1. *A.U.*, vol. 1, pp. 344-5; *Chron. Scot.*, pp. 142-3; *Ann. Clon.*, p. 138.

2. Relevant entries in *A.U.* are as follows:

   837.   Longas eile tre fhichet long for abaind Liphi . . .

   841.   Longport oc Duiblinn asrorta Laigin 7 Oi Neill etir tuatha 7 cealla, corice sliabh Bladhma . . .

   851.   Tetact dubgennti du Ath Cliath, co ralsat ár mór du fhinngallaibh, 7 co ro slatsat in longport etir doine 7 moine . . .

3. E.g., Young, J.I., 'A note on the Norse occupation of Ireland', *History*, vol. 35 (1950) and references therein.

4. The principal collection of artefacts of this type is that which was assembled by Thomas M. Ray during the years 1856-9. This material, together with other objects found in Dublin and formerly in the Hewson, Hassé, Verschoyle-Campbell and Frazer collections, is now preserved in the National Museum of Ireland. Some bone combs and iron knife-blades which have a Dublin provenance and which formed part of the Bell collection are now preserved in the National Museum of Antiquities of Scotland. Some of the Dublin finds are listed in Wilde, W.R., *Catalogue of the Antiquities in the Museum of the Royal Irish Academy* (1861); Wakeman, W.F., *Descriptive Catalogue of Objects in the Collection of the Royal Irish Academy* (1894); and Bøe, J., 'Norse antiquities in Ireland', in Shetelig, H., (ed.), *Viking Antiquities in Great Britain and Ireland*, pt. 3 (1940), pp. 65-9 and figs. 45, 56.

5. For a summary report and illustrations of some of the principal finds and structures see Ó Ríordáin, B., 'Excavations at High Street and Winetavern Street, Dublin', *Medieval Archaeology*, vol. 15 (1971), pp. 73-8, figs. 20-28 and plates V-X; see also Dolley, M. and Seaby, W.A., 'A find of 13th-century pewter tokens from the National Museum excavations at Winetavern Street, Dublin', *Spinks Numismatic Circular* (1971).

6. A small selection of finds from the Christchurch Place excavation is incorporated in Nat. Mus. Ire., *Viking and Medieval Dublin, National Museum Excavations, 1962-1973: Catalogue of Exhibition* (1973). Some objects and structures discovered on this site since the date of holding of the Seventh Viking Congress in Dublin have been included in this article.

7. Mahr, A., (ed.), *Christian Art in Ancient Ireland*, vol. 1 (1932), plates 57, 58.

8. Raftery, J., (ed.), *Christian Art in Ancient Ireland*, vol. 2 (1941), p. 155 and plates 113, 114.

9. MacDermott, M., 'The Kells Crosier', *Archaeologia*, vol. 96 (1955).

10. Raftery, *Christian Art*, plates 87, 88.

11. *Ibid.*, plate 82.

12. Henry, F., 'Remarks on the decoration of three Irish psalters', *R.I.A. Proc.*, vol. 61 (1960-1), sect. C.

13. Henry, F., *Irish Art in the Romanesque Period (1020-1170)* (1970), pp. 56-8 and fig. 4. The writer is indebted to Dr. Henry and Miss U. O'Meadhra for comments on the trial pieces.

14. Foote, P. and Wilson, D.M., *The Viking Achievement: the Society and Culture of Early Medieval Scandinavia* (1970), plate 26a.

15. The writer wishes to thank Professor Ole Klindt Jensen, Århus University, for this suggestion. The excavations at Bryggen, Bergen, have produced a number of examples, also, for which see Herteig, A., *Kongers Havn og Handels Sete* (1969), plate 49.

16. Many of the combs have been examined by Mrs. Mairead Dunlevy-Reynolds, who has kindly informed me that the majority of the single-sided combs are of types (her classes F and G) recorded from sites in Norway, Sweden and Scotland in particular. For Norway see Brøgger, A.W., *Osebergfundet*, vol. 2 (1928), figs. 136-8; Grieg, S., *Middelalderske Byfund fra Bergen og Oslo* (1933), figs. 190, 191. For Sweden see Arbman, H., *Birka I: die Gräber* (1940), plates 159, 160, 164; Blomquist, R. and Mårtensson, A.W., *Archaeologica Lundensia*, vol. 2 (1963), figs. 230, 231. For Scotland see Hamilton, J.R.C., *Excavations at Jarlshof, Shetland* (1956), fig. 69, nos. 11, 12 and plate XXXII, no. 4. Examples are also known from Frisia: Roes, A., *Bone and Antler Objects from the Frisian Terp-mounds* (1963), plate XXI, nos. 2-4; and from England: Waterman,

D.M., 'Late Saxon, Viking, and early medieval finds from York', *Archaeologia*, vol. 97 (1959), p. 88, fig. 16.

17. Fanning, T., 'The bronze ringed pins in the Limerick City Museum', *North Munster Antiquarian Journal*, vol. 12 (1969).

18. Identified by Mr. John G. Hurst, Senior Inspector, Department of the Environment, London. The writer is much indebted to Mr. Hurst and to Mr. K.J. Barton, Director, Portsmouth City Museums, for information and advice on the large collection of pottery recovered in the Dublin excavations.

19. Ó Ríordáin, 'Excavations at High Street and Winetavern Street', p. 77 and fig. 27a and b. Carvings of ships found on a stone from Gauldalen, Sørtrøndelag, Norway, illustrated in *Nicholay*, no. 13 (1973), fig. 17, depict a somewhat similar treatment of the furled sail to that on the larger of the Dublin examples. A study of the Dublin ship sketches, boat models and other finds of this nature is being carried out by Mr. Arne-Emil Christensen, University Museum of National Antiquities, Oslo, to whom I am indebted for many useful references and for information. [See now Christensen, A.-E., 'Ship graffiti and models', in Wallace, P.F., (ed.), *Miscellanea 1* (1988), pp. 13-26.]

20. For illustrations of rowlocks of similar type on the gunwales of boats found on board the Gokstad ship see du Chaillu, P.B., *The Viking Age*, vol. 2 (1889), fig. 923. Other examples have been found in Novgorod and Bergen.

21. Coins from the sites have been examined by Professor Michael Dolley, The Queen's University, Belfast.

22. Hurst, J.G., 'Saxo-Norman pottery in East Anglia', *Proceedings of the Cambridge Antiquarian Society*, vol. 51 (1958). The Crowland Abbey, Lincolnshire, bowl illustrated therein (plate V) is a close parallel to the Dublin examples of wheel-stamped ware. For a discussion on Andenne ware and its origins see Hurst, J.G., (ed.), 'Red-painted and glazed pottery in western Europe from the eighth to the 12th century', *Medieval Archaeology*, vol. 13 (1969).

23. Müller-Wille, M., 'Nya Stavbyggnader i Rhenlandet', *Viking*, vol. 32 (1968), pp. 7-18 and fig. 1.1 and references therein. I am much indebted to Mr. Patrick Healy for surveying these features and for his constant and enthusiastic assistance in recording other structures and material from the excavations. I wish also to express my thanks to Dr. A.T. Lucas, Director, National Museum of Ireland, and Professor David M. Wilson, University College, London, for helpful discussion and comments on the structures and artefacts discovered.

NOTES TO CHAPTER 9

[Reprinted from *R.S.A.I. Jn.*, vol. 20 (1890-1), pp. 36-43. The same author published two other brief studies of Christ Church Cathedral: 'On evidence of the plan of the cloister garth and monastic buildings of the priory of the Holy Trinity, now known as Christ Church Cathedral, Dublin', *R.I.A. Proc.*, vol. 16 (1879-86); 'The Christchurch of Dublin', *R.S.A.I. Jn.*, vol. 24 (1894). Meanwhile a major historical document was being prepared for publication: Mills, J., (ed.), *Account Roll of the Priory of the Holy Trinity, Dublin, 1337-1346* (1891). This in turn is the basis of the article printed in companion volume, pp. 112-22.]

1. In this Mr. Street was, in his dogmatic way, entirely wrong; a 'slype' is not usual in this position anywhere. A staircase communicating from the dormitories to the church *is*

usual, and there was abundance of evidence of this usual arrangement. It was evident on Reading's map, referred to by Mr. Street. The built-up doorway at the foot of the stairs is still evident; an under-flight of stairs leading to the crypt, opened and exhibited to Mr. Street, is still in existence.

2.   Quoted in *Reg. All Saints, Dublin*, p. iii, n. h.

3.   Messingham, T.,*FlorilegiumInsulaeSanctorum*...(1624), pp. 384-5: 'Ideo vir sanctus et timoratus siue religiosus, honestatis amator, et zelator religionis, operam dedit, industriamque adhibuit, et [ut?] clericos saeculares, qui in ecclesia Dublinensi erant instituti canonici, secundum exteriorem et interiorem hominem mutatos in melius in regulares canonicos transformaret. Et vt hoc summi pontificis au[c]toritate confirmaretur, duos e canonicis suis misit Romam, propter vsum et consuetudinem Aroasiensis ordinis, per quos sanctis viri desiderium adimpletum est. *Fecitque regulares stare cantores circa altare, vt laudarent nomen Domini, et dedit in celebrationibus decus, et in sono eorum dulces fecit modos*'.

4.   At present with the female effigy referred to, placed in the church.

5.   Peter Lewis continues: 'A great storme had brocken the great gabule of the hyge awter iii. panis, and had cast doune Plunckets armys, & he chaffed at hit, and was very angry for hit, Mr. Justes Plunckat, and there was iii. wyndows, the panys of glass was broken, and loussyd wth the great wynds and stormys of this yer': T.C.D., Proctors' accounts [on which see Robinson, J.L., 'Christ Church Cathedral, Dublin, proctors' accounts, 1689-90', *R.S.A.I. Jn.*, vol. 41 (1911)].

BIBLIOGRAPHY FOR CHAPTER 10

[Reprinted, with some additional material, from Gillespie, E., (ed.), *The Liberties of Dublin* (1973), pp. 16-23. The section of the post-medieval history of Newgate has been omitted. For the process of reclamation from the River Liffey that necessitated a northward extension of the town walls see Wallace, P.F., 'Dublin's waterfront at Wood Quay, 900-1317', in Milne, G. and Hobley, B., (eds.), *Waterfront Archaeology in Britain and Northern Europe* (1981), pp. 109-18. On the crucial north-eastern angle of the defences see above, pp. 144-56, and on the castle see above, pp. 193-201. The comparatively small size of the area enclosed by the town walls of Dublin is clearly demonstrated in Bradley, J., 'Planned Anglo-Norman towns in Ireland', in *Comparative Urban Origins*, fig. 17.4. The late medieval extramural gateways are shown on the map in Clarke, H.B., *Dublin c. 840 to c. 1540: the Medieval Town in the Modern City* (1978).]

Anc. Rec. Dublin.

Gilbert, J.T., *A History of the City of Dublin*, 3 vols. (1854-9, reprinted 1978).

Grose, F., *The Antiquities of Ireland*, vol. 1 (1791=1795).

Harris, W., *The History and Antiquities of the City of Dublin* ... (1766).

Leask, H.G., *Dublin Castle: a Short Descriptive and Historical Guide for the Use of Visitors* (1944).

McNeill, C., 'Hospital of St. John without the Newgate, Dublin', *R.S.A.I. Jn.*, vol. 55 (1925) [reprinted in companion volume, pp. 77-82].

Miller, L. and Power, E., (eds.), *Holinshed's Irish Chronicle ... continued till the Yeare 1547 by Richarde Stanyhurst* (1979).

N.L.I., surveys of Nicholas Street (1772), Newgate (1782) and Newhall Market (1788); Christ Church deed map of Back Lane (1780).

Orpen, G.H., (ed.), *The Song of Dermot and the Earl* (1892).

Price, L., (ed.), *An 18th-century Antiquary: the Sketches, Notes and Diaries of Austin Cooper* ... (1942).

NOTES TO CHAPTER 11

[Reprinted from *R.S.A.I. Jn.*, vol. 104 (1974), pp. 5-14. For a sequel see the same author's 'Dublin Castle: three centuries of development', *R.S.A.I. Jn.*, vol. 115 (1985). Recent excavations by the Office of Public Works have uncovered on the western side of the castle the foundations of the Bermingham and Cork Towers, a section of the moat 65 ft. wide and almost 30 ft. deep, and over 90,000 medieval and modern artefacts: *The Irish Times*, 24 April 1986.]

1. Gilbert, J.T., *A History of the Viceroys of Ireland, with Notices of the Castle of Dublin* ... (1865), p. 503.
2. Leask, H.G., *Dublin Castle: a Short Descriptive and Historical Guide for the Use of Visitors* (1944), p. 5.
3. Hughes, J.L.J., 'Dublin Castle in the 17th century', *D.H.R.*, vol. 2 (1940), p. 91.
4. Lawlor, H.J., 'The chapel of Dublin Castle', *R.S.A.I. Jn.*, vol. 53 (1923), p. 52.
5. Gilbert, *Viceroys of Ireland*, p. 116.
6. Lawlor, 'Chapel of Dublin Castle', p. 52.
7. N.L.I., MS. 3137.
8. N.L.I., MS. 2656.
9. Hayes-McCoy, G.A., *Ulster and Other Irish Maps* (1964), no. xviii.
10. *H.M.C. Rep. 9*, appendix, pt. 18, pp. 381-2.
11. Harris, W., *The History and Antiquities of the City of Dublin* ... (1766), p. 37.
12. *H.M.C. Rep. 15*, appendix, pt. 1, p. 117.
13. Ware, R., 'The History and Antiquities of Dublin', in Dublin, Central Municipal Library, MS. 1678, p. 23 f.
14. Hughes, 'Dublin Castle', p. 84 f.
15. *Ibid.*, p. 87.
16. Harris, *History and Antiquities*, p. 38.
17. *Ibid.*, p. 39.
18. Stanihurst, R., *De Rebus in Hibernia Gestis* (1584), p. 22.
19. Knowler, W., *The Earl of Strafforde's Letters and Dispatches* ..., vol. 1 (1740), p. 168.
20. N.L.I., MS. 392, p. 58.

NOTES TO CHAPTER 12

[Reprinted with minor revisions from *Archaeologia*, vol. 106 (1979), pp. 107-22. See further the same author's 'Irish Gothic and English fashion', in Lydon, J., (ed.), *The English in Medieval Ireland* (1984), pp. 65-86; Phillips, J.R.S., 'The Anglo-Norman nobility', *ibid.*, pp. 87-104. The evidence of the English pipe rolls complements that of the sculpture remarkably well: Clarke, H.B., 'The early English pipe rolls as a source for Irish history', in Mac Niocaill, G. and Wallace, P.F., (eds.), *Keimelia: Studies in Medieval Archaeology and History in Memory of Tom Delaney* (1988), pp. 416-34. There is a recent discussion of the architecture of Dublin's second medieval cathedral in Rae, E.C., 'The medieval fabric of the cathedral church of St. Patrick in Dublin', *R.S.A.I. Jn.*, vol. 109 (1979).]

1. The figures are based on information contained in Gwynn & Hadcock, *Med. Relig. Houses*, pp. 59-101. There is also a useful table showing the 'anglicization' of the Irish sees in Watt, J.A., *The Church in Medieval Ireland* (1972), p. 88. A clear-cut picture covering all 33 Irish dioceses cannot be obtained, since the identity of some bishops is unknown and several sees were neither consistently Irish nor consistently Anglo-Norman.

    Of the 12 cathedrals which retained Anglo-Norman bishops throughout the 13th century, insufficient remains at two of them — Connor and Down — to judge the character and extent of the buildings. A reconstruction of Down Cathedral had in fact started by 1220 when the monks appealed to Henry III for aid after its destruction through war: *Archaeological Survey of Northern Ireland: County Down* (1966), pp. 267-8. Limerick was rebuilt in the late 12th century before Anglo-Norman bishops took over: Clapham, A.W., 'Some minor Irish cathedrals', *Archaeological Journal*, vol. 106 (1949), supplement, p. 29. Leighlin belongs to the later 13th century: *ibid.*, pp. 26-7.

    For the impact of the Anglo-Norman invasion on the Irish Church see Watt, J.A., *The Church and the Two Nations in Medieval Ireland* (1970), chaps. 2, 3.

2. A detailed account of the conquest is provided in Otway-Ruthven, A.J., *A History of Medieval Ireland* (1968), particularly chaps. 2, 6. Dr. Tessa Garton has recently made a convincing case for a date of *c.* 1200 for Killaloe: 'A Romanesque doorway at Killaloe', *Journal of the British Archaeological Association*, vol. 134 (1981).

3. Watt, *Church and Two Nations*, pp. 52-4.

4. *A.L.C.*, vol. 1, pp. 166-7.

5. A detailed analysis of the arch is given in Leask, H.G., *Irish Churches and Monastic Buildings*, vol. 1 (1955), pp.153-4.

6. *Ibid.*, vol. 2, pp. 25-6. Leask also acknowledged a considerable period of overlap by dating a number of important Romanesque works after 1170. These include the elaborate doorway at Killaloe which he ascribes to *c.* 1180: Leask, *Irish Churches*, vol. 1, pp. 151-2. An alternative date of *c.* 1168 proposed in Henry, F., *Irish Art in the Romanesque Period (1020-1170 A.D.)* (1970), p. 167, seems too early, particularly as dragons similar to those on the jambs of the Killaloe doorway can also be found at Ballintober dated to 1216-25 (see below, n. 8).

7. Leask, *Irish Churches*, vol. 1, p. 154, suggests *c.* 1170 and Henry, *Irish Art*, p. 168, proposes *c.* 1152. The transitional form of abacus certainly rules out a date as early as 1152 and in fact confirms the documentary evidence for 1184.

8. *A.L.C.*, vol. 1, pp. 290-1.

9. Illustrated in Stalley, R.A., *Architecture and Sculpture in Ireland, 1150-1350* (1971), p. 115.

10. Stalley, R.A., 'A 12th-century patron of architecture: a study of the buildings erected by Roger, bishop of Salisbury, 1102-39', *Journal of the British Archaeological Association*, vol. 124 (1971), p. 79.

11. Henry, *Irish Art*, pp. 171-4.

12. The list is published in *Hist. & Mun. Doc. Ire.*, pp. 3-48. John Harvey has suggested to me that the dearth of masons may be explained by the use of the words *taillur, talliur, tailiator,* and variants in the sense of 'carver' not 'tailor'. Fourteen 'tailors' are mentioned in the late 12th-century list, and some of these could, therefore, have been stone-carvers. *Taillo* was used in the Middle Ages meaning 'to hew stone' and variants of *talliator, taylator,* etc., were employed in the sense of 'stone-cutter' and 'carver': Latham, R.E., *Revised Medieval Latin Word-list from British and Irish Sources* (1965), p. 475; Salzman, L.F., *Building in England down to 1540,* 2nd edn. (1967), p. 117. When the context does not indicate the exact meaning, as in the Dublin city roll, it is probably safer to translate the word merely as 'cutter'. In the case of Dublin there is, unfortunately, no way of determining what sorts of cutter were involved. The word is notoriously ambiguous in the Middle Ages. The Norman kings of England included in their household an official described as *tallator* or *taleator* and there has been considerable difference of opinion in this case as to whether he was a tailor or merely a tally-cutter: White, G.H., 'The household of the Norman kings', *R. Hist. Soc. Trans.*, 4th series, vol. 30 (1948), pp. 146-7.

13. *Hist. & Mun. Doc. Ire.*, p. 120.

14. It is possible that the Anglo-Normans built other cathedrals in the period 1170-1200, but these works do not survive. Connor is one possibility, for Bishop Reginald (1178-1225) was the first Anglo-Norman bishop in Ireland: Gwynn & Hadcock, *Med. Relig. Houses*, p. 66. Another is Down, which was turned into a Benedictine priory dependent on Chester Abbey in 1183 by John de Courcy: *ibid.*, p. 105. The Anglo-Normans did, of course, begin other types of religious building in the period. The Cistercian abbeys of Inch (founded in 1180), Dunbrody (1182) and Grey (1193) are obvious examples: *ibid.*, pp. 131, 134, 135.

15. The restoration is described at length by Street himself in Street, G.E. and Seymour, E., *The Cathedral of the Holy Trinity, commonly called Christ Church Cathedral, Dublin: an Account of the Restoration of the Fabric* (1882). See also McVittie, R.B., *Details of the Restoration of Christ Church Cathedral, Dublin . . .* (1878); Drew, T., 'Street as a restorer', *Dublin University Review*, June 1886, pp. 518-31; Butler, W., *The Cathedral Church of the Holy Trinity, Dublin* (1901). There are also numerous references to the restoration in the *Dublin Builder*. See especially vol. 13, nos. 275, 286 (1871); vol. 14, no. 296 (1872); vol. 23, no. 513 (1881).

16. Waterman, D.M., 'Somersetshire and other foreign building stone in medieval Ireland, *c.* 1175-1400', *U.J.A.*, 3rd series, vol. 33 (1970), pp. 63, 71.

17. Street and Seymour, *Cathedral of the Holy Trinity*, p. 108.

18. Illustrated in Gardner, A., *Wells Capitals* (no date), plate VIIIa.

19. Zarnecki, G., *English Romanesque Sculpture, 1066-1140* (1951), p. 32 and plate 39.

20. Zarnecki, G., *Later English Romanesque Sculpture, 1140-1210* (1953), p.14.

21. The coloured drawing is kept in a chest in the chapter room.

22. Zarnecki, *English Romanesque Sculpture*, pp. 22-3, 34-5.

23. *Ibid.*, plate 55. An animal playing a viol also appears in the Elder Lady Chapel of St. Augustine's, Bristol, *c.* 1220 (see below, n. 29).

24. T.C.D., MS. A.1.1, fo. 151.

25. Robinson, J.A., 'On the rebuilding of Glastonbury after the fire of 1184', *Archaeological Journal*, vol. 85 (1928), pp. 18-20.

26. Saxl, F., *English Sculptures of the 12th Century*, ed. H. Swarzenski (1954), pp. 67-8 and plates 96-8.

27. An indirect reference to the moving of the doorway is contained in Butler, W., *Christ Church Cathedral, Dublin: Measured Drawings of the Building prior to Restoration* (1878), p. 8. Plans of the cathedral made before the restoration of 1871-8 show the doorway in the south transept, as at present. It was certainly there by 1835, but not before 1821: *Dublin Penny Journal*, vol. 4 (1835-6), p. 105; Wright, G.N., *An Historical Guide to Ancient and Modern Dublin* (1821), facing p. 107.

    Its reconstruction during the restoration of 1831 is not therefore really in doubt. I am grateful to Mr. J. O'Callaghan for bringing the illustration in the *Dublin Penny Journal* to my attention.

28. The only discussion of these capitals of which I am aware is in McVittie, *Restoration of Christ Church Cathedral*, pp. 76-7. The author states that there were once two further heads, now missing, 'over the outer arch', and he also records that the doorway once had a bead moulding around the hood mould. The interpretation he provides for the capitals is intriguing: 'The capitals exhibit fitz Stephen's crest, a Sagittarius, and the eagles of the arms of Montmorency-Marisco'. The identification of a Sagittarius is dubious, to say the least, and there is no substantive evidence that the capitals refer to the arms of any Norman lords. Street makes only a passing reference to the capitals, saying 'it seems impossible to make out what subjects the figures represent': Street and Seymour, *Cathedral of the Holy Trinity*, p. 100.

29. Hill, R., 'A letter-book of St. Augustine's, Bristol', *B.G.A.S. Trans.*, vol. 65 (1944), p. 152.

30. 2 Samuel xviii. 9-17.

31. Beckwith, J., *Ivory Carving in Early Medieval England* (1972), catalogue no. 97, plate 170.

32. Zarnecki, *Later English Romanesque Sculpture*, pp. 12-13, plate 32. Samson also appears with long hair in 12th-century manuscripts (e.g., the initial in Cambridge, Pembroke College, MS. 16, fo. 30), and on many a 12th-century aquamanile, a fact pointed out to me by the late John Hunt.

33. It is just possible that this scene illustrates the anointing of David, which would have some relevance if placed next to the death of Absolom. The two scenes are placed together in at least one Romanesque manuscript, the famous Morgan leaf, painted at Winchester in the late 12th century: Rickert, M., *Painting in England: the Middle Ages* (1965), pp. 82-3, plate 86. But the arrangement of the scenes in the manuscript bears little similarity with the Christ Church sculpture, and at this stage it is more judicious to regard the subject of the Dublin capital as remaining unsolved.

34. Mr. J. O'Callaghan in the summer of 1970 was the first person to draw my attention to these.

    A huge quantity of stonework was stored in the crypt after the restoration. This includes almost complete chevron arches (from the north transept windows), parts of piers, numerous moulded stones, and several capitals. Amongst the latter is a fine water-leaf capital, no doubt from the choir or transepts. Originally there were at least three elaborate scallop capitals (illustrated in Street and Seymour, *Cathedral of the Holy*

Trinity, p. 91), but the whereabouts of these is now unknown.

There are also two carved heads cemented into the fabric of the crypt, which makes a thorough examination of them almost impossible. They appear to be medieval, and one at least could date from the late 12th or early 13th century.

35. The original location of this capital is unfortunately not known.

36. A discussion of this type of capital is given in Galbraith, K.J., 'The Sculptural Decoration of Malmesbury Abbey', unpublished M.A. thesis, University of London (1962), pp. 177-81. Its popularity in the west of England may partly be explained by its use in the buildings of Bishop Roger of Salisbury: Stalley, 'A 12th-century patron', p. 78.

37. See, for example, the canonical tables of the Winchcombe Psalter: T.C.D., MS. A.1.1.

38. Henry, *Irish Art*, p. 170.

39. The Elkstone sculpture is dated *c*. 1160 in Galbraith, 'Malmesbury Abbey', p. 181, which would mean that it is nearly thirty years later than Cormac's Chapel. But several elements of the Elkstone sculpture are related to Bishop Roger's work at Sarum Cathedral (*c*. 1125-39), and this may be the ultimate source for both Cashel and Elkstone.

40. Sculpture related to that of Kilteel is found near by at Timahoe and Killeshin (Co. Laois). The whole group of heads placed on the angle of the capitals is discussed in Henry, *Irish Art*, pp. 177-81.

41. The original position of the keystone is not clear. Since both this and the monster-head capital had relatively little dirt on them, it is likely they were walled up during the reconstruction of the choir after 1349. The moulding of the keystone ought perhaps to provide a clue to its location, but none of the arches in the existing building appears to have an equivalent profile. If Street had found it *in situ*, in a part of the cathedral that he wanted to preserve or restore, he would no doubt have left it in place.

42. Illustrated in Zarnecki, *Later English Romanesque Sculpture*, plate 46. A much-weathered mask, placed at the apex of an arch, can also be found at Cormac's Chapel, Cashel, and some derivative buildings: de Paor, L., 'Cormac's Chapel: the beginnings of Irish Romanesque', in Rynne, E., (ed.), *North Munster Studies: Essays in Commemoration of Monsignor Michael Moloney* (1967), pp. 135, 137. The example at Cashel (1127-34) must predate most of those in England, but one possible English source is Sarum Cathedral (*c*. 1125-39) which had at least one such mask, now preserved in the museum at Salisbury. It is illustrated in Zarnecki, *Later English Romanesque Sculpture*, plate 45. Indeed Sarum may have been an important source for Cashel, for it also had elaborate gables with rosettes, which cannot have been too dissimilar from the north porch at Cashel. For a brief discussion of the sculpture at Sarum see Stalley, 'A 12th-century patron', pp. 75-6.

43. It is illustrated *in situ* (in the arch leading from the north transept to the nave aisle) in Street and Seymour, *Cathedral of the Holy Trinity*, p.105.

44. The idea continued in early Gothic work, where such flowering shafts are often used in conjunction with more orthodox shafts and capitals, as in the nave of Christ Church, Dublin.

45. Greek key is another ornament popularized by Sarum Cathedral. In the west of England it appears at Malmesbury Abbey, on a 12th-century font at Hereford, and at Christon (Somerset); in Wales it can be found at Llandaff Cathedral and at St. Davids Cathedral; in Ireland the only example, apart from Christ Church, Dublin, is at St. Mary's,

Glendalough, where it was no doubt copied from Dublin.

46. Abaci profiles closely related to Christ Church appear at Droitwich, Deerhurst, Wells (north porch), Bristol, St. Mary Redcliffe (north porch), Llanidloes (from Cwmhir Abbey), Llanthony Abbey, Queen Charlton (Somerset), Kelmscott (Oxfordshire), and Bishop Cannings (Wiltshire). It is in fact a simplified form of a type used generally in the choir of Glastonbury Abbey.

47. Brakspear, H., 'A West Country school of masons', *Archaeologia*, vol. 81 (1931), provides a guide (though incomplete) to the stylistic features of the West Country school.

48. North, F.J., *The Stones of Llandaff Cathedral* (1957), p. 73 ff.

49. Waterman, 'Foreign building stone', p. 71. From a Dublin point of view the lack of surviving buildings in Bristol is a major problem, since the City of Dublin was granted to 'his men of Bristol' by Henry II in 1171-2: *Hist. & Mun. Doc. Ire.*, p. 1. However, the various lists of the citizens of Dublin show that its English population was drawn from a wide area and not restricted to Bristol itself, so that it is perhaps unwise to exaggerate the importance of Bristol in the artistic affairs of Dublin: *ibid.*, pp. 3-48, 112-23, 136-40.

50. V.C.H., *Gloucestershire*, vol. 2, p. 67. A dedication also took place in 1239: Luard, H.R., (ed.), *Annales Monastici*, vol. 1 (1864), p. 112.

51. V.C.H., *Worcestershire*, vol. 2, p. 387.

52. These are taken from the famous Black Book of Christ Church, which contains two rather dubious late medieval accounts of the cathedral's history. The passages are discussed in Gwynn, A., 'The origins of the see of Dublin', *I.E.R.*, vol. 57 (1941), pp. 46-9.

53. Leask, *Irish Churches*, vol. 2, p. 45.

54. Street and Seymour, *Cathedral of the Holy Trinity*, p. 109.

55. Robinson, 'Rebuilding of Glastonbury', pp. 18-20.

56. Colchester, L.S. and Harvey, J.H., 'Wells Cathedral', *Archaeological Journal*, vol. 131 (1974), pp. 200-3.

57. Gwynn, A., 'Archbishop John Cumin', *Reportorium Novum*, vol. 1 (1955-6), p. 289.

58. *Pipe Roll 27 Henry II*, pp. 15-16.

59. Gwynn & Hadcock, *Med. Relig. Houses*, p. 171.

60. Giraldus, *Expugnatio*, pp. 198-9.

61. Cal. Christ Church deeds, no. 5.

62. I have argued the case for Cumin in more detail in Stalley, R.A., *Christ Church, Dublin: the Late Romanesque Building Campaign* (1973), pp. 4-6.

63. The sculpture also helps in plotting the sequence of building. The earliest carving is found in the choir and the lower parts of the south transept, whereas the carving in the equivalent area of the north transept is somewhat more advanced. It thus appears that the south transept was built up to about string-course level, before work began on the north transept. No such division, however, is apparent at triforium and clerestory level, where construction seems to have been simultaneous.

64. Illustrated in Stalley, *Architecture*, plates 53, 55, 56.

65. *Ibid.*, p. 68.

66. These corbels include an ape head on a hood mould (third pier from the east). Similar

heads appear at Hawkchurch (Devon), Queen Charlton (Somerset), Wells (transept), and the Elder Lady Chapel, Bristol: Reeves, P.W., 'English Stiff Leaf Foliage', unpublished Ph.D. thesis, University of London (1952), pp. 362-4.

67. Leask, *Irish Churches*, vol. 2, p. 77; Stalley, *Architecture*, pp. 65-6.

68. *Cal. Doc. Ire., 1171-1251*, no. 2178.

69. The stylistic variations continue all the way up to clerestory level, giving a vertical break. This suggests that for a short time there was a temporary west wall on a line between the fifth piers, resting on the west wall of the crypt below.

I have discussed the architecture of Christ Church at greater length in 'Three Irish buildings with West Country origins', in Coldstream, N. and Draper, P., (eds.), *Art and Architecture at Wells and Glastonbury*, British Archaeological Association (1981), pp. 71-6.

70. See companion volume, p. 104. Building was probably under way at St. Patrick's soon after 1220. In 1225 a protection was issued for four years 'for the preachers of the fabric of the church of St. Patrick, Dublin, going through Ireland to beg for alms for the fabric of the said church': *Cal. Pat. Rolls, 1216-25*, p. 518.

71. Cal. Christ Church deeds, no. 22.

72. Archdall, M., *Monasticon Hibernicum* ... (1786), p. 155.

73. Champneys, A.C., *Irish Ecclesiastical Architecture* (1910), p. 142.

74. The date 1223 is provided in ab Ithel, J.W., (ed.), *Annales Cambriae* (1860), p. 76: 'Et inceptum fuit novum opus majoris ecclesiae Sancti Thomae Hauerfordiae'. This reference appears to have gone unnoticed in the past, perhaps because too many have trusted the index of *Annales Cambriae*, which is faulty! The derivation of the Haverfordwest sculpture from Wells is obvious. It even includes a toothache capital copied from the famous example in the south transept at Wells.

75. There are occasional similarities between the stiff leaf of Wells and that of the Christ Church nave. See, for example, a capital at the entrance to the undercroft of the Wells chapter-house.

Stiff leaf is a notoriously difficult subject to classify and discuss. The only major attempt to tackle the problem so far is Reeves, 'English Stiff Leaf Foliage', but it is far from complete and many of the conclusions are questionable (see below, n. 78). In the case of Haverfordwest, however, her date of *c.* 1220 (p. 366) has proved to be roughly accurate (see above, n. 74).

76. For a description of the church see V.C.H., *Worcestershire*, vol. 3, pp. 82-4.

77. Round abaci make their appearance in the crypt of the Trinity Chapel, Canterbury, *c.* 1178, but they were not universally employed in England until after 1200.

78. In 1971 I suggested a date of 1190-1200, which may be a few years too early: Stalley, *Architecture*, pp. 20-1. In a rather perplexing passage Reeves gives a date of 1225-30: 'The head sculpture presupposes Wells *c.* 1210, the foliage brings the likely period forward to *c.* 1225-40, and since the octagonal abacus is more like Wells than Pershore, and the point more like Hereford than the latter, we are narrowed down to *c.* 1225-30' (p. 199). On the basis of the Christ Church evidence, 1225-30 seems too late.

V.C.H., *Worcestershire*, vol. 3, p. 82, is content to ascribe the work to the early 13th century.

79. A description of the church is contained in V.C.H., *Worcestershire*, vol. 3, pp. 472-5.

80. Apart from general comments assigning the chancel to the early 13th century, the only

specific suggestion is 1220 given in Glynn, C., 'Overbury church', *B.G.A.S. Trans.*, vol. 19 (1894-5), p. 43. This date is probably close to the truth. I now think the date of *c.* 1200, which I gave in 1971, rather too early: Stalley, *Architecture*, p. 21.

81. I am grateful to Dr. Malcolm Thurlby for telling me of this example. The south porch at Cleobury Mortimer (Shropshire), a church closely related to Kinlet in style, has head capitals which may be the product of the same workshop, but they are heavily if not totally restored.

82. Hale, W., (ed.), *Register of the Priory of St. Mary's, Worcester*, vol. 2 (1865), pp. 4, 5, 8.

83. Crosthwaite, *Obits*, p. 3.

84. Nat. Mus. Ire., *Viking and Medieval Dublin, National Museum Excavations, 1962-1973: Catalogue of Exhibition* (1973), pp. 20, 42 and plate 15 (bottom).

85. Orpen, G.H., *Ireland under the Normans, 1169-1333*, vol. 1 (1911), p. 271.

86. The origins of the Christ Church elevation, involving a linked clerestory and triforium, must be related in some way to the early 13th-century work at Pershore Abbey, Lichfield Cathedral and Worcester Cathedral. See Stalley, 'Three Irish buildings'; Milburn, C., 'Pershore Abbey: the 13th-century choir', *Journal of the British Archaeological Association*, vol. 137 (1984), pp. 138-40; Thurlby, M., 'The early Gothic elevation of Lichfield Cathedral', in Dale, W., (ed.), *Transactions of the Third Canadian Conference of Medieval Art Historians* (1985), pp. 71-9.

87. Stalley, *Architecture*, pp. 75-80.

88. An interesting detail on one of the Athassel heads is a circular brooch below the neck, presumably as a clasp for drapery, though no clothes are depicted on the capital. Another circular brooch appears on a head capital in the south porch of Kilkenny Cathedral, and one of the Christ Church heads has a diamond-shaped one. In England a head capital in the north transept at Lichfield Cathedral has a conspicuous circular brooch, pulling tightly on the surrounding drapery, and a similar ornament appears on many of the west front statues at Wells Cathedral.

89. Gardner, *Wells Capitals*, p. 1.

90. Luard, H.R., (ed.), *Matthaei Parisiensis, Monachi Sancti Albani, Chronica Majora*, vol. 3 (1876), p. 391.

91. I have had the opportunity of discussing the Christ Church capitals with several people over the last four years, and in particular I should like to record my thanks to Professor G. Zarnecki, Mr. J. O'Callaghan, Mr. M. Thurlby, Mr. J.H. Harvey, and Professor A.J. Otway-Ruthven.

NOTES TO CHAPTER 13

[Reprinted from *R.S.A.I. Jn.*, vol. 47 (1917), pp. 109-38. The monuments of the Dublin churches are catalogued in Hunt, J., *Irish Medieval Figure Sculpture, 1200-1600: a Study of Irish Tombs with Notes on Costume and Armour*, vol. 1 (1974), pp. 134-44. For the general background see Stalley, R.A., *Architecture and Sculpture in Ireland, 1150-1350* (1971).]

1. *Chartul. St. Mary's, Dublin*, vol. 2, p. 266 f.; Plummer, C., (ed.), 'Vie et miracles de S. Laurent archevêque de Dublin', *Anal. Bolland.*, vol. 33 (1914), p. 121 ff., § 7.

2. *Chartul. St. Mary's, Dublin*, vol. 2, p. 287; Plummer, 'Vie et miracles', §§ 25, 26 and notes.

3. Plummer, 'Vie et miracles', §§ 27, 29.

4. *Ibid.*, § 31.

5. A photograph of the monument is reproduced in the *Irish Rosary*, November 1912.

6. Haines, H., *A Manual of Monumental Brasses . . .* (1861, reprinted 1970), p. lxii: 'Before the latter end of the 16th century hardly any attempts were made [in brass] to give the portrait of the deceased'. I had hoped to be able to present to the Royal Society of Antiquaries of Ireland a photograph of the figure taken from above, and showing the full face. But the war has made it impossible to procure such a photograph.

7. Lawlor, H.J., 'A calendar of the *Liber Niger* and *Liber Albus* of Christ Church, Dublin', *R.I.A. Proc.*, vol. 27 (1907-9), sect. C, p. 69.

8. More accurately, crystalline limestone, probably one of the Carboniferous Limestones of Ireland, common in Co. Dublin and elsewhere, as Professor Joly informs me. There are some traces of fossils in it.

9. The Rev. J.L. Robinson thinks that there are traces of lettering or ornament on the chamfer which surrounds the figure, at the head and sides, but not at the foot.

10. Even in position. But this cannot be used as an argument, for it was placed where it now is by Street. When he began the work of restoration it was 'in the cathedral'; but the ruins of the 'chapel of St. Laurence' lay outside, the ancient arch which now gives entrance to it having been built up: Street, G.E. and Seymour, E., *The Cathedral of the Holy Trinity, commonly called Christ Church Cathedral, Dublin: an Account of the Restoration of the Fabric . . .* (1882), p. 101. It is shown in the ground plan of the cathedral in Butler, W., *Christ Church Cathedral, Dublin: Measured Drawings of the Building prior to Restoration* (1878), under the built-up arch. In his *De Praesulibus Lageniae . . .* (1628), p. 10, J. Ware says that it was *in australi pariete chori*, which may seem to mean that it was in a recess under the wall of the choir. But *pariete* may be a misprint for *parte*, which is the word used in the corresponding sentence of the *De Praesulibus Hiberniae . . .* (1665), p. 106. In any case in Ware's time it was in the choir, on the south side. This may have been its original site.

11. Ware, *De Praesulibus Hiberniae*, p. 106. In all references to Ware I give the pages of that volume, though I quote it in Harris's translation, where I am satisfied that he has rendered it correctly. I refer to Harris's edition of Ware's works, *The Whole Works of Sir James Ware concerning Ireland . . .*, 2 vols. (1764), only for Harris's additions.

12. So also Butler, *Christ Church Cathedral*, ground plan. But he is less confident in his *The Cathedral Church of the Holy Trinity, Dublin . . .* (1901), p. 16.

13. A few examples of monuments in various places in memory of the same person are noticed in Haines, *Monumental Brasses*, p. lv f. But some are of late date, and the remainder do not supply parallels in the case of St. Laurence.

14. Crosthwaite, *Obits*, p. 4.

15. Plummer, 'Vie et miracles', §§ 26, 27, 31.

16. Robinson, J.L., *Handbook to Christ Church Cathedral, Dublin* (1914), p. 15; Butler, *Cathedral Church of Holy Trinity*, p. 16. Street can only say: 'The foundations of an old chapel were found, which *was said to be* that of St. Laurence O'Toole, and a new chapel has been erected on the old foundations': Street and Seymour, *Cathedral of the Holy Trinity*, p. 101.

17. In Canterbury Cathedral there is a monumental effigy of John Pecham (*d.* 1292) in wood — 'a fine bit of Irish bog oak', as Mr. J. McClemens, senior vesturer of the cathedral, tells me.

18. It is reproduced as the frontispiece of Gilbert, J.T., (ed.), *Crede Mihi: the Most Ancient Register Book of the Archbishops of Dublin before the Reformation* (1897).

19. *Cal. Doc. Ire., 1252-84*, no. 1549; *Cal. Papal Letters, 1198-1304*, pp. 457-60, 469; Luard, H.R., (ed.), *Annales Monastici*, vol. 4 (1869), p. 297; Riley, H.T., (ed.), *Willelmi Rishanger . . . Chronica et Annales* (1865), p. 108.

20. Ware, *De Praesulibus Hiberniae*, p. 110; *Chartul. St. Mary's, Dublin*, vol. 2, p. 323.

21. MacInerny, M.H., *A History of the Irish Dominicans, from Original Sources and Unpublished Records* (1916), pp. 378, 475.

22. *Chartul. St. Mary's, Dublin*, vol. 2, p. 334; *Cal. Papal Letters, 1305-42*, p. 20.

23. Ware, *De Praesulibus Hiberniae*, p. 112. The text quoted (Job xix. 25-7) is a commonplace on brasses: Haines, *Monumental Brasses*, p. xli. It is taken, not from the Vulgate text, but from the Officium Defunctorum of the Breviary, in which it serves as a Response (in most Breviaries the first Response) at Matins. The words *salvatorem meum* are apparently in all Breviaries.

24. Ball, F.E., 'Extracts from the journal of Thomas Dineley, or Dingley, Esquire, giving some account of his visit to Ireland in the reign of Charles II', *R.S.A.I.Jn.*, vol. 43 (1913), p. 291.

25. Harris, *Works of Sir James Ware*, vol. 1, p. 332.

26. So on the Cranley brass we find two shields, both of which bear the family coat; see also above, p. 234.

27. Eubel, C., *Hierarchia Catholica Medii Aevi*, 2nd edn., vol. 1 (1913), p. 72.

28. *Cal. Papal Letters, 1362-1404*, pp. 372, 382.

29. *Ibid.*, p. 297.

30. *Ibid.*, p. 535.

31. Ware, *De Praesulibus Hiberniae*, p. 114.

32. Ware is not exceptional. Even Harding, G.P. and Moule, T., *Antiquities in Westminster Abbey* (1825), p. 18, with the monument before them, make three bad mistakes in ll. 9-10.

33. He probably took this from Weever, J., *Ancient Funerall Monuments . . .* (1631), p. 481, where we read: 'His epitaph is quite worne or torne away from his monument, yet I found it in a manuscript in Sir Robert Cotton's Librarie'.

34. Harris, *Works of Sir James Ware*, vol. 1, p. 335.

35. There is perhaps a stroke over the word indicating the letters *ar*. But this is very uncertain, and in any case the word must be pronounced as if it were not there.

36. Error for *septini = septeni*. This must be read *septini*. Possibly the engraver mistook *m* in his copy for *ni* (*septem* for *septeni*).

37. So, I believe, the brass reads. A mistake of the engraver for *nouie*.

38. 1389-96: *D.N.B.*, vol. 13, p. 17.

39. Not 'the arms of the see of Dublin, and his own', as Harris says: *Works of Sir James Ware*, vol. 1, p. 337.

40. Gutch, J., (ed.), *The History and Antiquities of the Colleges and Halls in the University*

of Oxford (1786), p. 201. This edition seems to represent Wood's final revision of the work shortly before his death in 1695.

41. The reader will observe that the rhymes prove that ll. 3-4, as here printed, were intended to be consecutive, as were also ll. 7-8.

42. Read *eripitur*.

43. Crosthwaite, *Obits*, p. 26.

44. Ware, *De Praesulibus Hiberniae*, p. 115 f.

45. Harris, *Works of Sir James Ware*, vol. 1, p. 339.

46. 'On which heretofore might be read the following epitaph': *ibid*.

47. Mason, W.M., *The History and Antiquities of the Collegiate and Cathedral Church of St. Patrick near Dublin* . . . (1820), appendix, p. lviii.

48. Reproduced in Ball, 'Journal of Thomas Dineley', p. 281.

49. White, N.B., (ed.), *The 'Dignitas Decani' of St. Patrick's Cathedral, Dublin* (1957), p. 175.

50. *Ibid.*, p. 45; printed also in Mason, *Church of St. Patrick*, appendix, p. xxxiii.

51. The measurements are 9 x 8 in. and 6 x 7 in. respectively. The lost brasses of the Talbot monument are in the course of being replaced in the original matrix by copies designed after the drawings that have been preserved.

52. Ware, *De Praesulibus Hiberniae*, p. 111. In 1628 Ware had qualified the statement with the words *ut fertur*: *De Praesulibus Lageniae*, p. 20. The omission of this phrase in 1665 indicates that in the meantime he had convinced himself that it was supported by sufficient evidence.

53. In 1349 Old Style, i.e. after 24 March 1349 New Style. See Elrington, C.R., (ed.), *The Whole Works of the Most Rev. James Ussher, D.D.* . . ., vol. 1 (1847), p. cxxxi f.

54. Ware, *De Praesulibus Hiberniae*, p. 112: 'In ecclesia (ut opinor) Patriciana sepultus est'. The same words are found in his *De Praesulibus Lageniae*, p. 22.

55. Mason, *Church of St. Patrick*, appendix, p. lviii. It is true that Mason mentions Bicknor among a number of persons 'none of whose monuments are now to be found'. But the stone which lay over Bicknor's grave had lost its brass more than two centuries earlier, and by 1820 it may have been worn so smooth as to be unrecognizable as a 'monument', though held by tradition to mark the spot.

56. Ware, *De Praesulibus Hiberniae*, p. 113.

57. *Ibid.*, p. 114.

58. Harris, *Works of Sir James Ware*, vol. 1, p. 336.

59. Ball, 'Journal of Thomas Dineley', p. 283.

60. Macklin, H.W., *The Brasses of England* (1907), p. 3.

61. Beaumont, E.T., *Ancient Memorial Brasses* (1913), p. 185. See also below, n. 62.

62. Macklin, *Brasses of England*, p. 67 f. Cf. the brass of Margaret de Camoys, Trotton, Sussex, *c.* 1310, figured *ibid.*, p. 28. Of the canopy only the matrix remains, which increases its value as an illustration of our pictures. The same may be said of the matrix of the brass of Bishop Beaumont of Durham, 1333 : *ibid.*, p. 314.

63. Laurence de St. Maur (canopies in shafts) and Sir Hugh Hastings: Macklin, *Brasses of England*, pp. 49, 100; Haines, *Monumental Brasses*, p. clv.

64. Haines, *Monumental Brasses*, p. cxxxvii.

65. Macklin, *Brasses of England*, p. 70.

66. Beaumont, *Ancient Memorial Brasses*, p. 165 f.

67. So also says Haines, *Monumental Brasses*, p. cxxxix.

68. Another early feature in the projection under the mitre on the right of the archbishop's head. This indicates the bushy hair found in brasses of the first period: Macklin, *Brasses of England*, p. 100. Cf. the Beaumont matrix and the St. Maur brass: *ibid.*, pp. 101, 314.

69. Haines, *Monumental Brasses*, p. xliii.

70. For these brasses see Ward, J.S.M., *Brasses* (1912), pp. 11, 13.

71. Ware, *De Praesulibus Hiberniae*, p. 116. Cf. his will in Berry, H.F., *Register of Wills and Inventories of the Diocese of Dublin in the Time of Archbishops Tregury and Walton* (1898), p. 26.

72. The chapter appointed a committee to determine the place where it should be fixed, on 8 January 1722.

73. Berry, *Register of Wills*, p. 26.

74. See further about this monument *ibid.*, p. xxiii f.

75. Lawlor, 'Calendar of the *Liber Niger* and *Liber Albus*', p. 11.

76. Ware, *De Praesulibus Hiberniae*, p. 117. Ware may be wrong about the date, 29 November. See above, pp. 245, 247. It is easy to confuse xxviiii with xxviii.

77. Harris, *Works of Sir James Ware*, vol. 1, p. 346.

78. Wood, *Athenae Oxon.*, vol. 1, col. 563 f. The inscriptions are not quite accurately copied in the *Athenae Oxon.* The diocesan registrar of York, Mr. A.V. Hudson, has been so kind as to compare them with the original in Wolsey's register.

79. Anthony Wood omitted the word *cor*. Harris, by way of emendation, printed *Willielmus, Archiepiscopus, Vicarius, perpetuus,* instead of the corresponding genitives, thus making the inscription imply that Rokeby's body was to be buried in the Halifax chapel. Some of his readers may have inferred that that chapel was identical with the new chapel at Sandal. He may even have thought so himself.

80. Rokeby made a singular provision for a chantry priest for this chapel: 'Item, where I did obtain a Pardon for the Parish of Halifax, and the Parishings thereunto adjoyning, *pro lacticiniis in quadragessima edendis*, I will that mine Executors at their discretion obtain *sub plumbo* the said license to be renewed, and the Profit thereof to be imployed for a Priest to sing at Halifax in my said new Chappel as long as may be, by the advice and discretion of my Executors and the Church-Wardens': Wood, *Athenae Oxon.*, vol. 1, cols. 563-4.

81. So I gather from the references to him in Holmes, R., 'Dodsworth Yorkshire notes: the wapentake of Osgoldcross', *Yorkshire Archaeological Journal*, vol. 11 (1891), pp. 455-7.

82. Ware, *De Praesulibus Hiberniae*, p. 117.

83. Not on the south, as Rokeby desired.

84. The book was published in 1691.

85. Wood could not read the date. In supplying it I assume that the same date was given at Halifax as at Sandal.

86. Harris, *Works of Sir James Ware*, vol. 1, p. 345 f. Ware's language implies that Rokeby's body was not sent to England. According to Watson, J., *History and Antiquities of Halifax* (1775), p. 503, there is no proof of the burial at Sandal.

87. So called to distinguish it from another Sandal which lies between it and Doncaster: Hunter, J., *South Yorkshire: the History and Topography of the Deanery of Doncaster*, vol. 1 (1828), p. 198.

88. Printed in Wood, *Athenae Oxon.*, ed. P. Bliss, vol. 2, col. 719.

89. For the dedication see the will of Nicholas Riccard quoted in Hunter, *South Yorkshire*, p. 200.

90. To the west of the monument described below; not, as Torre says, 'above' it.

91. The window is protected by plain glass, on the inner side of which the spider has spun its web. The word *qui* and the year number are now illegible and the latter was also illegible in 1828: Hunter, *South Yorkshire*, p. 200. The inscription is not now continuous. We find *istius capellae fundatoris* at the bottom of the second light, reckoning from the west, *qui* (?) half-way up the same light, *Novembris die* half-way up the third light, and *xxviii* a foot from the bottom of the fourth. The date (28 November) is that of Archbishop Rokeby's death, as recorded on his monument, though Ware gives it as 29 November; see also above, pp. 243, 247.

92. Otherwise Cindercliffe or Thundercliffe.

93. Hunter, *South Yorkshire*, p. 199. He resigned on his appointment to the office of lord chancellor of Ireland about 1500. In 1502 he was presented to the vicarage of Halifax. Both benefices were in the gift of the Cluniac priory of St. Pancras at Lewes: Dugdale, W., *Monasticon Anglicanum*, ed. J. Caley, H. Ellis and B. Bandinel, vol. 5 (1825), p. 2.

94. Hunter, *South Yorkshire*, p. 199.

95. *Ibid.*, p. 200.

96. Drew, T., *The National Cathedral of St. Patrick, Dublin* ... (1900), p. 14. Sir Thomas Drew states that 'the surviving wall-ribs give all evidence requisite for a true restoration of' the groined roof. Of course, the wall-ribs would not indicate the design of the bosses. I have not been able to ascertain what evidence he relied on for them.

97. It is curious that the three monumental slabs in St. Patrick's Cathedral already mentioned are of the same length, which is nearly identical with the height of the Rokeby monument.

98. Argent, on a chevron sable, three mallets, between three rooks proper.

99. So Torre. Hunter, *South Yorkshire*, p. 200, describes it as bearing the arms of the see impaling those of Rokeby.

100. So I judge from a photograph, though both Torre and Hunter say, from his mouth. Cf. Haines, *Monumental Brasses*, p. cxli: 'scrolls, when they appear in this [14th] and in the beginning of the next century, issue from the hands of the figures'.

101. Nos. 5-8 are identical in size and form.

102. Ware, *De Praesulibus Hiberniae*, p. 117 f.

103. Eubel, *Hierarchia Catholica*, vol. 3, p. 204 [translated from Meath on 27 February 1523: *N.H.I.*, vol. 9, p. 311].

104. Harris, *Works of Sir James Ware*, vol. 1, p. 153, confirmed by the will of John Ynge of Croscombe (29 June 1512), who named 'the Reverend Father in Christ Hugh, Bishop of Meath' overseer, and bequeathed to him 'a cup called "a nut" with a silver cover': Weaver, F.W., (ed.), *Somerset Wills*, vol. 2, *1501-1530*, Somerset Record Society, vol. 19 (1903), p. 212.

105. I owe this suggestion to the learned antiquary, the Rev. F.W. Weaver. I regret that I

have not been able to read his account of Archbishop Inge in *Somerset Wills*, p. xxii.

106. Only the lower part of the letter D remains.

107. Only portions of the first A and the final T remain.

108. This paragraph is based on information kindly supplied by the dean of Canterbury and the late Dr. Purey-Cust, dean of York.

NOTES TO CHAPTER 14

[Reprinted from *R.S.A.I. Jn.*, vol. 41 (1911), pp. 391-3. The High Cross is shown as site 0 5 on the map in Clarke, H.B., *Dublin c. 840 to c. 1540: the Medieval Town in the Modern City* (1978).]

1.   Harris, W., *The History and Antiquities of the City of Dublin* . . . (1766), p. 88.

Index

Aldermen, archbishops, bailiffs, bishops, kings, mayors, and provosts listed without further qualification are those of Dublin. Many medieval mayors of Dublin served as provost/bailiff before assuming the higher office and these individuals have been indexed accordingly. All gates, wall towers and streets are those of Dublin. Page numbers in **bold** type refer to this volume; those in *italic* type refer to text figures; those in medium type refer to companion volume.